Anne Boleyn

Anne Boleyn

Joanna Denny

PORTRAIT

Visit the Portrait website!

Piatkus publishes a wide range of non-fiction, including biography, history, science, music, popular culture and sport.

If you want to:

- buy our books over the internet
- read descriptions of our popular titles
- take advantage of our special offers
- enter our monthly competition
- learn more about your favourite Piatkus authors

VISIT OUR WEBSITE AT: www.portraitbooks.com

Copyright © 2004 by Joanna Denny

First published in 2004 by **Portrait**
an imprint of
Piatkus Books Ltd
5 Windmill Street
London W1T 2JA
e-mail: info@piatkus.co.uk

Reprinted 2004

This edition first published 2005

Reprinted 2005

The moral right of the author has been asserted

A catalogue record for this book is available from the British Library

ISBN 0 7499 5051 X

Text design by Paul Saunders
Edited by Richard Dawes

This book has been printed on paper manufactured
with respect for the environment using wood from
managed sustainable resources

Data manipulation by Phoenix Photosetting, Chatham, Kent
Printed and bound in Great Britain by
Mackays of Chatham, Chatham, Kent

Contents

Royal Families of Europe

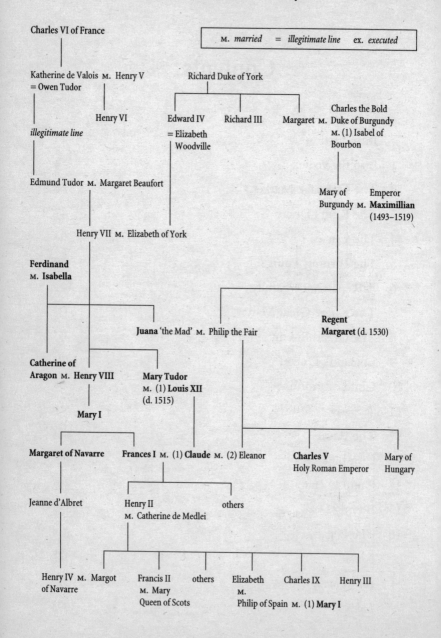

M. *married* = *illegitimate line* EX. *executed*

Charles VI of France

Katherine de Valois M. Henry V
= Owen Tudor

illegitimate line

Henry VI

Richard Duke of York

Edward IV   Richard III   Margaret M. Charles the Bold
= Elizabeth   Duke of Burgundy
Woodville   M. (1) Isabel of
                                               Bourbon

Edmund Tudor M. Margaret Beaufort

Mary of   Emperor
Burgundy M. **Maximillian**
               (1493–1519)

Henry VII M. Elizabeth of York

Ferdinand
M. **Isabella**

Regent
Margaret (d. 1530)

Juana 'the Mad' M. Philip the Fair

Catherine of
Aragon M. **Henry VIII**

Mary Tudor
M. (1) **Louis XII**
(d. 1515)

Mary I

Margaret of Navarre   **Frances I** M. (1) **Claude** M. (2) Eleanor   **Charles V**   Mary of
                                                                                    Holy Roman Emperor   Hungary

Jeanne d'Albret   Henry II   others
                       M. Catherine de Medlei

Henry IV M. Margot   Francis II   others   Elizabeth   Charles IX   Henry III
of Navarre   M. Mary   M.
                          Queen of Scots   Philip of Spain M. (1) **Mary I**

The Boleyn Family

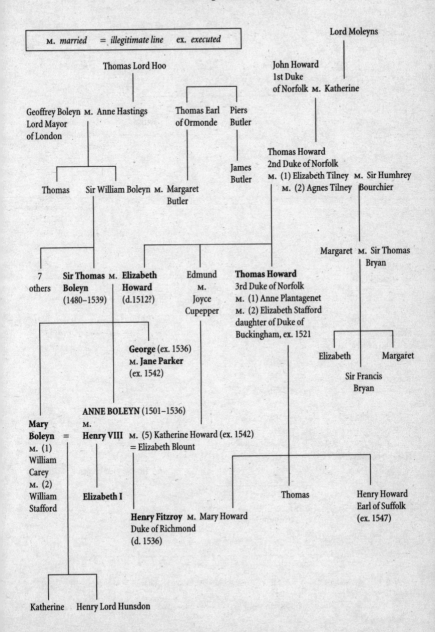

Who list [wishes] his wealth and ease retain,
Himself let him unknown contain.
Press not too fast in at that gate
Where the return stands by disdain,
For sure, *circa Regna tonat*
[thunder rolls around the throne].

The high mountains are blasted oft
When the low valley is mild and soft.
Fortune with Health stands at debate.
The fall is grievous from aloft.
And sure, *circa Regna tonat*

These bloody days have broken my heart.
My lust, my youth did them depart,
And blind desire of estate.
Who hastes to climb seeks to revert.
Of truth, *circa Regna tonat*.

SIR THOMAS WYATT,

'*V. Innocentia Veritas Viat Fides Circumdederunt me
inimici mei*' (Psalms 17, 9: 'My Enemies Have
Surrounded Me')

Dates

All dates given use the Julian Calendar, which was kept until February 1582 and in which the new year starts on 25 March. In 1582 Pope Gregory XIII introduced the Gregorian calendar, with the new year starting on 1 January, but Protestant England ignored this change, remaining ten days behind Europe until 1751–2.

Introduction

'The very ink of history is written with fluid prejudice.'

Mark Twain

NO ENGLISH QUEEN has made more impact on the history of the nation than Anne Boleyn, and few have been so persistently maligned. In her lifetime she was traduced, shamed and butchered. Since her death she has been pursued beyond the grave, subjected to accusations and vilification.

Tradition has presented us with a totally unconvincing one-dimensional picture. As Samuel Butler said, 'Though God cannot alter the past, historians can.'

The past is a reality that exists just beyond our reach. We try to stretch out and touch the lives of these astonishing men and women, seeking to understand their characters and motivation. Was Anne really the scheming temptress portrayed by her detractors, a woman accused of incest and witchcraft? Or was she the innocent victim of a campaign of malicious disinformation, the target in the bloody game of court factions?

There are few accepted facts about Anne's life. Virtually everything is still in dispute, from her date of birth to her appearance. Henry VIII's love letters to Anne were stolen in her lifetime by secret agents of the

Vatican. Other documents were destroyed during the reign of Bloody Mary. Much of the case against Anne is based on the reports of those who were her enemies. We cannot trust the mythology, but as E.H. Carr warns us, 'Study the historian before you study the facts.'

Take as an example two contemporary chroniclers of the period. Eustace Chapuys was ambassador and spymaster for the Holy Roman Empire in England and for seven years Anne Boleyn's greatest enemy. His mission was to preserve Catherine of Aragon as queen and England as a Catholic nation. Although he was fluent in several languages, his English was so poor that he could not understand what was being said around him. Yet he claimed to know all the inside information at court and repeated gossip and rumours from his paid informers.

To Chapuys, Anne was a 'whore', 'the Concubine', a she-devil, an Agrippina, the other woman, who, he claimed, used witchcraft to manipulate and control the King. Her daughter Elizabeth is consistently referred to in his dispatches as 'the little bastard'. Yet he refused to even meet Anne face to face.

Nicholas Sander is responsible for much of the black legend that surrounds her. A Catholic priest and propagandist, he was only five or six at the time of her death but he invented a monstrous picture of her as the instrument of evil. It seems incredible to us today that Anne bore any resemblance to the grotesque monster, with a sixth finger, warts and goitre, that he portrays. But in that period, as in Shakespeare's caricature of Richard III, the deformities of the body were believed to indicate the depravity of the soul.

If Anne was truly as unattractive as Sander describes her, she would never have captured Henry's attention and held it for more than ten years.

Sander also claimed that Anne had conducted notorious affairs with innumerable men, including her own brother. He states that Anne was sent to France as a child after being caught having a sexual relationship not only with her father's butler but also with his chaplain. He alleged that her mother had been the King's mistress, in effect saying that Anne Boleyn was Henry's own daughter. Such stories are so improbable that too much time need not be wasted upon them.

Many who knew her personally saw Anne in a very different light.

Thomas Cranmer, Archbishop of Canterbury, was Anne's pastor and friend. He had lived in the Boleyn household and knew the family at first hand. He stood up for Anne's reputation before the King, writing: 'I have never had better opinions of woman than I had of her.'

As she faced death, Anne showed real moral courage. The Renaissance flowered among the racks, the stake, the fires and butchery of the Inquisition. In the midst of this revolution in politics, religion and society, one woman transformed the nation from within.

It is time for a fresh look at the facts.

Chapter One

Into the Vortex

How strange England must have appeared, its white cliffs looming out of the mist like vast fortress walls protecting the island kingdom. From the rolling deck of a square-rigged carrack, Anne Boleyn and her father watched the approaching land as they finally made port in Dover. Eight long years had passed since Anne had set foot in her native land, but now she was no longer a child but a lively and brilliant young woman of 20.[1]

It was a rude awakening after the sunlit warmth and dazzling palaces of the Loire Valley, where she had attended Queen Claude, wife of Francis I of France. There Anne had received her radical education among the élite of Europe until abruptly summoned home. The political situation between France and England was rapidly deteriorating and it was no longer wise for Anne to stay abroad. Of even greater personal interest to her, Anne now learned that marriage had been arranged for her with James Butler, her father's rival for the title Earl of Ormonde, in order to settle their land dispute.

Anne's father, Sir Thomas Boleyn, was a diplomat and the trusted envoy for the Tudor King of England, Henry VIII. He was well used to making arduous journeys even at such a dangerous time of the year and travelled to the tiny English enclave of Calais to meet Anne and bring her home. Father and daughter were reunited and they took passage together, crossing the notorious Channel in fierce December gales. It was an exhausting journey as they struggled on horseback over mud-choked roads through the driving rain, no doubt breaking the ride to London at Hever Castle, the family seat in Kent.[2]

Thomas Boleyn was, at 40, an exceptional politician, typical of a new breed of courtiers who had risen to prominence through his own merit. He was very much the archetype of Renaissance man, athletic and well versed in arms as well as in politics and law. He was fluent in Latin and his French was considered to be the best at court.[3] In this he followed his great-uncle the Earl of Ormonde, a famous linguist. Thomas's intelligence and witty conversation full of classical allusions made him a favoured member of the King's close circle, whose business was concerned with many secrets.

Anne was coming home to make her court debut in that winter of 1521–2. Her first taste of the Tudor court was probably during the 12 days of Christmas, a great celebration of lavish banquets and pageantry culminating in the Feast of the Epiphany. Everyone who was anyone had gathered in London for the holy days to enjoy the seasonal food and masques, to watch the antics of the Lord of Misrule and the King's jesters and fools, and to hear carols sung as the wassail cup passed around the great hall decked with holly and ivy.

At some time during these celebrations Thomas introduced Anne to his sovereign, proudly showing off her sophistication and her cultured manners, newly acquired at the French court. Anne's continental education set her apart from other women. She was dressed stylishly in the very latest French fashions and at New Year, when presents were exchanged, Anne wore a yellow satin gown and a caul of Venetian gold. Cardinal Wolsey's usher, George Cavendish, remembered how she stood out among the other women at court 'for her excellent grace and behaviour'. As her contemporary the Spaniard Lancelot de Carles records: 'For her behaviour, manners, attire and tongue she excelled them all, for she had been brought up in France. No one would ever have taken her to be English by her manners, but a native-born Frenchwoman.'[4]

The life that Anne Boleyn had returned to at the English court was that of entertainer. Besides her daily duties as one of the waiting women of Queen Catherine, she would provide music and conversation as required and take part in masques and dancing. She was not at all amazed by the extravagance she saw around her. As just a young girl Anne had been sent to the greatest courts in Europe, in Burgundy and France, where she was daily in the presence of men and women who would shape history and bring about changes that would shake the world.

Burgundy was the very centre of culture and style, which the rest of Europe sought to emulate. From the days of Charles the Bold and his wife Margaret of York, there had flourished in the many palaces of Mechelen and Brussels a lavish and sophisticated court, famed in the 15th century for artists such as Van Eyck and composers such as Josquin Des Prés. It was in Burgundy that the printing revolution had begun, creating an exciting atmosphere of radical intellectual thought. There, under the tutelage of the Regent Margaret of Austria, Anne had started to acquire the learning and style for which she would become famous.

For someone who had spent her formative teenage years at the heart of Europe, it is possible that the Tudor court was something of a disappointment. England was just a tiny kingdom isolated on the periphery, struggling to recover after decades of civil war between the Houses of York and Lancaster. The Tudor dynasty was still insecure and fragile. The great houses of Europe looked down on a monarch they considered an upstart, son of an unknown usurper, and had been reluctant to enter into alliances. Ferdinand and Isabella of Spain imposed strict conditions for the marriage of their daughter Catherine of Aragon to the Tudor heir, Prince Arthur, Prince of Wales, and later to his younger brother, Henry VIII.[5]

Henry sought to ape the finesse and sophistication of Burgundy and France. To celebrate Shrove Tuesday in 1522, the Master of Revels, William Cornish, arranged at York Place in London a great pageant in the Burgundian style in which Anne was selected to play a role.

Every masque had a theme. The costumes and props were exotic, with courtiers disguised as anything from Robin Hood's outlaw band to devilish Moorish pirates. When Charles V, Emperor of the Holy Roman Empire, visited London, the city put on fantastic shows with leaping mechanical animals and singing birds. A masque was held in Windsor Castle in which a horse ran amok among the dinner guests.

The Shrove Tuesday masque in which Anne acted was called the *Château Vert*. An elaborate castle was constructed in which Anne and other young damsels in distress waited to be rescued by the King and his gallant knights. Dressed all in white satin, Mary Tudor, the King's sister, was playing Beauty, surrounded by Mercy, Pity, Honour, Bounty, Perseverance, Kindness and Constancy. Anne – somewhat prophetically – was Perseverance.

These pageants imitated the themes of the passing chivalric age, of King Arthur and the lost world of Camelot, when courtly love was still honourable. But the old order of chivalry had long since broken down and Henry had never been content to woo his lady from a distance. To the fanfare of live cannon, the King appeared dressed as Ardent Desire. We can only imagine what that must have been. Henry led his men in a barrage of fruit and sweetmeats thrown from the castle by their enemies, disguised as Indians. After a riotous battle the rescuers finally reached the damsels and carried them off to cheering from the suitably impressed audience of diplomats and courtiers.[6] These events often got out of hand when the King and his courtiers, disguised as outlaws or exotic foreigners, burst unannounced into ladies' chambers in the middle of the night.

Of all English monarchs, 'Bluff King Hal' is probably the most famous, but for all the wrong reasons. His extravagant tastes and marital adventures mask the schizoid personality of one of history's most brutal kings. But little of this was apparent when his reign began. After the dull oppression of his father's iron rule, the feeling in the country was that this would be a new beginning, a new age full of hope. The 17-year-old King was relatively unknown, having been kept out of the public eye during his adolescence. He now appeared like an omen of peace and harmony, promising much for the realm after many long years of hardship.

Henry married Catherine of Aragon and suddenly the future looked golden.[7] The Venetian ambassador Sebastian Giustinian recorded: 'Nature could not have done more for him… He is much handsomer than any sovereign in Christendom; a great deal handsomer than the King of France, very fair and his whole frame admirably proportioned.'[8]

Henry's first desire had been to cast aside all the inhibitions and prohibitions of his father's regime. Pleasure was now the order of the day. Henry was free at last to indulge himself in every way. He seemed determined to make his court the most spectacular in Europe, spending recklessly on banquets and outrageous clothes.

In 1514 Giustinian wrote:

His Majesty is the handsomest potentate I ever set eyes upon: above the usual height, with an extremely fine calf to his leg, his complexion very fair and bright, with auburn hair combed straight and short in the French fashion, and a round face so very beautiful that it would become a pretty woman, his throat being rather long and thick...[9]

From his many portraits we can exactly follow his physical decline from youthful paragon to crabbed monster. At six foot two, Henry was vain about his figure. In 1512 his waistline was a trim 32 inches, but by 1545 it matched his age: 54.

Henry was clean-shaven until 1518, but one of the Lucas Horenbout miniatures of 1526 still shows him without a beard. He was already overweight, with a small, cupid's-bow mouth that spoke of selfish petulance. His piercing blue eyes are seen in Joos van Cleeve's portrait, 1530, in the Royal Collection. He is very much an imposing and impressive figure in this and the Hans Holbein portrait of 1536, when he was 45.

His clothes are cloth of gold or silver, rich silk and sarsenet, ablaze with jewels. Henry's costume set the standard for fashion. 'His fingers were one mass of jewelled rings and around his neck he wore a gold collar from which hung a diamond as big as a walnut.'[10] But later Holbein portraits, and even more so the Cornelys Matsys in the Bibliothèque Nationale in Paris, show that physically it was downhill all the way.

Henry had red-gold hair inherited from his mother, Elizabeth of York, while his height came from her father, Edward IV. He was, in fact, a true York, no doubt much to the disgust of his father Henry VII, Henry Tudor. He took after his maternal grandfather rather than the thin and sallow, pinched-featured Henry Tudor and his domineering mother, Margaret Beaufort. Edward IV was a blond giant renowned for his good looks. His skeleton at Windsor shows that he was six foot four and strongly built, but by the time he was 40 he was inclined to corpulence through excess and debauchery. Mancini records that he 'pursued with no discrimination the married and unmarried, the noble and lowly' and once discarded, his mistresses became prey for his friends: 'as soon as he grew weary of dalliance, he gave up the ladies much against their will [to] courtiers'.[11] Edward was wilful and highly secretive, surrounding himself with sycophantic cronies – all traits he clearly passed on to his grandson.

Henry VIII continually had to be amused and those around him, even serious men such as Thomas Boleyn, were expected to join in the nonsense. The court had a veneer of culture, bolstered by ceremonial extravagance that would lead in time to heavier and heavier taxation and the near bankruptcy of the exchequer. The cost of a wardrobe lavish enough for attendance at court was enough to destroy some gentry. Sumptuous, jewel-encrusted clothes flaunted their wearers' wealth and status.

The King set out a strict dress code in order to separate the classes. Only those above the rank of earl or countess were permitted to wear cloth of gold or silver, and purple silk. Only barons, Knights of the Garter, Privy Councillors, their wives and those above them in rank could wear satin and silk, while only the eldest sons of knights and above could wear velvet. Heavy fines were imposed on those who defied these regulations. But Thomas Boleyn was heir to the title of Ormonde, with half its fortune and lands inherited from his Butler grandmother.

Tradition tells us that the Boleyns were upstarts, from a family of lowly London merchants, but tradition leads us astray. Anne Boleyn was better born than Henry VIII's three other English wives. She was of 'descent of right noble and high thorough regal blood' with great-grandparents who included a duke, an earl and the granddaughter of an earl.[12]

Thomas Boleyn's marriage to Elizabeth Howard was an ambitious match as her father and brother in turn inherited the dukedom of Norfolk, one of the greatest noble titles in England. The Howards had been out of favour for supporting the House of York but now regained much of their influence after Elizabeth's brother led the English victory against the Scots at Flodden in 1513. The Howards were influential patrons, but Thomas did not owe his success to his in-laws but rather to his own merit. He was never close to his aggressive brother-in-law and as years went on they clashed many times, in particular because Norfolk remained a staunch Catholic while the Boleyns became firm advocates of the evangelical faith.

By contrast with the immoral circle closest to the King, Thomas Boleyn appears a man of integrity, hard-working and diligent, a man without a hint of scandal attached to his name – at least not until his eldest daughter, Mary, became the King's mistress.

Boleyn was educated, a good companion for a King who considered himself to be an intellectual and was fascinated by the 'New Learning'. As the 16th century began a revolution was under way, an earthquake that would shake the very foundations of civilisation and change the face of Europe. It was a convulsion in society and class, in belief and education. Reform was suddenly on the agenda as the world began to open up through exploration and trade, shaking the old accepted traditions and status quo in politics, the economy, the arts – but most of all in thinking.

The invention of the printing press had created a new industry in literature and education. It was the beginning of the Information Age. And the great moving force behind this tidal wave of change? It was the Bible. The revolutionary concept was that, for the first time, the Scriptures should be available to the common man in his own language, no longer in Latin, the sole preserve of the authoritarian Roman Catholic Church. Literacy was on the march and with it came enlightenment and the heady promise of freedom.

For if a man might read for himself the very words of God, what need was there of a mediator or a priesthood? What need of confession, of fines and penance if God alone could provide salvation? What need of the Church?

There was panic in the Vatican. Reformist writings exploded on to the scene across Europe, reaching into every sector of society. The seeds of revolution had been planted. The movement began to spread like wildfire.

Erasmus of Rotterdam laid the intellectual foundations of the Reformation, visiting fellow scholars in England and being introduced to Henry VIII at court. His *Enchiridion, Handbook of the*

Christian Soldier (1503) and *Greek New Testament* (1516) ran into more than 20 editions. Erasmus had discovered that the Church's Latin Vulgate Bible was inaccurate. Not only that, but many of the beliefs taught by the priesthood had not been authorised by the Bible but invented by men. Worst of all, many of the Church's rituals were directly imported from pagan religions. But Erasmus was tolerated because his critique was limited to an intellectual debate. It was not until Martin Luther launched his very public attack on the Church in 1517 that Europe was really set on fire.

In England Cardinal Wolsey denounced the so-called 'heretics' and launched the whole machinery of his ecclesiastical police state against suspects. The Bible in English was banned. In the summer of 1521 a sinister and frightening scene had taken place in the shadow of St Paul's Cathedral in the heart of London. Crowds gathered to watch in awe as flames leapt high into the night sky and the priests added more books to the fire. The scarlet robes of the Cardinal gleamed in the torchlight. Wolsey had just issued his *fatwa* on the evangelical Christians for their heresy. The banned books that were too danger-ous for men and women to be allowed to read were excerpts from the Scriptures translated into English. The leaders of the Roman Church were burning the Bible.

Thomas Boleyn was a firm advocate of the 'New Religion'. He imported dangerous tracts that could have led to his condemnation as a heretic, one of which he translated and dedicated to his daughter Anne. He commissioned works from Erasmus, who wrote a com-mentary for him on Psalm 23 and called him '*egregie eruditus*', out-standingly learned.

Religion is what distinguished the Boleyn family from others at court and brought them enemies. Chief of these was Cardinal Wolsey himself, but Thomas could not be touched as long as he remained useful and close to the King.

The King spent his days amusing himself. He was a skilled horse-man who could tire out eight horses during a day's hunting. He was highly competitive in all forms of physical exercise and games with his close circle, which included Thomas Boleyn, but he must always win.[13] In 1510 Thomas was a star of the tiltyard, dressed up like a pil-grim to Santiago de Compostela in an extravaganza held to celebrate the birth of the King's short-lived son. Jousting was always dangerous, and the first time that Henry had tilted in public his favourite William Compton had nearly been killed. Henry himself was nearly killed on two occasions, although he performed 'marvellously' and 'looked like St George'.[14]

Henry also loved dancing and was said to be a gifted musician. He composed his own songs and enjoyed singing, accompanying himself on the lute and virginals. He was monumentally conceited about his skill in everything from tennis to theological discussion, regarding himself as naturally endowed with every good gift. He was encouraged in this fantasy by his sycophantic entourage, which flattered and fawned on him, competing for his favours 'in the tiltyard and on the hunting field, in the masque and the dance, in the discharge of official duties, and even in bed'.[15]

There was a lascivious atmosphere at court. Courtly pursuits were less amusing and glamorous than we might imagine. Drunkenness was common, even in the Queen's household. Foreigners regarded the English as 'licentious in their disposition'. The Spanish ambassador recorded that every woman at court was seen as a whore, every man as a pimp: 'You may imagine whether, being an Englishwoman and having been long at court, she would not hold it a sin to be still a maid.'[16]

It is doubtful whether Henry was ever faithful to Catherine of Aragon. The King's reputation was hardly a secret. Hugh Latimer, Bishop of Worcester, dared to send him a copy of the New Testament with the message: 'The Lord will judge fornicators and adulterers.'

It was said that Henry never spared a man in his anger nor a woman in his lust.[17] 'King Henry gave his mind to three notorious vices – lechery, covetousness and cruelty, but the two latter issued and sprang out of the former.'[18]

Although Henry was also considerably more discreet than his French rival, Francis I, William Thomas wrote: 'It cannot be denied but that he was a very fleshly man, and no marvel, for albeit his father brought him up in good learning, yet after he fell into all riot and overmuch love of women.'

William Compton acted as Henry's procurer, setting up liaisons and sharing women, as in the notorious case of the Duke of

Buckingham's sister, Lady Anne Hastings. When Buckingham had discovered his sister's affair with the King in 1510 he told her husband, who furiously withdrew her from court and shut her away in a convent. Compton reported this to Henry, who was outraged to lose his mistress and complained about those 'such as go about the palace insidiously spying out every unwatched movement in order to tell the Queen'. The royal marriage was already in difficulties.[19]

As he grew older, Henry surrounded himself with younger men as if to hang on to his fast-disappearing youth. The Duke of Buckingham complained that the King 'would give his fees, offices and rewards to boys rather than noblemen'.[20] These 'minions' were reminiscent of the hated cliques who had surrounded Edward II and Richard II. Both kings had paid a heavy price for choosing such degenerate favourites. But these youthful hangers-on provided Henry with amusement, flattering his ego while lining their own pockets. Their antics became the subject of gossip and parody in Hawes's *Conforte of Louers* and Skelton's drama *Magnyfycence*.

In May 1519 Cardinal Wolsey objected to the young courtiers and their 'French vices'. The Council went to see Henry to demand action. 'Certain young men in his Privy Chamber, not regarding his estate nor degree, were so familiar and homely with him, and played such light touches with him that they forgot themselves.'[21]

Henry resolved to turn over a new leaf. There was a minor purge of the worst offenders – at least for a month or so.[22] At the same time his latest mistress, Elizabeth (Bessie) Blount, gave birth to his son Henry, called Fitzroy. He soon married her off to Gilbert Tailboys, to give her some semblance of respectability, rewarding the couple with land grants and money.

Lady Hastings later returned to court, resuming an earlier affair with Compton, but the cat was out of the bag and the King's favourite was brought before Cardinal Wolsey's ecclesiastical court on charges of adultery. Henry got his own back just a few months before Anne Boleyn arrived at court. In May 1521 Henry took revenge on Buckingham on trumped-up charges of using divination to determine how long the sovereign would live. This smacked of witchcraft. Buckingham was duly executed, even though Queen Catherine pleaded on his behalf and London rioted.

Thomas More later wrote of the dangers of the court under Henry VIII: 'And so they said that these matters be Kings' games, as it were stage plays, and for the more part played upon scaffolds. In which poor men … that sometime step up and play with them, when they cannot play their parts, they disorder the play and do themselves no good.'

Behind the lavish display and extravagance lay the dark reality of life at the royal court. The poet Thomas Wyatt cynically advised that the way to self-advancement at court was to provide 'thy niece, thy cousin, thy sister or thy daughter'.[23]

This was an unstable world in which savage ambition lay just beneath the surface and information was the currency which brought patronage, the lifeblood of Tudor society. Client–patron relationships had advantages for both sides, opening doors through flattery and feigned friendship, nepotism and sinecures, extending the range of allies who might support one's case in times of trouble. Forming personal ties through service or marriage was the way to rise. Covert and backroom deals made the court a seething den of ambition and greed. Sir Anthony Denny wrote: 'The Corte … is a place so slipperie, where ye shall many tymes repe most unkyndnesse where ye have sown greatest pleasures, and those also readye to do you moch hurt, to whom you never intended to think any harme.'[24]

Every act was virtually a public performance. Thomas Elyot's bible for courtiers was *Pasquil the Playne*, recognising that they lived behind the masks of theatre, using deceit and flattery. '*Nescit dissimulare qui nescit vivere*' ('It is necessary to deceive in order to live') wrote Thomas Wyatt. 'Never let friendship get in the way of advantage – this is the only recipe.'[25] Erasmus gave this advice: 'Arrange your facial expression beforehand at home, so that it may be ready for every part of the play and so that not even a glimmer of your true feelings may be revealed in your looks… These are the rudiments of courtly philosophy… Put on a mask, as it were.'[26]

Henry's preference was for women rather than girls. Catherine of Aragon was six years his senior and the mistresses he took were not youthful. Mary, Anne Boleyn's elder sister, was already in her twenties when she became his mistress. Nor was Jane Seymour the shy young girl that many imagine her to be. In 1536 when she supplanted Anne in the King's affections, she was actually 28.

In 1522 Henry was 31, but how old was Anne? The traditional account gives her date of birth as 1504 or 1507, which would have made her either 18 or just 15. However, these are based on sources which have since proved to be unreliable. Could Anne have been scarcely more than a child when she first attracted Henry or was she a mature young woman, capable of taking on a king, just nine or ten years her senior?

In 1876 a headless corpse was unearthed at the Tower of London which an examination established was that of a female in her twenties. The idea that Anne was 'not quite twenty-nine' when she was executed comes from Jane Dormer. At her death, on 19 May 1536, Anne was just short of her birthday. If Jane Dormer was correct, she was therefore born in 1507. But how accurate is this report? Jane Dormer was not born until 1538, two years after Anne died. She was a good friend to Mary I, 'Bloody Mary', and later married Gómez Suárez, the Spanish ambassador, becoming Duchess of Feria. As an apologist for Roman Catholicism, Jane Dormer regarded Anne Boleyn as the cause and instigator of the 'heretic' Protestant Church in England and the epitome of all wickedness and her testimony is unreliable.[27]

Surprisingly, evidence that Anne was indeed older comes from one of her greatest enemies, the Imperial ambassador Chapuys. In 1536 he called Anne 'that thin old woman' – hardly appropriate for someone in her mid-twenties. In early 1533, when they married, Anne was still young and beautiful, a radiant queen, but three years later she had suffered several miscarriages and now suspected that her husband wanted to be rid of her.

Anne had earlier reprimanded Henry that for seven years she had sacrificed her youth and her chances of making another marriage elsewhere. Would she have said this if she was still only in her mid-twenties? More likely she was already in her thirties, born most probably in the early summer of 1501.

The corpse at the Tower may not have been Anne Boleyn, who was certainly in her thirties and most likely almost 35 when she was beheaded. It has never been proved that Anne was buried permanently in the Tower of London. Her family were said to have taken her body for burial elsewhere, perhaps even at Hever.[28]

Given that Henry was inclined towards women in their twenties, it is probable that Anne was of that age when she first attracted him. This was a woman, not a girl. Yet that spring of 1522 no one was prepared for the effect that she would have one day on the lives of everyone present, not least on the King himself.

What was she like, this young woman who was to captivate King Henry VIII? Certainly very different from the traditional picture that her enemies later concocted to denigrate her fame and reputation. Sander, who probably never saw her, wrote:

> Anne Boleyn was rather tall of stature, with black hair and an oval face of sallow complexion, as if troubled with jaundice. She had a projecting tooth under the upper lip, and on her right hand, six fingers. There was a large wen under her chin, and therefore to hide its ugliness, she wore a high dress covering her throat. In this she was followed by the ladies of the court, who also wore high dresses, having before been in the habit of leaving their necks and the upper portion of their persons uncovered. She was handsome to look at, with a pretty mouth.[29]

There are glaring contradictions in this report. Sander tells us that Anne had a pretty mouth yet a projecting upper tooth, and a large wen or tumour on her neck, which was thought to be a witch's teat on which an incubus or demonic male spirit could suck.

Sander does not explain how he knows this, but simply goes on to say that she wore high necklines to hide this defect. Yet portraits of Anne very clearly show that she wore low necklines in keeping with fashion. It would have been impossible to conceal either a goitre or unsightly moles with the strand of pearls or delicate gold chain we see in the National Portrait Gallery Anne Boleyn.

Neither is there any contemporary evidence that Anne had a sixth finger, or even an extra fingernail. These tales of deformity are part of the black legend that was created after her death to suggest she had been involved in witchcraft. By seeking to associate witchcraft with the Protestant religion, Catholic detractors were warning the gullible against deserting the Church of Rome. The allegations of a teat, with all its associations of demonic possession, were horrific later additions, calculated to alienate the people from Anne's daughter Elizabeth.

The phenomenon of extra digits, polydactyly, is extremely rare and anyone at court with such a difference would most certainly have provoked widespread comment.

It is known that Anne was an accomplished dancer and excellent musician. Anne was 'imbued with as many outward good qualities in playing on instruments, singing, and such other courtly graces, as few women were of her time,' records William Thomas, while De Carles says: 'She knew perfectly how to sing and dance … to play the lute and other instruments.'[30] Plucking lute strings would have shown off her hands and fingers, making it virtually impossible to hide such a glaring defect.

George Wyatt notes that Anne had introduced new fashions which included long, hanging sleeves. This is the basis for the story that Henry VIII wrote 'Greensleeves' in praise of Anne Boleyn. He claims that when she played cards with Catherine of Aragon she tried to hide the 'little show of nail, which yet was so small' on one of her fingers.[31] This scene is pure invention. Catherine did not play cards, although Anne did. She could not have excelled in these courtly skills had she been trying continually to hide an extra finger.

We must ask whether it is at all probable that any woman with such glaring physical traits would ever have been invited to court, given the attitude in that period that a monstrous appearance represented an evil soul? Until recent times, deformed children were hidden away, ostracised even by their families. It is inconceivable that she would have been received at the royal courts in Burgundy, France and England, selected to wait personally on the Queen of France and Catherine of Aragon or invited to take part in court masques designed to catch the King's eye.

Is it credible that someone of that appearance would be singled out by Henry, becoming the object of his very public desire and keeping him captivated for seven years? Disadvantaged in such a way, Anne would have had no hope of success in the marriage market, let alone have won and held the interest of the King of England.

The Venetian diplomat Francesco Sanuto describes her as 'very beautiful', De Carles calls her 'beautiful and with an elegant figure' and

Simon Grynee as 'young and good-looking'.[32] The cleric John Barlow stated that the King's mistress Bessie Blount 'was more beautiful', although Anne was very eloquent and gracious, '*competement belle*', or reasonably attractive, as well as '*de bonne maison*', from a good family.

Sander says she was tall, others 'of middling stature'. By contrast, Catherine of Aragon was extremely short and had put on weight by the time she entered middle age. In 1519 the Venetian ambassador described her as 'old and deformed'.

Women were supposed to be delicate little creatures with peaches-and-cream complexions and fluttering blue eyes. Blondes were said to be more cheerful in temperament and submissive to men. In her youth Catherine of Aragon had matched this template, although with the passage of time that freshness had faded and, with it, the King's love.

It was the fashion for women to use lotions to lighten their hair and skin. The blonde tresses of Pope Alexander VI's daughter, Lucrezia Borgia, were widely copied by the prostitutes of Rome by wearing wigs. Sunburned skin was to be deplored as suggestive of peasant women who laboured outside in the fields. A dazzling white skin was seen as a sign of wealthy indolence and various potions and herbs were used to achieve this, including concoctions made from ivy, saffron and sulphur.

So how dark was Anne? She has been said to be the opposite of the currently fashionable ideal, which held up the blonde Mary Tudor as the epitome of feminine beauty. Yet in her wedding portrait Mary is not shown as fair but with hair much darker than Anne's.

Anne was called sallow, *olivastra*, but then her daughter Elizabeth was also described as tall and even swarthy by Michieli, the Venetian ambassador, in 1557. According to Simon Grynee, Anne was 'rather dark' and Thomas Wyatt gave her the poetic name 'Brunet'.[33]

Although no contemporary portrait of Anne Boleyn has survived, this does not mean that none was ever painted.[34] In an era dominated by the genius of Hans Holbein, Anne would surely have chosen him to undertake her portrait for posterity. If so, this no longer exists. The contentious Holbein drawings reputed to be Anne remain supremely unconvincing, suggesting a missing masterwork and its mysterious, unhappy disappearance.

The National Portrait Gallery portrait is a copy from some lost original recreated later in the century by an unknown artist. This is no doubt the most authentic likeness we have of Anne. The oval face with high cheekbones and prim mouth bears certain similarities with portraits of her daughter.

It is a fallacy that Elizabeth bore no resemblance to her mother. They were both above average height and shared the same features and dark, expressive eyes. The main discrepancy is in the colouring of the hair, but as we have seen previously – and as the National Portrait Gallery portrait clearly indicates – Anne's hair is best described as a rich auburn rather than black. There is a reddish tinge that may be an inheritance from Irish ancestry. Her eyebrows are not dark but of the same colour. The eyes are hazel brown, not black.

Anne's mother, Elizabeth Howard, was a very great beauty, whom John Skelton compared to Cressida.[35] Her daughters inherited her striking looks, but Anne clearly got her colouring from her Irish ancestors on her father's side of the family. Her rich auburn hair can be seen mirrored in Thomas's fiery beard.

In the coloured drawing by Holbein, Thomas is shown as strongly built, with the same long nose and dark eyes as Anne. He cuts an impressive figure in his fashionable court clothes. The slashed doublet was a trend imported from the courts of Italy and France, while the long beard became the sign of evangelical reformers and was *de rigueur* at court in the latter years of Henry VIII's reign.

The painting in the National Portrait Gallery shows Anne also dressed in the height of fashion. The black gown with extraordinary sleeves trimmed in reddish fur accentuates her hair. The whole attire is perfectly coordinated to match the sitter's colouring, which is shown off by the fashionable French hood that Anne made so famous. This round, jewelled headdress sat on the back of the head, unlike the gable hood, which covered the hair. For the first time in more than 300 years women showed their hair. The innovation was regarded as very avant-garde and even shocking. Catherine of Aragon scrupulously adhered to the gable headdress to hide her hair and was followed in this by Jane Seymour after Anne's death. It was not until the 1540s that the fashion was revisited. Anne's daughter Elizabeth began wearing the French hood again, perhaps as a quiet sign of defiance or in homage to the memory of her mother.

The same style of French hood was repeated in an exquisite enamel miniature made for Elizabeth around 1575. This hinged double portrait with a matching likeness of Elizabeth herself was set into a secret compartment in a ring of rubies and diamonds.

This is surely proof that Elizabeth not only did not believe her mother to be an adulteress and a witch but also accepted Anne's portrait to be a good likeness. For years she kept the miniature portraits secret, but on her deathbed in 1603 the ring was taken from her finger by Robert Carey, who carried it straight to Scotland as proof that James VI was now also King of England. Later given to Lord Home, the ring passed into the collection at Chequers, the Prime Minister's official country residence.[36]

In the National Portrait Gallery portrait Anne is wearing long necklaces to emphasise the low-cut bodice, together with a pearl choker that displays her fine neck. This is hardly compatible with the view that she had some kind of deformity of the neck or a goitre. From the choker hangs a delicate golden pendant in the form of the letter 'B', for Boleyn.

Anne was described as thin, with small breasts. The fashion was for very low-cut necklines, although women flattened their breasts by binding them tightly under the stomacher. But less than modest women pushed their breasts up to make them spill over the tops of their gowns and so show off their voluptuous figures. Sanuto remarked that Anne did not follow this trend, for her breasts were 'not much raised'. He reports on her visit to Calais with the King in 1532: 'Madame Anne is not one of the handsomest women in the world; she is of middling stature, swarthy complexion, long neck, wide mouth, bosom not much raised, and in fact has nothing but the English king's great appetite and her eyes, which are black and beautiful.'[37]

Her eyes were among her most attractive features. De Carles wrote of them: '…eyes always most attractive which she knew well how to use with effect. Sometimes leaving them at rest and at others, sending a message to carry the secret witness of the heart. And, truth to tell, such was their power that many surrendered to their obedience.'[38]

The sophistication of her costume, with its very precise details and jewellery, suggests that this portrait was an exact copy of a genuine likeness of Anne. She was always noted for her style and elegance. George Wyatt wrote that in her attire 'she excelled them all' and even Sander acknowledged that Anne was 'well dressed, and every day made some change in the fashion of her garments'.[39] Black was a favourite colour at that time and regarded as highly sophisticated. It is recorded in the Privy Purse Expenses for 1532 that Henry bought his intended bride a black satin and taffeta 'night gown' or dressing robe.[40]

Other variations on an original portrait can be seen at Hever and in the miniature by John Hoskins the Elder (c.1590–1664/5) now in the collection of the Duke of Buccleuch and Queensberry. On the back of this someone has written: 'from an ancient original'. In both portraits Anne wears the same style of French hood. In the one at Hever she holds a rose, symbolising her link to the House of Tudor.

Providing a contrast with the images of the fashionable queen we have just considered, there are two Holbein sketches said to be of Anne, one in the Royal Collection at Windsor, the other in the British Museum, previously held at Weston Park.[41] The Windsor drawing portrays the sitter in a state of undress, wearing a furred dressing robe over undergarments or a chemise. The woman wears a tight-fitting coif, or 'biggin', tied firmly under the chin and showing hardly any hair. She appears to be an invalid or indisposed. It seems a nonsense to believe that the Queen would ever have agreed to sit for a portrait dressed like this, yet it has been argued that this is Anne because the sitter's double chin recalls Sander's description of her alleged abnormalities.[42]

Starkey suggests that Anne could have sat for a portrait in this state of undress because the standards of her household were so low that she thought nothing of appearing in *déshabillé* around men other than her husband. Yet far from running a lax moral household, Anne as Queen was renowned for her strict supervision of her ladies and maids. Jane Wilkinson, her silkwoman, recalled that her attendants and servants never had 'any leisure to follow such pastimes as daily seen now-a-days in princes' courts' but kept them busy with charitable works.[43] Anne's household was strictly moral and expected 'to embrace the wholesome doctrine and infallible knowledge of Christ's Gospel'. After her coronation Anne's Vice-Chamberlain, Sir Edward Baynton, wrote to her brother, George Boleyn, lamenting the fact that 'pastime in the Queen's chamber was never more'.[44]

This sketch by Holbein was labelled in the 18th century, copying an alleged identification after Holbein's death by John Cheke that this was 'Anna Bollein Queen'.

Starkey and Rowlands conclude this is Anne because, although Cheke was not at court in Anne's lifetime, he was Edward VI's tutor and must have had access to those who knew her. Cheke certainly attempted to identify Holbein's many sitters but he made several errors, notably in relation to Thomas More's family. It is possible that he mistakenly identified this sketch, too. Clearly it is not Anne, for the reasons previously stated, and because the hair was blonde.

The Holbein drawing in the British Museum (of which there are later painted versions at Hever and Hatfield) shows a woman in a gable hood, which Anne disliked. It was not inscribed as 'Anna Regina' until 1649, when in Latin was added: 'Anne Bullen was beheaded, London 1536.' This work is dated 1530 and the sitter's age is given as 27: 'HR 1530 – *aetatis* 27'. Friedmann took this as proof that Anne was 27 in 1530 and therefore born in 1503 or 1504,[45] but it is more probable that this is a portrait of Jane Seymour.

Other portraits said to be of Anne include a miniature by the Flemish artist Lucas Horenbolte, 'the King's painter' from 1528 to 1532.[46] The shape of the face, with its tiny glimpse of light-blonde hair under the ginger cap of the headdress, is plainly at odds with the description of Anne, yet Roy Strong claims the jewel on the bodice of the sitter is her falcon badge. Anne did not adopt the falcon as her badge until she became Queen, in 1533, and the jewel in the picture does not follow the design of the falcon in her badge. The provenance of the miniature reveals that it was originally in the possession of the Seymour family, which suggests that this also is Jane. A further portrait, formerly at Nidd Hall, shows another woman wearing a jewel with the initials 'AB'. An engraved version by Richard Elstrack in 1618 changed the 'AB' pendant to a square-cut jewel. Both show a strong resemblance to the Holbein mural at Whitehall depicting Jane Seymour.

Why these images of Jane Seymour should have been identified as Anne Boleyn remains a mystery. It appears that the campaign of defamation against Anne, which caused her downfall and did not diminish after her death, led to the deliberate destruction of many original portraits as well as documents. This may be seen in a medal dated 1534 in which the image has been defaced. It bears the initials 'A.R.', for 'Anna Regina', together with her motto, 'The Moost Happi'. Yet there is some doubt about the identification, because the sitter wears a gable headdress.[47]

Whether Anne was beautiful or not, there can be no doubt that she was stunning. Her impact was not limited to mere looks. From her very first appearance at court she set tongues wagging, dividing opinion and starting a wave of speculation that has not ceased since.

Chapter Two

The Marriage Market

WHAT MADE ANNE Boleyn so very different? Her looks, style and intelligence were to make her a beacon, shining out among Catherine of Aragon's dour Spanish ladies. Anne is perhaps the prime example of a new breed of Renaissance women who were literate and had received a formal education, unlike Jane Seymour and Katherine Howard, who could neither read nor write. Anne's keen mind was the reason why her father Thomas chose her above her elder sister, Mary, to be educated abroad.

In May 1512 Henry VIII had sent his troubleshooter Thomas Boleyn on a damage-limitation mission to the Habsburg court of Burgundy at Mechelen, ruled by the Archduchess Margaret of Austria. The daughter of Maximilian, the Holy Roman Emperor, she was a widow and a powerful woman in her own right, who chose not to remarry but acted as agent for her father and guardian of her nephew, who became the next Emperor, Charles V.

The Holy Roman Empire was a medieval revival of the ancient Roman Empire. It occupied most of central Europe and Italy and was ruled by the German Habsburg dynasty from 962 to 1806. Although emperors were officially elected, in effect a Habsburg was always chosen to take the crown of Charlemagne, who first sought to create a united Europe.

This vast European empire was organised into ten regions ruled by Imperial courts, such as that in Burgundy.[1]

Thomas the diplomat was not often at Hever with his family. Early in his career he had been present at the marriage of Prince Arthur to Catherine of Aragon and formed part of the escort for Princess Margaret when she travelled to Scotland in 1503 to marry James IV.[2] As envoy for Henry VIII, he travelled for months over great distances in terrible conditions. It took two days to cover the 70 miles from London to the English Channel, first by barge down the Thames, then by post horse to the coast. Richard III had established a system of couriers with mounted messengers posted at 20-mile intervals.[3] Cardinal Wolsey once set a record by travelling from Richmond Palace to the court of Burgundy in just 36 hours. He made the return journey in an equally impressive time, completing the entire mission in four days. When he got back, the King assumed he had not even started.

Thomas reported back that negotiating with Emperor Maximilian was like dealing with a man on a horse out of control.[4] Niccolò Machiavelli had written in 1505: 'The Emperor Maximilian is a secretive man – he does not communicate his designs to any one … those things he does one day he undoes the next.'[5]

Thomas made a greater success with the Regent, Margaret. They even bet against each other on whether a deal could be done within ten days, putting up horses as the prizes. As she lost the wager, Thomas now had her in his debt.[6]

The court of Burgundy was the pinnacle of style and sophistication. The New Learning received a welcome here, where printing had made its first impact. The arts and revolutionary religious ideas abounded. They knew 'the right way of doing things'.[7] It was this enlightened education that Thomas wanted for his younger daughter, Anne.

The Boleyns have generally been seen as examples of *nouveaux riches*, grasping *parvenus* and social climbers, but the times were apt for the rise of these 'New Men'. England in the 14th and 15th centuries was a society in flux after the ravages of the bubonic plague, 'the Black Death', which between 1348 and 1361 destroyed over two million or half of the country's population. In its wake, ambitious men with talent had unprecedented opportunities to rise in rank among the old aristocracy. The kingdom was in chaos. The Peasants' Revolt, the seizure of the crown by the House of Lancaster and murder of Richard II led to a century of intermittent civil war, culminating in what is known as 'the Wars of the Roses'. The incompetent reign of the apparently mad Henry VI permitted the rise of New Men who aspired to attain the highest offices of state.

The Duke of Suffolk came from a family of Hull merchants. The Beauforts rose to power through an extramarital affair, as did the whole Tudor line. Children who had been born on 'the other side of the blanket' were suddenly converted into the highest nobility. When 13-year-old Margaret Beaufort married Edmund Tudor, no one could have imagined their son would become King Henry VII of England.

It was in this shifting landscape of social revolution and savage war that the Boleyns first made their mark. They had always been an upwardly mobile family, originating from the English-held territories in France.[8] By the mid-15th century Geoffrey Boleyn had made a successful career as Master of the Mercers' Company, becoming alderman, Sheriff of London and then Lord Mayor of London in 1457–8. His second wife was the heiress of Thomas Lord Hoo and Hastings and his son Sir William became a baron of the Exchequer, one of the leading gentlemen in Norfolk and the Duke of Norfolk's deputy. He inherited manors in Hertfordshire and Bedfordshire from his maternal grandfather, and owned Blickling Hall and Hever Castle. He also married well, to Lady Margaret Butler, daughter and co-heiress of the Earl of Ormonde, with vast estates in Ireland. Their son Thomas was Anne Boleyn's father, born either in 1477 or 1480. He was therefore either 14 or 11 years older than King Henry VIII and a contemporary of Thomas More.[9]

The Boleyns were gentry but people said that Thomas had married above his station in life. Elizabeth Howard was the daughter of Thomas, Earl of Surrey, and granddaughter of the Duke of Norfolk, but until she received her jointure in the summer of 1501 the newlyweds were forced to survive on the returns from their house, Blickling Hall, near Norwich,[10] as Thomas himself complained: 'When I married I had only £50 a year to live on for me and my wife, so long as my father lived, and yet she brought me every year a child.'[11]

As they were married in 1498 or 1499 it is probable that by the date of Thomas's father's death Elizabeth had perhaps borne five children, of whom only three survived: Mary, Anne and George.[12] All the Boleyn children were born in Norfolk; later, Anne's private chaplain, Matthew Parker, Archbishop of Canterbury in 1559, stated unequivocally that she was from that county, as he was.[13]

There has been some confusion in ordering the Boleyn children. Historians have argued over who was oldest, who youngest, and which year Anne was born. There is evidence to show that George's first appearance at court was as a child in a Christmas play in 1514, when he would have been about nine or ten. Therefore he was the youngest of the Boleyn children, born between 1503 and 1505. Later he was a royal page until 1524, when he was awarded a grant just before he married at the age of 20. In 1529 he received a place in the Privy Chamber, waiting upon the King. That same year Jean du Bellay protested that George was still too young to be appointed as ambassador to France. He is unlikely to have said this had George been born in 1500.[14]

So, if George was the youngest child, which Boleyn sister was the elder? Boleyn family history confirms it was Mary, probably born in 1499 or 1500. Her grandson, Lord Hunsdon, stated beyond all doubt that she was older than Anne. In 1597 he claimed the earldom of Ormonde through Mary. Had Mary been younger than Anne, then Anne's daughter, Queen Elizabeth, would have had prior claim to the title. To suggest, as Friedmann did, that Hunsdon discounted the Queen's rights on the grounds of her alleged illegitimacy is frankly absurd. No loyal subject of Elizabeth ever believed that she was illegitimate and only a madman would have dared to challenge her publicly on an issue that smacked of high treason.[15]

Anne was the middle child, born most probably in the early summer of 1501. The later date of 1507 meant she would have been a child of only six when she was sent abroad,[16] yet 12 was the minimum acceptable age for a maid of honour at court. We are asked to believe that, although her years in France were spent not at court but in the children's nursery, she somehow became the accomplished courtier who dazzled Henry VIII. We know Anne was at court because De Carles tells us: 'la Boullant, who at an early age had come to court, listened carefully to honourable ladies, setting herself to bend all her endeavour to imitate them to perfection, and made such good use of her wits that in no time at all she had command of the language...'[17]

The children of the gentry were traditionally brought up strictly, following a tight schedule of education and exercise. Literacy, the Scriptures, good manners and skills such as riding to hawk and hunt, archery, music and dancing were on the syllabus for the Boleyn sisters and their brother George. With their father at court, their mother was left to run the household at Hever, with its home farm, woods and tenant farms belonging to the estate. Her managerial skills were passed on to her daughters, who one day would be expected to be able to supervise their own property as married women. As the only surviving male heir, George would receive a more formal education, at Oxford University, to prepare him for a more public career, following in his father's footsteps.

Thomas Boleyn wanted his daughters to have the opportunity of education at the highest level. They might not be able to share George's advantages by going to university, but the chance of a place for one of them at the courts of Burgundy and France, the birthplace of the New Learning, was an offer he could not refuse.

It had been the custom since feudal times for children to be sent away at a tender age for education or an apprenticeship. The nobility sent their sons to become pages to those above them in the hierarchy, and, although the practice was less common, some girls would serve as 'gentlewomen' or 'maids of honour'. This 'placing out' was seen by foreign visitors as a sign of the English 'want of affeccion' towards their children, but it provided the opportunity for advancement, as well as to widen social contacts and improve marital prospects. Certainly the practice was widespread at the great courts of Europe.

Thomas shrewdly called in his debt, persuading Regent Margaret to take Anne to be trained in her household, as a maid of honour. He clearly recognised that she had a brighter intellect than her sister Mary, as well as displaying an early enthusiasm for the French language. In the early summer of 1513 he returned to England and immediately arranged for Anne to go to Burgundy. The Boleyns were on the rise.

Margaret of Austria was a great patron of the arts, encouraging the composers Antoine Brumel, Pierquin de Thérache, Pierre La Rue and the poet Jean Lemaire de Belges. It was a very rare atmosphere for a girl of just 12, but Anne Boleyn was an immediate success with her exalted hostess. Margaret, clearly delighted by the girl's intelligence and character, speedily wrote back to Thomas praising her:

> I have received your letter by the Esquire Bouton who has presented your daughter to me, who is very welcome, and I am confident of being able to deal with her in a way which will give you satisfaction, so that on your return the two of us will need no intermediary other than she. I find her so bright and pleasant for her young age that I am more beholden to you for sending her to me than you are to me.[18]

The Regent announced she was pleased to find '*la pettite Boulain*' so well spoken at '*son josne age*', her young age. Anne was alone in a foreign land, and even at 12 she would have appeared vulnerable. It was probably her first time away from her family and Hever.

Even more traumatic is the suggestion that she may have just lost her mother. Conflicting dates are given for the death of Elizabeth Howard: as late as 1557, April 1538 or as early as 1512.[19] If Anne's mother died when she was only 11, while Thomas Boleyn was still travelling widely as a diplomat in Europe, this would have been a further incentive for Anne's father to have his daughter securely settled for the next few years. It is said that Thomas remarried, giving his children a stepmother, a new Lady Boleyn.

Anne was away from her family in a strange land, and even the excitement of the journey and her first sight of the elegant palaces could not dispel a natural nervousness. It was all such a contrast with Hever. Anne was a country girl plunged into the rarefied atmosphere of the Imperial court. The cost of this venture was considerable. A brand-new wardrobe suitable for court was a very great expense for Thomas and perhaps provoked envy in Mary.

Our first glimpse of the young Anne is the letter she wrote home to her father from Veure, a hunting lodge near Brussels where the court spent its summers. The letter, from around 1514, was written to practise her French, but the lines are evenly spaced, the letters stylish. Anne's handwriting suggests an adolescent rather than a small child who has just learned how to write the alphabet. She very neatly corrects her errors in the language above the line.

She was showing off her French, apologising for errors. The letter (here in the author's translation) must have pleased her father, for he kept it safe, and today it can still be read in Corpus Christi College, Cambridge.

Sir,

I understand by your letter that you wish that I shall be of all virtuous repute when I come to the Court and you inform me that the Queen will take the trouble to converse with me, which rejoices me greatly to think of talking with a person so wise and virtuous. This will make me have greater desire to continue to speak French well and also spell, especially because you have so recommended me to do so, and with my own hand I inform you that I will observe it the best I can.

Sir, I beg you to excuse me if my letter is badly written, for I assure you that the spelling is from my own understanding alone, whereas the others were only written by my hand...

I promise you that my love is based on such great firmness that it will never grow less, and I will make an end to my [word illegible] after having commended myself right humbly to your good grace.

Written at five o'clock by your very humble and obedient daughter

Anna de Boullan.[20]

The queen to whom Anne refers was Catherine of Aragon, whom she was expecting to serve after finally completing her education and taking up a place at the English court. Study and a strict regime of courtly etiquette were the rule of the Regent's household. Anne was set to perfect her French, learn music and comport herself in a manner that would set her apart in any court. It is interesting to note that her father had warned her about guarding her character and chastity. This could hardly have applied to a six-year-old girl. Anne ends the letter with a promise of obedience and obvious affection, showing how close she was to her father.

The Regent Margaret was an accomplished musician and

composer, encouraging Anne to develop her own musical talents. Anne played the lute and was probably taught the keyboard by the organist Henri Bredemers, sharing lessons with the future Emperor Charles V and his sisters, Eleanor, later to become Queen of Portugal and France, and Isabel, later Queen of Denmark.²¹ Anne may have brought back to England the book of compositions now found at the Royal College of Music in London.

Although she was in Burgundy for only a year, Anne clearly made a strong impression and quickly adapted to the sophisticated standards of the Imperial court. However, soon international politics and diplomacy rudely interrupted her idyll.

War with France had cost Henry VIII five times his annual revenue. In 1514, when his father-in-law, Ferdinand of Castile, made a separate peace, Henry considered it treachery. He devised a shrewd plan to counteract Spanish influence: marrying off his 18-year-old sister, Mary, to the ageing Louis XII of France. In this complex game the role of princesses was to pay the price of diplomacy. Almost from birth Mary had been used as a pawn in international politics, but she was remarkably strong-willed and famous for her tantrums. She was, in fact, a spoilt brat. Yet, in this instance, she plainly had good cause to be, for the people 'spake shamefully of this marriage, that a feeble, old and pocky man should marry so fair a lady'.²²

After refusing outright to go through with marriage to a man over 30 years her senior, she apparently came to some arrangement with her brother. She agreed to become Queen of France as he demanded, but with conditions. Knowing that Louis XII had gout and was reportedly sick, with not very long to live, she struck a deal by which, on becoming his widow, she would be free to choose her own husband the second time round.

Did she already have a candidate in mind? The legend is that she had already set her heart on Charles Brandon, her brother's boon companion and a much-hated *roué*. Brandon was an *arriviste*. His dissolute lifestyle and close personal resemblance to Henry had led to his being called the King's 'bastard brother'.²³ He was Henry's partner in tournaments and seemed to accompany him everywhere. The nobility loathed him as an upstart but Henry appeared willing to forgive him for every scandal.

Brandon left his first wife, Anne Browne, to marry her aunt, 43-year-old Margaret Mortimer. Two years later he abducted Anne Browne, by whom he had two daughters. When she died, in 1512, he betrothed his eight-year-old ward, the heiress Elizabeth Grey. On 15 May 1513 the King created him Viscount Lisle, in right of his future wife. Brandon finally had a noble title, but Margaret Mortimer still claimed their marriage was valid. Effectively, he had two, and even three, wives for years until the marriage was finally annulled by the Pope in the 1520s. None of this had any effect on the King's opinion of him. In February 1514 he raised Brandon to the very highest degree of society by creating him Duke of Suffolk, the title of the Yorkist de la Pole family.

Henry's drinking and whoring companion was now one of the three greatest noblemen in England, together with leading aristocrats Thomas Howard, Duke of Norfolk and Edward Stafford, Duke of Buckingham. 'From a stableboy into a nobleman,' commented Erasmus scathingly.[24] The fact that Brandon was considerably older than Mary and already had two ongoing marriages and innumerable affairs to his name, as well as currently wooing the Regent Margaret, seemed not to trouble her at all. Henry guessed that Mary intended to promote Brandon into the royal family, but he was satisfied that she agreed to go to France now as he desired. Nevertheless, knowing his friend's character all too well, he extracted a promise from Brandon that he would not pursue Mary in future.

A proxy royal wedding duly took place, and the Venetian ambassador Badoer records Mary's curious delight at the prospect of a husband who was 'an old man and gouty ... so pleased was she to be the Queen of France'.[25] On the following day, 14 August 1514, Thomas Boleyn wrote to the Regent Margaret from Greenwich asking her to release his daughter Anne and to return her in the care of the escort he had sent to Burgundy. Thomas was clearly deeply embarrassed by his master's strategy, knowing the rift it must cause with the Habsburgs: 'My very dear and renowned lady, I recommend myself as humbly as possible to your good graces.'

He explained that Mary Tudor had personally requested Anne's attendance upon her as Queen of France, perhaps because she spoke French. This may or may not have been true, but it was a ready excuse to cover his discomfort. The Regent was certain to be affronted by such a snub and proved slow to release Anne to take up her new position in France.

The royal bridal party was ready to set off for Paris, led by the Duke of Norfolk and, ironically, Brandon. Among the Princess's attendants was 15-year-old Mary Boleyn. Perhaps it was true that Mary Tudor had asked for both Boleyn girls to join her train, as they were closer to her own age than the matronly Lady Guildford. This is another indication of the true ages of Anne and Mary. It is improbable that the young bride would have requested the company of a child of seven.

The royal wedding took place on 9 October 1514. It is not known if Anne attended the ceremony. De Carles records her departure from Burgundy: 'My lord, I am well aware that you know and have known for a long time that Anne Boullant first came from this country when Mary [Tudor] left to go to join the King [Louis XII] in France to bring about the alliance of the two sovereigns.'[26]

Mary Tudor's marriage lasted for 82 days. Louis's gout did not prevent him from boasting that he had been an eager bridegroom and had 'crossed the river' three times. Just after Christmas Louis wrote to Henry telling him how pleased he was with his young bride. He then dismissed Mary's English retinue led by Lady Guildford, seeking to replace them with his own people. Mary was deeply upset and complained bitterly to her brother and Cardinal Wolsey. In the end Norfolk hand-picked just a few girls who would remain, including his Boleyn relative. Records show that payments for service between October and December 1514 were made to 'Marie Boulonne', not Anne, who must have joined Mary later in Paris.[27]

Meanwhile Wolsey was writing to Mary with advice should Louis suddenly die. Recalling her pact with Henry, he warned her that should her new husband shuffle off his mortal coil, she ought not, in any circumstances, think about a second marriage, 'and if any motions of marriage be made unto you, in no wise give hearing unto them'.[28]

As if to fulfil the Cardinal's prophecy, Louis was found dead on New Year's Day 1515. The marriage had obviously put a strain on Mary's ageing husband – he was 52.

Mary Tudor became briefly '*la reine blanche*', for the young widow dressed in traditional white robes. For 40 days there was to be official mourning, with the young widow in forced seclusion at the Hôtel de Cluny until it could be proved that she was not pregnant with her dead husband's heir. Twenty-year-old Francis I was crowned on 25 January. Charles Brandon returned to France but not in time for the ceremony.[29]

What happened next is highly controversial and the subject of much debate. Mary claimed that Francis came to her and confessed a passion for her, offering to put aside his wife, Claude, in order to marry her. When she refused, he tried to rape her. Mary fought him off, but had been badly frightened. She turned for help to her brother's best friend, Brandon, who, providentially, had just returned to France, and quickly married him for her own protection.

Francis's version is somewhat different. The King claimed that Mary had confided her love for Brandon and wanted his support to help them marry. She was worried that Henry was planning another dynastic marriage for her, perhaps with a Habsburg in an alliance against France. Naturally, Francis was pleased to assist her. Brandon's version confirms this in one respect. Shortly after his return to France he was summoned to a private audience with Francis to discuss his plans to marry Mary. He denied it, but, to cover himself, wrote urgently to Henry. Mary was afraid, he told him, that she would be sent to Burgundy and married off there. 'To the which she said she had rather to be torn in pieces than ever she should come there, and with that wept. Sir, I never saw woman so weep.' He ended, somewhat lamely, by saying: 'and so she and I was married'.

It was a secret ceremony, deliberately kept from the English diplomats at court, he explained. 'Therefore they know not of it, nor the writing of this letter on my faith and truth.'

A flurry of desperate letters across the Channel kept couriers fully occupied over the next few months trying to sort out the entire fiasco before it turned into an international scandal.[30] Brandon asked Wolsey to seek retroactive support for the marriage, telling him that Mary was already pregnant by him:

...and the Queen would never let me be in rest till I had granted her to be married. And so, to be plain with you, I have married her heartily, and have lain with her, in so much I fear me lest that she be with child.

My lord, I am not in a little sorrow if the King should know it, and that his Grace should be displeased with me. For I assure you that I had rather have died than he should be miscontent... Let me not be undone now, the which I fear me shall be, without the only help of you... for I assure you that I have as heavy a heart as any man living, and shall have till I may hear good [tidings] from you...

At Paris the 5 day of March by your most assured, Charles Suffolk.[31]

Wolsey can only have been shocked at this frank revelation. Brandon and Mary were playing a very dangerous game. It was a treasonable offence to marry a royal princess without the King's permission. Besides, it was far from certain that Brandon was free to marry anyone. Given the scandals attached to his name, not to mention at least two wives at home, this was tantamount to a great insult. Margaret Mortimer was still fighting the annulment of their marriage in a ten-year battle at the Vatican and meanwhile Brandon's betrothal to his child ward, Elizabeth Grey, was another impediment. It could be said he already had two wives, without adding a third.

'With sorrowful heart' Wolsey wrote that he must tell the King. For days Mary and Brandon must have waited in dread to hear Henry's reaction. Then a second letter from the Cardinal warned that Mary's brother seemed more concerned about keeping hold of her dowry and jewels than the scandal with Brandon. Wolsey suggested that if Brandon could secure these, then the King's approval might be won:

...for I assure you the hope that the King hath to obtain the said plate and jewels is the thing that most stayeth His Grace constantly to assent that ye should marry his sister; the lack whereof, I fear me, might make him cold and remiss and cause some alteration, whereof all men here, except His Grace and myself, would be right glad.'[32]

Brandon wrote flamboyantly to Henry: 'Punish me rather with prison, Sir, rather than you should have me in mistrust in your heart. Strike off my head and let me not live.'[33]

Mary also kept up the pressure, first submitting a draft of her letter to Wolsey. She reminded him that she had only 'consented to his request, and for the peace of Christendom, to marry Lewis of France, though he was very aged and sickly' on condition that if she survived him she should marry whom she liked:

> Whereupon, Sir, I put my Lord of Suffolk in choice whether he would accomplish the marriage within four days or else that he should never have enjoyed me; whereby I know well that I constrained him to break such promises he made Your Grace, as well for fear of losing me as also that I ascertained him that by their consent I would never come into England. And now that Your Grace knoweth the both offences of the which I have been the only occasion, I most humbly and as your most sorrowful sister requiring you to have compassion upon us both and to pardon our offences.[34]

The Boleyn sisters were witnesses to this whole fiasco. As attendants upon Mary Tudor, they were able to observe the scandal at first hand, but their responses proved to be very different.

Anne must have been delighted to see Mary again after they had been separated for a year. Mary would have found her younger sister remarkably changed from the timid girl at Hever. Anne had gained an advantage over her, growing into a sophisticated young woman who was accustomed to the Imperial court, who knew how to conduct herself and could speak the language.

By contrast, this was Mary's first venture into the wider world and the dazzling experience of the French court clearly went to her head. She had attended Mary Tudor over past months, two young women in an alien world. They shared the same excitable, flirtatious natures and enjoyed the flattery of handsome courtiers. Anne, on the other hand, had received a more restrained introduction to court life, supervised by the strict but cultured Regent Margaret.

The promiscuity of Francis I was to become notorious. The new King used his wife Claude as a breeding machine and soon established his own '*petite bande*' of courtesans. He installed secret doors and spyholes in his many palaces to serve his voyeuristic tastes. It was recorded that 'rarely did any maid or wife leave that court chaste'.[35]

Even if Mary Tudor's rape story was an exaggeration, Francis clearly drank 'water from many fountains'. One such spring was Mary Boleyn.

Perhaps encouraged by her mistress's sexual antics with Brandon, she had joined wholeheartedly in the depravity of the French court. Mary Tudor's example surely gave her namesake *carte blanche* to behave in a similar manner.

Surely here lies the reason for the obvious dislike that always existed between Mary Tudor and Anne Boleyn.[36] Anne's reaction to the promiscuous goings-on in Mary's chambers must have set her apart from the others. Her father's religious inclinations and injunction to keep her virtue had an impact. Perhaps she revealed her distaste or disapproval rather too openly, or perhaps she blamed her royal mistress for her own sister's wild behaviour and all its consequences.

Mary Tudor's manipulative strategy paid off. A second marriage ceremony took place in Paris on 31 March and another was planned for the couple's return to England, but the public reaction was still hostile 'because the Kingdom did not approve of the marriage'.[37] There were even calls for Brandon to be tried and executed, but Wolsey made a deal with the King. The newly-weds must get Francis's consent to repay Mary's dowry of 800,000 crowns, out of which they must pay Henry a fine of £4,000 a year.[38] Here Henry was showing the financial meanness of his father.

Mary signed a document agreeing to give up her dowry to Henry, but when she and Brandon left France in mid-April she also contrived to smuggle out the great diamond known as the Mirror of Naples, part of the French crown jewels.

Francis I never forgave her. Years later he described her as *'plus sale que royne'* – 'more dirty than queenly'.[39]

So unpopular was the marriage in England that while he and Mary were still in Calais, Brandon was attacked by a mob and had to hide in the Deputy's house.[40] Wolsey met them at Dover. The financial wrangling was still going on. It was finally agreed that they would pay Henry £24,000 in instalments over the next 12 years. Henry forgave Mary and for the rest of her life she insisted on being addressed as if she was still the 'French Queen'.

For a few brief months of 1515 Mary Boleyn attracted the French

King's attention and she became his mistress. Mary was already sexually notorious while still only 16 or 17, but Francis soon tired of her and passed her on to his courtiers, much as Henry VIII shared women with Brandon and Compton. Later Francis was to cruelly recall the girl, calling her 'my hack, my mule' – it was hardly a great romance. He described her to an Italian diplomat as '*una grandissima ribald et infame sopre tutte*' ('a very great whore, the most infamous of all').[41]

Mary passed on from man to man in what seemed to her to be a dazzling career of advancement, but Thomas, far from regarding his daughter's fall from grace as some kind of ambitious career move, which certain writers have claimed, swiftly recalled her to England in the wake of Mary Tudor. Despite her reputation, or perhaps because of it, in England she went on to become Henry VIII's mistress.

Anne remained in France for six years, waiting upon the ailing Queen Claude. There could not have been a greater contrast between sisters than that between the two Boleyn girls.

Traditionally, Thomas Boleyn has been viewed as a selfish schemer who used his daughters as political pawns, consecutively manipulating them into Henry's bed and then just as treacherously dropping them. Some historians insist that it is clearly impossible to defend Sir Thomas. They claim that he was avaricious and represented all that was bad about the court.[42] But is this picture of Thomas Boleyn realistic?

A closer examination shows us that, on the contrary, he was a man of principle, learned and daring in taking risks for his beliefs. He was a supporter of the New Religion, a Protestant, although this term was not in use until 1529. There had been Lollards in England for 100 years, followers of Wycliffe, who first had the temerity to translate the New Testament into English. 'Evangelical' perhaps describes these believers best. Secret churches met to read the Scriptures. Forbidden Bibles were being smuggled into the country from printers overseas. Tracts were passed from hand to hand and committed to memory, for possessing them was dangerous. An underground resistance ran this subversive operation. The Church had tried its best to eliminate the movement through denunciations, arrests and executions. Yet now here was another tidal wave of new opponents of papal authority and power.

Anyone who travelled was suspect. Merchants, tradesmen, students and government agents had been bringing the banned books into England. Copies were being discovered all over the country, hidden in vats and bales. They had to be rooted out. The Church paid informers to sniff out their trail. Denunciations settled old scores. One word could bring Cardinal Wolsey's men crashing into houses up and down the land. The pursuivants came with carpenters and masons with the expertise to measure walls for secret rooms and hiding places. They ransacked homes, broke through walls. The discovery of an English Bible led to arrest and imprisonment, usually with torture, the confiscation of all goods and perhaps even death at the stake.

It was one thing to round up the artisan and lower classes, but the Church faced the problem that the secret networks included gentlemen and even members of the royal court. Diplomats became suspect. Men of growing influence like Sir Thomas Boleyn were involved in bringing in the new religious works. They were brazen in such activities, almost flaunting their beliefs. Cardinal Wolsey had clashed with Boleyn over it, but it was regrettable that such ringleaders close to the King could not be touched. Not yet, at least.

Thomas opposed the kind of restrictions on female education that Catherine of Aragon imposed on her daughter Mary. The misogynist views and purdah-like conditions advocated by Juan Luis Vives were anathema to anyone who believed in religious reform.

Vives taught Princess Mary that women were the only imperfection in God's creation. They were the authors of original sin and, from birth, 'the devil's instrument, and not Christ's'. Unless strictly confined and controlled by fathers and husbands, they would give way to temptation and wickedness. Their inherent sinfulness was a threat to everyone around them. 'A woman that thinketh alone, thinketh evil,' declared Vives, believing that a woman should remain at home, out of sight of men and silent, with 'few to see her and none at all to hear her'. If it was ever necessary to leave the house at all, then she should be covered from head to foot, with 'scarcely an eye open to see the way', after the Islamic manner then found in Spain and in Arab society today.[43] By contrast, the new evangelical movement included many strong women who risked their lives for their beliefs. Fifty-six women were to be burned at the stake by the very Queen,

Mary I, who had been taught and indoctrinated by Vives' repressive mindset.

The idea that during Anne's time in France there was no network of evangelical believers is totally false. Jacques Lefèvre d'Etaples, the leader of religious reform in France, had spoken out openly against the tyranny of the Roman Church five years before Luther emerged on the scene. His commentary on Paul's letters, which Anne read, had been published in France in 1512. Lefèvre's life was in danger but he enjoyed the protection of Francis I's sister, Margaret of Angoulême, later Queen of Navarre. It is astounding that in the midst of the lascivious French court Margaret should become a courageous evangelical, using her privileged position to promote her faith and offer protection to persecuted fellow believers. All this was happening while Anne Boleyn was present at the French court.

Margaret found willing allies in Anne Boleyn and her father. The three shared not only an avid intellectual curiosity but also a decided leaning towards religious reform and the New Religion, the hot topic of the moment.

Anne was most certainly influenced by this remarkable woman, who was ten years her senior. They were so closely connected that Herbert of Cherbury even believed that Anne served in the household of 'the Duchess of Alençon [Margaret of Angoulême], sister to Francis'.[44]

An early French translation of the Bible by Jean de Rely was reprinted seven times between 1487 and 1521. Anne had her own copy. From 1519, when Anne was still in France, the great poet Clément Marot was a protégé of Margaret. He later made a translation of the Psalms that went into an amazing 500 editions.

In 1521 Lefèvre had to be rescued from a lynch mob at the Sorbonne. Through Margaret's influence, he was appointed tutor to the royal children and librarian in the château at Blois, where Queen Claude and Anne Boleyn were often resident.

Those who claim that Anne was corrupted by her experience at the French court have deliberately distorted reality in order to blacken her reputation. In the new Queen's household the atmosphere was very different from that of the court. Far from joining in the dissolute lifestyle of Francis I's entourage, as her sister Mary had done, Anne spent her days in attendance on the sickly Claude, keeping her company, reading together, playing music and doing silkwork. She would have caught rumours and whispers of the King's latest scandals, but she was not one of them.

Claude was 15, of an age with Anne, but plain, with a pronounced limp and a quiet, retiring disposition. As Queen of France she endured a succession of annual pregnancies, eventually bearing seven children before her early death in 1524.[45]

The Queen's household included several hundred young women who were being educated according to a strict code. They moved between palaces on the River Loire. King Francis remodelled Blois, where she had been born, between 1515 and 1524, and completed the palaces at Fontainebleau and Chambord. In 1516 Anne could have met Leonardo da Vinci when he was received at court in Amboise.

Anne kept company with women of the highest moral standards, devoting herself to the improvement of her skills in language, composition and the arts. She could 'handle cleverly both flute and rebec' and would sing, accompanying herself on the lute and virginals. There exists at Hever a nine-stringed lute which is said to have been hers. Anne wrote her own compositions but, like almost everything else she ever penned, these were later destroyed by her enemies.

Anne was 'very expert in the French tongue, exercising herself continually in reading the French Bible and other French books of like effect, and conceived great pleasure in the same'. She also knew some Latin.[46] Her earliest book is a traditional Latin work, a Book of Hours from Bruges in Burgundy from about 1450. She signed it and wrote in the flyleaf: '*le temps viendra*' ('the time will come'). This can still be seen at Hever. All her other books were evangelical works in French or English.

In January 1519 Thomas Boleyn was posted to Paris as ambassador. Henry VIII believed there was no skilled negotiator to equal him.[47] Thomas must have been in frequent contact with Anne at this time because he often mentioned Queen Claude's poor health in his official dispatches. Henri, Duc d'Orléans, born in March 1519, was her fourth child since 1515. Thomas stood as proxy for Henry VIII at the christening. That October an outbreak of plague forced the Queen's household to move to Amboise, as recorded by Anne's father.

The following year Thomas was responsible for all the arrangements for the lavish summit meeting between the Kings of England and France which became known as the Field of the Cloth of Gold. The English delegation, with a retinue of 5,000 nobles and knights, established an astonishing glass palace in the midst of their encampment. For two weeks in June Henry and Francis competed with each other in feasts, tourneys and even wrestling matches. Forty thousand gallons of wine and 14,000 gallons of beer and ale were consumed. The political extravaganza achieved nothing and was described by John Fisher as a symbol of the instability of the secular world.[48]

Anne was there with Queen Claude, who was expecting yet another child that August. When she dined with King Henry at Guisnes, the Boleyns were all reunited. Lady Boleyn had come from England with Anne's brother George and sister Mary.

Relations between the two sisters must have been uncomfortable. Mary had been recalled from France in disgrace, but now she was in attendance upon Queen Catherine of Aragon while simultaneously warming King Henry's bed. Francis I cannot have failed to notice that Henry was now riding his 'English mare'.

There could not have been a greater contrast than these two sisters, Mary and Anne. The elder had eagerly embraced the opportunity to make a mark for herself by copying the example of her mistress, Mary Tudor. Her road to advancement was through the use of her feminine wiles to manipulate men. Her reputation was sacrificed to be close to men of the highest influence and in this she was remarkably successful: two kings in quick progression. Her affair with Francis was extremely brief. With Henry she did not make the same mistake, holding out for some reward for her labours.

On 4 February, while Thomas Boleyn was still away from England, the King had married Mary off to William Carey, one of his attendants, much in the same manner as he had married off Bessie Blount to cloak their affair.[49] Henry himself attended the wedding, knowing that the bride's father was away on a diplomatic mission and could not object.

Anne's time in France was now drawing to an end. After her father gave up his post, diplomatic relations between England and France went into a sharp decline. Cardinal Wolsey now favoured a Habsburg alliance again and Thomas Boleyn was sent on a mission to Emperor Charles in September 1521. It was no longer advisable for Anne to stay in France or to imagine a time when she might marry some French nobleman. Besides, another opportunity in the marriage market had now presented itself. Late in 1521 Thomas unexpectedly asked for his daughter's return to England to marry the heir of the Earl of Ormonde.

How much of a surprise this was to Anne we cannot know. She had always been groomed to make the best possible match on behalf of her family. The Boleyns had always advanced through marriage, allying the family with nobility who could act as patrons for the future. Given her extraordinary education, Anne was now expected to draw a husband from among the very highest rank and title. This was why Mary's hasty marriage to the lowly second son of the Carey family was far below the family's expectations. Thomas was not about to make the same mistake with Anne.

It is likely that Thomas had been negotiating for this marriage for some years. In August 1515 the Earl of Ormonde had died, leaving his daughters, Margaret Boleyn and Anne St Leger, in dispute for his lands and titles. Thomas Boleyn was his favourite grandson, to whom he had earlier given the treasured relic of Thomas Becket's ivory drinking horn. He was also Ormonde's executor, with control of half of his English estates, including New Hall in Essex, which he later sold to the King for a sum equal to several million pounds today. Henry undertook his usual construction work and renamed it Beaulieu.

The remaining lands and the Ormonde title had been seized by the murderous Piers Butler with the backing of many leading Irish lords. In the spring of 1520 King Henry sent the Boleyns' relative Thomas Howard, Earl of Surrey, to Ireland as Lord Lieutenant. Howard proposed that the situation could be resolved through the marriage of Butler's son James to his niece Anne.[50] On 21 November 1521 Thomas Boleyn had written from Bruges in Burgundy to Cardinal Wolsey to try to hasten the prospective marriage.

The relationship between Thomas and the Cardinal was always poisonous. Thomas was a trusted diplomat, a confidant of the King, increasingly respected and influential, but Wolsey regarded him as a

heretic who sponsored the illegal trade in evangelical works and sub-
sidised the underground network of believers in England and abroad.
To Wolsey, Thomas was a dangerous canker right in the heart of the
court, worming his way into the King's confidence and spreading
heretical beliefs that threatened the Cardinal's own power base. Their
enmity grew more intrusive and perilous as the years passed.

Thomas Wolsey is the prime example of the rise of the 'new man'.
A butcher's son from Ipswich, he succeeded in obtaining a university
education, gaining his degree at Oxford at the age of 15. He took holy
orders as a means to advancement and a career at court. In 1507 he
became a protégé of Richard Fox, Bishop of Winchester, and was
made chaplain to Henry VII. Wolsey was soon trusted with diplomatic missions abroad to Scotland and Burgundy. He was made Dean
of Lincoln and, with the accession of Henry VIII, Royal Almoner.
Before long he was exerting influence over Henry, taking on the
work of government while the King hunted and amused himself. By
September 1515 Wolsey was a Privy Councillor, Archbishop of York,
Cardinal and the Pope's representative, as well as one of the richest
men in England.

He represented everything that was rebarbative to an evangelical
like Thomas. His increasing wealth and the scandal of his private life
made him the symbol of the corrupt soul of the Roman Church.
Wolsey had at least one long-term mistress, Joan Larke. He kept her
in his London house at Bridewell, just behind Fleet Street. He had two
children: Dorothy, born in 1512, who became a nun, and a son, who
was known as Thomas Winter. It is possible that Dorothy's mother
was another mistress of the Cardinal, Joan Clansey. It was common for
priests to call their illegitimate children nephews and nieces, and
Wolsey was no exception, but no one was fooled. Wolsey transferred
church revenues to provide for his son, making him Dean of Wells in
1526. After this he was sent to university in Louvain, Paris and Italy.
Winter's extravagance was one of the charges brought against Wolsey;
this referred to 'his son Winter' and 'the great treasure and charges and
the promotions ... converted to his own use thereby'. Clearly the
Cardinal's vows of celibacy meant nothing to him. But in this he was
hardly unique. Corruption was a byword for the Catholic Church and
the cause of much condemnation among the people.

As Thomas Boleyn's deadly enemy, Wolsey intercepted his mail and already had sought to bring about his downfall in 1515, when he had targeted him with complaints and false insinuations.[51] He succeeded for seven years in depriving Thomas of the post of controller of the royal household, even though the King had promised it to him. For, as Giustinian recorded: 'The cardinal of York is the beginning, middle and end.'[52] He had risen to unprecedented influence. At a banquet in 1517 for the Imperial ambassador he had dined at the King's table while the nobility of England sat at a lower table.[53] Gwyn argues that for Wolsey 'the most important thing was to dominate affairs, and by this means bring honour to his master – and, of course, to himself'.[54]

At this time there was no supporting evangelical court faction. Thomas Boleyn was very much a vanguard, daring to be different and trusting in his ability to keep the King's favour and therefore his protection.

Wolsey wrote to Henry from Calais before sailing for England on 28 November 1521. He pledged to 'perfect' the marriage between James Butler and Anne Boleyn. Although he took up the case, how sincere was the Cardinal? He was simultaneously telling the King that James Butler was too valuable a hostage to be freed:

I shall, at my return to your presence, devise with Your Grace how the marriage betwixt him and Sir Thomas Boleyn's daughter may be brought to pass, which shall be a reasonable cause to tract [delay] the time for sending his said son over to him; for the perfecting of which marriage I shall endeavour myself at my return, with all effect.[55]

Ives suggests the marriage was a political solution to unrest in Ireland and only temporary. James Butler returned to Ireland in August 1526. By then the Ormonde match was long dead.[56] The land dispute was finally settled in 1528 and the following year Thomas Boleyn became Earl of Ormonde. The Boleyns' influence was then at its zenith. The King's infatuation with Anne Boleyn had brought about Wolsey's ruin, but whatever part the Boleyns may have had in this, the Cardinal surely must have regretted not having seen Anne off to obscurity in Ireland.

The fruit of Anne's experience abroad had been her exposure to the wider world. The sumptuous palaces of Europe were very different from the quiet country manor houses where she had spent her childhood in England. At first hand she had seen how the movers and shakers of the great nations and empires lived and comported themselves. She had discovered the values and ambitions of three distinct kinds of women close to the apex of power.

She was appalled at the frivolous, pampered Mary Tudor, so briefly Queen of France. A witness of her tantrums and manoeuvres to bring about the marriage with Charles Brandon, she felt cold distaste for Mary. The secret liaison, the weeks of begging letters back and forth between England and France, followed by the financial haggling, laid bare the sordid nature of the 16th-century marriage market.

Anne's anger at her sister's antics and the disgrace that she brought to the Boleyn name never diminished. Her own reputation was scarred by Mary's careless disregard for the effect her wantonness would have upon her younger sister.

In stark contrast, Anne had witnessed the example of Queen Claude, the betrayed wife. In the face of her husband's notorious affairs, the Queen meekly accepted the role of brood mare, bearing child after child, year after year, and devoting herself to good works.

The whore or the saint: these seemed to be the prototypes set up by the Church's historic misogyny. But was there no alternative model to follow?

Yes, for Anne had seen for herself that it was possible to be an independent thinker, set free from the pattern of sinful Eve or patient Griselda. She had been in the company of clever, strong-willed women like the Regent Margaret of Austria and Margaret of Navarre. The influence of evangelism had enabled women of character to take an alternative path, one that offered Anne Boleyn a different future.

Chapter Three

The King's Desire

ANNE SOON WON admirers. One of those who became obsessed by her was Henry Percy, son of the Earl of Northumberland, who had been placed in Cardinal Wolsey's service. He was a year or so younger than Anne and heir to vast lands on the Northern Marches bordering Scotland. Wolsey's usher Cavendish claims he personally witnessed Percy's infatuation, but he was writing during the reign of Catherine of Aragon's daughter, Mary, the enemy of Anne and everything she stood for, and presents her as the instrument of Wolsey's destruction: 'The Lord Percy would then resort for his pastime unto the Queen's chamber and there would fall in dalliance among the Queen's maidens, being at the last more conversant with Mistress Anne Boleyn than with any other.'

Tradition has it that Anne returned Henry Percy's love and that the pair shared a brief romance. However, there is no evidence to prove conclusively what Anne thought of her new suitor. Although she remained the betrothed of James Butler, Ormonde's heir, Percy claimed that she had given her promise to marry him.

Eventually Wolsey summoned Percy and warned him to stop pursuing Anne: 'You have not only offended your own father but also your sovereign.' Wolsey was acting on orders from Henry, claiming that the King had other plans for Anne. He had 'already promised this lady to someone else and that though she is not yet aware of it, the arrangements are already far advanced'.[1]

Was this a reference to the Ormonde match? Surely Anne had already been told about this, as it was given as the reason for her recall from France. But Cavendish tells us this was just a ruse, used to conceal the fact that Anne was already intended for the King himself.

Both Cavendish and George Wyatt later stated that Henry was absorbed by Anne from the moment she made her first appearance at court. Cavendish writes that she showed such 'exemplary behaviour and excellent deportment that she quickly outshone all the others. To such an extent, in fact, that the flames of desire began to burn secretly in the King's breast, unknown to all, least of all to Anne herself.'

But how much of this is true and how much hindsight?

In April 1522, after the *Château Vert* pageant, Thomas Boleyn was appointed Treasurer of the Household, the position that had been kept from him by Wolsey's opposition to his evangelical faith. Why this promotion now? Mary Boleyn had been Henry's mistress for two years and anyway Thomas opposed their affair. Yet Henry was showing him special favour.

Wolsey was told to warn Percy off, but the suitor was not willing to give up Anne so easily. He told Wolsey that he was 'of sufficient age and in a good enough situation to be able to take a wife of my own choosing', and defended Anne's 'very noble descent': 'On her mother's side she has Norfolk blood and on her father's side she is a direct descendant of the Earl of Ormonde. Why then, sir, should I query the suitability of the match when her pedigree is of equal worth to mine?'

Wolsey rebuked and threatened him: 'I order you and in the King's name command you not to see her again if you intend to avoid the full wrath of his majesty.' He then summoned Percy's father from Northumberland. This took place in the summer of 1523, according to a letter written by Percy senior complaining about the expense of having to return to London to sort out his son's rash behaviour.

Percy had been betrothed to Lady Mary Talbot, daughter of the Earl of Shrewsbury, but Wolsey had intervened in 1516 to stop the marriage. Now he positively sanctioned it. This action highlights his continuing enmity with the Boleyn family, whom he most certainly did not want to see connected to the powerful and wealthy earldom of Northumberland.

It was later claimed by Chapuys that Percy and Anne had promised to marry and that this amounted to a legal pre-contract because the relationship had been consummated. But his story is wildly inaccurate, as he dates the whole affair to 1527, when Percy was already married to someone else.[2] By Cavendish's account, Anne was twice betrothed and simultaneously, but neither betrothal was binding under canon law as neither match had been consummated. He confirms that Anne remained a virgin until her marriage with the King.[3]

There is no evidence to show that Anne either promised to marry Percy or was ever deeply interested in him. However, it would have been a far greater marriage for her than to have wedded Ormonde. Marriage was first and foremost a hard-headed business contract based on land rights and social standing, not love. If husband and wife got along together, that was a bonus. Romance was just foolishness.

Percy married Mary Talbot in January or February 1524,[4] but did he ever really recover from his obsession with Anne? His marriage was childless and miserable. He inherited his father's title in 1527 and wasted the family's entire wealth in the decade before his death. In 1536 he was cruelly forced to sit in judgement at Anne's trial, which made him physically ill. The next year he was dead.

Cavendish claims that Anne never forgave Wolsey for preventing her marriage to Percy and that later she was to seek revenge against him.[5] But there already existed enmity between Wolsey and the Boleyns, based on their evangelical faith and opposition to the Catholic Church.

In 1523 Thomas Boleyn was on diplomatic business in Spain and perhaps ignorant of what had been going on. It is unlikely that he would have entered into negotiations for a new marriage for Anne while abroad, even if it was a much better match for her to marry into the Percy family rather than into the Ormondes of Ireland.

When Thomas did get back it seems that he removed Anne from court to the safety of Hever. While he could do nothing to prevent the King's affair with Mary, he could try to protect his younger daughter.

As to what Anne's movements were after Percy was sent away from London by his father in the summer of 1523, we can only speculate. Bishop Burnet stated that she returned to France to serve

Queen Claude, staying until 1527, but given that Claude died in 1524 and relations with France were at an all-time low, this is highly improbable.[6] It appears far more likely that her father, returning from a diplomatic mission and discovering what had occurred during his absence, immediately removed her from the dangerous orbit of the King to the family seat at Hever.

The rolling green countryside, soft contours of the hills, neat patchwork fields and apple orchards made Kent the Garden of England. Hever's moated manor house dated from the 13th century. The honey-coloured stone keep was surrounded on all sides by the River Eden, which was inclined to flood. The inner yard was small and cobbled, accessible by a drawbridge under a portcullis. Thomas Boleyn had moved with his wife and three young children from Norfolk after his father's death in 1505. The years of financial restraint were finally over and Thomas carried out dramatic alterations, creating a new Long Gallery over the Great Hall. These changes turned what had been a medieval manor house into a modern and fashionable family seat for the new Boleyn dynasty.

Was Anne's return to Hever a punishment, banishment?[7] Or was Thomas, as a cautious father who had already lost one daughter to a predatory king, simply removing her from danger? But even Hever did not prove to be a safe haven from the King, for it seems that he followed her there. Henry was frequently at neighbouring Penshurst Place in the company of her sister, Mary, dropping in while hunting or to pay a family visit.

Much of the affair with Mary Boleyn was conducted at Penshurst, which had been part of the estate of the Duke of Buckingham, managed by Thomas Boleyn since May 1521, when Buckingham was executed on trumped-up charges. Was Henry issuing a not very subtle reminder to Thomas of what happened to those who opposed him?

Buckingham's fate had shocked Europe, but those close to the King remembered his fury when Buckingham had interfered in Henry's affair with his sister, Lady Hastings.

Under his boisterous and frivolous public face, the King was stubborn, cold and calculating. He was peevish and totally unpredictable, subject to violent mood swings, abusing courtiers verbally and physically. His tantrums caused embarrassing scenes.

Henry had a pathological cold streak that made him truly danger-ous. He savagely punished ministers for failure and was obsessive about many things, including punctuality. His high-pitched voice could be heard savaging his attendants. He could change his opinion in an instant and transfer his favour without warning. For anyone ejected from the King's intimate circle, it was as if the sun had gone out.

All the more remarkable then that Henry should remain obsessed by the same woman, Anne Boleyn, for more than seven years.

Henry flaunted the affair with Mary, even naming one of his ships the *Mary Boleyn* in 1523.[8] She gave birth to a daughter, Catherine Mary, in 1524. Although Henry did not acknowledge the child, he did, in June of that year, award another grant of lands to the Careys. Mary's husband was appointed to stewardships and received royal annuities in 1522, 1523, 1524 and 1525.

Anne returned to court once her younger brother, George, came down from Oxford University.[9] Anne had always had more in com-mon with George than with Mary. They shared intellectual and artis-tic tastes, enjoying poetry, literature and theology, and, both fluent in French and with some Latin and Italian, were able to read the latest books brought from the continent.

George was about to marry Jane Parker, the daughter of Lord Morley, a family friend. Sir William Boleyn had acted as executor for the 7th Lord Morley. On 2 July 1524 the King had awarded George a grant for a manor in Norfolk. The Boleyns were high in favour. In 1526 George became the King's Cupbearer, an office of trust, and later a Gentleman of the Privy Chamber. In 1525 Thomas Boleyn was made a peer of the realm and became Viscount Rochford.[10] This was not, as some writers assert, a reward for turning a blind eye to Henry's affair with his daughter Mary, but partly a recognition of Thomas's increasing usefulness to the King and partly, perhaps, a move by Henry to smooth access to his younger daughter.

Anne was now in a vulnerable position. After the Percy negotia-tions, her betrothal to James Butler was suspended if not dead. She again took up her place in the Queen's household, for the first time an eligible prospect for a suitable husband, although, at 24, she was pressing against the upper age limit for the competitive marriage market.

She certainly attracted suitors, but not necessarily those seeking her hand. The royal court was a dangerous place for a single woman. The poet Thomas Wyatt, Anne's lifelong friend, attacked the deceit and depravity prevailing at court and the difficulty that someone of integrity faced in trying to survive there:

> None of these points would ever frame in me –
> My wit is nought, I cannot learn the way.
> ...never let friendship get in the way of advantage –
> this is the only recipe.[11]

Wyatt's acerbic satires are addressed to 'mine own John Poyntz', a minor courtier at one time in Anne's service, and to one of the most prominent men at court, her cousin Francis Bryan.

Traditionally, Henry has been portrayed as the Renaissance prince *par excellence*, artistic, crafty, with intellectual pretensions. Giustinian wrote: 'He speaks French, English and Latin, and a little Italian, plays well on the lute and harpsichord, sings from the book at sight, draws the bow with greater strength than any man in England, and jousts marvellously.'[12]

On the other hand, much that was written of him comes from the pen of those grovelling for his attention and patronage. A good example is William Roper's apologia for his dead father-in-law, Thomas More. Roper claimed that More had enjoyed a far more intimate friendship with the King than was the case. He tells of Henry habitually taking More

> into his private room, and there some time in matters of astronomy, geometry, divinity and such other faculties, and some time in his worldly affairs, to sit and confer with him, and other whiles would he in the night have him up into the leads [roof] there to consider with him the diversities, courses, motions and operations of the stars and planets.[13]

Flattery and sycophancy have distorted the real Henry. Erasmus was always seeking prospective wealthy patrons and his excessive paeans in praise of Henry VIII and his astonishing intellectual talents are not to be taken too seriously. As a second son unhindered by training for the weightier matters of state, Henry showed interest in the New Learning which was then the fashion. He was sufficiently enthusiastic to take Greek lessons from Richard Croke of Cambridge and later picked up some Spanish from his first wife, Catherine of Aragon.

After women, music was the King's greatest obsession. He had brought to his court some of the most famous musicians in Europe, including the violist Ambrose Lupo, the lutenist Philip van Wilder and Dionisio Memo, the great organist of St Mark's Cathedral in Venice.[14] There were 80 musicians in the Chapel Royal, where sacred music was sung by a choir that was 'more divine than human'.[15]

Anne's skill at music attracted a circle of talented young courtiers. In his handbook for courtiers, published in 1528, Castiglione writes: 'Gentlemen, you must know that I am not satisfied with our courtier unless he be also a musician, and unless, besides understanding and being able to read music, he can play various instruments.'[16]

Anne was not only a capable instrumentalist, but, 'when she sang, like a second Orpheus, she would have made bears and wolves attentive'. She also composed her own poems, some of which were set to music, but none of these songs has survived the deliberate destruction of everything connected with her at her fall.[17]

Henry considered himself to be a great composer, reading from sight and accompanying himself as he sang his own songs. Many of these focused on pleasure and the joys of youth, 'The time of youth is to be spent' and 'Lusty Youth should us ensue', or, sighing over some love affair, 'Alas, what shall I do for love?'[18] But perhaps the most famous remains:

> Pastime with good company
> I love and shall until I die.
> *Grudge who likes*, but none deny,
> So God be pleased, thus live will I.
> For my pastance: hunt, sing, and dance.
> My heart is set!
> All goodly sport for my comfort.
> Who shall me let?[19]

Also known as 'The King's Ballad', this is found in the Ritson Manuscript of 1510 and the songbook known as *Henry VIII's Book* or *Henry VIII's Manuscript*, of around 1513–18, which contains 33 compositions.

'Grudge who likes' as a motto was quoted by the Royal Almoner in a court sermon of March 1521.[20] It was also taken up by Anne in 1530 as '*Ainsi sera, groigne qui groigne*' ('That is how it will be, grudge who likes'), a response to a court which was full of deceit, as John Husse wrote to Lady Lisle: 'Your ladyship knoweth the court is full of pride, envy, indignation, and mocking, scorning and derision.'[21]

The motto also appeared in Burgundy at the court of Margaret of Austria, which Henry admired and sought to emulate and where Anne studied in 1513. Thomas Wyatt also cites it in 'If it ware not' of around 1530, which has the first line 'Grude on who liste, this ys my lott.'

Did Henry write 'Greensleeves' for Anne Boleyn? The sonnet, popular as a song of unrequited love, was first recorded in 1580 in the Stationers' Register as 'A new Northern Dittye of the Lady Green-Sleeves' and is twice referred to in Shakespeare's *The Merry Wives of Windsor*. The lyrics were printed in *A Handful of Pleasant Delights* in 1584:

> Alas, my love you do me wrong
> To cast me off discourteously
> For I have loved you oh so long
> Delighting in your company
>
> Chorus:
> *Greensleeves was all my joy*
> *Greensleeves was my delight*
> *Greensleeves was my heart of gold*
> *And who but my Lady Greensleeves.*
> *I have been ready at your hand*
> *To grant whatever you would crave;*
> *I have both wagered life and land*
> *Your love and good will for to have.*

> Then I will pray to God on high,
> That thou my constancy mayst see,
> And that yet once before I die,
> Thou wilt vouchsafe to love me.
>
> Chorus.

The romantic notion that Henry wrote this while pining over Anne could even be true, given his other compositions, such as:

> Whereto should I express
> My inward heaviness?
> No mirth can make me fain,
> Till that we meet again.[22]

Among Anne's circle, Thomas Wyatt was an old family friend. He had been born in 1503 at Allington Castle on the River Medway in Kent, not far from the Boleyn home at Hever. A scholar of St John's College, Cambridge, he was an aspiring diplomat as well as a poet, undertaking various missions abroad from 1524.

Wyatt's grandson, George Wyatt, recounts how the poet fell in love with Anne, ravished by 'the sudden appearance of this new beauty and then even more taken with her witty and graceful speech'. George Wyatt wrote his biography of Anne Boleyn in the late 1590s from the reminiscences of one of Anne's attendants, Anne Gainsford, later Zouche.[23]

According to her story, while flirting with Anne, Wyatt filched a small jewel as a keepsake and then always wore it on a cord next to his heart. One day during a game of bowls with the King, he saw that Henry himself was wearing one of Anne's rings. Suddenly jealous, he immediately produced his own token from around his neck, declaring that the lady was his. The King reacted with fury, crying: 'It may be so, but then am I deceived', and shortly afterwards sent Wyatt abroad on a mission to be rid of his rival.

This tale must be treated with a fair degree of scepticism. Wyatt and Anne were friends and shared a love of literature and music, but with the Percy fiasco still very much in her mind, Anne had no intention of encouraging another fruitless association. She could have had no thought of any relationship with Wyatt, as he was already married. When his interest took a serious turn away from the conventions of chivalric courtship, she promptly 'rejected all his speech of love'.

There is nothing to suggest that she and Wyatt were ever lovers. Anne and George Boleyn both wrote poetry and were good friends of Thomas Wyatt. George possessed two collections of 15th-century poems in French on love and marriage by Lefèvre, *Les Lamentations de Mathéolus* and *Le Livre de Leesce*. He and Wyatt had more than poetry in common. They were both victims of unhappy marriages, for Wyatt's wife, Elizabeth Brooke, was notorious for her affairs.

If Anne was the object of Wyatt's soulful yearning, then it was most certainly an unrequited love.[24]

> What word is that that changeth not?
> Though it be turned and made in twain?
> It is mine answer, God it wot,
> And eke the causer of my pain.
> A love rewardeth with disdain.
> Yet it is loved. What would ye more?
> It is my health eke and my sore.

The answer to this courtly riddle is 'An'er', or Anna.[25]

> Alas, madam, for stealing of a kiss
> Have I so much your mind there offended?
> Have I then done so grievously amiss
> That by no means it may be amended?
> And wilt thou leave me thus?[26]

Only a few of Wyatt's poems were published in his lifetime, in a miscellany compiled by Robert Singleton entitled *The Court of Venus*. He was among the first to introduce the sonnet, rhyming couplets such as the *rondeau* and the triplet form *terza rima* into England. A *rondeau* was a French poem, 10 or 13 lines long, with just two rhymes repeated throughout and the first words used twice as a refrain. Wyatt was inspired by the great Italian poet Petrarch's '*Pace non trovo*' ('I find no peace').

George Wyatt claims that the budding poet was still obsessed with the object of his desire, unaware at that time that he already had a rival.

The King had been 'struck with the dart of love', according to his own words in a letter to the absent Anne, 'above one whole year'. This suggests that his interest began in 1525,[27] but Cavendish insists that it had been Henry who had caused plans for Anne's marriage to Percy to be abandoned. He recorded that the King had been attracted to Anne from her first appearance at court on her return from France, possibly as early as 1522, although he was at that time involved in his affair with Mary Boleyn.

By 1525 Henry's interest in Anne was clear. Sometime during that summer Henry broke off his affair with Mary, even though she was pregnant again. She gave birth on 4 March 1526 to a boy she called Henry, who was to grow up to closely resemble his royal namesake. The King did not openly recognise him as his son, for even he had some scruples. By that time he was deeply involved with his former mistress's younger sister.

Captivated by Queen Catherine's new lady-in-waiting, he perhaps made some proposition to Anne which became the cause of her departure again from the court. Whereas other women would have been overwhelmed by such an offer and readily succumbed, Anne Boleyn, as Henry was about to discover, was different.

She no doubt thought that putting a certain distance between them would cool his ardour, but the King would not take no for an answer. Assuming that her refusal was all part of the pretty conventions of courtly love, he began his campaign to woo her by sending her the present of a deer he had killed in the hunt: 'I send you by this bearer a buck killed late last night by my own hand hoping that when you eat it, it will remind you of the hunter.'

He also complained that she had not been in contact with him since leaving court – a reaction he found inexplicable. No one refused the King. 'You have not been pleased to remember the promise which you made me ... which was that I should hear good news of you.'

There are 17 love letters in existence which Henry wrote to Anne. Nine of them are in French, undated and therefore open to controversy as to their order and timing. All are Henry's, written in his own hand. This was remarkable, given that he loathed writing anything and was always ready with an excuse to avoid entering into correspondence.[28]

The letters are now held in the custody of the Vatican, having been stolen from Anne by Catholic agents linked with the papal legate Cardinal Lorenzo Campeggio.[29] When the Cardinal left England on 5 October 1529 the King's agents searched his luggage at Dover, as the letters had gone missing. The thief was seeking to expose Henry's relationship with Anne Boleyn, no doubt expecting to prove his adultery. In fact the letters proved the exact opposite, namely that Anne had refused the King and preserved her virtue despite all speculation to the contrary.[30]

The letters are remarkable for the insight they give us into Henry's state of mind at this vital turning-point in English history. As for Anne's replies – if such there were – they have not reappeared. Possibly they were destroyed during Bloody Mary's reign or even earlier, when Anne's name was being blackened and her letters did not sit well with the 'spin' about her character.

What we do know from Henry's frantic deluge of love letters is that Anne was often absent from court and that he was reduced to demanding why she did not write to him. The most likely explanation is that she answered very few of his letters.

Clearly, he feared that she was deliberately avoiding him. Desperately uncertain of Anne's response, he resorted to bombarding her with letters, such as:

> Although it doth not appertain to a gentleman to take his lady in place of a servant, nevertheless, in compliance with your desires, I willingly grant it to you, if thereby you can find yourself less unthankfully bestowed in the place by you chosen than you have been in the place given by me. Thanking you right heartily for that it pleaseth you still to hold me in some remembrance.

This rather pathetic pleading for attention must have been a humbling experience for the King, but he was terrified of frightening Anne off for ever. This was still very much a secret relationship, even if it was one-sided. He ends the letter with the cryptic motto 'O.N.R.I. de R.O.M.V.E.Z.', before adding 'Henri Rex'.[31]

Only in these texts does he sign himself 'H Rx.'. To everyone else his signature is always given as 'Henry R.'.[32]

After her earlier disappointments in seeking to obtain a husband, Anne was not about to ruin her prospects now by becoming anyone's mistress – not Thomas Wyatt's, not even the King's. The story of her rejection of Henry is told even by her detractors; for example:

> she fell down upon her knees saying, 'I think your majesty, most noble and worthy king, speaketh these words in mirth to prove me without intent of defiling your princely self, who I find thinks nothing less than of such wickedness which would justly procure the hatred of God and of your good queen against us... I have already given my maidenhead into my husband's hands...'[33]

The King was beginning to understand that Anne was not like his other women, and very different in her morality and beliefs from her sister Mary. Anne knew 'how soon he was sated with those who had served him as his mistress'.[34]

Henry used Greenwich and Penshurst Place for his affairs, and his boon companion William Compton made his house in Thames Street available.[35] The King had sex there with the wives of courtiers such as Robert Amadas and Sir Nicholas Carew. Cardinal Wolsey was also accused of being 'the King's bawd, showing him what women were most wholesome and best of complexions'. These scandals could only confirm Anne's poor opinion of Wolsey as a symbol of the degenerate Catholic Church.

For centuries the Catholic Church had taught that women were corrupt and full of sin, the wanton daughters of Eve. They were so weak and inferior in intellect that all their lives they must be governed by men, first by their fathers, then through marriage. They must learn to be subservient and obedient, always deferring to the men who made the decisions in their lives. Beating was recommended to bring impudent and erring women into line.

All sex was evil and, unless restrained, women could become instruments of the Devil, luring men into lustful thoughts and therefore mortal sin. Only marriage could purify the vile act of sex, which was only for the procreation of children. Sex outside marriage was illegal, and fornicators and adulterers could be tried before the Church courts, whipped and forced to do penance by walking barefoot through the streets in public humiliation.

Women who did not fit the mould of either wife or whore were viewed with suspicion. As few families were sufficiently enlightened to bother to educate their daughters, any woman who showed the least trace of intelligence and independence broke with tradition and was seen as an outsider. If she also happened to be physically attractive to men, she was likely to be seen as a dangerous subversive, even a witch.

Forty years earlier two Dominican monks, Jacob Sprenger and Henry Kramer, had written a sensational book warning of the spread of witchcraft, the *Malleus Maleficarum* (The Hammer of the Witches). They now brought the Inquisition to the German states, armed with Pope Innocent VII's bull of 1484, to search out, torture and burn alive the witches of Europe. Over the next 200 years an estimated 160,000–250,000 alleged witches were executed in a wave of terror that principally targeted women.

It is not by chance that Anne Boleyn was accused of being a witch by her enemies.

We must set Anne in the context of the age in which she lived. She stood out from the other women of her time as literate, accomplished and intellectual. Her exceptional upbringing and radical education had produced a young woman who aspired to become something more than a mere chattel. Although not typical of the fashionable beauties of the time, she succeeded in drawing attention to herself wherever she went. Her self-confidence and strong, independent mind made her ready to engage in conversations and discussions that most women would shy away from, in particular on the subject of theology, which was the most controversial topic of the day.

Anne's daring participation in the sort of debate normally reserved for men had undoubtedly attracted the King. Her wit and intelligence marked her out; her very difference was a challenge. Significantly, Henry's letters to Anne indulge in intellectual language games, alluding to poems in French and playing on words.

Englishwomen certainly enjoyed far more freedom than those of continental Europe. They were not shut away in the kind of purdah practised in Spain, an inheritance of Islam, in which Catherine of Aragon kept her daughter Mary. Even before the demise of the Catholic Church in England, foreign travellers recorded with a mixture of horror and delight that Englishwomen were different.

The Italian Francesco Ferretti wrote that they were 'of marvellous beauty and wonderfully clever'. They were bold, 'astoundingly impudent', riding to hunt with the men and often showing their legs. Erasmus noted: 'You are received with a kiss by all; when you take your leave, you are dismissed with kisses; you return, kisses are repeated. They come to visit you, kisses again; they leave you, you kiss them all round.' It is no wonder that successive Spanish ambassadors saw Englishwomen, and in particular Anne Boleyn, as outrageously bold in comparison with their own strictly regulated and downtrodden women.

Evangelical believers such as the Boleyns viewed women and marriage in a way which differed sharply from the traditional Catholic outlook. A women was judged to be the partner and helper of her husband in a relationship which was even more strict on sexual misdemeanours. Such sins could not simply be wiped away by a visit to the confessional but must be purged by a change in behaviour. Sex before or outside marriage was an absolute taboo.

These religious attitudes, so strongly held by Anne Boleyn, make a nonsense of the stories spread by her enemies that she was a witch and seductress who had indulged in many illicit love affairs. As an evangelical Christian who believed in maintaining her chastity and virtue, Anne could never have sold herself so lightly. The example of her foolish sister was always before her. Mary had badly let down their father and sullied the family's name. In consequence she became something of a pariah.

Depending on the exact date of the King's letters, it is possible that, when he wrote to Anne, Mary had barely been delivered of a son commonly believed to be another of his bastards. Yet Henry could not believe that Anne would not flattered by his attention and eager to follow the same path as her own sister. Had he not ended his affair with Mary in order to take up with Anne?[36]

In February 1526, at the Shrovetide tournament, Henry arrived to joust wearing the device of a flaming heart with the motto 'Declare I dare not'.[37] This was the first public sign that he had a new romantic obsession. It must have set the court abuzz with speculation as to the latest object of the King's passion. The event was also remembered for the accident suffered by Sir Francis Bryan, who lost an eye and wore a patch ever after.

Henry's interest in Anne was not yet common knowledge, but he had broken with her sister and, so it seems, did not replace her with another regular mistress. For another year there was no suspicion at court that the King was becoming obsessed with this sparkling young woman with her charming manners, intelligent conversation and witty repartee. Nor was there any direct evidence of a relationship between Anne and Wyatt, let alone a passionate affair that might have provoked the King to jealousy.

Showing some impatience and exasperation – always a dangerous thing in a king – Henry now demanded that, after keeping him at bay for more than a year, Anne should make a firm decision whether to take him or not:

Debating with myself the contents of your letter, I have put myself in great distress, not knowing how to interpret them, whether to my disadvantage, as in some places is shown, or to advantage, as in others I understand them; praying you with all my heart that you will expressly certify me of your whole mind concerning the love between us two. For of necessity I must ensure me of this answer having been now above one whole year struck with the dart of love, not being assured either of failure or of finding place in your heart and grounded affection. Which last point has kept me for some little time from calling you my mistress, since if you do not love me in a way which is beyond common affection that name in no wise belongs to you for it denotes a singular love, far removed from the common.

Having acknowledged the fact that Anne may not be in love with him after all – however astonishing that may have been to a man of Henry's immense vanity – now he comes to the key point of the letter, his offer:

If it shall please you to do me the office of a true, loyal mistress and friend and to give yourself up, body and soul, to me who will be and have been your loyal servant (if by your severity you do not forbid me), I promise you that not only shall the name be given you, but that also I will take you for my only mistress, rejecting from thought and affection all others save yourself, to serve you only.

Written with the hand of your servant, who oft and again wisheth you [were here] instead of your brother – H.R.

Anne's brother George was an intimate of the King's Privy Chamber, with duties in the bedroom, where Henry clearly longed to place her.

What was the significance of this ultimatum? It looks as if the King was no longer willing to play the courtly game of love and was therefore raising the stakes.

Ives suggests that he was offering Anne the position of mistress before all the court, '*maîtresse en titre*', much as Francis I had Françoise de Foix and later Anne d'Heilly, the future Duchesse d'Etampes.[38] Henry clearly thought that he was paying her an enormous compliment. Although at that very time he was already beginning proceedings to annul his marriage to Catherine, he was not apparently thinking then of replacing her with Anne Boleyn.

But he was still only thinking of filling his empty bed.

Maddening Henry still further, Anne stayed at Hever and the ensuing silence drove him almost to despair:

Since I parted with you I have been advised that the opinion in which I left you is now altogether changed and that you will not come to court neither with my lady your mother, and if you could, nor yet by any other way. The which report being true I cannot enough marvel at, seeing that I am well assured I have never since that time committed fault…

I could do none other than lament me of my ill fortune, abating by little and little my so great folly.[39]

'My so great folly' must indicate that his earlier ultimatum had only served to offend her further.

Wilful, restless, Henry could take any woman he desired – except Anne Boleyn.

Chapter Four

The Curse

Henry's marriage to Catherine of Aragon was very far from a success. From the very start of the royal union, Henry and Catherine's sexual history was full of tragedy, scandals and lies.

He had always harboured severe doubts about the morality of marrying his own brother's widow, but these had been stifled to facilitate the alliance with Spain. The King's desire to be rid of Catherine was rumoured as early as 1514. As the years passed, Henry found his grand schemes frustrated by her inability to supply him with the heir he needed. A kind of desperation seized him. His obsession with perpetuating the Tudor dynasty now took centre stage. It was not a ploy to be rid of an ageing wife and replace her with a younger model, but the symptoms of an obsession which had haunted Henry from his childhood.

Henry's elder brother Arthur was Prince of Wales and would inherit all, whereas Henry was only the second son, the 'spare' as all second sons in the royal family are known. Henry had a cosseted youth and childhood, brought up away from court with his sisters. He adored his mother, Elizabeth of York, who indulged him perhaps because he reminded her of her father, the Yorkist King Edward IV. Until her death she protected him from her husband and her self-righteous mother-in-law, Margaret Beaufort.

Then, in 1501, everything changed. Arthur married the Spanish princess Catherine of Aragon and was dead within the year. Overnight 11-year-old Henry was propelled from the safe cocoon of life as a second son into the spotlight as Prince of Wales and heir to the throne. There has been a strange propensity for the English crown to pass unexpectedly to second sons, along with the heir's wife or fiancée, as happened in the 20th century to George V and Mary.

There existed a strained relationship between Henry VII and his second son. Shakespeare's stormy scenes of Henry IV and Prince Hal have some basis in truth, being inspired by the youth of Henry VIII.

As Henry entered puberty, his father arranged for him to stay in the room adjacent to his own and supervised his every move. Henry was kept on a tight rein and under constant observation as if he had been a girl in purdah, as the Spanish diplomat Fuensalida reported in 1508. He made few public appearances and was never permitted to talk without his father's permission.[1] It was a strict regime, unlike anything he had known before. Henry received a broad education but nothing in the way of preparation for government. The father clearly did not trust his son and let him leave the palace to exercise only when escorted by responsible guardians. Did he already suspect Henry's inner nature, his weakness for self-indulgence and promiscuity, or was there even more to alarm the father about the boy who would inherit his throne?

The Spanish ambassador considered this strange state of affairs, which lasted for almost eight years. His conclusion was that the King was 'beset by the fear that his son might during his lifetime obtain too much power'. He records many rows between them, including one particularly violent clash in 1508 that could not be covered up. Like Prince Hal, it seems that the King was afraid that his son was impatient to take the crown and 'sought to kill him'.

Was there any truth in this? No doubt that after being subjected to virtual imprisonment, Henry was eager to break free. Perhaps he even prayed for his father's death (which was to occur the following year). He must have looked forward to the day when he would command, rather than serve, and be free to indulge his own pleasures and repressed appetites. Yet he also saw at first hand the burden of government which crippled his father, driving him to an early grave.

Henry VII's insecure title lay at the root of his paranoia, which conveyed itself to his son. Henry VIII could not believe in the divine right of kings because he knew that his father was a usurper.

The medieval age had been dominated by the belief that God alone appointed and anointed the ruler, who represented His power on earth. Monarchs such as Richard II held an ineffable belief in their God-given authority, but this was not enough to prevent his overthrow and murder by Henry Bolingbroke of Lancaster in 1399. For the next century England suffered the consequences in bitter civil war. Richard, Duke of York had the better claim, stating that if a man steals the crown, it is no more his after 40 years than it was the first day.

It was widely believed that the House of Lancaster had sinned by usurping the crown and these sins passed on down the generations. Henry V died young. Henry VI lost France, then his throne and died insane. They were brought down by the agents of divine retribution and rightful heirs – the House of York. This was the 'Curse of England', which haunted all Lancastrian Kings and their Tudor successors.

The Tudors were the crop of a secret affair between Henry V's widow, Catherine de Valois, with a lowly groom, Owen ap Meredith ap Tudor. Catherine's father, Charles VI of France, was mentally deranged and her son by Henry V, Henry VI, inherited his grandfather's insanity. We can speculate whether this may be said to have an impact on later generations, notably in the dramatic character change and violent nature of Henry VIII.

The eldest son of the affair, Edmund, married Margaret Beaufort, dying before his 13-year-old wife gave birth to Henry Tudor, later Henry VII. Margaret was a descendant of the children from another scandalous affair, between John of Gaunt, Duke of Lancaster, and his mistress Katherine Swynford. The Beaufort line was legally barred by Parliament from the succession but this did not diminish Margaret's very elevated opinion of herself and her destiny or curb her relentless conspiracies. She had a paranoid loathing of the House of York and was instrumental in efforts to bring about its downfall. She maintained a network of secret agents, mostly priests, who conspired to manoeuvre her beloved son on to the throne.

The Tudors had no legal right or title to the crown. It was a claim based solely on the invasion of England. There was nothing heroic about Henry Tudor. He had never even lived in England. His early life was spent in Wales, separate from his mother. At the age of 14 he was forced into exile, penniless and forgotten until he became the political pawn of his French hosts. He called himself the Earl of Richmond, but the title had long been forfeit to the crown and this claim, as any other, was spurious. He was then pronounced a traitor by attainder in the English Parliament. In 1485 his invasion force included French and Breton jailbirds and foreign mercenaries – '3,000 of the loosest and most profligate persons in all that country' – who brought sweating sickness and the plague with them. After treachery at Bosworth delivered the King into the hands of his enemies, the victor, out of fear, travelled to London in a special armoured coach. Throughout all the years of his reign he lived in dread of Yorkist retaliation.

Henry VII's insecurity is demonstrated by an amazing series of acts passed in the first days of his reign. He immediately dated that reign to the day *before* Bosworth, thereby making his predecessor King Richard III and everyone who had fought for him guilty of high treason. At the same time he rushed to suppress the Act of Settlement, which on 23 January 1484 confirmed Richard's title to the crown. This document, *Titulus Regius*, had changed the course of English history and was of such momentous significance that Henry Tudor demanded that every single copy be destroyed unread.

What was so dangerous about this document that the new King feared its contents? It was already public knowledge. Only two years had passed since the greatest scandal of the century had rocked the nation.

After Edward IV's unexpected death in 1483 preparations for the coronation of his son Edward V were brought to an abrupt halt. Robert Stillington, Bishop of Bath and Wells, and Chancellor for seven years, broke his silence with the news that the prince could not become King because he was illegitimate. Edward IV's marriage to Elizabeth Woodville was never valid because he already had a wife. In an earlier secret ceremony, Edward had pre-contracted to marry another young widow, Eleanor Butler, daughter of John Talbot, Earl of Shrewsbury and hero of the French wars.

The news rocked the Council. A pre-contract was as legally binding as a public wedding ceremony if such promises led to sexual intercourse. Then only an ecclesiastical court or the Pope could grant an annulment. The problems of pre-contracts were to play a vital part in the future relationship between Anne Boleyn and Henry VIII.

Commynes reported that Eleanor Butler may even have had a child by Edward.[2] In 1464 she retired to the convent of the White Carmelites in Norwich, where she died in obscurity four years later. Once Eleanor was dead, a public marriage between Edward and Elizabeth Woodville could perhaps have legitimised any future children, but no such marriage ever took place. Instead, his earlier pre-contract was covered up and those who discovered the secret were hastily removed. Edward's own brother, the Duke of Clarence, learned of the pre-contract in 1478 and quickly realised that if his marriage to Elizabeth Woodville was invalid and their children illegitimate, then *he* would be the true heir to the throne. After a rash confrontation with Edward, Clarence was arrested and executed. It was a shock to the whole country that the King was willing to kill his own brother. Bishop Stillington was also thrown into jail but released on condition of his silence.

The 1483 crisis meant that the marriage's invalidity was widely publicised and became common knowledge. Parliament found the children of Edward and Elizabeth Woodville to be illegitimate, as was ratified in the Parliament of 1484 in *Titulus Regius*. The next in line to the throne was Edward's surviving brother, Richard of Gloucester, who became Richard III.

Henry Tudor's first act as Henry VII was to reverse *Titulus Regius* unread and to have every copy destroyed on pain of imprisonment 'so that all thinges said and remembred in the said Bill and Acte thereof maie be for ever out of remembraunce, and also forgott'.[3]

Yet although Henry VII tried to cover up the scandal, it was still 'common report', according to Polydore Vergil. In 1533 ambassador Chapuys told Emperor Charles V that he had a better claim to the English crown than Henry VIII: 'People here say you have a better title than the present king, who only claims by his mother, who was declared by sentence of the Bishop of Bath a bastard, because Edward IV had espoused another wife before the mother of Elizabeth of York.'[4]

Yet by reversing the act, Henry legitimised all the children of Edward IV, thereby making his sons Edward and Richard, the so-called 'Princes in the Tower', first in line for the throne. While Richard III had no motive to eliminate his nephews as they were illegitimate and no threat to him, Henry VII had every reason to destroy them once he reversed *Titulus Regius*.

He was obliged to marry Elizabeth of York, eldest daughter of Edward IV, because her claim was now once again far greater than his own. By repealing *Titulus Regius* he had restored the Yorkist claim. Despite the Tudors' efforts to suppress all copies of the Act, history was to play a trick on them. One copy survived in the Second Continuation of the *Croyland Chronicle*, a contemporary record of that era. 'King Edward's sons were bastards,' wrote the unknown chronicler, for 'he had been pre-contracted to a certain Lady Eleanor Butler before he married Queen Elizabeth'.[5]

Henry took revenge by refusing to marry Elizabeth of York until after his coronation or to crown her as Queen until after the birth of his heir, Arthur, when Parliament forced his hand, two years later. Henry did not attend. Bacon records that he was viewed by the public more as her consort or 'gentleman usher'. To retaliate, Henry then sent his mother-in-law, Elizabeth Woodville, into a nunnery at Bermondsey, where she died in 1492. True to his character, he also seized all her worldly goods. He was so self-conscious of his lack of any valid claim that he attempted to bolster his title by claiming descent from the mythical King Arthur, even naming his son and heir after him.

His imperious mother was the power behind the throne. Margaret Beaufort maintained a suffocating control over his actions. When separated, she kept up a barrage of cloying letters to 'My own sweet and most dear king and all my worldly joy'. She saw herself as the true sovereign, even signing herself 'Margaret R'. She despised and ill-treated her daughter-in-law, Elizabeth of York, who was far more popular with the people. The Spanish ambassador reported: 'The Queen is beloved because she is powerless ... she is kept in subjection by the mother of the King.' Elizabeth, he said, 'suffered under great oppression and led a miserable and cheerless life'.[6]

Henry treated his wife as the enemy. Not only was her presence a constant reminder that she had a better right to reign than he did, but the knowledge that she had made little secret of her preference for his predecessor destroyed any affection between them. Rumours of a romance had obliged Richard III to make a public denial at St John's Clerkenwell of any future marriage plans. Elizabeth was packed off to remote Sheriff Hutton in Yorkshire, but even distance could not diminish her hopes. She wrote to the Duke of Norfolk asking him to intercede with the King on her behalf 'in respect of the marriage propounded between them', for she was 'his in heart and thought in body and in all' and Richard was 'her only joy and maker in the world'.[7]

It was impossible for Henry to forget his wife's involvement with Richard. By his attitude and the cruelty towards her by her mother-in-law, he 'showed himself no very indulgent husband towards her, though she was beautiful, gentle and fruitful. But his aversion towards the House of York was so predominant in him as it found place not only in his wars and councils but in his chamber and bed.'[8]

Elizabeth of York bore Henry eight children, but only four survived. Arthur, the Prince of Wales, was born in 1486, followed by Margaret in 1489, Henry in 1491 and Mary in 1496. She died in childbirth in 1503, trying to bear another son to replace Arthur. She was just 38.

Henry's reputation was so poor among the courts of Europe that in 1507 he hired Polydore Vergil to rewrite history. Hay comments that he 'thoroughly accomplished his task of interpreting English history in favour of the Tudors'.[9]

Vergil blithely destroyed any documentary evidence which did not support the Tudor cause. Historical records were burned by the wagon-load while the Yorkists, and in particular Richard III, were painted as responsible for every crime and murder of the past 50 years.

Vergil's fiction stirred up great controversy, yet his version became the authorised and official history for future writers, including Hardyng, Grafton, Hall — and ultimately William Shakespeare. The Tudor myth was born.

Yet Vergil's assessment of his employer reveals Henry's true nature:

This avarice is surely a bad enough vice in a private individual, whom it forever torments; in a monarch indeed it may be considered the worst vice since it is harmful to everyone and distorts those qualities of trustfulness, justice and integrity by which the State must be governed...

The King wished to keep all Englishmen obedient through fear.[10]

The Milanese ambassador agreed: 'The King is rather feared than loved, and this was due to his avarice... The King is very powerful in money, but if fortune allowed some lord of the blood royal to rise and he had to take the field, he would fare badly owing to his avarice; his people would abandon him.'[11]

Bacon was even more honest, describing Henry as 'a dark prince and infinitely suspicious and his time full of secret conspiracies'.

The Tudors' phobia of Yorkists dominated the reigns of Henry VII and his son. After Bosworth there were 30 contenders with a better claim to the throne than any Tudor. These included all the children of Edward IV, now restored to legitimacy by the destruction of *Titulus Regius*, his seven nephews and, as time passed, all of their children. There seemed no end to the number of Yorkist heirs.

Bacon wrote that Henry had 'a settled disposition to depress all eminent persons of that house'. Between them over the years, Henry VII and Henry VIII succeeded in acts of judicial murder on trumped-up charges that removed them all. One of the first to die had been John of Gloucester, the illegitimate son of Richard III. His claim was better than that of Henry Tudor, who was merely the great-grandson of an illegitimate son of a younger son of a king.

In effect the civil war continued, for there were many who regretted the treachery at Bosworth Field. Two years later a rival claimant appeared in Ireland claiming to be Edward, Earl of Warwick, nephew of Edward IV. His coronation as 'Edward VI' took place in Dublin Cathedral in May 1487.

The following week an invasion army of 5,000 troops under the command of John de la Pole, Earl of Lincoln, set sail for England. On 16 June, at Stoke Field, near Newark, thousands were butchered, including Lincoln himself, although Henry Tudor had given strict instructions that all Yorkist leaders should be taken alive. Henry was frustrated by their deaths. Archbishop Morton said now they would never 'get to the bottom of the affair' – a reference to the mystery of the disappearance of the sons of Edward IV. Henry feared that one or more of his wife's brothers had escaped to Burgundy, waiting for the moment to mount a challenge for the throne. This demonstrates that the alleged murder of the 'Princes in the Tower' by Richard III had not yet been contrived.

In 1489 the traitor of Bosworth, Henry Percy of Northumberland, was lynched in revenge by the people of Yorkshire. In 1491 another challenger claimed to be one of the missing sons of Edward IV, Richard, Duke of York, now Richard IV. All the ruling figures of the time, including Emperor Maximilian and the monarchs of Spain and France, believed it. James IV of Scotland supported Richard and provided him with a wife.

Even Henry VII feared that Richard IV was genuine, and all official reports actually referred to him as the Duke of York.[12] Yet he still initiated a misinformation campaign claiming that this was another fraudulent pretender, Perkin Warbeck.

The Pretender was taken prisoner, yet, curiously, was not executed. Clearly Henry was still convinced that this could be a royal prince, his very own brother-in-law. The following year, however, after a bungled attempt to escape the country, Henry had 'Warbeck' dispatched to the Tower to join his cousin, the unfortunate Earl of Warwick, but he was still reluctant to have him killed, until the King of Spain forced his hand.

In Europe the Tudors were seen as usurpers. Their insecure hold on the crown meant that royal houses were loath to enter into any kind of alliance with them. Yet Henry wanted Catherine of Aragon as the bride for his son and heir Arthur. The King of Spain, openly disdainful of the new Tudor dynasty, refused the marriage while the Earl of Warwick and the Pretender Warbeck still remained a threat. King Ferdinand issued an ultimatum to Henry, insisting upon the execution of Tudor rivals to secure the dynasty.[13] Henry had little conscience in such matters and readily complied. The executions were witnessed by the Chancellor of Castile, and the Spanish ambassador, de Puebla, was now able to report back that 'not a doubtful drop of royal blood remains in England'.

Arthur married Catherine of Aragon on 14 November 1501 at St Paul's Cathedral. She was 16, he a year younger. The marriage, which was founded on blood, lasted just five months. In 1529 Catherine would claim that in all that period under constant public scrutiny Arthur shared her bed only seven times.[14] Later she was to insist that the marriage was never consummated and although she had slept in the same bed as her husband, she was still a virgin. Yet she said nothing of this at the time. Nor was there any suggestion or rumour of such a scandal among the many witnesses to the wedding night.

In that period it was the tradition for the bride and bridegroom to be 'bedded' together in the full glare of publicity. The newly married couple were obliged to suffer the humiliation of a raucous ceremony in which they were put to bed and expected to perform the necessary rituals, providing evidence on the bridal sheets of virginity deflowered for a whole spectrum of family members and even official government representatives.

The wedding of the Prince and Princess of Wales was no exception. All the traditional customs had been observed. Henry VII, his fierce mother Margaret Beaufort, his Queen Elizabeth of York, all the nobility of the English court and ambassadors of Spain and other nations present at the ceremony had no doubts that the marriage had been consummated.

There is no record that any of the many witnesses who by tradition and duty must have taken strict notice of the wedding-night requirements ever claimed it was a failure. On the contrary, the Dowager Duchess of Norfolk later brought evidence before the Blackfriars court that the marriage was indeed consummated.[15]

If the marriage was not a true one, then why did Catherine not say so at the time? This would have been a great insult to a royal princess, her country and family, invalidating the marriage contract with severe international implications.

Many couples were bedded at far younger ages than Arthur and Catherine. Henry VIII's sister Margaret married James IV of Scotland at the age of 14. Margaret Beaufort actually gave birth to Henry Tudor when scarcely 13. Why should Catherine's marriage to Arthur not have been consummated? At the time it was assumed by everyone that it had been.

Over 100 esquires of the bedchamber confirmed the bridegroom's proud boast: 'Gentlemen, I have been this night in the midst of Spain' and it had been thirsty work.[16] Thoroughly delighted with his bride, Arthur wrote to her father about his joy in the marriage: 'No woman in the world could be more agreeable.' He said he would make her a good husband.[17]

The couple took up residence as Prince and Princess of Wales at Ludlow Castle in the Welsh Marches. Then, on 2 April, Arthur suddenly died, perhaps of tuberculosis, seen as yet another victim of the curse on the House of Lancaster. He was buried at nearby Worcester.

There was no suggestion as yet that the marriage was unconsummated. In fact Catherine was now closely watched for signs of pregnancy. Tragically widowed though she was, it was assumed she might still produce an heir for the Tudor line. Accordingly, the Spanish ambassador kept himself fully informed about her menstrual health and even studied her bedlinen. Her father-in-law was less circumspect, asking her directly if she was pregnant; she denied it. This surely was the moment to finally confess that the wedding had not been consummated at all, but Catherine did nothing of the kind. She played the role of widow and was still watched for several months in order to confirm there would be no child of the marriage.

Prince Henry was now heir to the throne, and Catherine was to be returned to Spain, together with her dowry of 200,000 ducats. It was plain that Henry VII was far more reluctant to part with the money than with his daughter-in-law. He therefore proposed a marriage with his only surviving son.[18]

Catherine had been brought up to believe she would become Queen of England and was understandably loath to be sent back to Spain. For the next eight years she fought to stay in England in the hope of securing the new Prince of Wales, young Henry. Enduring poverty and insults, ignored by her own family, she insisted that because her marriage to Arthur had never been consummated she was free to marry his brother.

This highly debatable point lies at the very heart of English politics of the next 60 years.

Catherine of Aragon's upbringing as a princess of the reunited Spain had long prepared her to play a great dynastic role in the politics of Europe. Throughout her childhood she had been primed to become

Queen of England. The bride of Arthur, Prince of Wales, was a charming blonde, the epitome of the contemporary ideal of fashion and beauty, but under a submissive surface lay unchallenged pride and arrogance.

A portrait said to be the young Catherine shows that Henry's description of her as 'a woman of most gentleness, of most humility and buxomness' was accurate.[19] But this is probably not Catherine at all because it shows a French hood and there is a clear halo around her head, which suggests that this is a religious figure rather than a real person. In middle age she put on weight rapidly and whatever charm she might have had faded. Certainly she had lost Henry's interest within a few years of their marriage.

Catherine was extremely short, with a strangely deep, masculine voice. All her life she spoke English with a heavy Spanish accent. In her household she spoke her native tongue. Her waiting women, doctors, chaplains and confessor were all Spanish. She was always conscious of her superiority as a princess of Spain. She looked upon England as something of a backwater, provincial, inferior.

Her close contacts with Spain and her unbroken loyalty to her own nation were later to raise suspicions that she was employing spies and agents to work against her adopted country and its interests.

Her family were the leaders of Europe. Her parents, Ferdinand and Isabella, had reunited Spain and driven out Islam after 800 years. The fall of Granada in 1492 completed the *Reconquista* of the Iberian Peninsula and brought freedom from the threat of invasion for the next 500 years. Ferdinand was a changeable, duplicitous schemer. Isabella was a fiercely intelligent woman of great vision but ruthless cruelty who introduced the Inquisition. Catherine's elder sister, Juana, went insane, carrying the corpse of her husband from place to place and refusing to let him be buried.

The 11-year-old Henry had not yet been provided with a wife by his father, which was rare even for younger princes. His father resolved to solve two problems by one shrewd step: he would marry his surviving son to his elder brother's widow.

From the very beginning the validity of this marriage had been in doubt. There were many who objected strongly to such an idea. William Warham, Bishop of London, who had officiated at Prince

Arthur's wedding, disapproved of the match as 'not only inconsistent with propriety, but the will of God Himself is against it. It is declared in His law that if a man shall take his brother's wife, it is an unclean thing. It is not lawful.'[20]

Warham rejected the marriage on biblical grounds: 'If a man shall take his brother's wife, it is an unclean thing; he hath uncovered his brother's nakedness; they shall be childless' (Leviticus 20, 21).[21]

King Ferdinand was anxious on the same grounds, yet the Pope could be persuaded to grant a dispensation if it could be shown that the marriage to Arthur may not have been consummated at all. Immediately Catherine was instructed to play her part in these international negotiations and announce that she remained a virgin.

Catherine had never expected to be shipped back to her father, to a lifetime of ignominious widowhood or at best some inglorious second marriage. As a woman already in her mid-twenties, she fought not to be sent back to Spain penniless, in disgrace and facing an unknown future. She stuck to her story that her marriage to Arthur was a sham, and refused to change it for the next 20 years, against all evidence. She knew that her future depended upon staying on in England and winning the approval of her dead husband's younger brother Henry to become Queen. It was her second – and last – chance.

Henry VII agreed and kept her dowry. On 23 June 1503 12-year-old Henry was betrothed to his brother's widow but the marriage was not to go through until the Pope issued the dispensation.

Catherine was temporarily restored to some degree of status. But in 1504 her mother Isabella died and now her father lost interest in her as a political pawn, leaving her with neither means nor support. She and Henry were supposed to marry in 1505 when he was 14, but although the Pope's bull was issued in December 1503, it did not arrive in England until April 1506.

When the papal bull was opened it was clear that it stated that the first marriage had 'perhaps' ('*forsan*') been consummated. The fact that the document was necessary at all proves that the marriage was assumed to have been consummated. The Pope had not denied that Arthur and Catherine had truly been man and wife. This created an *impedimentum publicae honestatis*, grounds for doubting the bull's validity.[22]

Prince Henry had already expressed his own doubts. On 27 June 1505 he made an official protest before Bishop Fox, disowning the betrothal. The grounds given were that it constituted incest with his sister-in-law, contrary to the laws of God and the Church.

Whether this was the Prince's true opinion of the situation or whether he was advised or pressured into this get-out clause, the ensuing document was kept secret, hidden away for possible use at a later date if and when it should be required.[23]

Shortly afterwards another strange occurrence happened. In a letter of 20 October, Pope Julius II wrote to Arthur, Prince of Wales, who had been dead for three and a half years. The letter gave Arthur permission to restrain his wife Catherine from excessive religious practices injurious to her health (that is, fasting), which could prevent her from conceiving children.[24] This is further evidence that Arthur and Catherine had consummated their marriage, for clearly somebody had been worried enough about the fact that the bride was not yet pregnant to write to Rome.

Since her arrival in England Catherine had been under the spell of her confessor, Friar Diego Fernández. Like the notorious Rasputin, the friar was infamous for his sinful lifestyle, a rapacious womaniser who created sexual scandals in the Princess's household. Like many a priest, he was highly promiscuous, working his way through Catherine's ladies. He had free access to her private quarters at all times of the day and night. Like Rasputin, he controlled and manipulated his employer for many years, so that she fiercely defended him at all times, even at the cost of her own reputation.

When Henry VII heard about the outrageous goings-on in the Princess's household, he rebuked her 'in very strong words'. There was widespread gossip at court that Friar Diego had some sexual hold over her, very much at odds with her protestations of chastity. Yet Catherine continued to hotly defend the friar, declaring him to be 'the best that ever woman in my position had, with respect to his life as well as to his holy doctrines and proficiency in letters'.[25]

In March 1509 Catherine was furious with Fuensalida, the new Spanish ambassador, for reporting to her father that her confessor was 'unworthy' to hold his office. Fuensalida demanded that Friar Diego be recalled for he had 'neither learning, nor appearance, nor manners, nor competency, nor credit'. He warned that Catherine was completely dependent on this friar, who was 'haughty and scandalous in an extreme manner'.

Catherine flew into a rage and protested to the King of Spain: 'Your ambassador here is a traitor. Recall him immediately and punish him as he deserves.'[26] Fuensalida continued to press Ferdinand for the removal of 'this pestiferous person' but Friar Diego stayed on. Over seven years the betrothal of Henry and Catherine remained very much in doubt. Catherine was deeply embittered and changed by the experience, not least by the stress of waiting.

Henry VII died a miserable death from tuberculosis on 22 April 1509. His mother, Margaret Beaufort, followed on 29 June after eating a cygnet. It was nothing less than a liberation for the country. Yet under the gloss and heady excitement, young Henry's paranoia already raised its head. He had his father's hated ministers Empson and Dudley arrested and executed, the first of many thousands to die on his orders. It was a warning to everyone that he was not to be treated lightly.

On his deathbed Henry VII is said to have made his son swear not to marry his dead brother's wife.[27] But loathing his father as he did, Henry, as soon as he was King, immediately announced he would marry Catherine. Friar Diego remained and helped her through the spectacular transition from a seven-year widow to Queen of England and was instrumental in the mysterious cover-up which resulted in 1510.

Henry always had doubts about marrying his brother's widow, yet, having gone through with the match, just to spite his father's deathbed wish, he seemed determined to make the best of it, and expected Catherine to play her full part.

Within a year these hopes were shattered.

In public the couple seemed to be very happy, but as months passed and there was no sign of pregnancy, a certain anxiety appeared. Then, on 26 February 1510, an official warrant was sent to the Great Wardrobe for a cradle to be prepared for the Queen. 'God willing' there would soon be a royal heir.

However, in May Friar Diego wrote to the King of Spain informing him that Catherine had miscarried in late January, but this news was kept secret. Therefore when the warrant was issued in February, Catherine had already lost the child. It seems that no one knew of this but the Queen, Friar Diego, the King, two Spanish waiting women and the Queen's physician. In fact, Diego elaborated the story he told King Ferdinand, claiming that Catherine had been pregnant with twins, one stillborn in January while the other had 'lingered' in the womb until May.

On 27 May Catherine finally summoned the courage to write to her father herself, announcing that she had lost the child 'a few days ago', whereas it had happened – if it ever happened at all – four or five months before, in January. She begged him not to be angry with her because she was already pregnant again. This makes a nonsense of Friar Diego's claim that she could have carried a second baby.[28]

When this story came to the attention of the new Spanish ambassador, Caroz, he denied that any pregnancy had ever existed. It was part of his duty to keep a keen watch even on the most intimate details of the lives of Catherine and Henry. Through his contacts in their households Caroz knew exactly when the King visited his wife and the dates of her menstrual cycle. He could therefore state with authority that Friar Diego's story was pure fiction, for how could anyone believe the Queen was pregnant and still menstruating?

Caroz warned King Ferdinand that the priest behaved 'scandalously, in an extreme manner' and had an evil influence over Catherine. He had 'never seen a more wicked person in my life', he declared.

What had Catherine been trying to do? Perhaps she saw history repeating itself. There had been no sign of pregnancy after five months of marriage to her first husband and now again, after eight months of marriage to his brother, there was no indication that she had conceived. Perhaps Catherine was reminded of this by Friar Diego and rashly announced a false pregnancy. Whatever her motivation, she most certainly lied to her husband the King, to the court and to the nation, ordering a cradle to be prepared when she knew for certain she was not pregnant.

When the truth was known, Henry and his Council were astonished that they should have been deceived by the Queen and her household. The whole country had been looking forward to the birth of a royal heir, but now it could not be concealed that the Queen had lied.

In a move designed to save face, the blame was put on to her ladies for their 'error'.

Within a year of their marrying, Henry's wife had humiliated him by making him look a fool in public. Given his ego, it is inconceivable that he could forgive this enormous dent to his pride, which destroyed his trust and seriously changed his view of her. He now began to rethink their whole relationship.

Could it be that she had also lied to cover up the truth about her marriage to his brother Arthur? Had she really still been a virgin, although they had been wed for five months? If she could lie to her husband for five months about a pregnancy, might she not also have lied about the consummation with Arthur?

A seed of distrust had been planted that would never go away. As the years passed, Henry became ever more convinced that Catherine had lied to him in more ways than one. He had been duped into this marriage and made to look foolish. It was impossible to forgive her.

Yet the 'new' pregnancy proved to be very real. Henry waited in great expectation for the birth of his heir. Catherine duly complied, giving birth on New Year's Day 1511 to a boy, who was christened Henry. No one could have been more delighted – or relieved – than Catherine.

The event was greeted with great public celebrations and tournaments, but the royal couple's joy was to be short-lived. After a few brief weeks Henry's son and heir died.

Once again the suspicion was raised that Catherine had damaged her child-bearing possibilities because of extreme religious practices. It was the Queen's habit of fasting, Caroz believed, that had caused her irregular menstrual cycle and her failure to bear a child to full term: 'Some irregularity in her eating and the food she takes cause her some trouble, the consequence of which is that she does not menstruate as she should.'

Catherine was a devoted daughter of the Roman Church. She had been strictly schooled in the rigid traditions of Spanish Catholicism, convinced of the effectiveness of the intervention of the Virgin Mary and an entire calendar of saints. Her rooms were full of relics and statues. She spent hours day and night on her knees saying the offices of the Church. She fasted with a fanatic's zeal, so much so that the Pope himself had given her first husband permission to forbid the practice. The fact that even the Pope knew about this problem at the time of the first marriage shows that it must have been consummated. Her failure to conceive caused Arthur to communicate his concern to Rome.

Catherine appeared dissatisfied with her role in England. She resented the fact that Henry followed his father's practice, excluding his wife from politics, whereas earlier queens of England had played highly influential roles in the governance of the state. She had observed her own mother, Isabella, equal and co-ruler with her father Ferdinand, riding to battle against the Moors even when she was pregnant. Therefore when the chance finally came for Catherine to demonstrate what she was could do in her husband's absence, she seized the reins of power with both hands.

Henry's great design to take back the English lands which Henry VI had lost in France seemed little more than a vainglorious boast. By contrast, Catherine's skilful management of the Scots' attack in the north achieved a victory at Flodden Field worthy of her own warlike mother. The death of the King of Scots and all the flower of his nobility seemed like a direct challenge to Henry to treat her as an equal partner in politics rather than a breeding machine for sons.

Catherine had deeply wounded Henry's vanity by flaunting the victory when his own feeble exploits in France rang hollow. On 16 September 1513 she wrote as Queen Regent, sending a bloodstained portion of James IV's surcoat to Henry as a trophy:

Sir,

My Lord Howard hath sent me a letter open to your Grace within one of mine, by the which you shall see at length the great Victory that our Lord hath sent your subjects in your absence; and for this cause there is no need herein to trouble your Grace with long writing, but, to my thinking, this battle hath been to your Grace and all your realm the greatest honour that could be, and more than you should win all the crown of France; thanked be God of it, and I am sure your Grace forgetteth not to do this, which shall be cause to send you many more such great victories, as I trust he shall do.

The 24-year-old King was insulted. Probably, he never forgave her for submitting him to international ridicule. His pride was permanently wounded by his wife's presumption, but Catherine seemed blissfully unaware of her faults. At Henry's return she ridiculed the King before his court for capturing just one hostage in France, the Duc de Longueville, while she had three from Flodden.

Her sins were compounded by another miscarriage that autumn. The King's patience was wearing thin. Meanwhile the demonic Friar Diego continued to exert his malign influence over the Queen. By 1514 his activities had become such a scandal that he was brought before the ecclesiastical court on charges of fornication. The King took a very keen interest in the proceedings, but the friar was indignant and astonishingly impertinent. He publicly attacked the King's own notorious reputation, railing: 'If I am badly used, the Queen is still more badly used!' Henry finally had him removed and deported to Spain.

Henry acknowledged renewed qualms about his fateful decision to marry Catherine. In 1514 there were rumours that he wanted to be rid of her. Catherine's menstrual problems were common knowledge. Cardinal Wolsey hinted at 'secret reasons' why she could not share the King's bed: 'There are certain diseases in the Queen defying all remedy for which and other causes the King will never live with her.'[29]

Wolsey was eager to arrange an alternative marriage with a younger princess of France, but the whole scheme was halted when Catherine became pregnant.[30] In December 1514 she gave birth to another dead boy. Even for England at that time this was a high rate of fatality. One in five children died in their first year of life and perhaps one in four failed to reach the age of ten. But all of Catherine's children had died, and there was much rumour and speculation about the causes.

Within months she was pregnant again. During her lying-in her father died. Then, on 18 February 1516, she gave birth to a girl. This time the child survived. She was named Mary and would live to earn the unenviable – but well-merited – title 'Bloody Mary'.

A daughter was at least evidence that the Queen was capable of bearing a child. Henry could only pray that next time she would provide him with a son. But time was running out for Catherine. She was fast approaching 40, while Henry was still very much in his vigorous early thirties.

As their relationship steadily deteriorated, Catherine became increasingly superstitious and fanatical in religious excess. Meanwhile the King strayed to his mistresses and she was expected to turn a blind eye. She made desperate pilgrimages to shrines in the hope of divine intervention to save her marriage. She tortured her own body with further fasting, and in later years would wear the habit of the Lay Order of St Francis under her gowns and even put on a hair shirt – no doubt when she had given up on winning Henry back to her bed.

The court slavishly followed the King and increasingly ignored the Queen. Catherine made little effort to keep up with her still vigorous husband. She was no longer interested in attracting his interest and had given up dancing, often retiring early in the evenings to her own chambers. Her younger ladies, among them Anne Boleyn, were not included in her favoured inner circle. Henry's court began to talk openly about her failings as a wife. His expectation that his wife would provide him with an heir was long gone.

What is clear is that by 1524 Henry and Catherine had ceased having sexual relations, only occasionally sharing a bed for the sake of appearances. The effect of the age gap of five and a half years grew ever more pronounced and Catherine had not been pregnant for seven years. It is very likely that Henry was advised by his doctors that her child-bearing years were over.[31]

He was still a relatively young man but he had married a woman who was soon fighting her biological clock. From the very start time was limited for them, restricting their chances of producing the great family to which Henry aspired. Now he was doomed to live out the remainder of his days with a woman already past her prime and incapable of providing him with the sons he desired.

The realisation that there would be no son and heir was a hard blow to a man with Henry's ego. All his hopes and plans for the continuation of the Tudor bloodline were threatened. With no son to succeed him, there was only their sole surviving child, the Princess Mary.

To Henry it was a humiliation. Instead of the line of vigorous, healthy boys he had imagined, here was this sallow and dour child, educated by Vives to believe in women's inferiority and sinful nature, trained to be her mother's daughter in the strict Spanish tradition, in the expectation that she would marry Charles V and become Holy Roman Empress.

The thought that one day Charles would inherit England was a constant rebuke to Henry. He consulted his chief justices to discover how this could be avoided. Under English law women lost all property rights and income at marriage, their husbands taking everything. Canon law concurred. Yet surely there had to be an exception when the crown of England was at stake?[32]

It was of little comfort to learn the judges' opinion that Mary would become Queen but her husband could not by right call himself King even if he was effectively the ruler. At Henry's death the Tudor line which he and his father had fought and killed to preserve would vanish overnight. England would be swallowed up by the vast new European empire, reduced to nothing more than a colony.

Henry was disgusted. What had he struggled for all these years, waging wars and almost bankrupting the exchequer? Merely to hand his throne over to the man who married Mary? Hoping that his blood would continue through whatever children she might bear – unless she followed her mother in that, too, and proved barren.

Only one generation after his father had snatched the Plantagenet crown at Bosworth, he could lose it to some foreign prince whom Mary would marry, with England becoming absorbed into a foreign empire.

Then Charles V abruptly jilted nine-year-old Mary and betrothed Isabella of Portugal. Henry was outraged, blaming Catherine for the faults of her family. Although Charles was Catherine's own nephew, it seemed that Mary was not good enough for the Holy Roman Emperor.

Mary's rejection drove Henry into a rage, yet it changed little. Mary would still be obliged to marry a foreign prince in order for the Tudor line to survive. Henry was still an international laughing stock. Again he thought of escaping a marriage that had brought nothing but humiliation to him and England.

What if by some further twist of fate his life should be cut short? No one could predict the future and two recent accidents had shaken his sense of invincibility.

The year before he had almost died jousting with Charles Brandon, his brother-in-law. In the charge, Henry failed to drop his visor and Brandon caught him with his lance full in the face. The crowd had screamed as the lance sheared off the King's helmet and shattered.

As panic-stricken courtiers ran to his rescue, Henry shook off the shower of deadly wooden splinters which could have blinded or even killed him. Curiously, an almost identical accident was to happen to Henri II of France in 1559, an incident predicted by Nostradamus, when a lance pierced the King's eye and killed him.

Aware of how close he had come to meeting his Maker, Henry laughed off the incident, but fear had been implanted in his mind.

A few months later another accident seemed to reinforce this sense of his own mortality. His horse slipped while he was out hawking and he fell into a ditch of water, having to be rescued by a servant before he drowned.

Coming so close together, these two narrow escapes seemed like warnings. Henry began to consider what legacy he would leave behind if he should meet an untimely death.

The fault was not his. The sight of Fitzroy, his bastard son by Bessie Blount, was proof of that. He *was* capable. The 'goodlie manne childe' born in the spring of 1519 was a living testament to his virility. Henry had the boy brought up at court and educated by Richard Croke in Greek and Latin. Fitzroy was intelligent and bold and the more his father saw of him, the more he began to consider a different option for the future of the country.

On 18 June 1525 Henry surprised everyone by creating the boy Duke of Richmond and Somerset, Earl of Nottingham, Lord High Admiral of England and Warden General of all the Marches toward Scotland. These were royal titles which should have been granted to his son and heir, giving Fitzroy precedence over the nobles at court, even the Princess Mary. Among others ennobled on that day were his sister Mary Tudor's son, Henry Brandon, as the Earl of Lincoln, and Sir Thomas Boleyn, as Viscount Rochford.[33] Although by this time Henry was already attracted to Anne Boleyn, it was very clear that he was not intending to marry her for the sake of an heir.

Fitzroy was given his own lavish household in the north of England and Catherine feared that he was being groomed as an alternative heir to their daughter Mary. It was even rumoured that the King was planning to make this bastard son King of Ireland in preparation for his accession to the English throne. A possible marriage was even suggested between Fitzroy and Mary.[34]

Catherine now made the error of complaining to the King that this was an insult, but Henry was in no mood to take criticism from a barren wife. 'The Queen was obliged to submit and have patience,' records the Venetian ambassador as Henry took revenge on her by dismissing three of her Spanish waiting women and sending Mary away to Ludlow with her own household under the Countess of Salisbury, her Lady Governess. It was the first warning sign that Catherine had overplayed her hand at last.[35]

From the beginning Henry had wrestled with his doubts, torturing himself as dead child succeeded dead child. He was now facing a personal crisis of faith as a result of Catherine's failed pregnancies. Why had God not blessed his marriage? Of all the children Catherine bore, only Mary survived. Why had God not permitted his sons to live?

Henry now became convinced that God had shown him that all these years he had been living in sin and he was being punished 'by the curse of sterility'.[36] Once his mind was set, nothing could change this belief that his marriage to Catherine was against Holy Writ.

Ironically, Henry had made himself an international reputation as the defender of marriage in his famous theological attack on Martin Luther in 1521. The *Assertion of the Seven Sacraments* had been published after the Vatican issued a warning against the 'wicked pestilence' of Lutheranism, criticising Wolsey for lack of action against English heretics.[37] Wolsey gave Henry Luther's works to read, knowing the King's fascination with theological debate. Henry collected a library of more than 1,000 books, many on theology.[38] Soon the King had no time for affairs of state because he was too busy writing a response against Luther.[39]

Henry had written some sections as early as 1518. The chapters 'Of Indulgences' and 'Of the Pope's Authority' were later cobbled together to create an instant book, which was finished in ten days and ran to some 30,000 words in Latin.[40]

It was generally assumed that Henry had not written it himself, but that it was ghostwritten.[41] He had a shallow, butterfly brain, his interest drifting from subject to subject and never delving far beneath the surface of knowledge. According to Thomas Cranmer, he was in the habit of

> handing over books of this kind, which have been presented to him, and especially those which he has not the patience to read himself, to one of his courtiers for perusal, from whom he may afterwards learn their contents. He then takes them back, and presently gives them to be examined by someone else, of an entirely opposite way of thinking from the former party. And when he has thus found out everything from them, and has ascertained both what they praise and what they condemn, then at length he openly gives his own opinion on the same points.[42]

It appears to have been a book written by committee. Thomas More spoke of 'the makers' of the book and seems to have acted as some kind of editor. In May John Longland, the King's confessor, had been rewarded with the see of Lincoln. Henry said that he had been persuaded to write it at Wolsey's instance: he never intended any such thing 'afore he was by your grace moved and led thereunto'.[43] Pope Leo clearly assumed Wolsey had written it himself. Wolsey had 'been a diligent comforter and stirrer that the King's grace should this [sic] employ his time'.[44]

On 25 August Wolsey sent 30 copies to John Clerk, English ambassador in Rome, including one for the Pope, bound in gold and jewels. It went through some 20 editions and translations in Antwerp, Rome, Frankfurt, Cologne, Paris and Würzburg. Its major selling point was the fact that Henry claimed to be the author.

The Pope rewarded him by granting to him and his successors the title *Defensor Fidei* (Defender of the Faith).[45]

By writing his defence of marriage, Henry was probably seeking to win favour with God. His religious views were not entirely orthodox. He had a belief in good works to win salvation, and evolution towards perfection as 'sons of God'. God could be placated by good works of charity. He could be bribed not to bring disaster. This was essentially the view of the pagan world.

The Spanish marriage which had caused such controversy then

continued to create problems for him now. Without a prince to succeed him, civil war would surely follow. The Yorkist ghosts were always present, waiting in the wings.

Henry remembered the generational curse which had come down to him through his father's usurpation of the throne and was convinced that he was the victim of divine retribution.

Now he was facing a 'dark night of the soul' over the validity of his marriage to Catherine and the reasons why she could not give him a son. His fresh reading of Leviticus 20, 21 had shown him that far from being blessed by God, even though he was King, he would be under a curse until he was rid of her.

Once the idea was fixed in his head, nothing could dispel it. Neither politics nor Catherine's nephew the Emperor could alter the danger to his immortal soul of living a lie with his dead brother's wife. For the good of the nation he was obliged to seek an annulment at once.

Chapter Five

The Turning-Point

'The state of princes in matters of marriage is far of worse sort than the conditions of poor men. For princes take as is brought them by others, and poor men be commonly at their own choice and liberty.'[1]

Sir Anthony Denny

ANNE'S BLACK LEGEND claims she was a seductress, the 'other woman', plotting with her avaricious and ambitious family to usurp the crown from meek Queen Catherine. Others imply that Anne should have sent the King back to his wife, as though she herself was the cause of the marriage's break-up.[2] Yet Henry had already initiated legal proceedings to have his marriage with Catherine annulled before he resolved that he would make Anne her successor. Even given Henry's record of promiscuity and philandering, no woman could ever have expected him to cast off his well-connected wife, a foreign princess, in order to marry an Englishwoman and a commoner at that. Wolsey was making plans to replace Catherine with a foreign princess.

By escaping to Hever, Anne no doubt thought that putting a certain distance between them would cool the King's ardour, but Henry was not about to take no for an answer. He complained that she had not been in contact with him since leaving court, a reaction he found inexplicable. No one refused the King.

It was a dangerous and unhappy situation, similar in many ways to that of a modern-day stalker, but in this case the stalker was the King of England. Here was the most dangerous man in Europe, a fascinating and flamboyant figure, still very much in his prime. His ego was fed by a fawning court, eager to keep close to the centre of power by exploiting 'the politics of intimacy' and seeking to manoeuvre its own candidate into the King's bed, but Henry was never generous to discarded mistresses. He made a habit of marrying them off and rewarding complacent husbands with small grants of land, but, unlike the courts of Europe, there were no vast estates, noble titles, no role of chief courtesan or *maîtresse en titre* to which an ambitious young girl might aspire. Anne had the example of her own sister Mary's experience to warn her of the dubious fate which awaited the woman who surrendered to the King's desires.

It was a tempestuous relationship; for Anne, like keeping a man-eating tiger at bay. It was not her intention at any time to put herself in the King's way. She absented herself from court. She did everything to discourage him. She did not answer the constant stream of letters. No letters in reply exist; the one said to be hers is now regarded as a later fabrication.[3]

Anne faced a dilemma that had repercussions far beyond her personal hopes or preferences. It was not a good idea to cross Henry at any time. To refuse the King could spell disaster for her family's fortunes, for Henry was not a man to forgive a slight, let alone rejection on such a public scale. To offend him would bring ruin, perhaps even death.

Henry had a good memory for those who wronged him. His early years observing his father's paranoia at first hand had taught him that a pre-emptive strike was wiser than mercy. He would have approved of Machiavelli's advice in *The Prince* that it was better to be feared than loved. When, in 1521, Henry had executed Edward Stafford, Duke of Buckingham, the charges had been concocted but the underlying reason was his Plantagenet blood. While Henry continued to lack a male heir, Buckingham was the next in succession. There was outrage in Europe, where Emperor Charles V and Francis I believed England was on the brink of revolution.[4]

The golden reign which had started with such hope and expectation soon dissipated into fear and insecurity of the kind that had haunted the latter years of Henry VII. Henry told the French ambassador Marillac that he intended to eliminate the whole House of York. On the eve of his departure for France in 1513 he took care to remove Edmund de la Pole, Earl of Suffolk, who was beheaded on 4 May. His brother Richard, called 'the White Rose', was in exile but under surveillance. Henry also sought to have Cardinal Reginald Pole assassinated.

Henry never witnessed executions. The moment he rejected someone from his favour, he chose never to see them again. It was as if that person were completely erased from his memory. Instead of ensuring the security of the realm, Henry became increasingly suspicious as he grew older. So fearful was he about his own safety that he always took a locksmith with him to install his own personal lock on the door of the bedchamber wherever he was staying. The original lock is now said to be at Hever.

Marillac said of Henry that 'he will not cease to dip his hand in blood as long as he doubt his people'.[5]

This was the 'merciless prince', as Walter Raleigh called the King: 'For how many servants did he advance in haste and with the change of his fancy ruined again, no man knowing for what offence?'[6]

Apologists for Henry seek to show that his ruthlessness brought stability to the country and prevented a resumption of civil war: 'his dictatorship was the child of the Wars of the Roses'. They conclude that 'every drop of blood shed under Henry VIII might have been a river under a feebler King' and that 'it was better to draw blood of a few persons who were the corruption of a whole realm, than to suffer the whole realm to perish'.[7] Yet this was at a price. Some 50,000 people were executed during his reign.

It was perhaps his very public gamble in eventually staking all on marriage with Anne and the break with Rome that would later turn Henry's infatuation to humiliation and hatred. Anne did everything she could to show him that she was not interested in him as a lover, but it seemed that whatever she did only served to enflame him further. He was persistent in the chase and refused to accept rejection.

Henry's letters demonstrate barely suppressed sexual violence. He had begun his campaign by sending Anne a buck he had killed.[8] This was to remind her of the hunter, but clearly underlines his intention to pursue her to the end. Anne is the wild prey who must be tamed. Henry is making a threat, warning her that she cannot win. He is the King and gets everything he desires. He will stalk her, hunt her down and corner her so that there is no escape. He will have his way and, ultimately, discard her.

Anne knew at first hand how her sister Mary had been thrown aside when pregnant. She had not even fared as well as Bessie Blount, whose child had at least been acknowledged as the King's son. Mary's own poor marriage was a great disappointment to the Boleyn family.

Anne was not in love with the King. She had come home from France expecting to marry the heir to the Earl of Ormonde but this had been eclipsed by a much better match with Percy. The prospect of becoming the future Countess of Northumberland was a prize for the second daughter of Thomas Boleyn. Anne's expectation was to make a marriage that would propel the family into the heart of the aristocracy where her elder sister had failed.

She hoped for a husband who was 'more agreeable to her' than the King. Later she is said to have admitted: 'I never wished to choose the King in my heart.'⁹ Henry had invaded her life and that changed everything. His desire marked her out as his prey, setting her apart and untouchable. As soon as others at court, such as Thomas Wyatt, realised the King's interest in Anne they withdrew, fearing the unhealthy consequences of being seen as his rivals. No other match was possible.

This is explicit in Thomas Wyatt's most famous poem:

> Whoso list to hunt, I know where is a hind.
> But as for me, alas I may no more:
> The vain travail hath wearied me so sore.
> I am of them that farthest cometh behinde.
> Yet may I by no means my wearied mind
> Draw from the deer, but as she fleeth afore
> Fainting I follow. I leave off therefore,
> Sithens in a net I seek to hold the wind.
> Who list to hunt, I put him out of doubt,
> As well as I may spend his time in vain,

> And graven with diamonds in letters plain
> There is written her fair neck round about.
> '*Noli me tangere*, for Caesar's I am,
> And wild for to hold, though I seem tame.'[10]

This was inspired by the great Italian poet Petrarch's sonnet 190, 'Una candida cerva' ('A Snow-white Deer'). Here Wyatt reveals that behind the façade of courtly love lies a deeply sinister quality. The sophisticated veneer of false gallantry and mock chivalry disguises the ruthless hounding of the hind, who will be hunted to death to appease the King's lust. The phrase '*Noli me tangere*' ('Touch me not') is taken from the Latin Vulgate Bible, the words of Jesus the Christ in his newly resurrected body after his sacrifice to the death. Wyatt uses this to point to the King, who has all the authority of Caesar and has already staked his claim to the lady in question.

He was writing for a tiny élite, a closed intellectual community which used wordplay and codes as a disguise for real people. Here Henry is Caesar. The poem was clearly written after the King had claimed Anne for himself and thereby warned off all his rivals. Wyatt is drawing on deep wells of bitterness following Anne's rejection, complaining that he is the least of all her suitors: 'of them that farthest cometh behinde'.

There is no evidence that Anne and Wyatt ever had an affair.[11] There is no evidence that Anne ever had sex with anyone except her husband. Her firm religious belief became a force to be reckoned with.

Hers was no superficial faith. Since her education in France she had an abiding interest in the New Learning and the religious reformation that was spreading like a revolution in thinking across northern Europe. Her views were evangelical, many would later say 'Lutheran'.[12] She read the Bible daily and believed that everyone should be able to read God's word in a language they could understand.

Hers was an intensely personal and inward-looking faith of relationship with God through the work of the Holy Spirit, which any 'born-again' Christian of any era would recognise. Without God's grace, no one could be saved. No one could obtain this by taking the mass or by performing works of charity. God called his elect to salvation (Yeshua – the Hebrew name of Jesus the Christ, the Messiah of Israel), wiping out sin through new birth in the Holy Spirit. The experience, like that of Saul on the road to Damascus, was nearly always the great turning-point in life. Margaret of Navarre wrote later of her joy in conversion:

> I have found only one true and perfect remedy, which is reading the Holy Scriptures. In perusing them, my mind experiences its true and perfect joy; and from this pleasure of the mind, proceeds the repose and health of the body… I take up the Psalms and sing them with my heart and pronounce with my tongue, as humbly as possible, the fine hymns with which the Holy Spirit inspired David and the sacred authors.[13]

Here is the authentic experience of the convert, whose life is for ever transformed.

According to Roger Twysden, Margaret of Navarre was influential in Anne's religious conversion.[14]

A woman with such conviction and belief as Anne had could never have had the promiscuous background that her detractors claimed. Thomas Wyatt makes this point about Anne's morality and the role that religion played in her life. The hunted deer wears a diamond collar, an allusion to Petrarch's Laura, who wears it in devotion to the will of God. The poet sees it as restrictive, a symbol of slavery. Wyatt has been turned down because he is a married man, whereas the King has made Anne an offer she cannot refuse.

Anne's reputation later came under attack by many who sought to blacken her name by inventing sexual slanders about an affair with Wyatt. During the religious wars that followed the death of Henry VIII, Catholic writers undertook the task of defamation with relish, in order to cast suspicion on the claim of Anne's daughter Elizabeth, Queen Mary's rival. Gross inventions came from the pen of the Archdeacon of Canterbury, Nicholas Harpsfield, asserting that Anne had 'lived loosely and incontinently' and in a wholly imagined scene he claims that Wyatt went to the King to warn him of Anne's promiscuity: 'I beseech your grace to be well advised what you do, for she is not meet to be coupled with your grace, her conversation hath been so loose and base; which thing I know, not so much by hearsay as by my own experience as one that have had my carnal pleasure with her.'[15]

Similar nonsense later circulated among the Spanish community in London, who were vehemently opposed to Anne and her part in bringing reforming evangelism to England. The *Crónica del Rey Enrico* repeats the allegations about the Queen and Wyatt, stating that the poet was driven from court in order to prevent him from talking about Anne's wicked reputation.[16]

Anne's religious beliefs sit at odds with the traditional picture of a ruthlessly ambitious Jezebel. The evidence of her contemporaries proves that scurrilous accusations against her are malicious fiction. This was no strumpet, but a woman of vibrant courage and intelligence who had been propelled by Fate – or God – into the centre of the cauldron that was court intrigue.

If there was any rivalry between Wyatt and the King then it must date from 1526, before Wyatt departed for Italy on 7 January 1527.[17] In 1532 Wyatt wrote that he 'fled the fire' that burned him:

> And now I follow the coals that be quenched
> from Dover to Calais against my mind…
> I quit the enterprise of that that I have lost
> To whomsoever lust for to proffer most.[18]

Unlike others, he escaped Henry's jealousy with his life. He blamed the King for being able to 'buy' Anne but he took a risk in venting his reproach of Henry's success where he had failed. This is most clearly seen in his poem 'Ye old mule', a thinly veiled satire on the King:

> Ye old mule that think yourself so fair,
> Leave off with craft your beauty to repair,
> For it is true, without any fable,
> No man setteth more by riding in your saddle.
> Too much travail so do your train appair.
> Ye old mule
> With false savour though you deceive th'air,

Whoso taste you shall well perceive your lair
Savoureth somewhat of a Kappurs stable.
Ye old mule
Ye must now serve to market and to fair,
All for the burden, for panniers a pair.
For since grey hairs been powdered in your sable,
The thing ye seek for, you must yourself enable
To purchase it by payment and by prayer,
Ye old mule.

Wyatt never forgot Anne. A fourth poem was written after she died, when he had a mistress, here called Phyllis, really Elizabeth Darell, his last mistress in the period 1536–7, before his death in 1542.[19] This still harks back to his old obsession:

Then do I love again;
If thou ask whom, sure since I did refrain
Her, that did set our country in a roar;
The unfeigned cheer of Phyllis hath the place
That Brunette had: she hath and ever shall.[20]

He later decided it was safer to obscure the reference to Anne by changing the line 'Her, that did set our country in a roar' to 'Brunette, that set my wealth in such a roar'. Given the uncertain nature of the times, it is possible that he changed other poems, too, to hide references to Anne. He also wrote this advice to the 15-year-old son from his unhappy marriage:

Love well and agree with your wife, for where there is noise and debate in the house, there is unquiet dwelling. And much more where it is in one bed.

Frame well yourself to love, and role well and honestly your wife as your fellow and she shall love and reverence you as her head.

Such as you are unto her such shall she be unto you...

And the blessing of God for good agreement between the wife and husband is fruit of many children, which I for the like thing do lack, and the fault is both in your mother and me, but chiefly in her.[21]

It was now clear that something had happened between Anne and the King to trigger the turning-point in their relationship. Henry wrote to her of the 'fervency of love' and how her absence 'had so grieved my heart that neither tongue nor pen can express the hurt'. He complained of 'the great loneliness that I find since your departing' and 'the sufferings that I, by your absence, have sustained'.

Anne finally took pity on him and sent him a costly gift which is poignantly symbolic of the terrible situation in which she found herself. It was a rare jewelled figure of a woman alone on a ship riding a storm-tossed sea. Did she have it made for Henry, or come across the piece by some timely accident? She must have written back to him, in a letter accompanying her present, aware that such an offering could only be taken as encouragement. As it was:

> For so beautiful a gift, I thank you right cordially; not alone for the fair diamond and the ship in which the solitary damsel is tossed about, but chiefly for the good intent and too humble submission vouchsafed in this by your kindness: to merit it would not a little perplex me, if I were not aided therein by your great benevolence and goodwill, for the which I have sought, do seek and shall always seek by all services to me possible there to remain, in the which my hope hath set up his everlasting rest, saying *aut illic aut nullibi* [either here or nowhere]. The proofs of your affection are such, the fine poesies of the letters so warmly couched, that they constrain me ever truly to honour, love and serve you, praying that you will continue in this same firm and constant purpose, ensuring you, for my part that I will the rather go beyond than make *reciproque*, if loyalty or heart, the desire to do you pleasure, even with my whole heart root, may serve to advance it.

What was it that had taken place between them that made such a striking difference to their future plans? The King provides the answer himself in the remaining portion of the letter:

> Henceforth, my heart shall be dedicate to you alone, greatly desirous that my body could be as well, as God can bring it to pass if it pleaseth Him, whom I entreat once each day for the accomplishment thereof,

trusting that at length my prayer will be heard, wishing the time brief, and thinking it but long until we shall see each other again.

Written with the hand of the secretary who in heart, body and will is your loyal and most ensured servant.

H. autre AB ne cherche R.[22] [Anne's initials are enclosed in a heart.]

From this we understand that some deal has been done between them that radically changed their whole future. Anne had refused to become his mistress, yet the King now prays for God to intervene in order that they may be together:

My mistress and friend: I and my heart put ourselves in your hands, begging you to have them suitors for your good favour, and that your affection for them should not grow less through absence. For it would be a great pity to increase their sorrow since absence does it sufficiently, and more than ever I could have thought possible reminding us of a point in astronomy, which is, that the longer the days are the farther off is the sun, and yet the more fierce.

So it is with our love, for by absence we are parted yet nevertheless it keeps its fervour, at least on my side, and I hope on yours also: assuring you that on my side the ennui of absence is already too much for me: and when I think of the increase of what I must needs suffer it would be well nigh unbearable for me were it not for the firm hope I have and as I cannot be with you in person, I am sending you the nearest possible thing to that, namely, my picture set in a bracelet, with the whole device which you already know. Wishing myself in their place when it shall please you.

This by the hand of
Your loyal servant and friend

H Rex.[23]

The fact that the King now calls Anne his 'mistress' does not indicate any sexual connotation. If anything, there is a new reserve and awareness of proprieties apparent in this waiting period. There can be only one interpretation: Henry's intention to replace Queen Catherine with Queen Anne.

This was the resolution he had reached and which he now chose to share with his new love and future queen. He believed that God had shown him the truth that all these years he had been living in sin and 'an angel descending from heaven would have been unable to persuade him otherwise'.[24] The marriage was against God's law and it was this that had troubled his conscience from his youth. On the peril of his immortal soul Henry had no alternative but to seek an annulment at once. He was not married at all, but would soon be free to contract a legal marriage to a true wife, which God would bless with a son and heir.

This was what finally changed Anne's mind: the fact that Henry was now offering her marriage and what she must have thought a guaranteed future for herself and her family beyond their wildest dreams. Even if she had loathed Henry and found his attentions abhorrent, there was no way in which a woman of her time and status would have refused the King's proposal of marriage. It was make or break for the Boleyn dynasty and she could not be blind to the momentous opportunity that now presented itself. But personal ambition was not the reason for her change of heart. It was when Henry made his offer of marriage that she awoke to the role she alone was capable of playing.

We cannot escape the thought that Henry may have confessed his qualms about the validity of his marriage to Anne and the very real possibility that he was living under God's curse. William Latimer later described Anne's habit of debating theology when she dined with the King.[25] Her ability to discuss literature and theology on equal terms with the King was certainly one of the factors which attracted him to her in the first place. It was a meeting of minds and intellectual equals. Henry calls Anne his friend, one to whom he can open his heart even on troubled matters of conscience.

Until this time Henry had been very much a man's man, enjoying the macho world of the hunt and sport. Now, by giving Anne access, he signals an important move away from the exclusively male circle closest to the centre of power. He abandons his minions for the first real relationship of his life. No other woman, no mistress, not even his queen, had ever been so close.

Henry and Anne shared a love of music and literature. Louis de

Brun stated that Anne was never without 'some book in French' in her hand, 'as, for example, translations of the Holy Scriptures'. From her childhood Anne had devoted herself to biblical study, reading the Scriptures in the new French translation, a rare and decidedly dangerous activity.[26] She read Lefèvre, whom Margaret of Navarre had rescued from persecution. She read his *Fivefold Psalter* of 1509 and commentary on the Letters of Paul, first published in 1512. Other religious books and tracts were smuggled in from France.[27]

From this time Anne was able to share her beliefs with the King as her influence over him began to grow. Not everyone was delighted. Chapuys claimed she was more Lutheran than her father.[28] When Wolsey discovered Henry's interest in Anne he was 'extremely annoyed at a circumstance which boded no good to him'. His aversion to the Boleyns and their evangelical faith made them a danger to his own power over the King.

The Boleyns dared to use their influence to advance the cause of reform and also to protect those in the evangelical underground. Anne and her father interceded for those persecuted for the sake of the Gospel. Thomas kept in touch with French reformers such as Clément Marot. Thomas Tebold acted as his agent, reporting on the Inquisition in Europe. Beginning in 1525, many Christians were burned alive in France after Francis I brought in the Inquisition. His own sister Margaret was the leading evangelical believer who courageously tried to rescue Louis de Berquin, later martyred for his faith.

A story is told that after a diplomatic mission to Spain in 1523, Thomas Boleyn had abandoned the envoy of Emperor Charles V and left him to fend for himself in London. Well informed about the persecution of his co-religionists as he was, it seemed that his politeness did not extend to his religious opponents.[29]

Chapuys complained that Thomas Boleyn violently 'slandered' the Pope and cardinals, while Anne's brother George was always trying to strike up religious arguments. Theology was the only subject at the Boleyns' table. Lutheran books were circulating at the English court.[30] Diplomats like Thomas Boleyn were involved in bringing in new religious works. It was a dangerous gamble for the secret networks involved. They feared betrayal by informers which could lead to the stake.

Informers had always been paid, or harmless neighbours tortured, to denounce believers. Richard Hunne, a respected London merchant, had been arrested in 1514. After a search of his home, the bishop's men discovered a Wycliffe Bible in English and hauled him off in chains. He was later found hanging in his prison cell, but no one believed that he had killed himself. There were riots in London, yet the Church still decided to confiscate all his property. A charge of heresy could destroy an entire family and the Church could then confiscate all their goods. Later they dug up Hunne's corpse and burned it at the stake as a heretic.[31]

Eventually the case was put before Parliament, which reversed the verdict. Hunne had been murdered but no one was brought to justice. The Church immediately closed ranks to protect the killers and hired the lawyer Thomas More to write a whitewash of the affair, his *Dialogue Concerning Heresies* of 1529.

More was a most unattractive character, a dreadful gossip according to Erasmus, and a fanatic where his religion was concerned. Ridley calls him 'a particularly nasty sadomasochistic pervert' who enjoyed being flogged by his favourite daughter, as he also flogged 'heretics' and beggars in his garden.[32]

More's coarse and libellous book attacking Martin Luther reads like the scribblings of a dirty-minded schoolboy on a lavatory wall. Luther was 'filthier than a pig and more foolish than an ass ... deserving the applause of Jews, Turks and heathens'. He 'has nothing in his mouth but privies, filth, and dung' and was a 'privy-minded rascal ... shitting and beshitted'. More tells Luther to 'swallow down his filth and lick up the dung with which he has so foully defiled his tongue and his pen'. He calls on his readers to throw back into Luther's 'shitty mouth, truly the shitpool of all shit, all the muck and shit which your damnable rottenness has vomited up, and to empty out all the sewers and privies' over his head.[33] He thought that Luther should be 'overwhelmed with filth'.[34]

He wrote: 'The most absurd race of heretics, the dregs of impiety, of crimes and filth, shall be called Lutherans.' All evangelical women were 'foul prostitutes' and Lutherans publicly copulated in their churches, defiling images of the saints and the crucifix, to 'bespatter the most holy image of Christ crucified with the most foul excrement of their bodies destined to be burned'.[35]

'No other sixteenth-century polemicist, either on the Catholic or the Protestant side, sank to the depths which More reached in this work.'[36]

Cardinal Wolsey was embarrassed by the book, insisting it be published under the false name of William Rosse. More often invented fictitious characters, such as Raphael Hythlodeus in *Utopia*, and faked glowing reviews of his book by the non-existent foreign theologians Hermann of Prague, John Carcelius and Ferdinand Baravellus, the last 'a Spaniard remarkably learned in every branch of learning'. 'Rosse' claimed it was the fictitious Carcelius who had persuaded him to write the book in the first place.[37]

For centuries the medieval Church had controlled people's minds, providing answers to the great questions of life which few dared challenge. Shrines such as Walsingham in Norfolk were centres for the exploitation of tourist pilgrims. Pilgrimage was a thriving industry, a money-earning opportunity for the sale of indulgences, pardons, candles and relics. In an illiterate world, the gaudy carvings, wall murals and stained glass told the Bible 'story' for those to whom the book itself was completely unknown.

Erasmus criticised the excesses of the Church of Rome and its clergy, but what was needed was a complete overhaul and reform of self-serving institutions. Until men and women could read the Scriptures for themselves in their own language, the authority of the Church was relatively uncontested. The implication of reforming belief was to challenge the mythology and superstitions of mystical Catholicism. The consequences were to attack the Church as an institution, together with its teachings, interpretations and practices. This was a step too far. Those who rejected the claims of the mass were burned alive.

Bishop Longland feared 'the corruption of youth' at England's universities. In 1520 and again in 1521 Luther's books were burned opposite the chapel of King's College, Cambridge. William Tyndale, whose mission would be the translation of the complete Bible into English, was then just finishing his studies. Reformers met at the White Horse Inn, called 'Little Germany', between King's and St Catherine's. The Master of Queens' College, Cambridge, Dr Robert Forman, was instrumental in the illegal book trade. In Oxford, too, such radical literature was widely available. In 1520 a bookseller there offered a long list of reform literature for sale. The following year the Archbishop of Canterbury was told that Oxford was a hotbed of revolutionaries.

But it was at Cambridge that Bilney, Barnes and Latimer studied God's word in the English language and for the first time lectured directly from the Bible rather than from commentaries upon it, which is still the theologians' way today. These leading lights would become the victims of Bloody Mary's English Inquisition in the 1550s.

One early convert was William Roper, son-in-law to Thomas More. Having read Luther's *Babylonian Captivity*, he

> then thought that all the ceremonies and sacraments in Christ's Church were very vain... I have no more need of confession, of vigils, or of the invocation of saints. The ears of God are always open to hear us.
>
> Faith alone is necessary to salvation. I believe ... and I am saved... Nothing can deprive me of God's favour.[38]

Harpsfield states that Roper was a 'marvellous zealous Protestant' when he married More's daughter Margaret: 'He thirsted very sore to publish his new doctrine and divulge it.' More was fearful that his family would now be targeted by the authorities.

Roper made contact with fellow believers in the Hanse Steelyard in London and was caught in the drive against them. The German community's church was All Hallows the Greater, in Thames Street, which later dropped the ritual of mass as a false doctrine. Wolsey raided the Hanse Steelyard in February 1526, seizing illegal Bible tracts which were then burned. Roper was brought before him but, because of his connections, was let off with a caution while others had to recant at Paul's Cross, the open-air pulpit before St Paul's Cathedral. Clearly frightened by his close shave, Roper denied his new faith and regained More's favour in order to promote his career. He later wrote a self-serving account of his father-in-law's life. More took Roper as his model for the messenger in the *Dialogue Concerning Heresies*.

These evangelicals were the spawn of Satan to More, whose

persecution of them when Chancellor was to exceed Wolsey's. The authority of the word of God dared to challenge papal authority and in opposition to Rome there now grew up an incipient English nationalism.

A close-knit community promoted the cause and protected one another in a time of danger and oppression. Marriages and alliances were made within the network. They were all part of an underground circle of evangelicals dedicated to illegal and very dangerous work. This was the secret church of God, the first wave of evangelical believers, of which the Boleyns were the vanguard.

On 5 May 1527 Henry deliberately picked out Anne Boleyn as his partner before all the court and the French ambassadors at Greenwich. This signalled his public interest in her and his hopes for the relationship. 'We were in the Queen's apartments where there was dancing and M. de Turaine, on the King's command, danced with Madame the Princess, and the King with Mistress Boulan who was brought up in France with the late Queen.'

Other ambassadors did not recognise Anne's influence until August, while the Venetians did not know about Anne until February 1528.[39] Henry was highly secretive and without scruple or conscience: 'If I thought my cap knew my counsel, I would cast it into the fire and burn it.'[40] Cavendish describes the King as a self-indulgent, overgrown boy who recklessly handed over all the business of state to others. He quotes Wolsey's opinion of his master:

> rather than he will either miss or want any part of his will or appetite, he will put the loss of one half of his realm in danger. For I assure you I have often kneeled before him in his privy chamber on my knees the space of an hour or two to persuade him therefro. Therefore, Master Kingston, if it chance hereafter you to be one of his privy council (as for your wisdom and other qualities ye be meet so to be) I warn you to be well advised and assured what matter ye put in his head; for ye shall never pull it out again.[41]

The French ambassador Marillac said that the King was 'far from reckless and bets only on a sure thing'. He described three 'plagues' that ruled Henry: greed, distrust or fear, and inconsistency: 'The King, knowing how many changes he has made, and what tragedies and scandals he has created, would fain keep in favour with everybody, but does not trust a single man, expecting to see them all offended.'[42]

As Greenblatt states: 'Conversations with the King himself must have been like small talk with Stalin.'[43]

In the midst of the negotiations with the French for the marriage of Princess Mary, the Bishop of Tarbes actually questioned her legitimacy.[44] On 8 May Wolsey had officially been told of the King's doubts about the validity of his marriage. Nothing was said of Henry's relationship with Anne, but it seems incredible that the great spymaster did not know of his pursuit of her. Clearly he was under the impression that she would soon follow the path taken by her sister into the King's bed, and just as quickly be forgotten.

On 17 May Wolsey, as papal legate, convened a secret ecclesiastical court at Westminster in order to test the King's marriage. This court was headed by William Warham, the Archbishop of Canterbury, who had always believed that Henry's marriage to Catherine of Aragon was invalid and had warned Henry against the match 18 years before, when Bishop of London. The King appeared to the secret gathering of learned prelates, confessing his sense of sin in knowing his brother's widow and asking them to give him an annulment. But the shrewd canon lawyers recognised the minefield before them and decided to pass on a definitive ruling.

Henry was not about to give up now, and suddenly it seemed he had a second chance. His Privy Council sanctioned an approach direct to Rome for the Pope to settle the matter, but on 28 May extraordinary news arrived of events earlier in the month. Rome had been invaded and sacked by Charles V and the Pope had fled the rampaging troops. Looters and murderers stalked the streets while the pontiff cowered in the castle of St Angelo and was now the Emperor's prisoner.

On 22 June Henry went to Windsor to tell Catherine that they had never legally been married and that he had separated from her for ever. He read from Leviticus and explained to her that all these years they had actually been committing incest. Unsurprisingly, Catherine grew hysterical. Her temper was well known. She was arrogant, stubborn, even bloody-minded,[45] and she was outraged to be told by her husband that she was no better than one of his whores.

As a princess of Spain, she had her own resources. The news from Rome only confirmed that the Emperor was now the ruler of Europe. Catherine's nephew would surely support her against Henry. She sent him a secret letter about the crisis via one of her servants, Francisco Felípez. He claimed to be visiting his sick mother in Spain but Wolsey's agents had him arrested in Calais as a spy. Henry was furious that Catherine had been seeking to go to his enemies behind his back. Her loyalty to the crown was questioned. Even after all her years in her adopted country, it seemed that her first loyalty remained with Spain.

Archbishop Warham told her of his earlier conviction that her marriage to the King had always been illegal. Whatever Catherine thought, 'truth and law must prevail'.

In July Wolsey was dispatched to Europe to get the dispensation. At the very moment when Anne stepped on to centre stage, she deliberately withdrew from the limelight, rarely appearing at court. For the next two years she lived in seclusion at Hever, preserving both her distance from Henry and her reputation.

As the future Queen of England she realised she must be like Caesar's wife, just as Wyatt reflected in his poem.

'The long hid and secret love' described by Wolsey's servant Cavendish was now public knowledge. Henry was aware of new dangers which arose and feared that his letters to Anne had been intercepted. Here we see his concern expressed in the original English:

Darlyng, I hartely recommande me to yow, assertayneyng yow that I am nott a lyttyl perplexte with suche thynges as your brother shall on my part declare vnto yow, to home I pray yow gyffe full credence, for it wer to long to wryte. In my last letters i wrotte to yow that I trustyd shortly to se yow, whyche is better knowne att London than with any that is abowght me, weroff I nott a lytyll mervell. But lake of dyscrette handelyng must nedes be the cause theroff. No more to yow att thys tyme, but that I trust shortly our metynges shall nott depende vppon other menys lyght handyllynges but vppon yor Awne.

Wryttyn with the hand offhym that longyth to be yours –

HRx[46]

Henry wrote of the lack of 'dyscrette handelyng' and feared that his letters were being read by their enemies. Servants could be bribed, letters stolen. He was anxious that his passion for Anne would be 'tossed in every man's mouth, in all talks and at all tables, in all taverns, ale-houses, and barbers' shops, yea, and in pulpits too'.[47]

Throughout the period there was a general mood of caution about security of communications. The Governor of Calais, Lord Lisle, often wrote about the danger of putting pen to paper and sharing indiscretions. Sensitive issues such as politics should not be written down but told by a personal messenger who could be trusted:

> 'Touching news, this bearer will inform your lordship.' There should be nothing put down in writing which could be used as evidence. Yet to burn letters on receipt … might be dangerous. To have no letters to produce could be as fatal as to have indiscreet letters. Their absence could be interpreted as evidence that one had something to conceal.[48]

Once it was realised that Henry was serious about his intention to remove Catherine, his foreign enemies schemed to get their hands on evidence of his affair with Anne. Catherine in particular wanted to show the letters in court in order to prove that it was his lust for Anne which was driving the divorce.[49]

Pope Clement VII wanted to know if Anne was pregnant. He was to be disappointed. His envoy Cardinal Campeggio wrote back that Anne was of noble family and good education, while Cardinal Wolsey denied that she was the cause of the King's wish to set aside Catherine and defended her moral reputation:

> …the purity of her life, her constant virginity, her maidenly and womanly pudicity, her sobreness, chasteness, meekness, humility, wisdom, descent of right noble and high thorough regal blood, education in all and laudible qualities and manners, apparent aptness to procreation of children, with her other infinite good qualities…

The truth was Anne had not even slept with Henry. Cavendish confirms the fact that she remained a virgin until she married the King:

The noblest prince that reigned on the ground
I had to my husband. He took me to his wife;
At home with my father a maiden he me found.[50]

Even the Imperial ambassador had to admit there was no evidence of adultery. He wrote to Charles V in September: 'Both the King and his lady, I am assured, look upon their future marriage as certain, as if that of the Queen had actually been dissolved. Preparations are being made for the wedding.'

Obliged to show discretion, Henry wrote to his new betrothed: 'Mine own darling, I would you were in mine arms, and I in yours, for I think it long since I kissed you.'

Soon, he told her, 'you and I shall have our desired end, which shall be more to my heart's ease than any other thing in this world'.

Henry would marry Anne. They believed it would be but a matter of months.

Chapter Six

A Renaissance Family

THE DISCOVERY OF the King's infatuation with Anne was a severe blow for Wolsey.

Henry's duplicity and the fact that he had concealed the depth of his emotions from his first minister were dangerous signs that the King no longer trusted him. Henry had deliberately hidden his intention to cast Catherine away and replace her with an Englishwoman, not a royal candidate, not even a daughter of one of the great noble houses. This was an insult to the Cardinal's own intelligence network, which had failed to inform him about the true nature of their relationship.

Anne was the daughter of Wolsey's long-time enemy Thomas Boleyn, leader of the evangelical faction at court, and he himself had sabotaged her chances of becoming Countess of Northumberland some years before. The fact that he had done so on instructions from the King himself should have alerted him to Henry's interest, but he had foolishly dismissed Anne as lightly as her sister Mary.

When Wolsey had first reached the attention of Henry, the King was still young and relatively inexperienced, content to have him take over the administration of the kingdom, leaving him free to pursue his pleasure. Henry took all the credit for Wolsey's successes but turned against him when he failed; and he began to fail more and more often. His excessive demands of taxation, loans and grants caused fierce resentment in the country. Mendoza, the Imperial ambassador, reported that Norfolk, the Boleyns and their allies were now openly opposed to Wolsey.[1] The Cardinal realised that unless he could salvage his reputation, his whole career was in peril. He had to find a way to satisfy Henry's desire to be rid of Catherine while appeasing the Pope and Catherine's influential European relatives.

Anne Boleyn still came a long way down Wolsey's list of priorities. The idea that any daughter of Thomas Boleyn could become Queen of England was so remote and absurd that he dismissed it out of hand. He still believed that stalling negotiations with Rome would lead to the waning of Henry's infatuation and that the King would ultimately agree to look at a French princess as an alternative wife.

This decision of Wolsey, who once again failed to understand Anne and her growing influence over the King, was to prove fatal. While the Cardinal was away in Europe trying to play the great international statesman, Henry sent his own envoys, Dr William Knight and John Barlow, chaplain to the Boleyns at Hever, to the Pope for a special dispensation permitting the King to marry, 'for that is it which I above all things do desire'.

Anne was not mentioned, but a clause referred to the problem of a 'first degree of affinity' existing between the prospective bride and groom. This legal impediment, in Anne's case, was the fact that her sister Mary had slept with the King, but it also covered the difficulty of a pre-contract, where the bride (Anne) had some prior betrothal (with Percy of Northumberland) which had remained unconsummated.

Henry was trying to cover all possibilities. He clearly had no intention of letting his 'Great Matter' drop, despite Wolsey's prevarication.

Wolsey had been deliberately kept in ignorance of this double-dealing, but he soon found out how little Henry now trusted him. Aware that his position in England was under fresh attack, he hurried back from his abortive mission.

Even for England, it was the worst summer in living memory. The rain never stopped, pounding down from a sullen leaden sky that seemed to be an evil omen. Fields were flooded and crops ruined. The ancient highways turned to heavy mud and many bridges were washed away. The harvest was bad and was followed by a fierce winter in which the sea froze. There were serious food shortages, leading to hoarding and price rises. Half the flour in London had to be made out of beans. There were riots from Taunton to Tonbridge. Rebels marched to the Archbishop of Canterbury's palace, Knole Place in Kent, demanding that the King repay the money which the people had lent him to go to war under the 'Amicable Grant' of 1525. Thomas Boleyn and the local gentry were sent to arrest them and they were condemned to death at Rochester assizes.[2] The country was in trouble and Wolsey was seen as ultimately responsible for all these misfortunes.

The King's dissatisfaction with the performance of his first minister was now recognised in court circles, an indication that at last the influence of the hated Cardinal could be overthrown. Wolsey was seen as an enemy by not only the aristocracy but also the increasingly influential evangelical faction at court led by the Boleyns.

Although the nobility was headed by Anne's own uncle, Thomas Howard, 3rd Duke of Norfolk, there was little love lost between the two families. Norfolk was overbearing and arrogant, indulging in a scandalous private life. His wife was Elizabeth Stafford, daughter of the Duke of Buckingham (who had been executed in 1521) and heiress to the Plantagenet name, but she was treated shamefully by her husband, humiliated and beaten in public, while he flaunted his mistress, her servant Bess Holland. Norfolk was also a Catholic of the old school: superstitious, ignorant of the New Learning and opposed to the religion and progressive views of his Boleyn brother-in-law and radically educated niece, Anne.

According to the Imperial ambassadors Mendoza and Chapuys, Norfolk was secretly working against Anne, and this rift grew more intense in following years,[3] but in no way does this suggest that Norfolk opposed her sudden ascendancy or Henry's intention to make her his Queen.

He clashed openly with his rival, the Duke of Suffolk, Henry's old friend Charles Brandon, whose wife Mary Tudor used 'opprobrious language' against Anne. Mary had disliked Anne ever since she had witnessed the scandals surrounding their marriage in France.[4]

Norfolk was not inclined to oppose Henry's resolution to marry Anne. He saw, as Wolsey's servant Cavendish records:

> The King waxed so far in amours with this gentlewoman that he knew not how much he might advance her. This perceiving, the great lords of the council, bearing a secret grudge against the Cardinal ... who kept them low and ruled them as well as other mean subjects, whereat they caught an occasion to invent a means to bring him out of the King's favour ... perceiving the great affection that the King bare lovingly unto Mistress Anne Boleyn, fantasying in their heads that she should be for them a sufficient and an apt instrument to bring their malicious purpose to pass; with whom they often consulted in this matter. And she having both a very good wit, and also an inward desire to be revenged of the Cardinal, was agreeable to their requests.[5]

Cavendish attributes Anne's dislike of Wolsey to bitterness over his interference in her prospective marriage to Henry Percy, yet there were other long-existing and fundamental reasons for her low opinion of the Cardinal. These included the ongoing battle at court of Wolsey against her father which blocked his promotion, his opposition to the New Religion, and the fact that he epitomised the very abuses of the Catholic Church which reformers like the Boleyns decried: corruption and venal vices. The Cardinal had at least one mistress, with children whom he supported and advanced, and he used his high office to accrue vast wealth and ostentatious luxury.

However, Wolsey was still the King's chief minister, whom the Boleyns could not yet afford to alienate for fear that he would sabotage the annulment and prevent Anne's marriage. They were still waiting for news from Rome that would permit Henry to send Catherine away and publicly acknowledge Anne as his future bride.

Rome was still in an uproar after Emperor Charles V's invasion, but Pope Clement escaped to Orvieto. Wolsey pompously talked of overthrowing Charles for his insult to the Church,[6] expecting that the Pope would seek vengeance on the invader by agreeing to Henry's desire to put Catherine, Charles's aunt, aside. On 21 January 1528 the English rashly declared war on the Emperor in Burgos, although no one seriously anticipated a major campaign.

Henry believed that Wolsey could himself declare the dispensation permitting his divorce from Catherine, but as a precaution

Wolsey's man Gregory Da Casale and Henry's secretary Knight had been sent back to Rome to obtain a commission authorising the Cardinal to oversee the business, to pronounce the nullity of Catherine's marriage and to get a dispensation allowing the King to marry again. The mission backfired miserably when Cardinal Pucci changed the clause which would have permitted Wolsey to grant a final *decree nisi*. Henry was furious, but Wolsey took his chance and now stepped in to take full charge of the King's interests, sending Dr Edward Fox, Henry's almoner, and Dr Stephen Gardiner, Wolsey's secretary, to Rome.

The new envoys called at Hever en route in order to report to Anne in person. For since the King had declared himself and made his marriage proposal to Anne, the couple were extremely correct and circumspect about their behaviour. Anne had been briefly at court in late September 1527, but returned to Hever for the entire winter, only following the court to Windsor in March 1528, where her stepmother was a very public chaperone.

Now Anne was prompted by her family to make a discreet approach to the Cardinal through his agent Thomas Heneage. In March Anne invited Heneage to join her for dinner, a public signal of a new alliance of interests with Wolsey. From that time Heneage was the 'back channel' between his master and Anne's supporters at court. She thanked Heneage for Wolsey's 'kind and favourable writing unto her'. Clearly, despite their deep underlying differences, both players understood the importance of a temporary alliance.

In Orvieto Fox and Gardiner met the Pope and on 13 April obtained his agreement that the divorce could be heard in England by Wolsey and his fellow cardinal Campeggio. Fox returned in May with the news, finding the King at Greenwich. A contagious disease had broken out which infected Princess Mary and some of Catherine's ladies. This was said to be '*petite vérole*', smallpox, but was most likely measles. As a precaution, Henry had given Anne and her mother an apartment over the tiltyard, and it was here that the King and Anne heard Fox's news with 'marvellous demonstrations of joy'.[7]

Fox was sent straight to report to Wolsey in London, where he resided at Durham House in the Strand, rousing him from his bed. Suspicious by nature, Wolsey examined the agreement with a jaundiced eye and found that the cardinals in Rome had included a legal loophole which Gardiner, for all his experience, had missed. The next day, however, he summoned Fox, his adviser Dr Bell and Anne's father, declaring that Gardiner had achieved victory. Nothing could be further from the truth. In the fine print he had discovered the Pope's double-dealing, yet he dared not admit failure. His own position was in great danger, with the volatile King swinging from mood to mood. Wolsey was not about to take the blame alone. He warned Gardiner that if his mission should fail, he was 'never to return'.[8]

In private he commanded Fox to write immediately to Gardiner in Rome to undo the damage as swiftly as possible. He was to invent an accident which during the journey back to England had ruined the Pope's letter and required a second copy to be made. While dictating this copy, Gardiner was to be sure to insert his own clause in which the Pope decreed the divorce himself. Wolsey was willing to keep this secret if necessary, in order to save his reputation and the status of the Church in England: 'I would obtain the decretal bull with my own blood, if possible. Assure the holy father on my life that no mortal eye shall see it.'

Henry, learning of the letter, summoned Wolsey and publicly humiliated him. Wolsey is said to have shaken like a leaf, yet the King's full fury was directed at the Pope:

Shall I exhaust my political combinations, empty my treasury, make war upon my friends, consume my forces and for whom? for a heartless priest who, considering neither the exigencies of my honour, nor the peace of my conscience, nor the prosperity of my kingdom, nor the numerous benefits which I have lavished on him, refuses me a favour, which he ought, as the common father of the faithful, to grant even to an enemy. Hypocrite!

You cover yourself with the cloak of friendship, you flatter us by crafty practices, but you give us only a bastard document, and you say like Pilate: It matters little to me if this King perishes and all his kingdom with him…

I understand you … you wish to entangle us in the briers, to catch us in a trap, to lure us into a pitfall… But we have discovered the snare; we shall escape from your ambuscade, and brave your power.[9]

Henry at once invited Erasmus to London, but in a letter of 1 June the reformer said he could not come, offering the excuses of his poor health, the robbers on the road and the rumours of war.

Wolsey informed Rome that the whole situation was so precarious that if he fell from power then the Church would pay the price. 'It is only by acceding to his demand that we can preserve the kingdom of England to the popedom.'

Gardiner in Rome attacked the cardinals:

O perverse race, instead of being harmless as doves, you are as full of dissimulation and malice as serpents; promising everything but performing nothing. England will be driven to believe that God has taken from you the key of knowledge, and that the laws of the popes, ambiguous to the popes themselves, are only fit to be cast into the fire. The King has hitherto restrained his people, impatient of the Romish yoke; but he will now give them the rein.[10]

On 8 June the Pope granted a new commission, giving Wolsey and Campeggio the power to declare Henry's marriage null and void and to allow him to remarry. But instead of entrusting it to Gardiner, he gave it to Campeggio, with orders not to give it up until the political situation in Europe had resolved itself. If the Emperor was overthrown then it could be shown, but if he won, it could prudently be destroyed. A letter from Charles, intercepted by the French, stated that the divorce would bring revolution in England. Wolsey got hold of this and read it to the King, hoping it would make him think again. He claimed that peace in Europe, England's prosperity and particularly Henry's own security on the throne, were now at stake.

According to the French ambassador, Jean du Bellay, Henry's face grew black with rage and 'the king used terrible words'. He told him that he would gladly give a thousand Wolseys for one Anne Boleyn. 'No other than God shall take her from me.'

Anne had apparently been ill. On 6 June Heneage reported to Wolsey: 'Mistress Anne is very well amended, and commendeth her humbly unto your grace, and thinketh it long till she speak with you.'[11]

Soon afterwards sweating sickness broke out in London. Du Bellay records that the outbreak began on 14 June: 'It is a most perilous disease. One has a little pain in the head and heart; suddenly a sweat begins; and a physician is useless, for whether you wrap yourself up much or little, in four hours, sometimes two or three, you are dispatched without languishing.'[12]

Sweating sickness, or *sudor anglicus*, seems to have been a virulent form of influenza with pulmonary complications. It had first appeared in England in the summer of 1485, brought by the French mercenary troops of Henry VII's invasion force. Tens of thousands died in subsequent years, notably 1517 and July 1525, when 50 people a day had expired in London. It was a return to the terror of the medieval plague carried by rats, known as the Black Death, *yersina pestis*. This began in the East and spread to Europe, killing 25 million. In 1348–9 it had wiped out a third of the population, returning year after year until 1400.[13]

London had since grown into a vast city of sprawling slums. With poor migrants flooding in from the countryside in search of work, its ever expanding population lived in filthy conditions. All kinds of rubbish and waste polluted the streets. Horse droppings, chicken dung and mounds of refuse contaminated water supplies. The wealthy, notably Cardinal Wolsey, carried spiced or perfumed pomanders to counteract the vile stench. Lice and fleas were everyday problems, even for the nobility. Even the great houses were not immune to bedbugs and rats. Erasmus commented on English houses: 'above all, the dirty habit of spreading ... rushes over the clay floors of houses to catch food scraps, spilled ale and bones should be abandoned'.

Men would urinate anywhere, even in the corridors or fireplaces of royal palaces. Thomas Tusser wrote in his *Five Hundred Goode Pointes of Husbandrie*:

Some make the chimnie chamber pot to smell like filthie stink,
Yet who so bold, so soone to say, fough, how these houses stink?[14]

Only the highest in the land had access to an inside toilet. A *jordan*, or close-stool, was merely a chamber pot disguised inside a box which could be carried about as desired. Henry VIII's *jordan* was covered in black velvet and gilt studs. A *garderobe* was often communal, several seats side by side over a hole which dropped down into an open shaft outside the walls.

This was the breeding ground for summer outbreaks of 'the Sweat'. Thousands fled the capital, clogging up the roads in carts and wagons carrying prized possessions. As they fled unchecked, the disease began to spread from London into the countryside. Du Bellay wrote: 'We saw them thick as flies rushing from the streets and shops into their houses to take the sweat whenever they felt ill. I found the ambassador of Milan leaving his lodging in great haste because two or three had been suddenly attacked.'[15]

The Sweat brought high fever, stomach cramps, headaches and dizziness, often with a rash of black spots. It struck suddenly and in four hours the victim was 'stiff as a wall'. Those who died before a priest could be fetched to give the last rites were refused burial in consecrated ground, adding to the great resentment the common people already felt towards the Church.

> London ground to a halt as businesses closed and houses were shuttered up. In four days, 2,000 died. People collapsed without warning, some in opening their windows, some in playing with children in their street doors, some in one hour, many in two, it destroyed; ...some in sleep, some in wake, some in mirth, some in care, some fasting and some full, some busy and some idle; and in one house sometime three, sometime five, sometime more, sometime all.[16]

Within a day the disease had reached Greenwich, on the south side of the Thames, and one of Anne's own maids fell ill. The King reacted in terror, moving with the court and Catherine to Waltham Abbey, 12 miles to the north, leaving Anne to survive as well as she could.[17]

Du Bellay doubted whether Henry's relationship with Anne would survive an extended separation.[18] There was pressure on every side for the King to abandon her, but with Anne's absence he grew even more determined to have her.

Belatedly, his conscience pricking after Anne had apparently shown her disgust at his desertion, he wrote back to her from his place of safety:

The uneasiness my doubts about your health gave me disturbed and frightened me exceedingly, and I should have had no peace without knowing the truth, but now, since you have as yet felt nothing, I hope and believe that it will pass you by as I hope it has with us. I think if you would leave the Surrey side as we did, you would escape without danger.

And it may comfort you to know that it is true, as they say, that few women or none have this malady, and moreover none of our Court, and that few elsewhere have died of it.

Wherefore I beg of you, my wholly beloved, to have no fear nor to be uneasy at our absence; for wherever I may be, I am yours. And yet we must sometimes submit to our misfortunes, for whoever will struggle against fate, is generally but so much the farther from gaining his end. Wherefore, comfort yourself and take courage, and make this misfortune as easy to you as you can, and I hope shortly to make you sing for joy of your return...

I wish you between my arms that I might a little dispel your unreasonable thoughts.

Written by the hand of him who is, and always will be, your

Un-H-Rex-changeable.[19]

The King departed now for Hunsdon in Hertfordshire. He was there only two days when several members of his court fell ill and died in two or three hours. Without delay he left for Wolsey's house at Tyttenhanger, in the same county. He cut off all communication, even with his servants, and shut himself up in a room at the top of an isolated tower, eating alone.

He then summoned Sir Brian Tuke, who was sick in Essex, to come to him, even by horse-drawn litter if necessary. Henry was a hypochondriac, always anxious about his health and that of those around him. He recommended that Tuke take a cure *pro tumore testiculorum*, 'as any most cunning physician in England could do'.

Henry had a real horror of sickness and death. When he was a child, his elder brother Arthur and mother, Elizabeth of York, had died suddenly, leaving him with a morbid fear.[20] He had almost died from smallpox at Christmas 1513, and suffered in subsequent years from recurring migraines.[21] Smallpox and measles were often confused, as the measles-like eruption was followed by smallpox within two years. It has been suggested that as a young man Henry had contracted syphilis ('*roniole*', or 'the pox').[22] He could have caught it from any one of his numerous mistresses, including those he shared with Francis I, such as Mary Boleyn. The King of France was to die an agonising death of the disease, his body exploding in its coffin.

Henry suffered from one illness or accident after another. He had frequent bouts of malaria all his life, the first in 1524. Two years later he had a serious accident when jousting, which was followed by persistent migraine headaches and painful leg ulcers. These ailments, together with his mood swings and vicious temper, which worsened as he grew older and more frustrated with his lack of mobility, have been attributed to various diseases, including syphilis.[23]

Henry's extravagant indulgence only served to add to his problems. His diet was chiefly rich protein in the form of vast quantities of greasy, roast meats, accompanied by sweet confections and 'subtleties' carved from sugar for banquets. He was plagued with constipation, poor digestion and haemorrhoids. As his household accounts show, he was constantly supplied with pills, potions and enemas by his army of apothecaries, who were well known for their sharp practice.

Medicine was dominated by the theory of four 'humours' — fire: choler, yellow bile; water: phlegm; earth: black bile, melancholy; and air: blood. Urine was tested to determine imbalance in these humours, with bleeding recommended to restore good health. This could often prove excessive, the basilic vein below the elbow or even the jugular often slit to release bad humours. Rhubarb and liquorice was taken for digestive troubles; rue or rosemary for headaches; belladonna, fennel and St John's wort for fever; mandrake, hemlock and opium for surgery or sleep; and vervain for nerves and lust. There was an alleged cure for sweating sickness made from saffron, mustard seed, herbs and unicorn's horn.

After the Sweat had reached Pontefract, Henry took the precaution of moving his son, Henry Fitzroy, away from danger. He also sent him his own herbal remedies, which seemed to have worked. Fitzroy later wrote to his father:

Thanks be to God and to your said highness, I have passed this last summer without any peril or danger of the ragious sweat that hath reigned in these parts and other, with the help of such preservatives as your highness did send to me, whereof most humble and lowly I thank the same.[24]

Henry now complained of bladder problems and headaches. Separated from Anne, he had occupied himself writing an argument against his false marriage to Catherine, entitled *A Glasse of the Truthe*. He worked long hours, as Tuke records: 'His highness cometh by my chamber door, and doth, for the most part going and coming, turn in for devising with me upon his book.'

On 20 June, Henry, after hearing three masses (he had never done so much before in one day), said to Tuke: 'I want you to write my will.' He also advised Wolsey to follow his example and 'commit all to God'.[25] He recommended the Cardinal take pills of *rasis* (named after Rhazis, an Arab doctor) 'with more good wholesome counsel by His Highness in most tender and loving manner given to Your Grace'.[26]

Henry was increasingly worried about Anne's safety. He sent another messenger to Hever, where she had taken refuge: 'To acquit myself of the duty of a true servant, I send you this letter, beseeching you to apprise me of your welfare, which I pray may continue as long as I desire mine own.'[27]

Late at night, Henry heard devastating news: Anne was seriously ill. At once he sent for his doctors, meanwhile writing her a letter in French:

There came to me suddenly in the night the most grievous news that could arrive and I must needs lament it for three reasons: the first being to hear of the sickness of my mistress, whom I esteem more than all the world, and whose health I desire as my own, and would willingly bear the half of your illness to have you cured; the second because of my fear of being again endlessly tortured by my enemy absence, who until now has caused me every possible annoyance, and so far as I can judge is like to do worse, I pray God to rid me of so importunate a rebel; the third, because the physician in whom I most trust is absent at a time when he could do me the greatest pleasure; for I hoped through him, and his skills, to obtain one of my chief joys in this world, that is to say, that my mistress should be cured.

However, for lack of him I send you the second, and the only one left, praying God that soon he can make you well again, when I shall love him more than ever; praying you to be governed by his advice regarding your illness, by doing which I hope soon to see you again, which will be better medicine for me than all the precious stones in the world.

Written by the secretary, who is, and ever will be
Your loyal and most assured servant

H AB R.[28] [Anne's initials are enclosed in a heart.]

Dr Chamber, the King's chief physician, was not available, so Henry sent Dr William Butts of Norfolk galloping through the night to Anne at Hever. He later reported back to the King that her case was indeed serious 'by the turning in of the sweat before the time'.[29]

History now turned on Anne's survival. Who can say what might have happened if she had not come through the sickness, or who would have succeeded Henry to the throne? But to the King Anne remained 'the woman in the world that I value the most' and he was determined that Dr Butts would cure her.[30]

The epidemic was still spreading, attacking Anne's own brother George, who was still with the King's household. He recovered, but Henry's favourite Sir William Compton caught it and died. Eighteen died in the household of the Archbishop of Canterbury within four hours. Wolsey's own palace was also infected. Within days of Anne's arrival at Hever, her father Thomas had come down with the fever. Soon afterwards her sister Mary's husband, William Carey, succumbed.

When Henry finally received the news that Anne had survived and was past danger, he wrote to her again, enclosing copies of letters he had just received from his French ambassador.[31] France supported the divorce, but the military situation had deteriorated. Should the Emperor prove victorious, the Pope would not dare support their cause. Therefore it was vital that the papal legate, Cardinal Campeggio, should arrive soon.

Henry's correspondence was the subject of international espionage. Letters went missing or were stolen or copied, passed on to agents of the Emperor or the Pope. In late June a vital letter from Orvieto failed to arrive. This missal, 'longed longest for', had been intercepted somewhere in France by enemy agents.[32]

Anne convalesced away from court, at Hever. On her recovery Wolsey sent her 'a kind letter' accompanied by a 'rich and goodly present'. She wrote back:

My lord,

In my most humble wise that my poor heart can think, I do thank your grace for your kind letter, and for your rich and goodly present, the which I shall never be able to deserve without your help, of which I have hitherto had so great plenty, that all the days of my life I am most bound of all creatures, next the King's grace, to love and serve your grace, of the which I beseech you never to doubt that ever I shall vary from this thought, as long as any breath is in my body. And as touching your grace's trouble with the sweat, I thank our Lord that them I desired and prayed for are escaped; and that is the king's grace and you, not doubting that God has preserved you both for great causes known only of His high wisdom.

And as for the coming of the legate, I desire that much. And if it be God's pleasure, I pray him to send this matter shortly to a good end; and then I trust, my lord, to recompense part of your great pains. In the which I must require you in the mean time to accept my goodwill in the stead of the power; the which must proceed partly from you, as our Lord knoweth, whom I beseech to send you long life, with continuance in honour.

Written by the hand of her that is most bound to be your humble and obedient servant,

Anne Boleyn.[33]

Henry now moved from Tyttenhanger to Ampthill in Bedfordshire, delighted with the clean air.[34] He continued to bombard Anne with letters:

The cause of my writing at this time, good sweetheart, is only to understand of your good health and prosperity, whereof to know I would be as glad as in manner mine own; praying God (that it be his pleasure) to send us shortly together for I promise you I long for it, howbeit trust it shall not be long so; and seeing my darling is absent, I can no less do than to send her some flesh representing my name, which is hart's flesh for Henry, prognosticating that hereafter God willing you must enjoy some of mine, which, He pleased, I would were now.

As to your sister's matter, I have caused Walter Weltze [Walshe] to write to my Lord mine own mind therein … for surely whatsoever is said it cannot so stand with his honour but that he must needs take her his natural daughter now in her extreme necessity.

No more to you at this time, mine own darling, but that a while I would we were together of an evening.

H R.[35]

The reference to Anne's sister relates to her concern that William Carey had died of the Sweat on 23 June. Mary was now a widow with two children, Catherine, four years old, and Henry, two. Even so soon after her own brush with death, Anne was worried about her sister's financial problems.

She had written to the King for help, but Henry was not at all interested in the welfare of his rejected mistress. Although he referred to Mary's 'extreme necessity' and soon gave Anne the wardship of her nephew (very probably his own son), he questioned Mary's poor reputation. He wrote that 'Eve shall not have the power to deceave Adam' and complained that it was their father's duty to help his daughter. Considering that Thomas Boleyn was still very much at death's door himself, this shows the callous nature and meanness of Henry. Anne later secured an annuity of £100 for Mary.[36]

Mary Boleyn had also irritated the King because, before his death, William Carey had encouraged her to use Anne's influence with Henry to obtain advancement for his sister Eleanor. She wanted the position of abbess at St Edith's Nunnery at Wilton in Wiltshire and the Careys clearly expected to benefit from Anne's association with the King. Anne was willing to suggest Eleanor to Henry, but Wolsey had another candidate in mind, the prioress Isabel Jordan. Immediately this became a small crisis between rival factions.

To resolve the problem, Henry ordered Wolsey to find a third candidate. He told Anne he had learned that Eleanor Carey's reputation was not suitable, for she had several children by a priest. Nor was Isabel Jordan beyond reproach, having also taken lovers in the past. Such scandals were common, given the low state of morals in the Church, and such behaviour was one of the main reasons why evangelicals such as the Boleyns advocated reform.

However, Wolsey ignored the King's orders and went ahead and promoted his choice, Isabel Jordan. When he heard of this, Henry soundly rebuked him in a letter from Ampthill on 14 July. He wrote that out of 'the great affection and love' he had for Wolsey, following Christ he must say: 'He whom I esteem, I castigate':

Wherefore whatsoever I do say, I pray think it spoken of no displeasure, but of him that would do you as much good both of body and soul as you would yourself. Methink it is not the right train of a truly loving friend and servant, when the matter is put by the master's consent into his arbiter and judgment (specially in a matter wherein his master hath both royalty and interest) to elect and choose a person which was by him defended [forbidden].

And yet another thing which much displeaseth me more, that is, to cloak your offence made, by ignorance of my pleasure.

Written with the hand of him that is and shall be your loving sovereign lord and friend,

Henry R.

The Cardinal was forced into a humiliating apology and Henry promptly forgave him:

Wherefore, my Lord, seeing the humbleness of your submission, and though the case were much more heinous, I can be content for to remit it, being right glad that, according to mine intent, my monitions and warnings have been benignly and lovingly accepted on your behalf, promising you, that the very affection I bear you caused me thus to do.[37]

Anne was reunited with Henry at the end of July, probably at Ampthill. She was chaperoned by her mother, as Thomas Boleyn was still too weak and regaining his strength after suffering from the Sweat. Together again, they wrote a joint letter to Wolsey. Anne began:

My Lord,

In my most humblest wise that my heart can think, I desire you to pardon me that I am so bold, to trouble you with my simple and rude writing; esteeming it to proceed from her, that is much desirous to know that your Grace does well, as I perceive by this bearer that you do.

The which I pray God long to continue, as I am most bound to pray; for I do know the great pains and trouble that: you have taken for me, both day and night, is never like to be recompensed on my part, but only in loving you, next unto the King's Grace, above all creatures living.

And I do not doubt, but the daily proofs of my deeds shall manifestly declare and affirm my writing to be true; and I do trust you do think the same.

My Lord I do assure you, I do long to hear from you news of the legate; for I do hope, and they come from you, they shall be very good; and I am sure you desire it as much as I, and more, and if it were possible, as I know it is not.

And thus, remaining in a steadfast hope, I make an end of my letter, written with the hand of her that is most bound to be...

Here Henry took over, apparently reluctantly:

The writer of this letter would not cease, till she had caused me likewise to set to my hand; desiring you, though it be short, to take it in good part.

I ensure you, there is neither of us, but that greatly desireth to see you, and much more joyous to hear that you have scaped this plague so well; trusting the fury thereof to be passed, specially with them that keepeth good diet, as I trust you do. The not hearing of the legate's arrival in France, causeth us somewhat to muse; notwithstanding, we trust by your diligence and vigilance (with the assistance of Almighty God) shortly to be eased out of that trouble. No more to you at this time; but that I pray God to send you as good health and prosperity, as the writer would.

By your loving sovereign and friend, Henry R,
Your humble servant, Anne Boleyn.[38]

Henry promised that from now on Anne's new status would be recognised. No longer was she formally one of Catherine's ladies, but would have her own household and servants at Durham House: 'As touching a lodging for you we have gotten one by my lord Cardinal's means, the like whereof could not have been found here about.'

At the end of August Anne came to London, taking up residence in the mansion on the Strand, with its grand battlements, towers and gardens leading down to the river. Wolsey had lived there until recently and, symbolically, it was where Catherine herself had lived before her marriage to Henry.

The French ambassador recorded on 20 August: 'Mademoiselle Boulan has returned to court. The King is so infatuated that none but God can cure him…'[39]

Wolsey knew his influence would not survive Henry's marriage to Anne, but he kept his hostility secret and 'ordered himself to please as well the King as her, dissimulating the matter that lay hidden in his breast, and prepared great banquets and solemn feasts to entertain them both at his own house'.[40]

Anne and her father, now fully recovered, pressed their advantage to obtain favours from Wolsey. They both wrote to him requesting the living of Sonridge for the Boleyns' chaplain, Barlow, who had taken Henry's request for a dispensation to Rome.

In her letter Anne also wrote: 'I beseech your grace with all my heart to remember the parson of Honey Lane for my sake shortly.'[41]

All Hallows, Honey Lane, near Cheapside in the City of London, was a centre for evangelicals, attracting large crowds to hear sermons.[42] Dr Robert Forman, and his curate, Thomas Garett, were under investigation by the Bishop of London and Thomas More for 'the secret sowing and setting forth of Lutheran heresies'.[43] Forman was Dean of Queens' College, Cambridge, and with Garett passed so-called 'heretical' books to scholars and students and preached on the New Religion. The 'Oxford scandal' of 1528 reveals Anne's support for the new wave of evangelical scholars whom Wolsey and the Church establishment regarded as dangerous and heretical.[44]

Her contact with Cambridge came through the very doctor whom the King had sent to her during her illness, Dr William Butts. He was a Gonville College man and also an evangelical. Butts had qualified in 1518 and was appointed for a time to Princess Mary at Ludlow with his wife, Margaret Bacon. Together with the great preacher Hugh Latimer, many Cambridge scholars were favoured by Anne and later promoted to positions where they could influence the advance of the reform religion.[45]

Anne now took the opportunity of her growing influence to save some of the evangelical network from arrest, torture and even death. She influenced the King to write to Wolsey on behalf of another victim of the heresy laws, the Prior of Reading, who had been seized with Forman for possessing Lutheran books. Latimer also records Anne's intervention on behalf of the French poet Nicholas Bourbon de Vandoeuvre:

> Dr Butts receiving letters out of France from one Nicholas Borbonius, a learned young man, and very zealous in the scriptures, declaring his imprisonment in his own country for that he had uttered certain talk in the derogation of the bishop of Rome and his usurped authority, made his suit to [Anne] ... in his behalf, did not only obtain by her grace's means the King's letters for his delivery but also after he was come into England his whole maintenance at [her expense] ... only charges in the house of the said Mr Butts.[46]

Anne 'was a special comforter and aider of all the professors of Christ's gospel'. The Imperial ambassador was to state that the Boleyns were the 'principal instruments' of rescuing 'heretics' from prison and that Anne was 'the principal cause of the spread of Lutheranism in this country', which made her the enemy of the Catholic Church.[47]

During her time in France Anne had access to books that were banned in England. When she returned she kept her contacts and obtained many new evangelical works through underground channels and networks. Anne owned the *Epistle and Gospel for the Fifty-Two Sundays in the Year* and *Le Pasteur Evangélique* (The Gospel Shepherd) by the anti-establishment and reformist poet Clément Marot.

William Locke and Richard Herman in Antwerp were among those who supplied books for her.[48] Thomas Alway, prosecuted by Wolsey for having banned books, wrote to Anne: 'I remembered how many deeds of pity your goodness has done within these few years…without respect of any persons, as well as to strangers and aliens as to many of this land, as well to poor as to rich.'[49]

Anne's chaplain, William Latimer, records that she supported a French refugee, Mrs Marye, who 'fled out of France into England for religion'. Anne also wanted the scholar John Sturmius to come from Paris and sponsored Tyndale's forbidden *New Testament*.[50]

William Tyndale, like many leading evangelical reformers, was in exile. He lived in Antwerp, a free city surrounded by the Holy Roman Empire, whose agents had tried many times to seize him. His *New Testament* was smuggled into England from March 1526. The Bishop of London had publicly burned it, even buying copies abroad in order to destroy them. The Bishop recruited Thomas More to write tracts against 'the crafty malignity of these impious heretics', whom he called 'simple-minded people', even though they included some of the greatest scholars of the age.

Hired by the Bishop, Thomas More, in his *Dialogue Concerning Heresies*, rewrote history to suit his patron, blaming the sack of Rome, with its atrocities, on Luther's followers, when in fact it was carried out by mercenaries of the Catholic Emperor Charles V. More supported the burning of heretics such as Tyndale: 'and for heretics, as they be, the clergy doth denounce them; and, as they be well worthy, the temporality doth burn them; and after the fire of Smithfield hell doth receive them, where the wretches burn forever'.[51]

Tyndale had been joined in exile by the young barrister Simon Fish and William Roy, who had written a satire against Wolsey in 1525 and had to flee England.

Racket, Wolsey's appropriately named agent in Antwerp, reported that the exiles were now producing an Old Testament in English and informed against them. Tyndale and his friends had to escape up the Rhine in order to avoid arrest.[52]

Anne was in possession of Tyndale's *The Obedience of a Christian Man* as soon as it was published in 1528. The Dean of the Chapel Royal, Richard Sampson, took it from her but she dared to go to the King in order to get it back, for it was 'the dearest book that ever dean or cardinal took away'. She then persuaded Henry to read it, notably those passages she had marked with her nail, which was her habit.[53]

> The King is in the room of God in this world. He that resists the king, resists God; he that judges the King, judges God. He is the minister of God to defend thee… Let kings, if they had rather be Christians in deed than so to be called, give themselves altogether to the well-being of their realms after the example of Jesus Christ, remembering that the people are God's, and not theirs; yea, are Christ's inheritance, bought with His blood.
>
> The most despised person in his realm (if he is a Christian) is equal with him in the kingdom of God and of Christ. Let the king put off all pride, and become a brother to the poorest of his subjects…

Tyndale believed the Pope had usurped the authority of Christ and God's Word: 'The pope, against all the doctrine of Christ, which saith, My kingdom is not of this world, hath usurped the right of the Emperor. Kings must make account of their doings only to God.'[54]

Henry later stated: 'this is truly a book for all kings to read, and for me particularly'. The book, together with Simon Fish's new work, *A Supplication for Beggars*, urged emancipation from Rome's control. The Church owned a third of England's land and resources, and its priests were 'ravenous wolves'. They

> have gotten into their hands more than the third part of all your realm. The goodliest lordships, manors, lands and territories are theirs. Besides this they have the tenth part of all the corn, meadow, pasture, grass, wool, colts, calves, lambs, pigs, geese and chickens.
>
> Over and besides, the tenth part of every servant's wages…
>
> And what do all these greedy sort of sturdy, idle, holy thieves with

these yearly exactions that they take of the people? Truly nothing but exempt themselves from the obedience of your grace.[55]

The martyrologist John Foxe claimed it was George Boleyn, appointed esquire of the body to the King on 26 September 1528, who first suggested that Anne give these books to the King, but Louth gives full credit to her:

> In a short time the King, by the help of this virtuous lady, had his eyes opened to the truth. He learned to seek after that truth, to advance God's religion and glory, to detest the pope's doctrine, his lies, his pomp, and pride, and to deliver his subjects from the Egyptian darkness and Babylonian bonds that the pope had brought him and his subjects under.[56]

Henry was so interested in these ideas that he offered immunity to Fish and his wife and they eventually returned to England. After Fish died in 1531, his wife continued to bring evangelical works into the country and married Bainham, who was later martyred for his faith. The Imperial ambassador later asserted that Henry was considering permitting reformist and evangelical works to be printed in England.[57]

Henry could discuss these matters only with Anne, whom he called his friend.

Anne believed she had been called like Esther, chosen from all other women by a great King 'for such a time as this' (Esther 4, 14). At the King's side, she could promote religious reform and her deeply held evangelical beliefs. Like Esther, she would become Queen in order to save her people. The marriage to Catherine would be dissolved, Henry rescued from that sinful union and set free from the bonds that bound him to Rome. It was a role she alone was capable of playing.

By September Anne was back at Hever.[58] Campeggio had finally arrived in Paris and Henry wrote to Anne, informing her of the latest news:

> The legate which we most desired arrived at Paris on Sunday or Monday last past [14 September] so that I trust by the next Monday to

hear of his arrival at Calais, and then I trust within a while after to enjoy that which I have so long longed for to God's pleasure and our both comfort; no more to you at present mine own darling for lack of time, but that I would you were in my arms or I in yours, for I think it long since I kissed you; written after the killing of an hart at 11 of the clock, minding with God's grace tomorrow mightily timely to kill another; by the hand of him which I trust shortly shall be yours.

Henry R.

On 29 September, after a journey which took almost three months, Campeggio landed in England. In October Henry wrote:

Mine own sweetheart,

These shall be to advertise you of the great elengenes [loneliness] that I find here since your departing, for I assure you methinketh the time longer since your departing now last than I was wont to do a whole fortnight; I think your kindness and my fervencies of love causeth it, for otherwise I would not have thought it possible ... but now that I was coming toward you methinketh my pains been half relieved ... wishing myself (especially of an evening) in my sweetheart's arms, whose pretty duckies [breasts] I trust shortly to kiss; written with the hand of him that was, is, and shall be yours by his will

HR[59]

This, the most intimate of all Henry's love letters, was surely a sign that their marriage would come soon. On 18 September the Spanish ambassador, Mendoza, had reported to the Emperor that Henry was already preparing for the event.[60]

From a first reaction of alarm, even repugnance, at becoming the target of the King's unwelcome advances, Anne's feelings now changed dramatically. It was not the barrage of letters and gifts, the pestering attention or songs of love which brought about this sea change. It was not a growing affection for Henry or a desire to become his wife. Least of all was it personal ambition to be lauded as Queen with all the riches and dazzling privileges which Henry could give her. All Anne's ambition was now focused on what she could achieve for her faith should she be thrust into that exalted position.

This is a very different picture of Anne from that later concocted by her enemies. She believed that God was with her, steering her towards her destiny. If it was God's will that she should become England's Queen, then the annulment would go through. She waited in the wings, her whole fate in the balance. She could have said, like Winston Churchill in 1940: 'I felt as if I were walking with destiny and that all my past life had been but a preparation for this hour and for this trial.'

William Latimer later wrote that she owed the 'kyndness of almightie God' for raising her to be Queen. She was to tell the Venetian ambassador how God had 'inspired his Majesty to marry' her. Many years later her daughter Elizabeth was told by Alesius, the Scots reformer Alexander Ales: 'True religion in England had its commencement and its end with your mother.'[61]

Anne Boleyn was the catalyst for the Reformation, the initiator of the Protestant religion in England. The religious controversies of her day were Anne's motivation and driving force. Anne 'lived for one thing: to see the Reformed religion overcome the opposition to it both within the Church and outside it... [she] ached to see the Reformation triumph'.[62]

D'Aubigny writes:

The divorce of Henry Tudor and Catherine of Aragon is a secondary event; but the divorce of England and the popedom is a primary event, one of the great watersheds of history, a creative act (so to speak) which still exercises a profound influence over the destinies of mankind... it was only by emancipating themselves from this priestly dictatorship that modern nations could advance safely in the paths of liberty, order, and greatness.[63]

Chapter Seven

The King's Great Matter

T HERE WAS GREAT ANTICIPATION at court after Cardinal Campeggio's arrival in England to oversee the divorce proceedings of the King. Yet it seemed that nothing could hurry the exalted visitor. He travelled from Dover by horse-drawn litter because of his gout, taking a full week to reach London. While Campeggio recovered from his journey at Bath Place, the King was impatient to present his case to be rid of Catherine.

The Church's failure to act meant that popular feeling in the country was rising against the clergy everywhere. The government had come to a virtual standstill, a point that Wolsey stressed to the Pope. England stood at the crossroads, facing renewed civil war and anarchy as long as the succession remained in doubt.

Campeggio finally made a public appearance on 22 October. Henry had arranged a lavish reception at his palace at Bridewell, but violent storms and flooding ruined even these plans and the ceremonies had to be abandoned.[1] Henry visited him the next day, eager to urge the Cardinal to action. In June of the previous year the Pope had actually signed a decretal bull annulling the marriage, which was now in Campeggio's possession. He was under instructions to show this vital document to the King but not to hand it over: 'He could not be brought to part with the decretal bull out of his hands, or to leave it for a minute, either with the King or the Cardinal (Wolsey).'[2]

The Pope seemed surprised that Henry had not simply gone ahead and married Anne at once, considering that he regarded his marriage to Catherine as null and void. In January he had suggested that their legal status could be regularised later, as had happened before in countless other cases when the Pope had turned a blind eye to bigamy.[3] This was precisely what Henry's own sister Mary had done when she married Charles Brandon in 1515, ignoring the fact that he already had two wives and perhaps three. Although Brandon was made Duke of Suffolk and Henry had given his sister a vast wedding banquet at Greenwich, Mary's subsequent children with Brandon were not finally recognised as legitimate until 12 May 1528.[4] It was entirely due to Wolsey that a papal bull had been obtained, but Brandon was not the kind of man to remember old debts and he was shamelessly to abandon his old ally within the year.

The King should have learned from the Suffolk case that the Pope was right. If Henry truly believed that he had never been legally married to Catherine he should, like his friend Brandon, have gone ahead and married a new wife without worrying about the legal niceties. But Henry delayed and dithered, giving way to superstitious fears that lay at the heart of his religious beliefs. Like so many of his countrymen, he sought to appease God's wrath by good works and pilgrimages, hearing mass every day as though it was some protective talisman. These primitive fears were in conflict with his intellect, which Anne fed with fresh theological arguments seeking to enlighten and change his view, to show him that salvation could not be bought but was a matter of faith. Although he listened to her and read the books she gave him, at heart he was unable to shake off his terror that the Pope had the power to excommunicate him, putting his immortal soul in peril.

Campeggio now advocated a solution to Henry's dilemma without the necessity of a public trial. Following many precedents, Catherine should be encouraged to retire into a contemplative life in some nunnery. Many noble women chose this path, living out their latter years in comfortable luxury, including Henry's grandmother, Margaret Beaufort, who had taken a vow of chastity. Campeggio could then officially dissolve the marriage, leaving Henry free to marry Anne.[5]

The King enthusiastically endorsed this idea, sending Wolsey and Campeggio to see Catherine the very next day with promises of future rewards if she agreed. It was the first time that Campeggio had met Catherine and he was amazed to learn she was just 43, for she looked so much older. Yet she was far from meek or docile, demonstrating her obstinate, unyielding nature and the imperious vanity of her Spanish heritage. In a furious tirade, she rejected the cardinals' proposals and insisted that only a trial in Rome before the Pope would satisfy her. Campeggio was astonished by her attitude, reporting to the Pope: 'I have always judged her to be a prudent lady, [but] her obstinacy in not accepting this sound council does not please me.'[6]

Catherine now revealed how shrewd a political manipulator she could be. All these years she had kept hidden the 1503 dispensation of Pope Julius II which permitted her marriage to Henry. This was a bombshell, for it did not contain the irritating little word '*forsan*' (perhaps) from the original bull of dispensation which suggested her first marriage to Arthur had been consummated.

No one had known this extra document even existed. Henry immediately assumed it was a forgery, concocted by the Spanish. Upon examination it proved to be a copy, not an original. Catherine now admitted this, claiming that the original was still in Spain, in the possession of her nephew, the Emperor.

Catherine showed no scruples in attempting to deceive them, even openly humiliating the King whom she professed to love and serve. Henry must have remembered the earlier scandal of 1510 when she had carried out an elaborate pretence to be pregnant for months before being exposed. Then she had lied to Henry, his Council and the King of Spain.[7]

Henry demanded that Catherine send for this document at once. Meanwhile Wolsey suggested that their agents in Rome make a search in the Vatican archives to check that such a document existed.

The King was full of resentment. He took immediate action, officially informing his Privy Council of Catherine's refusal to listen to reason. He cited examples of her collaboration with the enemies of England through the Imperial ambassador Mendoza. He believed she was forming a political faction around her in opposition to the crown, secretly plotting an uprising to seize the throne and make their 13-year-old daughter, Mary, Queen. Henry even believed that Catherine was capable of planning his murder.

The Privy Council recognised the danger, understanding 'in their consciences that his life was in danger' and 'if it could be proved she had a hand in it, she must not expect to be spared'. They recommended that the King send Catherine away and separate her from Mary. He bluntly threatened those involved in such a conspiracy: 'If I find anyone – whoever he is – who speaks in unsuitable terms of his prince, there is no head so fine but I will make it fly.'

On 8 November Henry now chose to make his case public. He summoned a meeting of nobility and prelates to Bridewell to hear a statement on the urgent dangers facing the nation: 'for want of a legitimate King, England should again be plunged into the horrors of civil war'. He announced that the status of Princess Mary had changed: 'neither she is our lawful daughter, nor her mother our lawful wife'. This had been acknowledged by the ambassadors of France who had questioned her legitimacy several years before. This was the reason why he had to put Catherine aside, he claimed, for 'I assure you she is a woman of most gentleness, humility and buxomness – she is without comparison. So that if I were to marry again, I would choose her above all women.'

He was 'sorrowful to leave such a good lady and loving companion' but they had 'lived in adultery to God's great displeasure' and these 'be the sores that vex my mind, these be the pangs that trouble my conscience'.

The strategy seems to have worked, winning the sympathy and support of many Londoners now that they had heard the reasons for his actions rather than rumour and gossip. Yet Hall recorded that they were still suspicions about his true motives: 'The common people, being ignorant of the truth and in especial women and others that favoured the Queen, talked largely and said that the King would for his own pleasure have another wife.'[8]

Henry was still careful to keep Anne in the background. While Campeggio prevaricated and delayed the opening of a trial, the King invited his future wife to Greenwich for Christmas, but gave her separate apartments. Officially Catherine was still the Queen and she boldly presided over the 12 days of celebrations. The new Venetian ambassador assumed the couple were living in perfect harmony. They even kept up the pretence of sharing a bed, even though Henry had not slept with her for many years. Cardinal Campeggio had told the Pope that Catherine 'had not had the use of his royal person for more than two years', and this was confirmed by Wolsey when he wrote urgently to the Pope to inform him that, because the Queen suffered from certain irremediable diseases, Henry and Catherine would never again live as man and wife.[9]

While Anne kept a discreet distance, many members of the court visited her. Du Bellay records: 'Greater court is now paid to her every day than has been paid to the Queen for a long time.' Henry was extravagant with his gifts. His goldsmith, Cornelius Hayes, supplied him with wonderfully crafted jewels for the future Queen.

Campeggio wrote to Rome in January:

The King caresses her openly and in public as if she were his wife. Notwithstanding this, I do not think he has proceeded to any ultimate conjunction, but that he awaits the answer and decision of His Holiness, from whom he fully expects to obtain some remedy whereby to gratify his desire.

A month later he related in cipher:

So far as I can see this passion of the King's is a most extraordinary thing. He sees nothing, he thinks of nothing but his Anne; he cannot be without her for an hour, and it moves one to pity to see how the King's life, the stability and downfall of the whole country, hang upon this one question…[10]

False hopes were raised in February with news that the Pope had died. For a moment Wolsey revived his ambitions to replace him and finally resolve Henry's problems. Charles Brandon was sent to France to persuade Francis I to delay throwing in his lot with the Emperor at Cambrai. For a few months it appeared that the political crisis could be solved if Wolsey became Pope. Then news arrived that Clement had survived his illness and was now even more under the Emperor's influence.

On 6 March Catherine sent a secret letter demanding that the trial be held in Rome, with the King of England summoned to appear in person before the Pope.[11]

When Henry learned of this manoeuvre he ordered the Archbishop of Canterbury, Warham, to warn her that she was playing a dangerous game. Her public posturing, seeking to gain the people's sympathy, was as deceitful as her secret plotting. He promised that he would separate her from her daughter.[12]

After Easter Anne wrote to the King's agent in Rome, Gardiner, a letter of encouragement, sending a gift of cramp rings which the King had blessed on Good Friday to distribute as favours for their cause:

Master Stephen, I thank you for my letter, wherein I perceive the willing and faithful mind that you have to do me pleasure...

I pray God to send you well to speed in all your matters, so that you would put me to the study, how to reward your high service:

I do trust in God you shall not repent it, and that the end of this journey shall be more pleasant to me than your first, for that was but a rejoicing hope, which causing the like of it, does put me to the more pain...

I do trust that this hard beginning shall make the better ending... have me kindly recommended to them both, as she, that you may assure them, will be glad to do them any pleasure which shall be in my power. And thus I make an end, praying God send you good health.

Written at Grenwiche, the 4th day of April.
By your assured friend, Anne Boleyn.[13]

Henry was relying on Gardiner to counteract Catherine and her influential relative, Emperor Charles. Gardiner's mission was to obtain a new papal decree, even by alleging that the original had been lost on the journey. He was to try to obtain a duplicate, rewritten in such a way that it provided everything that had been missing in the first, but the ruse failed.[14] A warning against the Pope came from Gardiner's colleague in Rome, Sir Francis Bryan, one of Henry's favourites, an adventurer and intriguer nicknamed the 'Vicar of Hell': 'Always your grace hath done for him in deeds, and he hath recompensed you with fair words and fair writings, of which both I think your grace shall lack none; but as for the deeds, I never believe to see them, and especially at this time.'

He confessed in a letter to the King on 21 April:

> I dare not write unto my cousin Anne the truth of this matter, because I do not know your Grace's pleasure whether I shall so do or no; wherefore, if she be angry with me, I most humbly desire your Grace to make mine excuse.
>
> I have referred to her in her letter all the news to your Grace, so your Grace may use her in this as ye shall think best.[15]

Two English prelates sent to Spain to see the missing papal dispensation now wrote to Wolsey stating that it was undoubtedly a forgery. Eventually the Emperor sent the document to Henry, claiming it to be genuine and witnessed by a bevy of Spanish bishops. Henry's agents had searched the Vatican but found no mention of the dispensation. Suspicious Wolsey declared it a forgery, complaining to the Pope he should denounce this chicanery, but Clement lacked the courage to come out against the Emperor.

In a move that reflected the cooling of relations with England, Mendoza was recalled to Spain. The Imperial ambassador ended his tour of duty in England with the conclusion: 'nothing annoys this King so much as the idea of not accomplishing his purpose'.[16]

Campeggio could postpone it no longer. The Legatine court sat on a surprisingly cold May morning in the grand Dominican Priory of Blackfriars. Cardinals Campeggio and Wolsey took their seats of cloth of gold in a great show of pomp and pomposity to preside over the trial of the validity of the King's marriage. Even then, legal arguments and delays held back the appearance of witnesses until mid-June.

The whole business proved a fantastic sham. Catherine had been awaiting the arrival of Vives as her counsel, but when he was asked to defend her, he left for Bruges. Catherine stopped his pension.

The King and Catherine were summoned, but she did not take her seat, moving directly to Henry's side. A short figure in bright yellow and crimson, she knelt before him and made a theatrical and carefully rehearsed appeal designed to win her sympathy from 'all the court and assembly'. In her thick Spanish accent she said, according to Cavendish's version quoted almost verbatim in Shakespeare's *Henry VIII*:

Sir, I beseech you for all the love that hath been between us and for the love of God, let me have justice and right. Take of me some pity and compassion, for I am a poor woman and a stranger born out of your dominion. I have here no assured friend, and much less impartial counsel. I flee to you as the head of justice in this realm. Alas, Sir, wherein have I offended you? Or what occasion of displeasure have I deserved against your will that you intend to put me from you? I take God and all the world to witness that I have been to you a true humble and obedient wife, ever conformable to your will and pleasure. I have been pleased and contented with all things wherein you had delight and dalliance. I never grudged a word or countenance, or showed a spark of discontent. I loved all those whom ye loved only for your sake, whether I had cause or no, and whether they were my friends or enemies. This twenty years and more I have been your true wife, and by me ye have had diverse children, although it hath pleased God to call them out of this world, which hath been no default in me. And when ye had me at the first, I take God to be my judge I was true maid without touch of man.

And whether it be true or no, I put it to your conscience.

If there be any just cause by the law that ye can allege against me, either of dishonesty or any other impediment, to banish and put me from you I am well content to depart, to my shame and dishonour. If there be none, I must lowly beseech you, let me remain in my former estate...

It is a wonder to me what new inventions are now invented against me ... therefore I most humbly require you, in the way of charity and for the love of God, who is the just judge, to spare me the extremity of this new court...

And if ye will not extend to me so much impartial favour, your pleasure then be fulfilled, and to God I commit my cause.

Then she rose and left the chamber, refusing to return although summoned and denounced for contempt of court.[17]

Henry had said nothing until now. He addressed the court, repeating his Bridewell speech and stressing the doubts which 'pricked, vexed and troubled' his mind about the validity of his marriage. His treatise *A Glasse of the Truthe* demonstrated his reasoning from Leviticus, and he now appealed to the court.[18]

The King sent Thomas Boleyn to Wolsey at York Place with orders to speak to Campeggio. The two cardinals must visit Catherine and tell her it would be 'much better for her honour than to stand the trial of the law and to be condemned'.

Wolsey thought they would be wasting their time. He told Anne's father:

> Ye and other my lords of the Council, which be near unto the King, are not a little to blame and misadvised to put any such fantasies into his head, whereby ye are the causes of great trouble to all the realm.
>
> And at length get you but small thanks either of God or of the world.

Yet they did visit Catherine, passing on Henry's warning. She was not pleased to see them, complaining: 'I am a poor woman, without friends in this foreign country and lacking wit to answer persons of wisdom as ye be.'

They withdrew into a private room and Cavendish could not hear the others, only her raised voice attacking Wolsey:

> I know who has given the King the advice he is following: it is you.
>
> I have not ministered to your pride – I have blamed your conduct – I have complained of your tyranny, and my nephew the Emperor has not made you Pope... Hence all my misfortunes. To revenge yourself you have kindled a war in Europe and have stirred up against me this most wicked matter.
>
> God will be my judge ... and yours![19]

The legal wrangling went on for weeks, with Henry's side arguing from Leviticus, Catherine's from Deuteronomy. Catherine claimed she had been a virgin when she married Henry and that her first husband, his brother Arthur, had shared her bed only seven times. Yet at the time she had not complained, nor was there any suggestion that the marriage had not been consummated. Nineteen witnesses now gave evidence at the trial of that wedding night, among them the Duke of Norfolk, Charles Brandon, the old Duchess of Norfolk, the Earl of Shrewsbury and the Marquis of Dorset, who confirmed that, according to Prince Arthur's boastful account of the night, the marriage had indeed been consummated.

If it had *not* been consummated there was nothing to prevent Henry from marrying Catherine. The Pope 'dispensed upon nothing and so his bull was nothing worth'. Yet Pope Julius II had stated that her first marriage was 'perhaps consummated' (*forsan consummatum*) and therefore gave her a special dispensation which she needed only if there *had* been a sexual relationship. Ironically, by stressing the importance of the Pope's decision, Catherine's counsel contradicted her protestation of virginity.[20]

Wolsey argued that besides the debate on consummation there was still the fact that Catherine and Arthur had married '*in facie ecclesiae*', 'in front of the church' – that is, before everyone – and '*impedimentum publicae honestatis*', by which all the world recognised their marriage as valid. Nothing in the Pope's decree dealt with this.[21]

Catherine's chief supporter was the Bishop of Rochester, Fisher. He had been chaplain and confessor to Henry's grandmother, Margaret Beaufort, and was also the Chancellor of Cambridge University. He astonished the trial by stating he was ready to die in support of the Queen's case. Henry was so furious that he wrote an answer to the court in Latin. Fisher's copy of this contains comments in the margin where he disagreed with the King's opinion. Henry did not forget this opposition.

Henry was supported in a learned work by the Carmelite friar Giacomo Calco, whom he wanted to appoint Bishop of Salisbury, but Calco died from plague before the appointment could be made. Only brought to light in 2002, 'This treatise is of immense historical importance to the nation. The argument set out in its pages was part of the process that led to a critical moment in English history.' The Calco Treatise argues that conscience takes 'moral priority' over the laws of Rome.[22]

Henry's conscience was part of the problem. If Catherine's marriage to his brother had been valid, then his marriage to her had never been valid at all; therefore he was free to marry. Never having been legally married, he had always been at liberty to marry anyone he chose at any time.

Those around him had the courage of their convictions. His friend Charles Brandon had gone ahead and married Mary Tudor years before he received his divorce from the Pope, while his other sister, Margaret of Scotland, obtained a divorce from her second husband on highly questionable grounds. Henry had lectured her that she was 'under peril of God's everlasting indignation' and faced 'inevitable damnation' for her open adultery which tainted the Tudor name through all the courts of Europe.

Yet it was this caution, combined with a superstitious fear of excommunication, which prevented Henry from simply marrying Anne. For more than three years now he had been obsessed with her, yet, contrary to public speculation, they had not shared a bed. The French ambassador typifies the rumours abroad: 'I much fear that for some time past the King has come very near Mademoiselle Anne, therefore you need not be surprised if they want to hasten it, if her womb swells everything will be ruined.'[23]

Henry and Anne knew this as well as anyone. All Henry's problems stemmed from his lack of a legitimate male heir, so he was determined that when Anne bore him a child there would be no doubts at all about its status. It was marriage or nothing.

Therefore he would wait for the verdict of the court.

Henry had braved the heat and dirt of London all summer. The whole nation waited for the trial to end as Campeggio finally rose to his feet at the end of July, but instead of a resolution he suddenly announced an adjournment until October. The news was received with outrage. Charles Brandon gave a great clap on the table and said: 'By the Mass, now I see that the old said saw is true, that there was never legate nor cardinal that did good in England.'[24]

Henry could not conceal his disgust with the game of deception the Vatican had played upon him and the nation through Campeggio. His pride was deeply affronted that he should have been so humiliated in public and he searched for someone to take the blame for the whole fiasco.

The obvious target was Wolsey himself, who had always claimed that all would be resolved to England's favour. Wolsey realised at once that his own future was now endangered. He saw himself caught between Henry and the Pope: 'How shall I avoid Scylla, and not fall into Charybdis?'

It was not difficult for the King to find support for his move against the power of the Cardinal. The truth was that Wolsey now found himself virtually friendless, his popularity at an all-time low. He was loathed and resented at court for his pomposity and avarice, while mocked by the House of Commons as political satires and rhymes against him were heard in the streets:

> Why come ye not to Court?
> To which court?
> To the King's court, or to Hampton Court?
> Nay, to the King's court;
> The King's court should have the excellence;
> But Hampton Court hath the preeminence.

John Skelton's work ridiculed Wolsey for arrogantly seeking to displace the great aristocrats, even challenging the King. Skelton's patron was the Duke of Norfolk, leader of the court faction against Wolsey. He attacked the arrogance and greed of the great Cardinal who made England 'his footstool', and the clergy's obscene wealth:

> To ride upon a mule with gold all betrapped … there
>   may no cost be spared;
> Their mules gold doth eat, their neighbours die for meat…
> Ye are so puffed with pride that no man may abide
> your high and lordly looks…
> Ye boast, ye face, ye crake,
> And upon you ye take to rule both king and kaiser…
> Their rule is very small, almost nothing at all.

Another poet was Jerome Harlow, a former Franciscan converted to an evangelical, exiled in Germany, who denounced Wolsey as all that was evil:

> Of the proud Cardinal this is the shield,
> Born up between two angels of Satan...
> Mortal enemy unto the white lion (Norfolk)
> Carter of York the vile butcher's son...
> The mastiff Cur bred in Ipswich town
> Gnawing with his teeth a king's crown.[25]

The fact that it was Henry who had raised up Wolsey from lowly beginnings to great power was judicially ignored now as the hounds scented blood and saw their chance to bring him down.

Both Henry and Anne now suspected that Wolsey had been deceiving them, working against the divorce all along. He had shown his true colours, proving where his loyalties really lay – with Rome, not his native country. Anne was certain that the Cardinal was secretly conspiring with the Pope, and perhaps even with Catherine and the Emperor, to ensure that she would never become Queen. He was her enemy and her family's enemy because of their evangelical faith and growing influence upon the King. The Boleyns were educating Henry, feeding him with new ideas. Wolsey's treachery made Anne all the more determined to lead the King towards reform and a permanent break from the shackles of a corrupt religion:

> It was the pleasure of God [that] this noble prince should ... shake off that most unworthy yoke that long had been thrust upon us, contrary to the laws of God and those very ancient [laws] of our country [so that, together] with the Gospel, they both by him recovered their former force and vigour ... this excellent lady [Anne Boleyn] showing him the way ... both of them having the thread of the Gospel [as] their guide, by God put into their hands through her means who ever watched every opportunity for the same...[26]

Henry now deserted London on his summer progress, boldly taking Anne with him. There could be no greater public sign of his intention to go ahead with his plans than to show her off to the country as his future wife. Through the month of August they progressed to Waltham Abbey, Windsor, Reading, Woodstock, Buckingham and Grafton (Northamptonshire), hunting and hawking, sharing a house but not yet a bedroom.

News from abroad was discouraging. The French had not the military prowess to stand up to the armies of Charles V. Pope Clement was once more under the Emperor's control and secret negotiations now brought Francis I to sign the Treaty of Cambrai in August, allying all Henry's enemies. At this time Mendoza was replaced as the Imperial ambassador to England by Eustace Chapuys, a lawyer from Savoy and graduate of the University of Turin. For the next seven years he acted as the Emperor's spymaster at court, having been commanded by Charles to restore Catherine as Queen. Behind this agenda was the need to preserve England as a Catholic nation.

Chapuys set about denigrating Anne at every opportunity, calling her 'the Concubine', although there was never any evidence that she had become the King's mistress. His brief was to discredit Anne and her evangelical supporters and his campaign of defamation described her as an instrument of the devil and a witch.

Yet Chapuys never once met Anne and his verbatim accounts of her private conversations with Henry, when he could not possibly have been present, are totally uncorroborated. On many occasions he was not in the same palace or even in the same town.

Chapuys was a professional, working for a foreign power. He employed paid informers and spies, inventing disinformation and spreading rumours. Catherine's own usher, Juan de Montoya, was his secretary and this Spanish cabal at the heart of the court was a thorn in the King's side.[27]

At their first interview in August, Henry put to Chapuys his reasoning for believing that his marriage to Catherine was against God's laws. He then freely moved into an all-out assault upon the corruption of the Church and the need for major reform, which could only horrify the Imperial ambassador.[28]

Wolsey wrote to Rome warning Clement that 'the authority of the See Apostolic in the kingdom will be annihilated':

Pray, believe me... The divorce is the secondary question; the primary one is the fidelity of this realm to the papal see. The nobility, gentry and citizens all exclaim with indignation: 'Must our fortunes, and even our lives, depend upon the nod of a foreigner? We must abolish, or at the very least diminish, the authority of the Roman pontiff.'...

Most holy father, we cannot mention such things without a shudder.[29]

There was now little doubt that a break with Rome was inevitable. From a simple matter of annulment, the whole business had become a major schism in international politics, which would split England from Europe and ensure her independence for the following five centuries.

On his return from the summer progress, Henry made the decision to call Parliament, the first in seven years. The French ambassador, Du Bellay, reported on 23 August: 'It is intended to hold a parliament here this winter, and then bring about the divorce by their own absolute power in default of justice being administered by the Pope.'

Writs were issued on 25 September, Du Bellay commenting: 'I fancy that in this parliament the priests will have a terrible fright.'[30]

One priest most certainly had – Wolsey. A few days earlier, on 19–20 September, Wolsey and Campeggio had ridden to see the King at Grafton. Campeggio was taking his leave before returning to Rome, his mission a failure. Wolsey's servants left differing accounts of the meeting. Thomas Alward wrote immediately after it, while Cavendish wrote years later, claiming that Wolsey was deliberately snubbed by being refused accommodation at Grafton. Alward says the manor was small and both cardinals had to travel on to lodgings in Easton Neston.

Cavendish describes Henry dining alone with Anne that night, when she turned him against Wolsey, reminding him of the heavy taxes the Cardinal had brought on the people: 'Is it not a marvellous thing to consider what debt and danger the Cardinal hath brought you in with all his subjects?'

Cavendish says Anne insisted that Henry left early next day to see a new hunting park so that when Wolsey and Campeggio returned, the King told them he had no time to talk and deserted them.[31] Alward states that Henry did meet Wolsey, but went hunting after dinner. Whatever the truth, Wolsey must have felt the cold edge of the King's disfavour. Once Henry turned his back on a favourite, it was for good. This was the end for the humble butcher's son from Ipswich. He was 56, Henry 38.

Campeggio also received a last demonstration of the King's anger. As he set out to leave England, the King sent agents after him with orders to search his baggage. Henry had heard disturbing news: his letters to Anne had been stolen. Wolsey had a spy in Anne's household who had taken the King's correspondence to Campeggio to deliver in person to the Vatican. It was hoped that something in Henry's private letters would provide evidence against the King that could be used to make him give up Anne and take back Catherine. Henry was also told that Wolsey had sent treasure abroad with Campeggio in case he had to flee into exile at some future date.

At Dover the Cardinal was stopped, but nothing incriminating was found. The King's letters could have been sent out of England by another courier, Campeggio's son Rodolph.[32] They were certainly stolen from Anne in London and are now held in the Vatican Library. Nothing could be found in them, however, that could be used to prove that Anne was Henry's mistress. Although he must have been aware of the King's suspicion, Wolsey proceeded with much ceremony to open the Court of Chancery for the Michaelmas term on 9 October. At that very time Sir Christopher Hales, the Attorney General, was in the Court of the King's Bench filing charges against him. Wolsey was accused of *Praemunire*, acting in a manner which infringed the royal prerogative by allowing a foreign power (the papal legates' court) to challenge English law.[33]

Astonishingly, Wolsey did not contest the charges. He preferred to swallow his pride and endure what he must surely have hoped would be a brief period in the shade. He realised that any show of resistance now would only incite the King to take even more dramatic measures against him and against the Catholic Church. It was, however, too late. Du Bellay records that Wolsey was 'put out of his house and all his goods taken into the King's hands'. Cavendish records his master's fall, describing how, before he left York Place, he set out all his gold and jewels, silver and rich tapestries so that Henry would see the wealth he was confiscating. He left by barge, watched by a vocal crowd lining the river who thought he was being taken as a prisoner to the Tower of London: 'There were no less than a thousand boats full of men and women waffeting up and down the Thames: but Wolsey boarded his barge at his private stairs surrounded by his own gentlemen and sailed to Putney, where horses were waiting to take him to Surrey.'

Wolsey's destination was not the Tower but a house in Esher belonging to the bishopric of Winchester. According to Cavendish, Henry sent Sir Henry Norris with a ring and told him to be 'of good cheer, for he was as much in his Highness's favour as ever he was, and so shall be'.[34]

Cavendish claims that Henry retained some respect, even affection for Wolsey, keeping him in reserve for some future return. At the time, however, it appeared that the Cardinal was finished. Campeggio warned Rome:

> Immediately after my departure from London, the design against the Cardinal of York began to develop with great violence, so that before I had crossed the sea, they had deprived him of the Seal and of the management of all affairs... He has done nothing in the past so far as ecclesiastical matters are concerned to merit such disgrace, and therefore it may be thought his Majesty will not go to extremes, but act considerately in this matter.[35]

Wolsey was dismissed as Chancellor, with Norfolk and Suffolk hastening to Esher to collect the Great Seal. Du Bellay reported:

> Besides the robberies of which they [his enemies] charge him, and the troubles occasioned by him between Christian Princes, they accuse him of so many other things that he is quite undone. The Duke of Norfolk is made chief of the Council, Suffolk acting in his absence, and at the head of all, Mademoiselle Anne.[36]

Henry wanted to appoint Charles Brandon Chancellor, but this was opposed by the Duke of Norfolk, who argued that Suffolk had already accumulated too much power. On 25 October Chapuys wrote to the Emperor, his master: 'The Chancellor's seal ... has continued in the hands of the Duke of Norfolk till this morning, when it was delivered to Sir Thomas More. Everyone is delighted at his promotion, because he is an upright and learned man and a good servant of the Queen.'[37]

More presided over the opening session of Parliament in the role of prosecutor. After lavishing praise on the King, who was present, calling him 'a good shepherd which not only keepeth and attendeth well his sheep', More launched a vitriolic attack on his predecessor, Wolsey. His invective was absurdly exaggerated. Among the 44 charges in the Bill of Attainder were the allegations that Wolsey had risen above himself by using the phrase 'the King and I', that he had bought beef at knockdown prices, fiddled his accounts, and that, by breathing 'upon your most Noble Grace with his perilous and infective breath', he had endangered the King's life.[38]

Henry stripped Wolsey of his offices and seized his fabulous palaces and property, but he would not press charges further, as some desired. Wolsey was permitted to retire to his diocese of York. It was seen that the King still retained a certain friendship for his old minister.

The King took Anne and her mother to view his new acquisition, York Place, technically still part of the archdiocese of York. All the fantastic wealth that Wolsey had gained had been laid out, on his orders, in room after room like some vast treasure trove. Henry eagerly set about putting his own stamp on York Place, later renamed Whitehall, and Wolsey's impressive new palace at Hampton Court, where he carried out extensive and costly building for a Great Hall, council chamber and gallery with oriel windows.

Wolsey's fall had unleashed a wave of fierce anticlerical feeling. Henry took advantage of the mood in the country to enact a number of measures in Parliament to curb the corruption and excesses of the Church, including a restraint on absentee priests and plurality of offices. Priests demanded heavy fees for the probate of wills and ran businesses, many living as well as the nobility. Now the clergy were banned from keeping shops or taverns, gambling, hunting and hawking or visiting disreputable houses. There were heavy fines for those committing gross and unnatural vices.[39]

In an angry speech in the Lords, Catherine's supporter Fisher, Bishop of Rochester, concluded 'that the Commons would nothing now but down with the Church'. The Commons, through their speaker, complained to the King that the bishop had disparaged

Parliament. Henry summoned Fisher before him, but the bishop was clever enough to appease him.[40]

Anne could only have been delighted by this public move away from Rome, and was further helped by the introduction of a new figure on the scene who would prove to be her valuable ally.

In August, on their return from Rome, Henry's agents Gardiner and Edward Fox had stayed at a house in Waltham. Over dinner they met the family tutor, Thomas Cranmer, a Fellow of Jesus College, Cambridge, who was discoursing on the theological case for the King's divorce. Cranmer had impressed them by arguing that instead of looking to Roman canon law, Henry should win the support of theologians at the great universities.

What right had the Pope to command a divinely appointed king? Henry was under God's authority, not that of Rome.

These ideas were put to the King, echoing those he had already read in the works of Tyndale and Fish given him by Anne. In October Henry interviewed Cranmer at Greenwich and was highly impressed, commissioning him to write an appeal to the appropriate academics in continental Europe, notably in the states of Germany, Switzerland and the Lowlands, where the reform movement had gained ground.

Cranmer was lodged with Thomas Boleyn at Durham House. They shared the same evangelical views, Cranmer having gone to Germany after his first wife died in childbirth. All this time he kept secret the fact that he had married the niece of the Lutheran theologian Andreas Osiander, with whom he had three children, as the King still believed clergy should be celibate. So well did Cranmer and the Boleyns get along that Thomas made him the family chaplain, and he remained Anne's pastor until her death and a friend to her memory thereafter.

Armed with his thesis, Cranmer set out for Paris with Anne's brother George, now Lord Rochford, on his first diplomatic mission. Du Bellay recommended that the French receive him warmly, for the family's influence was very strong:

[Boleyn] allowed everything to be said, and then came and suggested the complete opposite, defending his position without budging, as though he wanted to show me that he was not pleased that anyone should have failed to pay court to the lady [Anne], and also to make me accept that what he had said before is true, that is, that all the rest have no influence except what it pleases the lady to allow them, and that is gospel truth. And because of this he wanted with words and deeds to beat down their opinions before my eyes.[41]

Francis I supported Henry's case, but the conservatives of the Sorbonne were strongly Catholic. George Boleyn obtained a letter from Francis to the French Parliament full of fury that these academics should dare to cross him and threatening action 'that would be an example to all others'. The rebuke had the desired effect and the decision was reversed in Henry's favour. George had done well on his first mission.[42]

Catherine is alleged to have now told Henry that for every academic he could produce to support divorce, she could 'find a thousand to declare that the marriage was good and indissoluble'. She was clearly prepared to draw out the whole process of divorce as long as possible.

According to the Imperial ambassador, Chapuys, Henry related this to Anne on the evening of St Andrew's Day, 29 November, and she flew into a rage, screaming:

Did I not tell you that whenever you disputed with the Queen she was sure to have the upper hand? I see that some fine morning you will succumb to her reasoning, and that you will cast me off.

I have been waiting long, and might in the meantime have contracted some advantageous marriage, out of which I might have had issue, which is the greatest consolation in this world; but alas! farewell to my time and youth spent to no purpose at all.[43]

Both of these conversations are uncorroborated, as Chapuys was certainly not present. Either this is pure fiction or backstairs tittle-tattle given by servants as paid informers, yet it is true that Anne was now 29 and Henry's prevarications and inability to act decisively were wasting precious time. Had the King not intervened in her life, she may well have made a happy marriage elsewhere, even to Harry Percy of Northumberland. Years were passing and Henry was already past his prime, putting on weight and suffering from a variety of maladies.

He would not go ahead and marry her yet, but he was eager to make it up to her.

On 8 December Thomas Boleyn was created Earl of Wiltshire and also of Ormonde, finally inheriting the long-disputed Irish title with its heraldic badge of a black lion rampant. Anne was now Lady Anne Rochford and George, Lord Rochford, given a place in the Privy Council. The next day a great banquet was held where the King seated Anne in the place of honour at his right hand, the place traditionally reserved for the Queen.

Henry was giving her precedence over his own sister, Mary, Duchess of Suffolk, who still insisted on being acknowledged as Queen of France, although she had been married only a matter of weeks. Her vanity, and the remembered disapproval shown by Anne when she had scandalously married Brandon, turned Mary into Anne's enemy. The Duchess of Norfolk, although Anne's aunt by marriage, was also affronted by the rise of the Boleyns. Chapuys wrote to the Emperor:

> Such is the blind passion of the King for the Lady, that I fear one of these days some disorderly act will take place...
>
> It never crossed my mind that the King's blindness could be so great...
>
> The King's affection for La Bolaing increases daily. It is so great just now that it can hardly be greater, such is the intimacy and familiarity in which they live at present.[44]

Henry provided for Anne as if for his wife. Not only had he celebrated their betrothal with gifts of extravagant jewels, but he bought her intimate items of clothing, including linen for her underwear. The Privy Purse accounts record £23 'for linen cloth for my lady Anne for shirts and other necessaries'. He paid for furs to keep her warm, lengths of cloth of gold, purple satin and velvet for new gowns, and pearls with which to adorn headdresses. He spent thousands of pounds, a fortune at that time, with Cornelius Hayes: 'For Mistress Anne ... nineteen diamonds for her head, 29 December. Two bracelets for her set with ten diamonds and eight pearls. A ring with a table diamond, nineteen diamonds set in the form of lovers' knots and twenty-one rubies set in roses of crown gold.'[45]

He did everything to demonstrate that Anne was the future Queen of England, everything but marry her.

Henry was for the first time in complete charge of the kingdom. Now that Wolsey had fallen, the duties of state fell heavily upon his shoulders. Henry had relied on the Cardinal to take the burden of day-to-day affairs, but now he found an administration in chaos and this preoccupied him for much of the time. He rounded furiously on his council, saying Wolsey was 'a better man than any of them for managing matters'.

At Christmas, hearing Wolsey was ill, Henry sent him, with 'the most comfortablest words', several cartloads of furnishings to warm himself in Esher. He also sent back a ring engraved with his likeness and persuaded Anne to send 'her tablet of gold hanging at her girdle'.[46]

These were seen as ominous signs by Wolsey's enemies. As 1530 dawned they began to fear that the King might call him back and even restore him to his former position of power. Something had to be done quickly to prevent the Cardinal's return.

Chapter Eight

The Grand Enemy

WOLSEY HAD FALLEN like Lucifer. At last the aristocratic faction at court under Norfolk and Suffolk had contrived to bring down the butcher's son, 'bearing a secret grudge against the Cardinal because that they could not rule the commonweal as they would'. Their hope was that from now on the King's Council would consist of 'those who from birth and circumstances were more competent'.[1]

The Boleyn family were now immensely influential at court. In January Thomas, now Earl of Wiltshire, was promoted to the Privy Council as Lord Privy Seal. Among those who had reservations about their rising power was his brother-in-law, Norfolk. Compared with the witty, intellectual Boleyns, Norfolk was entrenched in the past, scarcely literate and had always resented his evangelical in-laws. He supported his niece as long as it suited his own purposes, and in this he found a temporary ally in his old rival, Charles Brandon, Duke of Suffolk.

The Suffolks were renowned for their arrogance and snobbery, even though Brandon had far worse credentials than the Boleyns. They were well-matched manipulators who, while professing support for the King and Norfolk, still maintained strong ties with Catherine and her household.

The New Year celebrations of 1530 continued the uncomfortable *ménage à trois* of the King and his competing wives. Catherine was still prominent on all state occasions but Anne had been elevated to the semi-official position of Queen-in-waiting and fêted by foreign ambassadors. After the celebrations Catherine was sent to Richmond while Henry gave Anne a conducted tour of York Place, soon to be refurbished and to become her favourite residence.[2] A great banquet was held there on 12 January for the French ambassador Du Bellay, now finishing his tour of duty.

From his place of exile at Esher, Wolsey kept a close watch on all these events through his agent, Thomas Cromwell, to whom he wrote: 'If the displeasure of my lady Anne be somewhat assuaged, as I pray God the same may be, then it should [be devised] that by some convenient mean she be further laboured [for] this is the only help and remedy. All possible means [must be attempted for the] attaining of her favour.'[3]

Cromwell went to visit his master, who was deeply depressed and suffering from dropsy. Wolsey claimed that his life was in danger. He had written to Anne, but she did not reply and now he clearly saw himself as some kind of martyr: 'Norfolk, Suffolk, and Lady Anne perhaps, desire my death. Did not Thomas Becket, an archbishop like me, stain the altar with his blood?'

But the Spanish ambassador raised doubts about the authenticity of Wolsey's illness, claiming that he was trying to win Henry's sympathy.[4]

Wolsey kept up a barrage of correspondence, including a letter to Gardiner, with a list of complaints about the hardships and deprivations that were making him ill. Henry took pity on him and now Norfolk's worst fear was confirmed – that Wolsey would be brought back and reinstated at court, eager for revenge.[5] Henry had been in two minds about the loss of his most able minister, refusing to permit a Bill of Attainder in Parliament, leaving him Archbishop of York with its vast income and even sending him gifts of furniture, tapestries and 10,000 costly angels. On 12 February Wolsey was pardoned, granted a pension of another 3,000 angels and allowed to move to a better house in Richmond Park.[6]

Wolsey still tried to win Anne around, granting an annuity on George Boleyn from his church holdings, but in private to Cromwell and Cavendish he blamed her for his downfall and called her 'the continual serpentine enemy about the King'.[7] After years of pretence, in which he had sat on the fence, Wolsey now made his fatal mistake. He turned decisively against the King, pinning his colours to the future of the Church and Catherine's supporters in Europe. He began to conspire against Henry and Anne with the ambassador of Emperor Charles V.[8]

On 29 February Pope Clement VII placed the crown of Charlemagne upon Charles's head as Holy Roman Emperor. A new imperialism sought to unify Europe and the whole world as the resurrected Roman Empire under the Catholic Church. This included England, which was meant to have been secured by the marriage of Catherine and Henry. But the New Religion had proved to be a revolutionary force in northern Europe and England was resisting the Imperial plan through its own nascent Protestantism. The stage was set for a titanic struggle for the soul of Christianity, with the vast resources of the Holy Roman Empire and Spanish-American gold on one side and the tiny David of England on the other.

Henry still entertained the hope that a divorce could be obtained. He sent a new diplomatic mission to Bologna, where the Emperor and the Pope had reconciled their differences. The ambassador he chose was his most proficient linguist and future father-in-law, the Earl of Wiltshire, Thomas Boleyn.[9]

The mission was doomed from the start: 'The personal interest which the Earl felt in the divorce made him odious both to Charles and Clement.' In an audience before all the cardinals, the ambassador was expected to show subservience by kissing the Pope's foot. Thomas refused. As a good evangelical, he did not recognise the

> Vicar of Rome's authority. A story is told that a little spaniel, brought as a gift for the Pope, went further in defiance, biting Clement's toe so that the chamber erupted into laughter.
>
> 'That dog was a protestant,' said a reverend father.
>
> 'Whatever he was,' said an Englishman, 'he taught us that a pope's foot was more meet to be bitten by dogs than kissed by Christian men.'[10]

The discussions fared no better. Thomas had prepared sound theological reasons for the annulment of the marriage to Catherine, but it was his warnings of the political repercussions which alarmed his audience. If denied its chance for a new marriage and a legitimate heir, England would simply declare its independence from Rome and the Catholic Church, and this example 'will not fail to be imitated by other kingdoms of Christendom'.

Thomas's following interview with Emperor Charles was more subtle. He knew the concerns facing Europe's southern flank from the renewed Islamic threat and played upon Charles's fear of facing war on two fronts.

From its initiation in the seventh century, Islam sought to spread its religion by conquest. All non-Moslem lands are *kuffar* (infidel) and to be Islamised by force if necessary. Christian Europe, called Urufa by Moslems, was always the main target for invasion, with Spain and Portugal occupied for 800 years. The *Reconquista* from Moslem rule ended with the liberation of Granada in 1492, but the threat from a resurgent Islam was not over; in 1521, Belgrade fell to Suleiman I, and he was only repulsed from the gates of Vienna in 1529. Regular attacks by Moslem pirates continued across the Mediterranaean, and as far north as Cornwall and Ireland.[11]

Charles was more preoccupied with the defence of his empire. As Thomas Boleyn shrewdly calculated, compared with the Islamic threat the problems of his aunt Catherine's divorce seemed but a petty distraction. But Charles was a crafty politician and refused to hear the English case presented by someone who was party to it. Thomas coolly replied: 'Sire, I do not speak here as a father, but as my master's servant, and I am commissioned to inform you that his conscience condemns a union contrary to the law of God.'

He stated that his king refused to accept the Pope's judgement as he had shown himself ignorant of the law of God. Henry's position was to wait: 'England will be quiet for three or four months. Sitting in the ballroom, she will watch the dancers and will form her resolution according as they dance well or ill.'[12]

The following month his words were echoed at Augsburg in the north German states as the evangelical factions united in protest against the Catholic Church, gaining the name of 'Protestants'. Martin Luther addressed delegates, also calling for action against the Islamic threat to Europe from the Danube to Ireland.

Meanwhile the Pope had responded to Henry's ambassador with a public condemnation of the King for failing to appear in person in Rome before his tribunal. 'This ordinance of the Pope was not only posted up at Rome, but at Bruges, at Tournai, and on all the churches of Flanders.' The King was fined 10,000 ducats and forbidden to marry again under threat of excommunication from the Church. When news of this insult reached England, Henry was beside himself with fury and threatened to launch an attack on Rome.[13]

It was rumoured that he was unable to sleep, worn out by the diplomatic wrangling and the increased tedium of administrating the country since Wolsey's departure.[14] His fears of excommunication had now come back to haunt him. Had he simply taken the advice given him by the Pope two years before and announced the marriage null and void, so that he was free to marry anyone, he and Anne could already have been man and wife and England have an heir.[15] Yet how secure this heir might be was the question. With the legality of the marriage in doubt, any child born to Henry and Anne might be denounced by their enemies as illegitimate. This was the reason why Henry was willing to wait for Anne as more than a mistress, and the reason why he now waited before making her his wife.

What Henry needed now was sound advice, but there was no Wolsey to share his burden. The Cardinal was now moving north with a great train of wagons laden with goods and furniture and accompanied by 160 followers. He occupied Cawood Castle, the residence of the Archbishops of York, planning at last for his enthronement at York Minster and rebuilding his life in the Church by visiting dioceses and performing acts of charity. But behind this charade Wolsey had entered into a secret correspondence with Rome, betraying Henry.

Hall records:

grudging his fall and not remembering the kindness the King showed to him, he wrote to the court of Rome and to several other princes letters reproaching the King, and as much as he was able stirred them to revenge his case against the King and his realm...

The King, who knew of his doings and secret communications, all this year pretended to ignore them to see what he would eventually do.[16]

Norfolk and his party feared Wolsey's return. He found Chapuys a ready listener, but the ambassador was using Norfolk to threaten the King that, if he married Anne, his own subjects would rebel in favour of Catherine and the Emperor.

Henry once again began to backtrack on a break with Rome. He appointed a commission of bishops to assess religious reform, with Warham, Gardiner, Cuthbert Tunstall, who had just become Bishop of Durham, and the Chancellor, Thomas More. On 24 May the King stood up in St Edward's Hall in Westminster and said: 'Many of my subjects think that it is my duty to cause the Scriptures to be translated and given to the people.'

But the commissioners came down against any radical change, forbidding the reading of the New Testament in English and banning a long list of evangelical books, including Simon Fish's *A Supplication for Beggars* and Tyndale's *The Obedience of a Christian Man*, which Anne and her father possessed. Offending copies of Tyndale's New Testament, sold very cheaply, were ceremoniously burned outside St Paul's. Hall records that believers protested the burning as blasphemous.[17] Bishop Latimer, who had been invited to preach at court in March, boldly opposed this repression:

'The Bible should be permitted to circulate freely in English...
'Christ's sheep hear no man's voice but Christ's.
'Trouble me no more from talking with the Lord my God.'[18]

But Henry declared that the teaching of the priests was sufficient for the people: 'The holy scripture in English is not necessary to Christian men... but rather be to their further confusion and destruction than the edification of their souls.'[19]

What must Anne have thought of this turnaround? Only months before she had lent Henry copies of the very books he now banned. He seemed maddeningly contradictory, one moment receiving new ideas with great enthusiasm, the next superstitiously afraid to carry through decisions. But if Henry was no longer listening to her, if she could not influence him to support reform, then she had no role to play.

Wolsey's demise had given reformers hope, but his successor as Chancellor, Thomas More, was proving a greater threat to their religion than the Cardinal had ever been. There had been no burning of 'heretics' for eight years, but now More set out to quash reformers with extreme violence. In his *Apology* he boasted that he had prisoners flogged for sacrilege, they 'well deserved pain' and the burning of heretics was 'lawful, necessary and well done'. The evangelical and artist Holbein, having lived in More's household, knew him well enough to flee from England as soon as he became Chancellor.

Six protesters were burned under More's chancellorship, and perhaps 40 were imprisoned. More had a far from humble opinion of himself as persecutor and judge. He told his son-in-law Roper, once an evangelical himself, that 'we seem to sit upon the mountains treading heretics under our feet like ants'.[20]

More is renowned as a martyr for individual conscience but this was a right he denied to those he persecuted as Chancellor. He banned the Scriptures in 'our rude Englysshe tonge' and condemned evangelicals with abuse better suited to the gutter. His heresy hunters raided houses and terrorised Christians. His first victim came in January 1530 when Thomas Hitton was seized at Gravesend with letters 'unto the evangelycall heretykes beyonde the see'. Hitton was tortured but kept his faith to the last, rejecting the mass and purgatory. He was burned in Maidstone on 23 February. More wrote that he had learned his 'false faith and heresies' from Tyndale: 'The spirit of errour and lyenge hath taken his wretched soul with him strayte from the shorte fyre to ye fyre ever lastyng. And this is lo sir Thomas Hitton, the dyuyls [devil's] stynkyng martyr, of whose burnynge Tyndale maketh boste.'

For years More had battled to stop Tyndale's work from reaching England, writing diatribes attacking his beliefs. He told Erasmus that Tyndale was 'nowhere and yet everywhere'. He wanted to 'fynde hym with an hote fyrebronde burnynge at hys bakke, that all the water in the world wyll neuer be able to quenche'.

Through Sir Thomas Elyot, ambassador at the court in Brussels, More paid agents and informers, determined to hunt him down.

Having brought in the new restrictions on reform, the King tried again to force the Pope to grant him a divorce. On Sunday 12 June he compelled his nobles to sign a petition urging Clement to comply, but they prevaricated, saying there must first be more discussion. Appalled by their refusal, Henry sent the petition to each one individually, with his commissioners standing over the bishops and lords until they had signed and added their seals to the document.[21]

Among the signatories was Wolsey. At the same time he was corresponding with the King's enemies to push forward Catherine's case. He was still assuming that Henry would eventually tire of Anne and be forced to return to Catherine, and things would be as they were before, with he himself back in favour. Norfolk had intercepted some of the Cardinal's correspondence and believed that Wolsey 'desired as much authority as ever'.[22]

Norfolk boasted foolishly to Chapuys that he had his own informants among Wolsey's servants. The ambassador reported that Norfolk was 'a bad dissembler' and the Boleyns had 'not ceased to plot against the Cardinal, especially the Lady'.[23] It was said that one of Norfolk's agents was Thomas Cromwell, who now left the Cardinal's service, obliging Wolsey to use Agostini, a Venetian physician, to smuggle his letters abroad.

The Emperor had boasted that 'he will get the King driven from his realm, and that by his majesty's own subjects'. Chapuys had told him that England was ready to revolt in favour of Catherine, even to throw Henry off the throne to replace him with Princess Mary. The King immediately reacted, raising the fear of invasion. In July and August all ports were closed in an alert against enemy agents trying to leave the country. Henry deported over 15,000 foreigners from London alone. Other suspects in Catherine's household were denounced as Imperial agents who kept 'a great and constant watch' for the Emperor.

Catherine showed her husband no 'spark or kind of grudge or displeasure'.

Meanwhile she plotted with the Emperor. She wrote to her nephew assuring him of her continued 'readiness for his service'. Cavendish was convinced of her duplicity in masking her indignation while she conspired to bring England into renewed civil war.[24] Catherine was neither sweet nor saintly. She was a proud, embittered woman who had fought all her life to retain her position and status in a court she secretly despised as inferior to that of Spain. It was Catherine's pride that had kept her in England after Arthur's death. She had lied in order to protect her position – lying to her father and husband over her false pregnancy, perhaps even her virginity. She applied a double standard, protecting the lecherous Friar Diego for years. She had always surrounded herself with Spanish supporters and brought up her daughter Mary imbued with Spanish traditions and concepts that made her as much an alien in England as Catherine herself had been. She was arrogant, believing in Spain's superiority and maintaining spies of a foreign power that was working against the English crown.

There was a vast difference between Henry's England and the totalitarian state which the united Spain became under Catherine's parents, Ferdinand and Isabella. With the Pope's support, they had created the Spanish Inquisition in 1480. It had already established a notorious reputation in Languedoc, the German states and Italy. In 1492 Spain ordered the mass expulsion of 'all Jews of both sexes forever from the precincts of Our realm'. Up to a quarter of a million Jews were thrown out of their homes.[25] Others lived in constant dread of denunciation by informers, who were well rewarded, often with a proportion of the victim's property. Tribunal records show how flimsy the evidence could be to send someone to be burned alive. Confessions were achieved by interrogation using the *garrucha*, where the victim was hung up by the wrists with weights tied to the feet, the *potro* or rack, where limbs were pulled apart, and the *toca* or water torture. Even women of ninety are recorded as suffering these tortures.

Non-Catholic foreigners could be seized as 'heretics' and taken before the Inquisition. Evangelicals such as Thomas Boleyn, who had been English ambassador to Spain, was playing with fire when he travelled with a copy of the Scriptures in English. But 99.3 per cent of those tried in Barcelona between 1488 and 1505 and 91.6 per cent in Valencia between 1484 and 1530 were Jewish *Conversos*, Jews who had converted to Christianity.[26]

The new Spain saw herself as an imperial power. The Emperor's motto was '*Imperio y España*'. With the discovery of the Americas and the gold that followed, the nation saw itself able to dominate a new Europe as the active arm of the Roman Catholic Church. In northern Europe the Reformation and the printing revolution had combined to re-educate the masses but Ferdinand and Isabella controlled all literature entering Spain, while the office of the Inquisition was free to publish its own propaganda. Hebrew Bibles were seized and destroyed.

Vives wrote to Erasmus: 'We live in such difficult times that it is dangerous either to speak or be silent.' This view was echoed by Antonio de Araoz: 'The times are such that one should think carefully before writing books.'[27]

As Spanish imperialism spread, new forms of oppression, including the Inquisition, followed. In Galicia a priest commented: 'If the Holy Office had not come to this realm, some of these people would have been like those in England.'[28] There were many subsequent uprisings against Spanish rule. Foxe warned England: 'This dreadful engine of tyranny may at any time be introduced into a country where the Catholics have the ascendancy; and hence how careful ought we to be, who are not cursed with such an arbitrary court, to prevent its introduction.'[29]

An invasion from Spain in support of Catherine and Mary would inevitably bring about civil war, with the dangers inherent of England being sucked into Charles's repressive empire when Mary married some foreign Catholic prince. (This was exactly what would happen in the future.) Exasperated, Norfolk told Chapuys that he wished both Anne and Catherine dead.[30]

The years were passing and yet Henry could not be free of Catherine. The endless delays and the frustration of his private life deeply affected the King's character. His natural suspicion of those about him increased as he began to see enemies everywhere. He could no longer trust his ministers and began to give way to the paranoia and jealousy which dominated his latter years.

This made it easy for his favourite Brandon to try to turn him against Anne. Suffolk and his wife had long wanted the opportunity to destroy Anne and now he spread malicious rumours about her long friendship with Thomas Wyatt.[31] But the plot misfired and Henry sent Brandon away for the summer.

He was back in London in September when Norfolk and the Boleyns were persuading the court to abandon Catherine and to again press the idea of immediate marriage without the Pope's approval.[32] But Brandon stirred up sufficient opposition in Council to bury the idea. Henry was irritated by the Council's decision, ominously lamenting: 'Every day I miss the Cardinal of York.'[33]

Then Wolsey's agent Agostini was arrested with letters written in cipher. Norfolk was away from court but the King immediately demanded definitive proof of a conspiracy between his old friend and the Vatican.[34] Norfolk found proof in the intercepted letters from Agostini to the Sieur de Vaux of 'presumptuous sinister practices made to the court of Rome for restoring him to his former estate and dignity'. Possibly Agostini was bribed or encouraged to give proof of Wolsey's treachery. He could even have been one of Norfolk's double agents, for after his arrest Chapuys noted that he 'has been, and still is, treated as a prince in the house of the Duke of Norfolk, which clearly shows that he has been singing to the right tune'.[35]

Anne, recognising that a coup in support of Catherine had been planned, now used all her influence to finish Wolsey. She exposed his duplicity, talking of the years that had been wasted while he pretended to act on their behalf with Rome. All the time he had been their enemy, fooling Henry and wasting their chances of marriage. She spoke so eloquently that he grew very emotional and even began to cry. She said she could not go on as her youth was passing – she was now almost 30. Henry grew afraid that she would desert him and immediately took the necessary action against Wolsey.[36]

The Cardinal had planned a magnificent ceremony of enthronement in York, but on 4 November he had an unexpected visitor at Cawood. Ironically, it was Henry Percy, Anne's former suitor, now 6th Earl of Northumberland, who was sent to arrest him, the man who on the King's orders had blocked their marriage.

When Percy read out the charges of high treason, Wolsey protested:

> You have no such power for I am both a cardinal and a peer of the College of Rome, and ought not to be arrested by any temporal power, for I am not subject to that power... I wonder why I now should be arrested, especially considering that I am a member of the apostolic See, on whom no temporal man should lay violent hands.
>
> Well, I see the King lacks good counsel.[37]

Sickened by this reversal in his fortunes, Wolsey set out on his last journey.

At Sheffield Park he was told that Sir William Kingston had come to conduct him to the King. He knew that when he reached the Tower of London he would surely face execution. Ill now, he barely reached Leicester, lodging at the abbey, where he greeted the Abbot with the words: 'Father, I am come to lay my bones among you.'

On 29 November he was found dead, 'through weakness caused by purgatives and vomiting', Hall comments. His last words were allegedly: 'If I had served God as diligently as I have served the King, he would not have given me over thus in my grey hairs.'[38]

Cavendish rode south to tell Henry the news but was kept waiting while the King took his exercise. Wolsey's death was not lamented. A masque, *Of the Cardinal's Going to Hell*, was put on at court. Even the canons of Norwich, in recording a great storm on the night he died, commented that the Devil had come for one of his own.

Wolsey's former agent Thomas Cromwell now succeeded in gaining an introduction to the King by the Attorney General, Sir Christopher Hales. Cromwell's ability to take over much of the tedious daily grind of administration appealed to Henry, who had grappled for the first time with the burden of paperwork and resented his loss of freedom. Appointing Cromwell increased his liberty to spend more time in his old pleasures again.

Thomas Cromwell was as much a self-made man as his former master, but without the benefit of a scholarship to university. Cromwell grew up in Putney, then just outside London, making his way in trade and travelling widely in Europe. He hired himself out as a soldier in Italy, fighting for the French. In Venice he became an accountant to wealthy merchants. In Antwerp he made money and returned to England to marry and study law. He had taught himself Italian, French, Latin and some Greek. By 1514 he was Collector of Revenues for the archdiocese of York, becoming an expert administrator and rising to work with Wolsey ten years later. It was then that he devised a way of raising revenue by closing several small religious houses, an idea that would later make him invaluable to the King.

After Wolsey's disgrace Cromwell had to restart his career. His experience lay in being able to present an idea plainly, without flattery or apparent guile. As Cardinal Pole asked: 'Who will tell the prince his fault? And if one such be found, where is the prince that will hear him?' But here was Cromwell eager to make a name for himself by pushing startlingly radical advice on negotiations with Rome: why ask the Pope for permission? Why should a foreign bishop share the King's God-given power? 'Rely upon your parliament; proclaim yourself the head of the Church in England. Then you shall see an increase of glory to your name and of prosperity to your people.'[39]

This was the very same argument which Anne had outlined to Henry from Simon Fish's book. Cromwell was now the King's adviser and had established links with evangelicals, including the Boleyns, but always put his own interests above his religion. He was known to have a copy of Castiglione's *The Courtier* and was 'vigilant', studying his fellow men to 'fishe out' his motives from the very 'bottom of his stomake' to test how a true man can be distinguished from the false. He would say, with Machiavelli: 'He who has known best how to employ the fox has succeeded best.'[40]

Machiavelli wrote: 'the first opinion which one forms of a prince, and of his understanding, is by observing the men he has around him'. In *The Prince* he could almost have been writing of Henry's relationship with Wolsey: 'there is one test which never fails; when you see the servant thinking more of his own interests than of yours, and seeking inwardly his own profit in everything, such a man will never make a good servant, nor will you ever be able to trust him'.[41]

Cromwell's time in Italy had coincided with Machiavelli's period as a diplomat for the Republic of Florence, when he travelled to the Romagna and France as envoy to Cesare Borgia, son of Pope Alexander VI, who tried to unite the Italian states. Machiavelli admired Borgia's meteoric career and also praised his father:

> Alexander VI did nothing else but deceive men, nor ever thought of doing otherwise, and he always found victims; for there never was a man who had greater power in asserting, or who with greater oaths would affirm a thing, yet would observe it less; nevertheless his deceits always succeeded according to his wishes, because he well understood this side of mankind.[42]

During this period the great city of the Medicis declined to become a colony of the new Spanish empire. In 1513 Machiavelli was briefly imprisoned and tortured, but released when Giovanni de Medici became Pope. *The Prince* was Machiavelli's guide to political expediency in this unpredictable and dangerous world. Ironically, Emperor Charles was said to keep a copy by his bed. The court of princes in particular was 'a place so slipperie, where ye shall many tymes repe most unkyndnesse where ye have sown greatest pleasures, and those also readye to do you moch hurt, to whom you never intended to think any harme'.[43]

Flattery and feigned friendship were traps to deceive. Machiavelli recommends that

flatterers should be avoided by choosing the wise men in his state, and giving to them only the liberty of speaking the truth to him... but he ought to question them upon everything, and listen to their opinions, and afterwards form his own conclusions... outside of these, he should listen to no one.[44]

Henry was now listening to Cromwell, to whom Thomas More offered some advice:

Master Cromwell, you are now entered into the service of a most noble, wise and liberal Prince, if you will follow my poor advice, you shall, in your counsel giving unto his grace, ever tell him what he ought to do, but never tell him what he is able to do; so shall you show yourself a true, faithful servant and a right worthy councillor. For if a Lion knew his own strength, hard were it for any man to rule him.[45]

The King's new adviser had absorbed Machiavellian principles. As Man is more inclined to do evil than good, moral people are under constant threat from the immoral majority. If we want peace, then we must win the war. Don't allow your enemies to fight another day; deal decisively with them now.

'Never let any Government imagine that it can choose perfectly safe courses; rather let it expect to have to take very doubtful ones ... but prudence consists in knowing how to distinguish the character of troubles, and for choice to take the lesser evil.'[46]

Don't worry about what the world thinks of you, just concentrate on success. If you win they will praise you; if you lose, they will pillory you.

> It is much safer to be feared than loved, when, of the two, either must be dispensed with. Because this is to be asserted in general of men, that they are ungrateful, fickle, false, cowardly, covetous, and as long as you succeed they are yours entirely ... but fear preserves you by a dread of punishment which never fails.[47]

A judicious use of violence, rewards and punishment can bring security. If you have to do unpleasant things, do them all at once so it is quickly forgotten. But when you do good, spread it over time so it will be remembered.

'Princes should delegate to others the enactment of unpopular measures and keep in their own hands the distribution of favours.'[48]

It was advice like this which provided the King with the strategy he needed to force compliance upon the bishops. As the year drew to an end he indicted them under the same charge of *Praemunire* used to attack Wolsey. By accepting the Cardinal's jurisdiction, they were guilty of usurping the King's power with that of a foreign authority, the Pope, thereby committing treason. Henry left the prelates to absorb this while he went to Greenwich to celebrate Christmas.

Anne had ordered new liveries for her household with the motto '*Ainsi sera, groigne qui groigne*'. This was a deliberate play on the motto of the Regent Margaret of Austria, her patron as a child, '*Groigne qui groigne, Vive Bourgogne!*' (Grudge who grudges, long live Burgundy!) But the court reacted badly to Anne's sense of humour and she decided to withdraw the design. The Duchess of Norfolk openly declared that Anne would be the ruin of the Howards.[49]

Elizabeth, the much-wronged duchess, was heiress to the executed Duke of Buckingham and had many grudges. She could not attack the murderer of her father but she could hit back at him by working with Catherine to prevent his marriage to her Boleyn niece. She maintained a secret correspondence with Rome, concealing messages for Catherine inside gifts of oranges. Her outspoken criticism of Anne eventually led to her dismissal from court.[50]

Anne's household was suborned, with informants richly rewarded by Chapuys and the Catholic faction. He wrote expansively, attacking her and quoting probably entirely fictitious conversations:

The Lady Anne is braver than a lion... She said to one of the Queen's ladies that she wished all Spaniards were in the sea. The lady told her such language was disrespectful to her mistress. She said she cared nothing for the Queen, and would rather see her hang than acknowledge her as her mistress.[51]

Anne may have objected to the Spanish influence at court, but the image Chapuys creates of 'the great whore', who wishes to see Catherine hang, is sheer character assassination. Anne was neither Henry's mistress nor some evil Messalina. On the contrary, her firm religious beliefs had kept her from the King's bed (and anyone else's) so that now, at 30, she despaired of ever being able to enjoy a normal family life.

For six years of the chase Anne had been chaste. Her virginity was confirmed by Henry to Catherine herself on Christmas Eve and by the Imperial ambassador to Rome, Micer Mai, in January when, regretfully perhaps, he confirmed: 'There is no positive proof of adultery, none having yet been produced here at Rome but, on the contrary, several letters proving the opposite.'[52]

That same month the King approached the Archbishop of Canterbury to give judgement on the divorce in his favour, but Warham feared the split this would cause in the Church. As part of an exercise in persuasion, Cromwell now sent his agent Stephen Vaughan to meet the great evangelical Tyndale in Antwerp, offering him a safe conduct to return from exile and support Henry's bid for a divorce. Vaughan had strong evangelical beliefs and his offer was genuine, but Tyndale evidently did not trust the King or his Chancellor, Thomas More. Vaughan had discovered that More was paying two English monks in Antwerp to spy on Tyndale.

Tyndale's suspicions were proved correct as a resentful Henry continued his ruthless drive against evangelical Protestants, with Bilney being burned in August that year and James Bainham, a barrister of the Middle Temple, in April 1532.[53] As Chancellor, Thomas More dealt with fiscal questions and civic justice, but he had extended his role to cover questions of heresy, his obsession. 'A bitter persecutor he was of good men and a wretched enemy against the truth of the Gospel,' wrote Foxe.[54]

More enjoys a reputation as a man who stood up for freedom of conscience. Pope John Paul II claimed that More defended the Church against Henry VIII's 'uncontrolled despotism... in the name of primacy of conscience, of the individual's freedom vis-à-vis political power'.[55] Catholic hagiographies by Hilaire Belloc, Evelyn Waugh, G.K. Chesterton and Robert Bolt have created a martyr, but the irony is that More was intolerant of all dissident opinion. His zeal for public order verged on the fanatical. His early desire to become a priest exacerbated a repressed nature that led him secretly to wear a hair shirt and practise self-flagellation. He even imprisoned evangelicals in his own house in Chelsea and had them whipped on a tree in the garden. He was present during the torture of Tewkesbury, where they 'twisted in his brows with small ropes, so that the blood started out of his eyes'. Tewkesbury was later racked in the Tower of London until almost lame. His death at Smithfield was celebrated by More: 'burned as there was never wretche I wene better worthy'. Bainham suffered a similar fate, tortured in More's presence, then burned at the stake, where he declared: 'I come hither, good people, accused and condemned for a heretic, Sir Thomas More being my accuser and my judge.'[56]

In February the bishops submitted to the King's accusation of *Praemunire*, paying a great fine, but Henry's challenge continued. Now he demanded that they acknowledge his authority as *Caput Ecclesiae*, Head of the Church of England, 'sole protector and supreme head of the English church and clergy'.[57] Another bitter theological debate ensued, with Warham stating bluntly that Christ is Head of the Church, and on earth power is divided into the temporal and spiritual realms, governed respectively by kings and the Church.

The Pope claims sovereignty over all the world's Christians, whether Roman Catholics or not, as 'Father of Kings and Princes, the Vicar of Christ and Ruler of the World'. The 'Vicar' of Christ means one who substitutes or takes the place of Christ: an anathema to Protestants, who saw Catholic Europe as the forces of the Antichrist: 'The Pope hath his power out of hell, and cometh thence.'

Thomas Boleyn confronted Bishop Fisher, telling him 'that when God departed from this world he left behind him no successor or vicar on earth'.[58]

The Boleyns' influence was all too apparent. Faced with the bishops' reluctance to agree to accept Henry as their superior, they came up with a solution. Anne's younger brother George, Lord Rochford, was as deeply involved in evangelical reform as she and their father were. He was a noted debater on theological issues and now proposed the addition of the words 'as far as the law of Christ allows'. Warham and the bishops had no option but to agree.

The King was now the acknowledged sole authority in the land: 'The Bishop of Rome [the Pope] hath no jurisdiction in this realm of England.' There was a new self-awareness of English nationalism as Henry declared his separation from Rome: 'This realm of England is an empire.'

Chapuys reported this devastating seismic blow to the Catholic faction to his master the Emperor. He states that at the news Anne made 'such demonstrations of joy as if she had actually gained Paradise'. He called her 'the Grand Enemy' – not just of Catherine but of the Pope and the Roman Church. The Boleyns were 'more Lutheran than Luther himself'.[59]

Henry saw the benefits of political supremacy over the Church to strengthen the crown, while resisting the most radical religious reforms, such as Anne was advocating. His entrenched superstition deprived him of the liberty that accompanied her resolute evangelical faith. He chose appeasement over full-blooded revolution. Reformers like the Boleyns saw the whole Catholic system as anti-Christian.[60] Luther and Calvin believed that the Roman Catholic institution was Mystery Babylon, the Mother of Harlots, vividly described in Revelation 17.[61] The title of Mary as 'Queen of Heaven' is used in the Bible to refer to the Babylonian goddess Semiramis and other pagan deities such as Astarte and Diana of the Ephesians.[62]

The pietà of Mary with the dead Christ echoes the pagan cults of Tammuz and Osiris. Reformers preferred to focus on the resurrected Messiah.

The rediscovery of the written word of God, put into the language of the people, was a liberation from the superstition and corruption of the established Church. For the first time they discovered that the worship of images was forbidden by the Ten Commandments (Exodus 3, 4–6) and echoed by the apostles (Romans 1, 18–25). Indulgences were banned in 1 Peter 1, 18–19, the existence of Purgatory disproved by Matthew 25, 46 and Revelation 21, 1–8. The apostles were married, not celibate (1 Peter 2, 4–10, 1 Corinthians 9, 5 and 1 Timothy 4, 3). Even the mass and the idea of transubstantiation (later to be the veritable 'burning issue' which sent so many to die under Henry's daughter Mary) was disproved by 1 Corinthians 11, 23–32 and the book of Hebrews.

Such revelations spread by word of mouth and through access to the Scriptures in English.

London and the south-east of England contained the greatest number of evangelical believers, given their access to the continent and imported literature. Whereas Wolsey had generally turned a blind eye to this movement, More used his new power as Chancellor to send out hunters searching for victims, creating a wave of terror and persecution across the south. But his ambition had caught him in a trap, for as Chancellor he was required to present the verdict of the universities on the King's marriage before Parliament.

The universities had given the King their support, decreeing that Henry's union with Catherine had flouted God's law and the Pope should never have granted them a dispensation of any kind. They judged Henry's marriage to Catherine null and void on the grounds of incest. If More did not support this statement, he could have resigned. Yet he held on to office, doing the King's will, putting his career before his conscience. On 30 March he declared to Parliament: 'You of this worshipful House, I am sure, be not so ignorant but you know well that the King our sovereign lord hath married his brother's wife, for she was both wedded and bedded with his brother Prince Arthur.'[63]

When he was asked for his own opinion More refused to answer. Yet he was playing a double game all this time. On 11 March Charles V had written from Brussels to thank him for acting as Catherine's 'true father and protector'. Alarmed that this correspondence might be intercepted, More warned Chapuys that although he gave the Emperor 'his most affectionate service', he must 'for the honour of

God to forbear, for although he had given already sufficient proof of his loyalty that he ought to incur no suspicion, whoever came to visit him, yet, considering the time, he ought to abstain from everything which might provoke suspicion'.[64]

More was right to be cautious. At last the King felt confident enough to separate from Catherine. That summer when Henry left Windsor on progress, he took Anne with him and told Catherine to leave before he returned. He did not even say goodbye.[65]

Chapter Nine

England's Queen

CATHERINE WAS GIVEN Wolsey's former palace, The More, at Rickmansworth in Hertfordshire. Although she did nothing but complain of her deprivation and poverty, this was a magnificent mansion which had been rebuilt and entirely refurbished by the Cardinal. Du Bellay regarded its luxurious rooms and lovely gardens as even better than Hampton Court. Although Catherine lived in great state and entertained foreign ambassadors, she complained of suffering 'the pains of Purgatory on earth'. In a letter to Charles V she wrote:

My tribulations are so great, my life so disturbed by the plans daily invented to further the King's wicked intention, the surprises which the King gives me, with certain persons of his council, are so mortal, and my treatment is what God knows, that it is enough to shorten ten lives, much more mine.[1]

Yet the reality was that Catherine still maintained a household of over 200 servants. She had 50 ladies-in-waiting, with 30 who stood by her table while she dined.

Meanwhile Anne had returned from Hever for the New Year of 1532 and was given Catherine's old apartments at Greenwich. Lavish presents were exchanged between the King and Anne, but Henry returned the gold cup which Catherine had sent him.[2]

Catherine's removal from court made it more difficult for her faction to communicate. Her daughter Mary, now 15, moved from Richmond to Beaulieu with her cousin Margaret Douglas, the daughter of Margaret Tudor. Their governess was the aged Countess of Salisbury, the niece of the Yorkist King Edward IV, mother of Cardinal Pole. Catherine was in contact with all these through agents like Thomas Abell, her chaplain, who was arrested in August that year and sent to the Tower of London for some months.

In the New Year Mary visited her mother. Henry was now so certain that Catherine was plotting against him that he wanted them kept apart so as to insulate Mary from the conspiracy. The King was furious that Catherine had complained about her treatment in secret correspondence to the Pope. When the papal nuncio arrived at court, he was spurned.[3] Henry, on learning that the Pope had ordered him to send Anne away and take Catherine back, was beside himself with fury and indignation: 'Never was prince treated by a pope as Your Holiness has treated me. Nor painted reason but the truth alone must be our guide.'[4]

It was as Anne and Cromwell had advised him. The Pope had no right to command the King of England, the anointed of God. England was a sovereign realm, subject to no other state or authority. Neither the Pope nor the Holy Roman Empire had the power to override its laws and freedoms.

Henry now pressed forward energetically with reform. Parliament resumed its agenda, to liberate the nation from the control of foreign institutions. An Act in Restraint of Annates was designed to axe all revenues to Rome, making it a crime of *Praemunire*. The King was now given the right to appoint his own archbishops and bishops, bypassing the Pope, and alleged 'heretics' were now to be tried only by the King's commissioners. The Act for Submission of Clergy attacked the corruption and abuses of the Roman Church.

Henry pleasantly informed the papal nuncio that he had been obliged to take these measures because of pressure from the common people. Public opinion was so much against the Pope and the powers of the Church that he had no other option but to take control himself. By March Henry had succeeded in pushing through these revolutionary measures. He was now legally designated 'Protector and Supreme Head of the Church of England'.

The campaign culminated in another damaging fine on the bishops for their previous support for Rome. The following day Thomas More resigned as Chancellor. Sir Thomas Audley was appointed to the post. For months past More had overseen these dramatic changes without protest, but now he realised that it was no longer possible to play two roles. He had acted as the King's instrument to bring down the Roman Church while also taking it upon himself to initiate his own vicious campaign persecuting evangelical reformers. For a man who saw 'heretics' everywhere, notably at court close to the King, More had delayed an astonishingly long time in putting conscience above ambition.

The success of the 'heretics' at court had been reported by Chapuys. On 13 May he informed on a sermon which had attacked the Pope, claiming that the Duke of Norfolk, a conservative Catholic, had declared the preacher 'more of a Lutheran than Martin himself and that, had it not been for the Earl of Wiltshire [Thomas Boleyn] and another personage whom he would not name [meaning no doubt the Lady Anne herself] he would have had the said preacher ... burnt alive'.[5]

It was part of Chapuys' brief as ambassador to work against the Boleyns and for the restoration of Catherine and her political faction. Not only did he maintain a secret network of informers and agents in England, keeping Catherine informed of events, but also spread false rumours and disinformation. One such invention was the story of a rift between Anne and her father, in which Thomas was now opposed to her marrying the King. Nothing could have been further from the truth. Anne, her father and Henry now believed they should marry as soon as possible in 'the most solemn manner', as the King himself told Chapuys.[6]

Henry was all too aware of the Imperial ambassador's games and as a precaution, he now ordered Catherine to move house, thus disrupting their lines of secret communication. As a result she left The More for Hatfield, the red-brick palace built by Cardinal Morton in 1497, and after the summer he moved her again.

Chapuys retaliated with fresh stories against Anne, 'the whore', 'the heretic'. He claimed that the King's summer progress had to be cut short by crowds of women who attacked and threatened Anne, screaming abuse. 'The Lady is hated by all the world,' Chapuys reported to his master, the Emperor.[7]

The King was now firmly allied with France against the Empire. In June a mutual treaty had been signed, encouraging Henry to believe he had French support for his marriage to Anne. Henry invited Jean Du Bellay, who combined the roles of Bishop of Bayonne and Imperial ambassador, to accompany them on progress, where they made arrangements for a new summit meeting at Calais that autumn.

Anne's affinity with the French was now an obvious advantage. Hunting at Ampthill in July, Anne made Du Bellay the present of a greyhound and they watched the run while discussing politics. This was by Henry's design, for 'what the said Lady does is always by order of my lord the said King'.[8] As Starkey comments, 'Anne functioned, like her daughter Elizabeth, as an honorary man. She was one politician among others … Anne handled power like a man.'[9]

Henry was elevating Anne's position and status as a signal to the country of his intentions. He granted her the manors of Coldkenynton and Hanworth in Middlesex and provided her with clothes fit for his Queen. She was preparing a trousseau for her wedding, including a stunning robe of black satin to be worn as a house gown.

He also ordered Catherine to return all the jewels that rightfully belonged to the Queen of England. Predictably enough, Catherine raged and stormed against this very public rebuff. She claimed the royal jewels were her personal property and wrote at once to complain to the Emperor, but finally she had to submit, handing over the crown's jewellery.[10]

In July Henry had visited his sister Mary. He wanted her to accompany the royal party to Calais that autumn, but he found her seriously ill and unable to travel. The Venetian ambassador reported that she had refused to go, but her health was very poor and she died the next year.

Now suddenly a ghost from the past returned to haunt Henry. The Countess of Northumberland sought a divorce from Henry Percy on the grounds that he had first been betrothed to Anne Boleyn. She cited a legal pre-contract of marriage which made her own marriage void and meant that Anne herself was not free to marry.[11]

Henry knew very well who had caused the break-up of that betrothal. He had been the one to order Wolsey to intervene and stop the match, sending Percy away and insisting on his marriage to Lady Mary Talbot. Now the King recognised this as an attempt to sabotage his chance to finally marry Anne.

Under canon law, it was Edward IV's pre-contract with Eleanor Butler which had invalidated his later marriage to Elizabeth Woodville and made all their children illegitimate, including Edward V. Then the country had been thrown into crisis as the succession was disputed, leading to a renewal of civil war.

If this news was a manoeuvre by his political enemies, then Henry could not afford to ignore the danger. He immediately ordered the Archbishops of Canterbury and York to examine the matter, and summoned Northumberland to swear on oath there had never been any pre-contract with Anne. Parliament was obliged to hurriedly discuss the business; it decided against the Countess's petition for divorce, leaving the unhappy pair still married but Anne completely free.

Shortly after this issue was resolved, the Archbishop of Canterbury died. William Warham was over 80 and had been in office for 28 years, but his demise now offered Henry the opportunity to appoint his own man. For the first time it was the King's decision and not that of the Pope. The Archbishop was a potential ally, capable of granting Henry a divorce and the right to marry again.

Henry sent Nicholas Hawkins to Regensburg to replace the ambassador and to recall Thomas Cranmer to England to become his Archbishop of Canterbury.

Cranmer was born in 1489, the son of a squire, educated at Jesus College and then a Fellow there until his marriage ended a clerical career. When his wife died in childbirth, he was ordained and became an authority in theological debate, being recommended to the King to argue on behalf of his divorce. Cranmer stayed with the Boleyns and had acted as their chaplain. He was then sent with Thomas Boleyn as a diplomat to the courts of Europe, in 1532 appointed ambassador to the court of Charles V in Germany. During this time he had married Margaret, the niece of the Lutheran theologian Osiander. They lived so discreetly that few people, including the King, were ever to know of her existence.

In England division among the clergy largely resulted from their university backgrounds. Oxford men were conservative, while Cambridge scholars were far more radical and open to evangelical beliefs. Anne continually favoured Cambridge men such as Cranmer, Dr Butts and Anthony Denny. In Germany Cranmer had been open to increasingly radical reforms in church and society through contact with the leading lights of the Reformation. Religion was intrinsically linked with politics. The patchwork of German states saw their chance for freedom from the Holy Roman Empire through the Protestant revolution, a grassroots movement spreading like wildfire across northern Europe.

Henry was dismantling papal control in England but unwilling to accept Lutheranism. By selecting Cranmer he frightened Chapuys and Catherine's faction, while securing his marriage to Anne. Chapuys duly reported

> of the reputation Cranmer has here of being devoted heart and soul to the Lutheran sect... He is a servant of the Lady's and should be required to take a special oath not to meddle with the divorce. It is suspected that the new Archbishop may authorise the marriage in this Parliament.

Chapuys blamed Anne for Cranmer's appointment, but the true responsibility was Henry's alone.

Cranmer said later that 'there was never man came more unwillingly to a bishopric than I did to that'. His loyalty to Henry was unwavering. He had a duty to serve the King, anointed by God, whatever his faults. Studious and personally unambitious, Cranmer was 'either blessed or cursed with the ability to see his opponents' point of view'.[12] He served Henry even when he turned against those who Cranmer knew to be true believers like Frith, Lambert and Anne Boleyn. Yet before long he condemned the worship of saints, mass for the dead and, naturally enough, clerical celibacy. He was also Anne's chaplain.[13]

Henry now decided to elevate Anne to the peerage in order that she could accompany him to France as his consort. He created her Marquess of Pembroke, with lands valued at £1,023 13s 2d per annum.[14]

At a ceremony at Windsor on 1 September, Anne was escorted into Henry's presence by two countesses, Eleanor, Countess of Rutland, and Mary, Countess of Sussex. She was 'in her hair', her long auburn hair hanging loose down the back of her crimson velvet gown edged in ermine and 'completely covered with the most costly jewels'. Her cousin, Lady Mary Howard, carried her train. The King was attended by Norfolk, Suffolk and Du Bellay. Stephen Gardiner, Bishop of Winchester, read out her patent, creating her a peer in her own right, unprecedented for a woman, and with the income to support herself. Then Henry set a mantle of estate around her shoulders and a golden coronet on her head.

Anne gave a banquet for the King and the French ambassador, looking forward to the summit in France, but Henry had not calculated on the problems over protocol. Claude, Francis I's long-suffering Queen, whom Anne had attended for many years, had died, and although he had taken a new wife, Anne was not yet Queen and of equal status. Anne herself suggested that the French King's sister Margaret, now Queen of Navarre, should come to the summit meeting, for she was someone she 'hath ever entirely loved'. She said: 'there was no one thing which her grace so much desired ... as the want of the said Queen of Navarre's company with whom to have conference, for more causes than were meet to be expressed, her grace is most desirous'.

Margaret replied that she was ill and could not travel but Chapuys, as ever, added his own interpretation: that she had refused to meet the King of England's 'whore'.[15] That Chapuys was wrong is proved by Margaret's remembrance of Anne with genuine affection in her remarks to the Duke of Norfolk. She was 'as affectionate to your highness as if she were your own sister... My opinion is that she is your good and assured friend.'[16]

The two women's relationship continued to be excellent, with Anne writing to Margaret the following year 'that my greatest wish, next to having a son, was to see you again'.[17]

Francis now suggested that his *maîtresse en titre*, the Duchess of Vendôme, should be there to meet them, but this was immediately seen as an insult to Anne.[18] It was finally decided that the two monarchs should meet with no women present. Anne would remain in Calais while Henry went to meet Francis. In any case, the meeting was meant to be a chance for serious discussion.

In October the King's party set out for France with an entourage of 2,000 courtiers, including Henry's 13-year-old son, the Duke of Richmond. To avoid an outbreak of disease, they stayed en route on the Isle of Sheppey, stopping to visit Lady Bridget Wingfield, and again in Canterbury with Cromwell's patron, Sir Christopher Hales. Anne had written to Bridget in August about her 'trouble' when she was widowed for a second time, from Sir Nicholas Harvey:

Madam, I pray you, as you love me, to give credence to my servant this bearer, touching your removing and any thing else that he shall tell you of my behalf; for I will desire you to do nothing but that shall be for your wealth. And, madam, though at all times I have not shewed the love that I bear you as much as it was indeed, yet now I trust that you shall well prove that I loved you a great deal more than I made feign for; and assuredly, next mine own mother, I know no woman alive that I love better: and at length, with God's grace, you shall prove that it is unfeigned. And I trust you do know me for such a one that I will write nothing to comfort you in your trouble but I will abide by it as long as I live; and therefore I pray you leave your indiscreet trouble, both for displeasing of God and also for displeasing of me, that doth love you so entirely. And trusting in God that you will thus do, I make an end.

With the ill hand of your own assured friend during my life,

Anne Rocheford [sic].[19]

This 'indiscreet trouble' which threatened to disrupt their friendship and displease God might well have been Bridget's liaison with Sir Robert Tyrwhit, whom she shortly married. Although she was Anne's lady of the bedchamber, Bridget may not have reciprocated her friendship. She died the next year in childbirth, reputedly leaving a

Anne Boleyn (1501–1536). The original and most authentic portrait of Anne by an unknown artist. This shows her rich auburn hair, echoed in the fur trim of her elegant gown. National Portrait Gallery, London.

Anne Boleyn's daughter Elizabeth at about the age of 13. Note the remarkable similarity in features and even colouring with her mother. By William Stretes, *c.* 1546–7. The Royal Collection.

Henry VIII *c.* 1526 when he was aged 35 and first adopted a beard. A miniature by Lucas Horenbout.

Henry VIII painted after Hans Holbein in 1536, the year of Anne's execution. Aged 45, Henry wanted to show he was still at the height of his powers. National Portrait Gallery, London.

Henry VIII when only in his fifties, showing the results of excess and disease, including perhaps syphilis. Engraving by Peter Isselburg, after Cornelius Matsys. National Portrait Gallery, London.

Mary Boleyn (1500-1543), Anne's elder sister, mistress to Henry VIII and mother of two of his illegitimate children. By Holbein, Hever Castle.

Sir Thomas Boleyn, Earl of Wiltshire, Anne's father, c. 1477-1539. Note the fiery auburn colouring he shared with his daughter. A great linguist and ambassador, he was a patron of religious reform and took great risks for his faith. The Royal Collection.

BELOW Henry arrives at Hever Castle. This romantic Victorian print is wildly inaccurate in its depiction of costumes from the Elizabethan era, but shows the internal courtyard of Anne's family home in Kent, which was restyled and modernised by her father.

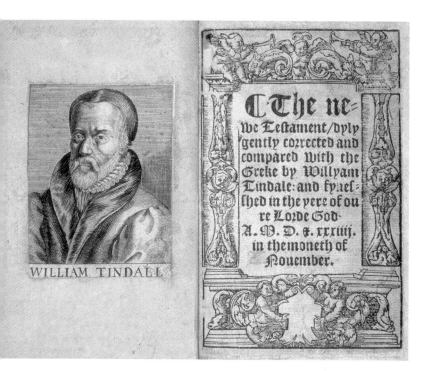

WILLIAM TINDALL

¶The newe Testament/dylygently corrected and compared with the Greke by Willyam Tindale: and fynesshed in the yere of oure Lorde God A. M. D. & xxxiiij. in the moneth of Nouember.

ABOVE The reformist martyr William Tyndale and the title page of his English version of the New Testament which was banned by the Church. He was betrayed by a spy and strangled then burnt at the stake in Brussels in 1536.

Smuggling Bibles into England, 1520s–30s. A wood engraving showing how Tyndale's English translation of the gospels was brought into the country and concealed from the Church authorities on pain of death.

Sir Thomas Wyatt the Elder, poet and diplomat (1503-1542). His love for Anne went unrequited, resulting in some of the most moving and evocative love poetry of all time. Engraving after a portrait by Holbein.

Tho. Wiatt. Knight.

Young Women Musicians at court dressed in the latest fashions, including the French hood made so popular by Anne Boleyn. Mansell Collection.

HENRY VIII TO ANNE BOLEYN

Y MISTRESS AND MY FRIEND— My heart and I surrender themselves into your hands, and we supplicate to be commended to your good graces, and that by absence your affection may not be diminished to us, for that would be to augment our pain, which would be a great pity, since absence gives enough, and more—than I ever thought could befell. This brings to my mind a fact in astronomy, which is, that the further the poles are from the sun, notwithstanding, the more scorching is the heat. Thus it is with our love: absence has placed distance between us, nevertheless, fervour increases, at least on my part. I hope the same from you, assuring you that in my case the anguish of absence is so great that it would be intolerable, were it not for the firm hope I have of your indissoluble affection towards me. In order to remind you of it, and because I cannot in person be in your presence, I send you the thing that comes nearest that is possible – that is to say, my picture, and the whole device, which you already know of, set in bracelets, wishing myself in their place when it pleases you. This is the hand of

Your servant and friend,

H. R.

One of the many effusive love letters from Henry VIII to Anne Boleyn.
His campaign to win her became a dangerous obsession lasting seven years.

ABOVE RIGHT Cardinal Thomas Wolsey c. 1520s, at the height of his power and influence. His double-dealing over the king's divorce destroyed his heady career. By an unknown artist. National Portrait Gallery, London.

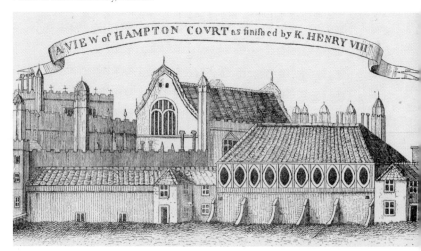

A view of Hampton Court Palace c. 1530 after the fall of Cardinal Wolsey. Henry VIII spent a fortune rebuilding it as his show palace.

Catherine of Aragon (1485-1536) while still Queen of England, before Henry annulled their marriage and replaced her with Anne. A miniature attributed to Lucas Horenbout. National Portrait Gallery, London.

Henry VIII and Catherine of Aragon's only child, Mary, c. 1554 when she was aged 38 and in her first year as queen. Attributed to 'Master John.' National Portrait Gallery, London.

Sir Thomas More (1478-1535) when Henry's Chancellor and repressive hunter of 'heretics.' A sketch by Hans Holbein.

EARL OF ESSEX.

Thomas Cromwell (1489-1540) who stepped into Wolsey's shoes as Henry's most powerful minister. After Hans Holbein the Younger. National Portrait Gallery, London.

ABOVE *The Ambassadors*: this fascinating and enigmatic portrait of Jean de Dinteville and Georges de Selve not only demonstrates the rich style of fashions *c.*1530s, but highlights the cultural accomplishments of the age. The distorted skull is a constant reminder of man's mortality. National Gallery, London.

Henry VIII surrounded by his councillors in the latter part of his reign. A print from Grafton's 1548 edition of Hall's Chronicle.

ABOVE *The Family of Henry VIII: An Allegory of the Tudor Succession.* This shows the figures of Peace and Plenty on the far right escorting Elizabeth into the presence of past rulers: her father Henry VIII in the centre, Edward VI to his right, and on the left, Mary and her husband Philip II shadowed by the figure of War. By Lucas de Heere.

Jane Seymour *c.* 1536 aged 28, having been manipulated by her family and Thomas Cromwell to win Henry's attention away from Anne. Painting by Holbein, Kunsthistorisches Museum, Vienna.

Thomas Howard, 3rd Duke of Norfolk, Anne's uncle (1473–1554) and leader of the Catholic party at court, who presided at Anne's trial and pronounced her sentence of execution. By Holbein. The Royal Collection.

Thomas Cranmer (1489–1556), Henry VIII's great reforming Archbishop of Canterbury, later burnt at the stake by 'Bloody' Mary I as a martyr. By Flicke. National Portrait Gallery, London.

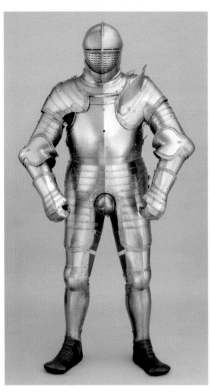

Suit of armour tailor-made for Henry VIII in his portly late forties for field and tournament *c.* 1540. Royal Armouries, the Tower of London.

BELOW A jousting tournament at court, *c.* 1530s. Henry VIII prided himself on his athletic prowess but suffered several dangerous falls, notably in January 1536, when Anne miscarried with shock on hearing the news.

The Water Gate to the Tower of London, better known as 'Traitor's Gate', in a print of 1798.

Anne Boleyn's Book of Hours, *c.* 1528, which she may have carried to her execution, still to be seen on display at Hever Castle.

Anne Boleyn in the Tower, a romantic painting by
Edouard Gibot in 1835, Musée Rolin, Autun, France.

stinging statement criticising Anne's relationship with the King. As this no longer exists it is impossible to judge the authenticity of her remarks.[20]

The royal party reached Dover early on 10 October and set sail on the *Swallow* at five a.m., reaching Calais with a fair wind by ten o'clock.[21] Anne's old family friend Thomas Wyatt accompanied them. He had been High Marshal of Calais from 1528 to 1530, having returned from diplomatic service in Italy and was soon to become a member of the Privy Council.

After resting, the King went to Boulogne to meet Francis on 21 October. Their discussions centred on the Islamic threat to Europe and resulted in a treaty to assemble a joint army in the event of a Moslem attack on France or England. Henry, of course, was also eager to win Francis's support for his marriage to Anne. He must surely have grown even more determined when he saw the French King's 'fair, joyous *Dauphin*', just one of many sons he had by Queen Claude. Among all the monarchies of Europe, the House of Tudor was seen to be the least productive.

But in other ways the two kings competed to outshine each other in sheer extravagance. Henry wore a collar made up of huge rubies, pearls and diamonds, while Francis's doublet was covered in diamonds valued at over 100,000 crowns.

Both kings came to Calais on the 25th, greeted by a 3,000-gun salute. Francis gave Anne a diamond worth 15 or 16,000 crowns.

For four days they enjoyed festivities 'with many goodly sports and pastimes', including wrestling and bear-baiting. At night there was feasting and dancing.

Anne took part with her ladies in a masque, dressed in 'maskyng apparel, of straunge fashion, made of clothe of golde'. She was attended by 30 ladies, including 'Lady Mary', Anne's aunts Dorothy, Countess of Derby, and Elizabeth Lady Fitzwalter, her sister-in-law, Lady Rochford, Lady Lisle and the wife of the ambassador to France.[22] Within a week news of the summit was lauded all over London in a pamphlet by Wynkyn de Worde, *The Maner of the Tryumphe*. He lists the ladies present, with Anne at the head, followed by 'my lady Mary', taking precedence over a countess and Anne's own aunts. Ives has argued that it would have been quite improper for this to refer to Mary Boleyn-Carey, Anne's widowed sister; nor could it be Mary Tudor, Duchess of Suffolk, who had not gone to Calais because of illness. He therefore proposes it was Henry and Catherine's daughter, Lady Mary, now a young woman, who had been included in the visit along with her half-brother Henry Fitzroy, Duke of Richmond, who went on to Paris with Francis to complete his education. This would demonstrate that Henry and Anne were not as opposed to Catherine's daughter as many have suggested.[23]

Of interest is the belief of the Milanese ambassador to France that Henry and Anne had already married in secret. He referred in his reports to Anne as 'the King's beloved wife'.[24]

Fierce storms now prevented Henry and Anne from crossing the Channel. For two weeks, they were obliged to stay in Calais at the Exchequer, a large house with gardens and a tennis court, where Anne's suite of rooms were next to the King's and linked to his by connecting doors.[25]

This unforeseen delay was to have unexpected results. Trapped in the English enclave by bad weather, Henry and Anne now seemed to throw caution to the winds and after seven long years they became lovers.

Although Anne's enemies called her whore and concubine, and the Venetian ambassador had even alleged that she had a son, Catherine's supporters could never prove that the King had committed adultery with her.[26] Anne remained a virgin until late 1532. Her religion and morality could allow her to act no differently, for she believed God had chosen her to be Queen of England in order to restore the true religion. The evidence shows that she finally surrendered to Henry at Calais.

Why did this happen now? Surely it was not premeditated, for the weather was beyond Henry's control. Perhaps it was simply the fact that they were thrown together without the pressures of state and away from the prying eyes of the court.

For years Henry had accepted with ill grace Anne's cautious assent to be his wife, not his mistress. Even though this goal seemed far closer now, nothing had really changed. For years Henry had dithered, unwilling or unable to find sufficient courage to take the step of marrying without the need for anyone's permission, as so many others had done. Nothing could allay the fear that pregnancy might produce a questionable heir.

Did they marry in secret? There was a rumour in Calais that they would marry there, but Anne was alleged to have objected to marrying outside England. This is clearly false, for Calais was at that time still very much part of England and a bastion of the English presence in France. Later it was claimed that a secret marriage took place on St Erkenwald's Day, 14 November, when they had just returned to Dover. The chroniclers Hall and Holinshed both give the date of 15 November.

Such secrecy surrounds the date and place of Anne's wedding to Henry that it was also believed that they married that November at her birthplace, Blickling Hall.[27] It has even been suggested that two ceremonies took place, one in November to unite the couple by a pledge, a kind of pre-contract agreement or hand-fasting that would appease Anne's conscience, and a second in January in the presence of a priest.[28]

Certainly by November Henry's strategy to curb the power of Rome over his affairs was under way, assisted by the appointment of a more flexible Archbishop of Canterbury. Married or not, Anne now gave way, committing herself totally to the man who had stalked her for so many years, commandeering her life. Through her surrender Anne put all her hope and expectations in Henry and his promise to be true to her as his only wife.

She immediately became pregnant, although she would not know this until mid-January. From the date of the birth of her child (7 September) we can see that she must have conceived in late November or early December. According to custom, the Queen would go into confinement for a month or six weeks before the birth, but in Anne's case it was only ten days before. Either she had miscalculated her dates or the baby was born more than a fortnight early.

Anne and Henry kept their secret. If they seemed far closer than usual, no one appears to have commented on it. The storms abated but the return voyage took 29 hours. Henry sent word of their safe arrival to London, staying a few days in Dover to recuperate and perhaps continue their chance of relative seclusion. They travelled back at their leisure, finally reaching Eltham Palace on 24 November.[29] That Christmas was celebrated at the newly refurbished York Place, but it was probably only in the second half of January that Anne realised she might be pregnant.

Suddenly all was activity. This supports the theory that they had not married in November, for as soon as Henry heard Anne's news it became vital that the marriage went ahead in order that the child would be legitimate. Even Cranmer did not know the exact date of the marriage. He wrote to Hawkins the following June that

> Anne was married much about Saint Paul's day last, as the condition thereof doth well appear by reason she is now somewhat big with child. Notwithstanding, it hath been reported throughout a great part of the realm that I married [them after the Coronation]; which was plainly false, for I myself knew not thereof a fortnight after it was done. And many other things be also reported of me, which be mere lies and tales.[30]

Chapuys agrees with this date, 'on the day of St Paul's conversion', the same day that Dr Bonner returned from Rome.[31] On 24 January Cranmer's appointment as the new Archbishop of Canterbury had been made public. Although he had now returned from Germany, he could not be called upon to officiate at their wedding as Henry required him to act as judge for his divorce from Catherine.[32] Very likely it was Rowland Lee, future Bishop of Coventry, who married the couple on 25 January at York Place. The witnesses were the King's Privy Councillors Henry Norris and Thomas Heneage, while Anne was accompanied by Anne Savage, later Lady Berkeley.[33]

The following day Parliament assembled under the new Chancellor, Thomas Audley, and on 3 February confirmed the Act of Appeals and the breaking of all Rome's judicial powers over England.[34] This enabled the King's divorce to be decided in England, removing the last obstacle for his marriage to Anne.

Chapuys claims that at this time Anne told Norfolk that she planned to go on pilgrimage to the shrine of the Virgin at Walsingham if she was not pregnant by Easter, at which the court were horrified, he says. This is plainly nonsense, for while it is highly doubtful that

Anne would have confided anything quite so personal to an uncle she loathed and distrusted, it would be even more incredible that someone with her evangelical beliefs would ever contemplate going on pilgrimage. Anne and her fellow reformers regarded shrines and the worship of saints not only as idolatry but also as an outrageous sham to milk the gullible and superstitious of their money.

Another story born of Chapuys' imagination refers to Anne publicly boasting of her pregnancy to Thomas Wyatt of a craving to eat apples 'and the King had told her it was a sign she was with child'. This invention was eagerly believed by Anne's enemies, including many Catholic biographers.[35]

At this time the King's marriage was still kept secret, although Anne sat at his right hand at a banquet held at York Place late in February. Chapuys reported that Henry fawned on Anne like a bridegroom and had never 'talked so much or so openly' about their marriage.[36] Catherine heard all of this via Chapuys and was worried that the Pope would now abandon her. She wrote to the Emperor in high melodramatic style: 'The thunders of the earth do not cast thunderbolts except to strike at me.'[37]

Thomas Cranmer's consecration as Archbishop took place in March. A week later Bishop Fisher was arrested. This was clearly a precautionary measure designed to silence Catherine's most vocal supporter, and he was released soon after Anne's coronation. Henry summoned Chapuys to York Place in mid-March. In an unsubstantiated conversation held in the gardens, Henry talked freely of his disgust with the Church, assured that the ambassador would repeat his words to his master the Emperor:

he began to say a thousand things in disparagement of the Pope, and among the rest how vainglorious he was to have his feet kissed [by princes] and what authority and power he unduly assumed over the Empire and also over the rest of Christendom, creating and deposing Emperors at will... As to himself, he was about to apply a remedy to the Pope's inordinate ambition and repair the errors of King Henry II and King John, who in a moment of need had been tricked into making England and Ireland tributaries to the Holy See. He was also thinking of uniting to the Crown the lands which the clergy of his dominions held thereof, which lands and property his predecessors on the throne could not alienate to his prejudice. This he was bound to do by the very oath he had sworn at his coronation.[38]

Henry meanwhile sent Anne's brother George, Lord Rochford, to France on 13 March to secretly inform King Francis of his marriage. In a private letter to Francis Henry even hinted that an heir was on the way.[39] That month work had begun on the royal nursery at Eltham Palace 'against the coming of the prince' and Henry informed the Privy Council that Anne was to be crowned after Easter but the formal announcement of his marriage was delayed until Parliament had completed its programme.[40]

In April Henry sanctioned Archbishop Cranmer to officially begin his assessment of the divorce case: 'Albeit we, being your King and sovereign, do recognise no superior in earth, but only God, and not being subject to the laws of any.'[41]

He also sent Norfolk and Suffolk to Catherine to tell her to co-operate with the hearing. From now on she would be called the Dowager Princess of Wales, as befitted the widow of Prince Arthur, his brother.

Catherine reacted characteristically to this news. She refused to be called anything but the Queen of England and insisted that all her servants continue to address her as such. In exasperation Suffolk commented: 'We find here the most obstinate woman that may be.'[42]

Chapuys was in a panic. He tried to obtain another audience with the King but was refused. He then warned Norfolk and Thomas Boleyn that the Emperor would retaliate if his ambassador was sidelined. Henry was persuaded to see him on Maundy Thursday, just before Easter. Chapuys made a formal protest at the news of the marriage and the measures taken in Parliament and by the bishops of the Convocation. Then he dared to question Henry's conscience, but Henry told him it was *because* of his conscience that he had put away his brother's wife. He was no more Catherine's husband than Chapuys was. They had never been married in the sight of God or the law. The Pope had no power to permit such a marriage for it was incest.

The Imperial ambassador claims he then told the King that he had no guarantee of a son by another marriage. This was a step too far, impugning Henry's virility, and the King lost his temper. Very aware of Chapuys' methods of spreading scurrilous gossip, Henry suspected that the Emperor was behind a new campaign to malign Henry's manhood and his right to the throne. He warned Chapuys that his master should mind his own affairs and not try to interfere in England. Going further, he vowed that if the Emperor should think of using force against him the English nation would defeat him.

The whole audience had been recorded by Chapuys' secretary. When Chapuys escaped Henry's wrath, the ambassador wrote to his master Charles recommending an immediate invasion of England. He stated that Henry was ruled by Lutherans and the whole country would soon become Protestant. He claimed that the masses would support a Spanish invasion and there were even those among the nobility, such as Norfolk, who would welcome the Emperor's armies. He also pointed out that England had no allies, for France would not risk alienating Charles by coming to Henry's aid.[43]

This was the duplicitous ambassador at the heart of the English court. Through agents and informers, he worked against the King and the government, keeping in constant communication with Catherine. There was no longer any pretence that Henry's rejected wife was loyal to her adopted country. Hoping to depose him and set her daughter on his throne, Catherine had long since joined wholeheartedly in this conspiracy against England.

By contrast, another alliance was forming between the King's new adviser, Thomas Cromwell, and the new Queen. The evangelical Stephen Vaughan, Cromwell's agent, had been approached by Anne the year before as a channel between them to assist other believers. These included Thomas Alway and Richard Lyst, to whom she had provided aid when Lyst was being persecuted by the Observant Friars of Greenwich. Lyst later went up to Clare College, Cambridge. Thomas Patmore, parson of Hadham in Hertfordshire, had been imprisoned in the Lollards' Tower for two years when he sought Anne's help. He was released after she personally took up his case with the King.[44]

Henry now made appointments for Anne's household. These included her uncle James Boleyn as Chancellor, Lord Burgh as Chamberlain, Sir Edward Baynton as Vice-Chamberlain and John

Uvedale as her secretary. William Cosyn, another relative, was to be her Master of Horse. Among her ladies-in-waiting were Anne Saville, Anne Gainsford (later Lady Zouche) and Anne Savage, the witness at her wedding, plus Anne's cousin Madge Shelton, Elizabeth Holland (who was her uncle Norfolk's mistress) and one Jane Seymour. They took oaths of allegiance and Anne gave them a little pep talk, saying that she expected them to be both discreet and virtuous.

On 12 April Henry attended Easter services with Anne in robes of state as Queen of England. The same day the Venetian ambassador Capello reported that they had already been married for several months.[45]

In mid-April Catherine was informed that to suit her new status as dowager she would be moved to Enfield with a reduced allowance. She immediately appealed to Chapuys to tell Emperor Charles of her plight, complaining that she could not live three months in such reduced circumstances and would be obliged to beg:

I am separated from my Lord, and he has married another woman without obtaining a divorce: and this last act has been done while the suit is still pending, and in defiance of him who has the power of God upon earth. I cover these lines with my tears as I write.

I confide in you as my friend. Help me to bear the cross of my tribulation. Write to the Emperor, bid him insist that judgment be pronounced.

The next Parliament, I am told, will decide if I and my daughter are to suffer martyrdom. I hope God will accept it as an act of merit by us, as we shall suffer for the sake of the truth.[46]

Chapuys duly reported to the Emperor that she feared for her very life:

Forgive my boldness, but your Majesty ought not to hesitate. Your Majesty must root out the Lady and her adherents.

When this accursed Anne has her foot in the stirrup, she will do the Queen and the Princess all the hurt she can, which is what the Queen fears most… [the King was] in great hope of the Queen's death.

Since he was not ashamed to do such monstrous things, he might, one of these days, undertake some further outrage against her.

Whereas the reality was that it was Catherine and her intrigues with the Emperor which now posed the most serious threat. Bishop Fisher also appealed to the Emperor to use force against England: a clear act of treason.[47] Chapuys was carried away by his fantasy of a nation in revolt:

> You cannot imagine the grief of all the people at this abominable government.
>
> They are so transported with indignation at what passes that they complain that your Majesty takes no steps in it; and I am told by many respectable people that they would be glad to see a fleet come hither in your name to raise the people... It is not to be thought that the King will be brought to the point by mild treatment, for his sin carries him away, and he is bewitched by this cursed woman in such a manner that he dares neither say nor do except as she commands him.[48]

Chapuys wrote to Henry on the Emperor's instructions challenging the ecclesiastical court convened at Dunstable to try the divorce. He had already advised Catherine not to cooperate with Cranmer and to refuse to appear there.[49]

He was duly summoned to appear before the Privy Council. Some years before, Wolsey had ignored the diplomatic immunity of the Imperial ambassador Praet, placing him under house arrest. Now Thomas Boleyn, Earl of Wiltshire, accused Chapuys of deceitful dealing, putting on 'two faces', and he was given a caution not to interfere in English affairs. Chapuys kept away from court, never once meeting Anne, but this in no way restrained him from having an opinion on everything that happened there.[50]

On 8 May the bishops gathered at Dunstable as Cranmer wrote to Hawkins:

> touching the small determination and concluding of the matter of divorce between my Lady Catherine and the King's Grace... it was thought convenient by the King and his learned Council that I should repair unto Dunstable, which is within 4 miles unto Amptell [Ampthill], where the said Lady Catherine keepeth her house, and there to call her before me, to hear the final sentence in this said

matter. Notwithstanding she would not at all obey thereunto, for when she was by doctor Lee cited to appear by [the end of] a day, she utterly refused the same, saying that inasmuch as her cause was before the Pope she would have none other judge; and therefore would not take me for her judge.[51]

The new Act of Restraint of Appeals made any plea to Rome illegal, but Catherine claimed that she was Queen of England and therefore not subject to English law but above it. Her reckless and astonishing arrogance could only alienate the court and when she did not appear they simply proceeded without her.

On 23 May the decision was reached that the King's marriage with his brother's widow had always been illegal. On 28 May, at Lambeth Palace, Cranmer decreed that Henry's marriage to Anne was valid for he was free from 'Catherine, widow of his brother, having been contracted contrary to the law of God, null and void'.[52]

The banks of the Thames outside the palace were lined with crowds eager to see their new Queen. That day the Lord Mayor had set out in a great procession of 50 barges downriver to Greenwich to escort Anne into London. Cranmer later took time to write an account to Hawkins:

The Thursday next before the feast of Pentecost, the King and the Queen being at Greenwich, all the crafts of London thereunto well appointed, in several barges decked after the most gorgeous and sumptuous manner, with diverse pageants ... came all unto Greenwich, where they tarried and waited for the Queen's coming to her barge; which so done, they brought her unto the Tower, trumpets, shawms, and other diverse instruments all the ways playing and making great melody.[53]

The Lord Mayor's barge, bearing the Tudor symbol of the red dragon, headed the great fleet, followed by a second with Anne's heraldic symbol, the white crowned falcon surrounded by red and white Tudor roses. Other barges carried trumpeters, musicians and singers, and even spectacular displays of 'wyldfyre', fireworks showering golden rain over the shimmering river.

At Greenwich Anne came out to greet them, dressed in a gown of cloth of gold. The whole river seemed covered with boats.[54] The most luxurious was the Queen's own barge, powered by 24 oars and hung with cloth of gold and heraldic banners, accompanied by those of the nobility, including her own father. Chapuys later sourly reported that Anne had 'seized Catherine's barge', but this was all part of the regal trappings belonging to the Queen of England, which title Catherine had legally lost.[55]

The return upriver was marked by 'divers peales of gunnes' as she entered London. The river façades were beautiful, with neat gabled houses and gardens sloping down to the Thames. The white stone of the Tower of London, with its fine turrets and cupolas, gleamed high above the outer wall, where the procession came to the Water Gate (later ominously to become known as Traitors' Gate), leading to St Thomas's Tower. 'And so her Grace came to the Tower at Thursday at night, about 5 of the clock.'[56] Henry was there waiting for her, greeting her with a kiss and a 'loving countenance'. Now Anne stopped to thank the great crowd who had gathered to see her.

For many years to come, these enthusiastic Londoners were to remember the magnificent processions and celebrations which greeted Anne Boleyn as Queen, passing the story down to their children. Anne's popularity owed something to the fact that many in the city were staunch believers in reform. Hall reports that 'he that sawe it not would not believe it'.[57]

The Tower was still very much a royal palace, with few of the lingering fears and memories that are associated with its imposing walls now. The royal apartments consisted of presence chamber, privy chamber and a great bedchamber with wall murals and stained-glass windows. Henry had everything lavishly refurbished just for Anne. Cranmer records:

> And the same night, and Friday all day, the King and Queen tarried there; and on Friday at night the King's Grace made eighteen Knights of the Bath, whose creation was not only so strange to hear of, as also their garments stranger to behold or look upon; which said knights, the next day, which was Saturday, rode before the Queen's Grace throughout the City of London towards Westminster Palace.[58]

The creation of these Knights of the Bath was a singular honour, normally only associated with the King's own coronation.[59]

On Saturday, 31 May Anne made her ceremonial entry into the City of London on her way to Westminster. She wore white cloth of gold, edged in ermine, and her long auburn hair hung loose under a jewelled circlet. She travelled 'in a white litter of white cloth of gold' drawn by two palfreys through the narrow streets filled with excited Londoners. Men, women and children lined the entire route and leaned out of overhanging windows, their cheers competing with the fanfare of trumpets and salute of the cannon.

At the head of the procession were a dozen envoys of the King of France in colours of blue and gold and the Knights of the Bath in purple. Behind the Queen came ladies of the nobility on horses or riding in chariots. They were followed by a vast procession of nobles in crimson with archbishops and bishops stretching back over half a mile.[60]

At the Eleanor Cross in Cheapside, a monument to Edward I's queen, the City Recorder presented Anne with a purse containing 1,000 marks in gold and she graciously thanked him with 'many goodly wordes'. At certain sites, such as Fenchurch Street and Gracechurch Street, Anne's litter would stop so that she could hear choirs of children or watch the amazing pageants that had been prepared in her honour by the City Guilds. One of the finest was designed by Hans Holbein for the Hanse Steelyard, recreating Mount Parnassus under a vast arch where Apollo and the Muses played instruments and sang Anne's praises. Streams of wine poured freely from the marble fountain of Helicon.[61]

This exhibit was surely the most significant to Anne, for it was sponsored by her fellow evangelical reformers in the City of London. Holbein had returned from exile since Thomas More had resigned as Chancellor and with the Hanse was celebrating the fall of their persecutor and the success of their patroness, Anne the new Queen.

Another evangelical, Nicholas Udall, later Provost of Eton College, wrote verses for the other pageants:

> Scarce had the Falcon found rest for the sole of its foot
>   in the rosebed,
> when an Angel descending crowned the empire-worthy bird –
> a sure presage of Heaven's smiling on your marriage, O Anna.
> Therefore fear not to take your crown.

Another reformer, John Leland, was even more effusive:

> Beflower the way, citizens; offer your thank-offerings, burn your incense. Wreath your brows with laurel, and with roses… Go to meet your lady mistress, poor man and rich man. Anna comes, bright image of chastity, she whom Henry has chosen to his partner. Worthy husband, worthy wife! May heaven bless these nuptials, and make her a fruitful mother of men-children. Fruitful Saint Anne bare three Manes; the offspring of her body, by a strange conception, bare the first founders of our holy Faith. Of that daughter was born Christ our Redeemer, foster-father of a vast family. Not without thought therefore, Queen Anne, do the citizens form this pageant in your honour. By her example, may you give us a race to maintain the Faith and the Throne.[62]

It was an impressive spectacle.[63] Only Anne's enemies, including Chapuys, tried to pretend that the new Queen was not received with amazing warmth and enthusiasm: 'The coronation pageant was all that could be desired, and went off very well, as to the number of the spectators, which was very considerable, but all looked so sad and dismal that the ceremony seemed to be a funeral rather than a pageant.'[64]

Anne continued down the high road to the village of Charing (now the Strand) and so to Westminster, as Cranmer describes:

> as she came along the City, were shewn many costly pageants, with divers other encomiums spoken of children to her; wine also running at certain conduits plenteously. And so proceeding throughout the streets, passed further unto Westminster Hall, where was a certain banquet prepared for her, which done, she was conveyed out of the back side of the Palace into a barge, and so unto York Place, where the King's Grace was before her coming, for this you must ever presuppose that his Grace came always before her secretly in a barge as well from Greenwich to the Tower as from the Tower to York Place.[65]

The next day, Sunday, June 1, was Pentecost or Whit Sunday, which celebrated the descent of the Holy Spirit. Many reformers saw Anne's elevation to Queen as the act of God to liberate England from the oppression of Roman domination. The Venetian ambassador reported Anne's belief thus: 'She knew that God had inspired his majesty to marry her and that he could have found a greater personage than herself, but not one more anxious and ready to demonstrate her love.'[66]

Since More's persecution with its arrests and burnings, London was increasing inclined to evangelical reform.

At seven that morning the Mayor and aldermen went to Westminster Hall, where Anne's coronation procession was formed of knights, judges and all the nobility of the land. Anne followed, walking under a canopy lifted by representatives from the Cinque Ports. She was dressed in purple edged in ermine fur and wore her hair loose under a caul of pearls. Her train was carried by the Dowager Duchess of Norfolk with an escort of ten ladies wearing robes of scarlet and golden coronets. She was led across to Westminster Abbey by the monks all dressed in gold, followed by bishops and archbishops in their jewel-encrusted copes and mitres. The crown jewels were borne in state by those of the highest rank. Cranmer himself records: 'my Lord of Suffolk bearing before her the crown, and two other lords bearing also before her a sceptre and a white rod, and so entered up into the high altar, where diverse ceremonies used about her, I did set the crown on her head, and then was sung *Te Deum*'.[67]

On a high dais before the altar, Anne was anointed by Cranmer, who placed the crown of St Edward on her head. This was a singular honour, for no other consort has ever been crowned with the same crown as the reigning monarch. Effectively, Henry was creating Anne as his queen regnant. The King himself watched the whole ceremony from a hidden vantage point in order not to take pre-eminence.[68]

Two prominent characters did not attend the coronation. Henry's sister Mary Tudor had made her last appearance in London for the wedding of her daughter Frances to the Marquis of Dorset. She was chronically ill and returned to Westhorpe in Suffolk, to be briefly visited by her husband Charles Brandon, who was organising Queen Anne's coronation. Yet surely the success of the young girl who had once been her own waiting woman must have irked her. She died on 24 June.

Neither could Norfolk be there to witness his niece's triumph because Henry had sent him as his envoy to France. His mission was to prevent an alliance between Francis I and the Pope through the marriage of his second son, Henry, Duke of Orleans, and the Pope's niece, Catherine de Medici. How ironic it was that at the very time when England had gained its first Protestant queen, France was about to welcome the arrival of a woman who would prove to be her very antithesis: a murderess and poisoner who would be responsible for the slaughter of evangelicals in the St Bartholomew's Day Massacre.

The coronation proceeded. After anthems and taking communion, Queen Anne processed the length of the cathedral to a triumphant fanfare of trumpets, supported by her father and Lord Talbot. She carried the ivory rod and dove in her left hand and the golden sceptre in her right. In Westminster Hall a great banquet for more than 800 guests took place, lasting until six that evening. Henry was watching everything from a closet in St Stephen's Cloister, deferring to his wife and her unchallenged glory on this one spectacular day.

On the dais at the top table, Queen Anne sat all in solitary state, attended by two countesses and served by Knights of the Bath. Her old family friend Thomas Wyatt attended her as chief ewerer, pouring scented water over her hands. Then the great feast began with a procession of the courses borne in by an army of servants. The first part of the banquet had 28 different dishes, the second 23 as the abundance seemed to begin all over again. These ranged from every kind of roasted meat to the most sophisticated sugar 'subtleties'. Beer and wine flowed freely. Much food was distributed to eager crowds and the poor waiting at the doors.

At the end of a long afternoon Anne gave her thanks to the Lord Mayor of London and citizens, presenting him with a gold cup in commemoration. The next day the celebrations continued with jousting and feasting as the whole court rushed to pay her homage.[69]

Anne issued her own coronation medal, which bore the device 'The Most Happy'.[70] This was her declaration before all the world that the frustrations and divisions of the past had finally been swept aside and now at last she was in the place appointed for her by God and destiny.

Chapter Ten

Child of Promise

THE VATICAN WAS not slow to retaliate against England. The Duke of Norfolk was in Lyons when he first heard that on 11 July the Pope had excommunicated Henry.

This was the mightiest weapon in the arsenal of the Pope, who claimed the authority to deny Henry salvation, cut him off from the Church and cast him out into eternal darkness. Excommunication could also make the King of England subject to arrest by any Church or secular authority.

Indeed the Pope had dared to excommunicate not only Henry, but also the new Archbishop of Canterbury, Cranmer: he 'hath cursed the four bishops of England the which have been the cause of the King's grace's marriage'; the other three were Gardiner, Lee of York and Longland of Lincoln.[1]

Luther had defiantly burned his bull of excommunication but to Norfolk, still very much a Catholic, this was a terrible blow. He is said to have fainted. When he recovered he quickly sent George Boleyn, Lord Rochford, back to England to break the news. Perhaps he thought it would come better from Anne's brother.[2] George discovered the court had fled sweating sickness by retreating to Guildford. No sooner had he delivered his news than Henry immediately ordered him back to France to tell Norfolk to return.

The Pope had given Henry until September to put Anne aside and take Catherine back as his wife. Coming as it did after their marriage and the coronation, this was, of course, quite impossible. By September Queen Anne would be about to deliver his son and heir. Henry was firmly of the belief that now he had removed Catherine, symbol of his sin before God, he would be blessed with the prince he had been waiting for – Prince Edward, as he had already decided.[3]

In July Lord Mountjoy, Catherine's former Chamberlain, forwarded a list of 'remembrances' to Cromwell for the Queen's lying-in.[4] Henry now ordered Catherine to send him the robe last used for the christening of their daughter, Mary. She had claimed to be obedient to the King, but she refused absolutely to hand over the robe and even compelled her household to take an oath to continue to address her as Queen.[5]

On 23 August Anne was still with Henry at Westminster. She did not travel down to Greenwich for her confinement until three days later.[6] Given that it was the custom for queens to take to their chambers in preparation for the birth at least a month beforehand, this seems very late. Anne and her doctors were clearly not expecting the birth until late September, even early in October. She might have been confused about the dates, this being her first pregnancy, but it would have been highly dangerous for the King to endanger his heir's life by putting Anne's health at risk by delaying her confinement. In this case a genuine marriage date of January appears all the more likely.

The apartments at Greenwich were duly prepared. Despite the summer heat, the delivery room was cocooned with heavy tapestries and thick carpets, with all but one window shut to keep out evil airs and odours. The great bed itself was curtained like a tent to give the Queen greater privacy. There were also other beds for the midwives and her ladies, and the 'groaning chair' was prepared for the delivery of the child.[7] Anne also had her own area for religious devotion, which under a Catholic like Catherine would have been festooned with every kind of statue, crucifix and religious talisman, but to the new Queen these were anathema.

The time came for Anne's seclusion. She was escorted to the door of her chambers in a great procession. It was an impressive moment.[8] Many queens had not come out of confinement alive. Childbirth was

still the most dangerous time in a woman's life and there was no guarantee that either mother or child would survive the experience.

The assembled procession were called upon to pray for her safety
and then the men drew aside as the women accompanying the Queen
shut themselves inside. For the next month or six weeks until the
birth, followed by 30 days afterwards, until she was 'churched', the
Queen and her ladies remained incommunicado with the outside
world.

Henry stayed hunting. He ordered prayers for her safe delivery to
be said in churches. At this very time Chapuys relates a story of cold-
ness and arguments between them because Henry had allegedly given
Anne 'legitimate cause' to be jealous. According to the Imperial
ambassador, he had been caught out in an affair with an unknown
mistress but had rounded on his wife, commanding that 'she must shut
her eyes and endure as those who were better than herself had done'.

Whether Chapuys can be believed is demonstrated by his report
the year before that Henry had abandoned Anne for another woman.[9]
The ambassador was now rarely at court because he had refused to
acknowledge Anne as Queen and was never even to have a meeting
with her.

Henry was absorbed and preoccupied with the coming birth.
Astrologers were predicting a son at last. The King was so convinced
that Anne would have a boy that formal documents had been prepared in advance announcing his birth and thanking God for 'good
speed in the deliverance and bringing forth of a prince'. Great celebrations were already arranged, including jousting tournaments and
pageants, to welcome the long-awaited heir.

'The 7th of September, being Sunday, betweene three and foure of
the clocke at afternoone, the Queene was delivered of a faire Ladie;
for whose good deliverance *Te Deum* was sung incontinently, and
great preparation was made for the Christening.'

The birth came quickly, far earlier than anyone had predicted. The
newborn child was wrapped tight in swaddling clothes and that very
day Anne had recovered enough to write personally to Lord Cobham
giving thanks for the 'good speed in the deliverance and bringing
forth'.[10]

The King was now permitted to see his wife and child. The

meeting must have been strained as both of them tried to disguise the real sense of disappointment they felt that the baby was a girl.[11] After such high hopes and confidence during the months before the birth, Henry and Anne must have wondered at their poor luck in producing another daughter for the King. Already scribes were at work altering the documents which had welcomed a prince, adding an extra 's'. The child would be named for both her grandmothers, Elizabeth.

On the very day that Anne was in labour, in another part of the palace the King's favourite Charles Brandon was getting married to a 13-year-old bride. It was only weeks since his wife, Mary Tudor, Henry's sister, had been buried. She had died on 24 June but such was the callousness of Suffolk's character that he raced ahead to break his own son's betrothal and take the girl who should have been his daughter-in-law as his own new bride. He was 35 years older than Katherine, who had been his ward, the heiress of Lord Willoughby and Maria de Salinas, one of Catherine's closest friends.

When she gave birth to a boy the following year, Suffolk's heir, Henry of Lincoln, her former betrothed, was said to have died of grief. De Carles unkindly claims that Anne remarked: 'My Lord of Suffolk kills one son to beget another.'[12] Katherine Willoughby, however, was soon to prove her own strength of character, becoming as strong an evangelical believer as Anne and a great defender of the Protestant martyrs.

Henry hid his feelings about the birth of his daughter, insisting that the elaborate christening ceremony should go ahead. It was always considered wise to christen the baby as soon as possible, for according to Catholic tradition an unbaptised child was prey for the Devil and should it die without the protection of the Church, it would be doomed to eternity in Limbo. Thomas More was typical of those who believed 'those infantes be dampned onely to the payne of losse of heauen'. Death was always waiting to threaten the newborn and infants. One in five children died in the first year of life.[13]

On 10 September the christening took place in Greenwich, but according to the custom, neither parent was there.

Sir Stephen Peacocke, in a gowne of crimsin velvet, with his collar of esses, and all the Aldermen in scarlet, with collars and chaines, and all the Councell of the Cittie with them, tooke their barge at one of the clocke; and the Cittizens had another barge, and so rowed to Greenwich, where were many Lords, Knights, and Gentlemen assembled: all the walles betweene the King's Pallace and the Fryers were hanged with arras, and all the way strewed with greene rushes.

Because it was cold, the walk to the chapel of the Observant Friars was hung with tapestries and a fire lit inside. Princess Elizabeth was carried by the Dowager Duchess of Norfolk while Lady Mary Howard carried a new robe 'very rich of pearl and stone' for the christening.

Significantly, Cranmer became Elizabeth's godfather, while the Dowager Duchess and the Dowager Lady Dorset were her godmothers. The Bishop of London plunged the baby three times in the waters of the font and

the Childe was named Elizabeth, and after that all things were done at the church doore, the Child was brought to the font, and christned; and that done, Garter chiefe King of Armes cried aloud, 'God of his infinit goodnesse send prosperous life and long to the high and mightie Princesse of England Elizabeth.'

And then the trumpets blew; then the Childe was brought up to the altar, and the Gospel said over it.[14]

The procession returned to the palace lit by 500 torches. In the Queen's apartments Anne waited with Henry to receive their daughter and the many gifts presented by their guests.[15] The whole ceremony was described by the Imperial ambassador's poison pen as 'very cold and disagreeable both to the court and to the City, and there has been no thought of having the bonfires and rejoicings usual in such cases'.

Chapuys asserted that the birth of a girl was a sign that God had abandoned Henry. He reported maliciously 'the great disappointment and sorrow of the King, of the Lady herself and of others of her party, and the great shame and confusion of physicians, astrologers, wizards and witches, all of whom affirmed it would be a boy'.[16]

To Catholics Elizabeth would always be seen as 'the little bastard', child of 'the Concubine' and subordinate in the line of succession to Catherine's daughter, Mary.

Conscious of the ill-concealed delight of their enemies, Henry felt humiliated.

His poor sexual reputation now turned against him. Henry had always been a hypochondriac, but his health had deteriorated ever since a heavy jousting fall some years before. He suffered from recurrent headaches which were changing his personality, making him more irritable and subject to violent mood swings. He was no longer the handsome, athletic young monarch who had taken Europe by storm. He had begun to put on weight and was going bald, hiding it under stylish hats. As he grew older and his girth grew greater, he radically changed men's clothing into a wider and more exaggerated silhouette. The codpiece, which in Henry VII's time had been concealed, was now revealed, puffed, slashed and even bejewelled.[17]

One explanation for this fashion, apart from boastful vanity, was the increased spread of syphilis. Those infected, who could have included Henry, needed to cover up heavy bandages and protect outer garments from balms and medication. It is possible that if Henry developed syphilis this might have affected his fertility. John Erley, secretary of the Bishop of Bath, suggested that the King was impotent and incapable of bearing sons.

Such rumours only made Henry even more anxious that Anne should produce more children. He is said to have told her: 'You and I are both young and by God's grace, boys will follow.'[18] But Anne's failure to keep her side of their bargain by producing a son must have always been in the back of his mind. Anne had made him look like a fool.

A woman was seen as unclean after giving birth, requiring to be 'churched' a month or so afterwards before marital relations could be resumed. Anne was clearly churched quickly, for on 15 October Sir Richard Page wrote that the royal couple were together again and merry.[19]

Anne proved to be a loving and protective mother. Aware that there were enemies at court, she refused to be parted from Elizabeth and kept her at her side, even lying her on a velvet cushion beside her throne. Anne supervised everything in the lavishly prepared nursery at Greenwich under the charge of Margaret, the widow of Thomas Bryan. There were golden trimmings for Elizabeth's cradle and satin gowns and caps for 'the lady princess'.

She had wanted to breastfeed her daughter herself, going against all tradition. It was unthinkable for a woman of her status to do so when a wet-nurse could be employed for her. Henry was decisive in refusing to permit Anne to have her way. He now laid down the law as her husband and master, thinking no doubt of a rapid resumption of sexual relations and the chance of her conceiving another child.

Marriage had brought them into a very different relationship. While previously Henry had found Anne's independence of spirit and intellectual bantering highly attractive, now the hunt was over these very attributes suddenly became liabilities. The King expected his wife to obey him in everything. After Catherine's example of wilful opposition, he was looking for a woman who would not set herself against him but know her duty as a wife and mother.

On 1 October the King reinforced the status of his new heir by informing his daughter Mary that she could no longer style herself 'Princess'. He was willing to set her up in her own household with a staff of more than 160 servants under Lady Salisbury. Mary, now 17, was formally declared illegitimate, to which pronouncement she reacted violently, crying there was no princess in England except herself. She threw such a tantrum that even her ally Chapuys thought she was being unreasonable. Henry was understandably furious. He wrote that she was 'arrogantly usurping the title of Princess' to which she was not legally entitled.

As a child Mary had been cosseted as princess and heir to the crown. Foreign ambassadors praised the child for her long, red hair, 'pretty face, a very beautiful complexion, well-proportioned physique'. But the conflict between her parents took its toll and by the time she was in her teens her health and appearance had suffered from stress and her unstable future. She was short and grew very thin, notably difficult about her food and always taking herbal medicines concocted for one illness or another. She had strange, piercing eyes, the result of poor eyesight.

When she read a letter she had to hold it right up to her face. It was also said that she had lost most of her teeth.

Mary had a limited education. She spoke several languages but was not scholarly, preferring music. She played and sang well, although her voice was very deep and masculine, like her mother's. Vives had taught her that women were the tools of Satan, weak and subject to evil temptations. Through her mother's overwhelming influence, Mary maintained a rigid Catholic faith which would accept no criticism of the Church of Rome or its practices. Like Catherine, Mary believed that the New Learning and the New Religion were heretical works of the Devil and that Anne Boleyn was responsible for seducing her father and ruining their lives.

Mary deceived herself. Henry had been contemplating a split with Catherine long before. Nor was it Anne who was keeping Henry away from his daughter. Although Mary blamed her for every setback in her life, she later discovered it was the King himself who had determined to teach her a lesson by humiliating and ignoring her.

He was now convinced that Catherine and her daughter were working against him. Immediately it was arranged for 'the Dowager Princess of Wales' to be moved to Buckden in Huntingdonshire, while Mary was sent to live at Hertford. They were forbidden to visit or to write to each other for fear of the conspiracy he believed the Emperor was plotting.

Anne now made a brilliant match for Lady Mary Howard, her protégée, cousin and evangelical member of her household, with Henry's son by Bessie Blount, the Duke of Richmond. He had just returned from the French court and was married on 25 November. Chapuys took advantage of this marriage to suggest that next Anne was planning a match for Mary. He reported that she wanted to 'marry her to some varlet' or even to poison her.[20] This kind of nonsense was fed to the ambassador by his spies and collaborators at court.

These included Gertrude Blount, Marchioness of Exeter, who, although she had been honoured as godmother to Princess Elizabeth, betrayed this trust by working for Catherine and Chapuys. In November she had written to the King denying any involvement with the notorious 'Nun of Kent' and claiming that, because she was only a woman 'whose fragility and brittleness is easily seduced', she had been deceived.[21]

This nun, Elizabeth Barton, had entered the convent of St Sepulchre at Canterbury, sponsored by Edward Bocking, a monk. She would go into trance like a medium, her eyes starting from their sockets, and a hoarse 'voice speaking within her belly' would make dire predictions, which he wrote down for publication.[22]

She would prophesy on all manner of subjects, in particular the King's divorce, bluntly denouncing his decision to put Catherine aside, so endangering his immortal soul. She claimed God had chosen her 'to restore the power of the Roman pontiff in England'. Barton soon became a spectacle, drawing crowds to hear the letter of gold which Mary Magdalene had written to her from heaven.[23]

Catherine was impressed by reports about her. Her agent Abell, Bishop Fisher and Thomas More believed in all her 'prophecies' and others close to her were equally won over, including the Marchioness of Exeter, who was pregnant. She told Catherine that the nun had made predictions for her unborn child and later brought her to meet Catherine.

Barton also appeared before the King, when she went into a prepared trance and writhed around on the ground proclaiming:

> Satan is tormenting me for the sins of my people, but our blessed Lady shall deliver me by her mighty hand... Abominable heresies, impious innovations! ... King of England, beware that you touch not the power of the holy Father... Root out the new doctrines...
>
> Burn all over your kingdom the New Testament in the vulgar tongue. Henry, forsake Anne Boleyn and take back your wife Catherine...
>
> If you neglect these things, you shall not be king longer than a month, and in God's eyes you will not be so even for an hour. You shall die the death of a villain, and Mary, the daughter of Catherine, shall wear your crown.[24]

The King was 'so abominable in the sight of God that he was not worthy to tread on hallowed ground'. England would be swept by a terrible plague sent from God.[25]

Whether or not Barton was being used by Catherine and her supporters for political purposes, a woman with such psychic powers was generally regarded to be a witch. The Scriptures were very clear about its opinion of such soothsayers:

'Do not turn to mediums or seek out spiritualists… Do not
practise divination or sorcery.' (Leviticus 19, 31, 26)

'Do not permit a witch to live.' (Exodus 22, 18)

Common superstition combined with Catholic mysticism to provide
Barton with many naïve supporters. Clairvoyants were fashionable at
court. The wife of the Master of the King's Jewel House, Robert
Amadas, also dabbled in the occult, claiming that the King, whom she
called 'Mouldwarp', was 'cursed with God's own mouth' and would
be overthrown by Scotland. Her vitriol against Henry may well be the
result of their brief affair some years before in William Compton's
house in Thames Street. Chapuys also recites a story that Anne told
Henry of a prophecy in which the Queen would be destroyed and
burned, a warning echoed by George Wyatt, but Anne's 'Christian
and faithful counsel' had 'so armed' Henry that he did not believe
these superstitious predictions.[26]

Barton was speaking treason. She proclaimed that Henry was not
the rightful King and God would bless any rebellion to remove him.
Barton and Bocking were arrested and questioned. She confessed that
she had invented her revelations, telling Cranmer that she had never
even had a real vision. According to Chapuys, it was the King himself
who led the attack on the 'lewd nun' and turned it into a purge of
Fisher and More. Barton was sentenced to death and hanged at
Tyburn in April 1534.[27]

The Marchioness of Exeter was not the only courtier playing a
double game.

Chapuys sought to create division at court by suggesting that
Norfolk – and even Anne's father – were opposed to her marriage to
the King. In reality Thomas was always Anne's greatest supporter.
Chapuys wanted to minimise the popularity of the new Queen by
inventing an atmosphere of seething resentment against her and in
favour of Catherine throughout the country. This was designed to
induce his master the Emperor to invade England and overthrow
Henry, a conspiracy he pursued for years.

Many of Thomas Wyatt's poems reflect his unease with this atmosphere of deceit at court:

What vaileth truth or by it to take pain,
To strive by steadfastness for to attain
To be just and true and flee from doubleness,
Sithens all alike, where ruleth craftiness,
Rewarded is both false and plain?
Soonest he speedeth that most can feign;
True meaning heart is had in disdain.
Against deceit and doubleness
What vaileth truth?
Deceived is he by crafty train
That meaneth no guile and doth remain
Within the trap without redress
But for to love, lo, such a mistress
Whose cruelty nothing can refrain.
What vaileth truth?[28]

During the summer of 1533 a papal envoy wrote that Henry would soon tire of his new bride. Claiming to be close to Norfolk, he suggested the Duke could persuade the King to take Catherine back. In December Chapuys claimed that Sir Nicholas Carew had told him of further rows between the King and Queen over a new mistress.[29]

That Christmas they were in good spirits, 'merry and lusty', and celebrated in high style.[30] The King and Queen exchanged gifts, including a golden bowl from which water flowed from a diamond fountain. Perhaps a reason for their closeness was the fact that Anne was pregnant again. Another cousin, Lord William Howard, broke the news in Rome, having left London in early December.

Now that, hopefully, a prince was on the way, Henry arranged that Princess Elizabeth, although only three months old, should be sent away from court to live with her own household at Hatfield. Given Anne's exceptionally close attachment to her daughter, this was cruel.

Margaret, Lady Bryan, wife of Anne's cousin Sir Francis Bryan, and Lady Margaret Douglas were to go with her. The girl who rocked her cradle, Blanche Parry, was to stay in Elizabeth's service for the next 57 years. Elizabeth later referred to her childhood: 'We are more bound to them that bringeth us up well than to our parents, for our parents do that which is natural for them, that is bringeth us into this world; but our bringers up are a cause to make us live well.'

Anne now stood second only to the King in authority. She became an important patron, maintaining a separate household from Henry's and able to promote her own people.[31]

Anne's servants came from varied backgrounds. Her ladies included several family members, among them her sister Mary, now brought back to court; her sister-in-law Jane, Lady Rochford; her cousin, Lady Mary Howard, Norfolk's daughter; another cousin, Mary Shelton, daughter of her aunt Anne; and Elizabeth, wife of her uncle Sir James Boleyn. There was also the King's niece, daughter of Margaret Tudor of Scotland, Margaret Douglas; Elizabeth, Countess of Worcester, and Jane Seymour, who had previously attended Catherine of Aragon.

The younger ladies were all supervised by Mrs Marshall. Unfortunately, one of the older ladies was also in need of supervision. Mary Boleyn, now aged 34, secretly married William Stafford, a commoner and soldier, the younger son of Humphrey Stafford of Blatherwick in Northamptonshire. This was seen as a terrible match for someone of the status of the Queen's sister. Even though she was a widow, Mary should have done better for herself than sliding several steps down the social ladder. Her family were horrified as she was sent away from court again, but Mary sought out Cromwell's assistance, writing that 'love overcame reason': 'For well I might have had a greater man of birth, but I assure you I could never have had one that loved me so well. I had rather beg my bread with him than be the greatest queen christened.'

She begged for help to win back the 'gracious favour of the King and Queen'. Anne provided assistance through Cromwell and the newly-weds settled at Rochford in Essex, living in relative obscurity.[32]

Mary's son Henry, now aged seven, still lived at court as Anne's ward. The boy increasingly looked like his namesake and was generally recognised as the King's son, but was never officially acknowledged because his aunt was now in fact his stepmother. This did not stop Catherine's supporters spreading salacious stories of Henry's sexual habits. Cardinal Pole actually accused the King of having affairs not only with Mary and Anne but also with their mother.

One of Anne's major goals as Queen was to set higher moral standards at court. Latimer describes how she told the members of her household 'to take especiall regarde, and to omitt nothing that may seeme to apperteigne to honour'. Foxe tells how Anne's silkwoman, Jane Wilkinson, confirmed there had never been 'better order amongst the ladies and gentlewomen of the court than in Anne's day'.

Her household attended religious service once a day and the Queen gave each one a book of Psalms in English. But these were not always appreciated. Latimer records how Anne warned her cousin Mary Shelton about writing romantic verses in hers.[33] Mary was one of the Queen's younger attendants, whose poetry was discovered with some early versions of Thomas Wyatt's work and is now in the Devonshire Manuscript at the British Library. Previously, when historians still saw Anne as flighty and a temptress, it was thought that she was the author, but this has now been disproved and the handwriting recognised as that of Lady Mary Howard, Margaret Douglas and Mary Shelton.

Anne condemned any 'licentious libertie' and insisted her court should set an example by 'vertuous demeanor' with 'godly conversation': 'They talked theology. Their inner circles of court ladies were twenty-four hours a day Bible studies. They saw everything that happened to them through two lenses: the lens of the providence of God and the lens of the furtherance of the Reformed Religion.'[34]

William Latimer reports that Anne and Henry never dined 'without some argument of Scripture thoroughly debated'. The King once had 'such pleasure' in this that he partnered Anne's uncle, Sir James Boleyn, against Nicholas Shaxton and Hugh Latimer that 'diverse and sundry times he would not only hear them but sometime would argue and reason himself'.[35]

Anne's intellect and her flashing, witty repartees had always excited the King. Only in future years did Henry look back on these times and react by forbidding later wives ever to argue with him but submit to his opinions.

Anne now saw that, like Esther, she should use her position as Queen to influence the rise of good men and women into court, fellow evangelical believers whose moral standards were of a higher order than those who had obtained office in the past. Foxe wrote of her influence on the King: 'So long as Queen Anne, Thomas Cromwell, Archbishop Cranmer, Master Denny, Doctor Butts, with such like were about him and could prevail with him, what organ of Christ's glory did more good in the church than he?'[36]

Anthony Denny, a relative of Mary Boleyn's dead husband, William Carey, although working for Sir Francis Bryan and Thomas Cromwell, was sent on a mission for Anne in London. He had attended the King in Calais and was later to become his most trusted personal servant and member of the Privy Council. He was also a strong evangelical with 'sincere affection to God and His holy word'.[37]

Some of Anne's staff had previously served Cardinal Wolsey, such as Dr Bartlett and her auditor, John Smith, while others had been in the King's household.[38]

Anne appointed evangelical chaplains to her household, such as William Betts and Robert Singleton. George Wyatt states: 'She had procured to her chaplains, men of great learning and of no less honest conversing, whom she with hers heard much, and privately she heard them willingly and gladly to admonish her, and them herself exhorted and encouraged so to do.'

Latimer records that she told them: ' "I have carefully chosen you to be the lanterns and light of my court," to teach them "above all things to embrace the wholesome doctrine and infallible knowledge of Christ's gospel." '[39]

When Anne's chaplain, William Betts, died in March 1535, she chose Matthew Parker as his successor. Her choice was driven by their shared faith and belief in making education available to the poor through the creation of grammar schools. She sent Parker a barrage of letters through her secretary to convince him to take the post, including two in one day: 'I pray you resist not your calling, but come in any wise to know further of her pleasure. Bring with you a long gown, and that shall be enough until you shall return to Cambridge.'[40]

Parker accepted and was made Dean of Stoke-by-Clare in Suffolk, founding one of the first grammar schools. He later became Elizabeth's Archbishop of Canterbury.

Alesius later described to Elizabeth 'the evangelical bishops whom your most holy mother had appointed from among those scholars who favoured the purer doctrine of the gospel'.[41]

Seven of the ten bishops elected between 1532 and 1536 were appointed through Anne's influence. Latimer names Cranmer, Hugh Latimer of Worcester, Nicholas Shaxton of Salisbury (who been persecuted for his own beliefs while at Cambridge), Thomas Goodrich of Ely and John Skip of Hereford. Others were Edward Fox, John Hilsey, a protégé of Cranmer, and John Salcot of Bangor. William Barlow, an old family friend of the Boleyns, whose brother John was a member of Anne's household, was given St Asaph's and then St David's, where his possession of the New Testament in English created opposition. Hugh Latimer and Shaxton preached controversial sermons before the King. Two others, Nicholas Heath of York and Thomas Thirlby of Westminster, later turned against their evangelical supporters, so that Foxe records: 'would to God they were now as great professors of the gospel of Christ'.[42]

Anne asked Cromwell to give a post to Robert Power, later Abbot of Vale Royal. John Smith, who had served at her coronation, petitioned her to aid him for the 'diligent love and service' he had shown her.[43] The French ambassador told Chapuys in February 1534 that Anne had wept when she heard of the death of Cranmer's correspondent Nicholas Hawkins. He had been recalled from Spain to become Bishop of Ely, but died on his way home.[44]

Foxe states that Anne: 'who, without controversy, was a special comforter and aider of all the professors of Christ's gospel...

'What a zealous defender she was of Christ's gospel all the world doth know, and her acts do and will declare to the world's end.'[45]

Anne maintained her support for the illegal trade in Scripture coming from abroad.

Anne's silkwomen included evangelicals who were involved in importing illegal Bibles with William Latimer. Another was the wife of Stephen Vaughan, Cromwell's agent abroad. Their daughter Anne married Henry, the son of William Locke, who supplied fabric for the ladies of the court. His daughter Rose Hickman later recalled: 'I remember that I have heard my father say that when he was a young merchant and used to go beyond sea Queen Anne Boleyn ... caused him to get her the gospels and epistles written in parchment in French together with the psalms.'[46]

Such close ties typified the interconnected network of evangelical believing families. These courageous ladies were forced into exile when Bloody Mary became Queen.[47]

Tyndale's English translation of the New Testament was still banned but Anne kept it on display for anyone to read.[48] Now in the British Library, it was printed on vellum and hand-coloured with wonderful woodcut illuminations and the words '*Anna, Regina Anglia*'.

In 1535 Miles Coverdale dedicated his translation of the whole Bible to the King and Queen.

Anne's family's overseas connections were strengthened by her elevated role. When Francis I turned against the evangelical reformers sheltered by his sister Margaret, Anne did her best to support the exiles and refugees. Thanks to her protection, many reformers now returned to England. After the intense persecution of Thomas More and his 'heresy hunters', and the burning of Frith in July, they now saw the new Queen as a great heroine who was working behind the scenes to save many lives.

Robert Barnes returned and was able to give sermons in London. Latimer records that Anne supported 'Mrs Mary', a refugee from France, and succeeded in obtaining the release of Richard Herman, an Antwerp merchant. Her appeal to Cromwell reads:

Anne the Queen.

Trusty and right well-beloved, we greet you well. And whereas we be credibly informed that the bearer hereof, Richard Herman, merchant and citizen of Antwerp in Brabant, was in the time of the late lord cardinal put and expelled from his freedom and fellowship of and in the English house there, for nothing else, as he affirmeth like a good Christian man, but only for that, that he did, both with his goods and policy to his great hurt and hindrance in this world, help to the setting forth of the New Testament in English.

We therefore desire and instantly pray you, that with all speed and favour convenient, you will cause this good and honest merchant, being my Lord's true, faithful, and loving subject, to be restored to his pristine freedom, liberty, and fellowship aforesaid. And the sooner at this our request: and at your good pleasure to hear him in such things as he hath to make further relation unto you in this behalf.

Given under our signet at my Lord's manor of Greenwich, the xiv day of May.

To our trusty and right well-beloved Thomas Cromwell, principal secretary [Secretary of State] to his Majesty, the king my lord.

After his release, Herman worked for Cromwell, intercepting certain diplomatic letters in November 1535.[49]

It was Dr Butts who obtained Anne's patronage for the French poet Nicholas Bourbon, whom Margaret of Navarre had failed to save from imprisonment for his faith. Where her friend had failed, Anne now secured his release.

A poor man, I lie shut up in this dark prison:
There is no one who would be able or who would dare to
     bring help:
You alone, Oh Queen: you, Oh noble nymph, both can and dare:
As one whom the King and whom God himself loves.[50]

In March 1534 he came to England to meet her, staying with Dr Butts, 'my Maecenas and my father'. Out of gratitude Bourbon wrote the following and dedicated his future work to her:

Your pity lighted upon me from the ends of the earth,
Snatching me in my affliction, Anna, away from all my troubles.
If this had not happened, I should be chained in that darkness,
Unhappily languishing, still under restraint.
Express my thanks, still less, Oh Queen, repay you,
How can I? I confess I have not the resources.
But the Spirit of Jesus which enflames you wholly with his fire,
He has enough to give you satisfaction...
Just as the golden sun dispels the gloomy shadows of night
and at daybreak makes all things bright: So you, Oh Queen,
restored as a new light to your French and brightening everything,
bring back the Golden Age...
Live on, you and your consort who, joined by His grace
and linked by His love, burn with ardour
for the honour of Jesus the Saviour.[51]

Bourbon described the evangelical circle at the English court which included Dr Butts, Cranmer 'a gift from God', and Hugh Latimer, 'the best of preachers'. There was also the King's goldsmith, Cornelius Hayes, his astronomer, Nicholas Kratzer, the great artist Hans Holbein, and Thomas Cromwell, whom Bourbon described as 'aflame with the love of Christ'. Bourbon also attacked the hypocrisy of the reformists' enemy, Thomas More:

> I have seen and know someone named More…
> which wickedly deceives acted – who would believe it –
> against his people and his King in a way sacrilegious …
> short-lived bubble.[52]

Anne was also a patron of the New Learning. Erasmus prefaced two books to 'the most gracious and virtuous Queen Anne', dedicating them to her father, his friend Thomas Boleyn. Clémont Marot dedicated a special edition of his *Le Pasteur Evangélique* to her with Anne's arms among Tudor roses on the cover:

> a lady Anne, a queen incomparable, may this good shepherd
> with whom you find favour give you a son,
> the image of his father the king, and may he live and flourish
> so that you may both see him come to manhood.

In her first year on the throne Anne donated £40 each to Oxford and Cambridge, doubling this the following year. Matthew Parker's reforms included Bible studies as well as preaching, grammar schools with free pupils and scholarships which could lead to a six-year bursary at Cambridge. Anne gave grants to study at university for poor students like William Barker and William Bill, who had been recommended by her chaplains. John Cheke, the protégé of Dr Butts, praised Anne's generosity. John Beckensall received £40 a year for study in Paris with Thomas Winter, Wolsey's son. Anne later gave Winter funds as a result of Cromwell's intervention. She insisted that the Abbot of St Mary's York send John Eldmer to Cambridge.[53] Nicholas Bourbon was given a position teaching Anne's nephew Henry Carey, Henry Norris's son Henry and Thomas Harvey, son of

Anne's friend and fellow evangelical. Bourbon instantly praised her:

> You, Oh queen, gave me the boys to educate,
> I try to keep each one faithful to his duty.
> May Christ grant that I may be equal to the task,
> Shaping vessels worthy of a heavenly house.[54]

When Anne was travelling, her almoner made contact with needy villagers 'overcharged with children'. She gave alms valued at 100 crowns a week to poor relief, helped pregnant women and even paid for farming families in difficulties to buy new livestock. Hugh Latimer wrote to the Queen about a farmer called Ive and his wife who had lost their cattle. They were evangelicals and he called them a modern Aquila and Priscilla, co-workers of the apostle Paul. As a result Anne gave Mrs Ive a gift of £20 in gold.

> It hath been reported unto us by divers credible persons who were about this Queen ... how her grace carried ever about her a certain little purse, out of which she was wont daily to scatter abroad some alms to the needy, thinking no day well spent wherein some man had not fared the better by some benefit at her hands.[55]

A treatise on poor relief, *The forme and maner of subvention for pore people, devysed and practysed in the citie of Hypres in Flaunders*, was dedicated to Anne, the 'floure of all queens', by William Marshall.

Anne was very discreet, not publicising her charitable work. From her own accounts George Wyatt calculated that, as Queen, Anne gave the enormous sum of £1,500 a year to charity. This was far more than her income as Marquess of Pembroke, amounting to some £15,000 during her reign as Queen.[56]

In December 1533 Suffolk had received orders to move Catherine from Buckden as a precaution against conspiracy. But she refused, saying that even if she was 'bound with ropes' she would not go. She locked herself away in her suite of rooms and would not come out until he had gone. Not long afterwards she did move, this time to Kimbolton near Fotheringhay Castle in Huntingdonshire.[57]

Henry now decided to teach his daughter Mary a lesson by assigning her a place in her half-sister Elizabeth's house. Her arrogance and petulant moods had angered him, reminding him painfully of Catherine's years of stubborn resistance to his will. He saw in this girl everything he had come to dislike in her mother and sent Norfolk to fetch her to Hatfield.

Once again Mary reacted with outrage and hysteria, but she had met her match in Norfolk, who had once ordered his wife to be held down on the floor while he beat her. He now wasted little time in bundling the girl into the waiting litter and moving on. But Mary was determined to make trouble, complaining in secret correspondence to Chapuys that she was assigned 'the worst lodging of the house', unfit for even a servant. As a result some of her staff were dismissed for 'encouraging her in her disobedience'.[58]

Lady Shelton had the unenviable duty of supervising her, with permission to beat her if necessary, but given that she was Queen Anne's aunt, it was unlikely that Mary would submit to her discipline. Refusing to eat with others, Mary demanded special food. She claimed to be ill and would not attend her baby half-sister. Henry sent his own physician, Dr William Butts, to see her. He diagnosed stress, but Henry was tired of her histrionics and thought Butts was exaggerating. The King believed Mary was trying to get moved to live with her mother, an idea he could never tolerate because of Catherine's persistent plotting.

When Henry visited Elizabeth in January, he refused to see Mary. She was ordered to her room, where Chapuys alleged that she was locked in with the door nailed shut. He describes her mournfully watching the King from a tower as he rode away.[59]

Chapuys naturally blamed Anne, claiming that she was the wicked stepmother. He said she had ordered her aunt to be sure Mary was 'slapped like the cursed bastard she was'. He wrote that someone 'of good faith' had told him how she had threatened to murder Mary 'by hunger or otherwise ... even if she were burned alive for it after'.[60]

The truth is far less melodramatic. Anne simply did not know what to do with her intransigent stepdaughter. She tried many times to win Mary round. In early 1534, when visiting Elizabeth at Hatfield, Anne offered to welcome Mary if she would reach a reconciliation with the

King and acknowledge their marriage.[61] Mary retorted that she knew no other Queen than her mother, but the King's mistress could still intercede with her father. This insult was hardly intended to endear her to Anne.

Some months later, when Elizabeth and Mary were at Eltham Palace, they met again in the royal chapel but Mary left before the Queen, breaking etiquette. Anne was told afterwards that Mary had actually curtseyed to her, although she had not seen it. Trying to warm to the girl, Anne sent her a brief note offering her friendship:

> The Queen salutes your grace with much affection and craves pardon, understanding that at your parting from the oratory, you made a curt-sey to her, which if she had seen she would have answered you with the like; and she desires that this may be an entrance of friendly cor-respondence, which your grace shall find completely to be embraced on her part.

Mary replied it was impossible for the Queen to have been there, for Catherine was

> so far from this place. You would have said, the Lady Anne Boleyn, for I can acknowledge no other Queen but my mother, nor esteem them my friends who are not hers. And for the reverence that I made, it was to the altar, to her maker and mine; and so they are deceived, and deceive her who tell her otherwise.[62]

It is hardly surprising, if this is true, that Anne cooled towards the teenager.

Chapuys claims she said she would 'pull down this high spirit' and 'bring down the pride of this unbridled Spanish blood'. Henry too referred to Mary's 'obstinate Spanish blood' and blamed Catherine for teaching his daughter such impertinent disobedience. Her obstinacy was as great as her mother's and only served to enrage the King. He certainly told one ambassador that he intensely disliked his daughter.[63]

Surely Henry would have treated Mary better if Catherine had not been plotting to give her his crown. Henry said Catherine had grown 'so haughty in spirit' that she believed she could 'raise a number of men and make war as boldly as did Queen Isabella her mother'.[64]

Anne Hussey, wife of Mary's former Chamberlain, had visited her at Hatfield and was heard calling her 'Princess'. Henry had her arrested and sent to the Tower, but the true reason was that she had been acting as a conduit for secret correspondence between Mary and the rebels focused around her mother and Chapuys. She was later released, but other members of her staff had also been suborned. It was claimed that Mary was suicidal.[65]

Henry saw Catherine and Mary as a danger. Their refusal to accept the validity of his new marriage undermined its acceptance in the country. Excommunication meant that the King himself was under threat and could become a target for rebellion by Catholics loyal to Rome.

Mary still claimed to be heir to the throne, a rival to Henry and to his new daughter Elizabeth. So the stage was set for the troubled relationship between the sisters, and the political and religious conflict of the next 50 years.

Chapter Eleven

Tragedy

Now, AFTER SEVEN long years, the Pope finally gave judgement on the validity of Henry and Catherine's marriage, but he had prevaricated so long that his opinion was irrelevant. Clement's announcement that the marriage 'always hath and still doth stand firm and canonical, and the issue proceeding standeth lawful and legitimate' was seen as an insult to the King, especially as he was required to pay the costs of the whole fiasco.

In England Parliament gave its support to Henry. On 23 March the Act of Succession to 'the imperial crown of England' was passed. Now only children of the King's marriage to Anne were his legal heirs. Should Henry die, Anne would become Regent and 'absolute governess of her children and kingdom'.

At Easter the churches were full to hear the new prayers for the King and Queen and Princess Elizabeth, whom the Pope had claimed was a bastard. They visited Elizabeth in her newly refurbished apartments at Eltham Palace: 'Her Grace is much in the King's favour as a godely child should be, God save her.'[1]

Henry had gambled by at last marrying Anne and making her Queen. He had anticipated that her pregnancy would deliver the longed-for prince and heir, but although Elizabeth had been a setback, he was determined to bolster his reforms with all the force of the law. It was duly decreed in Parliament that all the King's subjects 'shall truly, firmly, constantly, without fraud or guile, observe, fulfil, maintain, defend and keep the whole effect and contents of this Act'.

Any 'slander or derogation of the lawful matrimony [with] his most dear and entirely beloved wife Queen Anne' would be charged with treason. This decision was supported by the bishops, meeting on 5 May in York, where they renounced all allegiance to the Church of Rome.

Catherine had been abandoned by all except the Vatican and the Emperor. In alarm she now wrote to Chapuys demanding that her nephew Charles invade England immediately. 'She now realises that it is absolutely necessary to apply stronger remedies to the evil ... what they are to be, she durst not say.' She was clearly playing with fire, for this was high treason.

An Act of Attainder for treason was passed against the 'Nun of Kent' Elizabeth Barton and her supporters, including Catherine's old advocate, Bishop Fisher. He had been sentenced to life imprisonment but was treated leniently and released after merely paying a fine. The King was still unaware that Fisher was in fact a traitor who was actively involved in the Spanish plot to invade England. State papers from 27 September 1533 later revealed that he was involved in Catherine's conspiracy for a foreign army under the Emperor to seize England and depose Henry.[2]

Thomas More's name was not included in the Attainder, although he had given credence to Barton's treasonable 'prophecies'. According to his son-in-law Roper, More received with reservation the news that he would not be charged, telling his daughter: 'In faith, Meg, *quod dilfertur non aufertur'* – what is postponed is not abandoned.[3]

More had already admitted to Cromwell that he had visited the nun. He even wrote her a warning letter:

It sufficeth me, Good Madam, to put you in remembrance of such things as I nothing doubt your wisdom and the Spirit of God shall keep you from talking with any persons, specially with lay persons, of any such manner things as pertain to Prince's affairs, or the state of the realm, but only to commune and talk with any person, high and low, of such manner things as may to the soul be profitable for you to show and for them to know.[4]

It was said that More had resigned as Chancellor because he opposed the King's new policies, but he claimed in a letter to Erasmus that it was simply because he was ill. For nearly two years he had been spending his time writing tracts denouncing 'heresy' as 'the worst crime that can be' and praising the burning of martyrs like Tewkesbury 'as there was never wretch I ween better worthy'.[5]

Yet More knew he was under suspicion. He had written to Cromwell stating that he never opposed the King's divorce, insisting that he would 'neither murmur at it, nor dispute upon it'. He even described Anne as 'this noble woman really anointed Queen':

> So am I he that among other his Grace's faithful subjects, his Highness being in possession of his marriage and this noble woman really anointed Queen, neither murmur at it nor dispute upon it, nor never did nor will, but without any other manner meddling of the matter among his other faithful subjects, faithfully pray to God for his Grace and hers both long to live and well, and their noble issue too, in such wise as may be to the pleasure of God, honour and surety to themselves, rest, peace, wealth and profit unto this noble realm.[6]

More supported the divorce in the House of Lords, but on 13 April he was summoned before the commissioners at Lambeth Palace for questioning. His protestations of innocence were not believed and four days later he was arrested and sent to the Tower. A week later Barton and her associates were executed for high treason at Tyburn. On 26 April Bishop Fisher refused to acknowledge the Act of Succession and was again imprisoned.

Catherine was now housed at Kimbolton under the watchful eye of her governor, Sir Edmund Bedingfield. He had the task of trying to prevent all contact with the King's enemies but, as he told Cromwell, 'my fidelity in executing the orders of the King renders me no favourite with the Princess Dowager, therefore she conceals everything from me'.

This duplicity was characteristic of Catherine. She had always claimed to be subservient and obedient to Henry, but this was demonstrably untrue. All her life she had been a rebel, resisting her father and Henry VII, fighting to stay in England when she faced being sent home to Spain. She seems to have lied to all the world about the consummation of her first marriage to Arthur and as a young wife, she lied to cover up a false pregnancy and save face. She also fought to protect her rascal of a priest-confessor, Friar Diego, even when all the evidence proved that he was a notorious lecher.

Catherine had always viewed her adopted country as something less than the reunited Spain: an offshore provincial island on the periphery of world politics. That Henry should ever have dared to set aside a woman of her breeding and influence was an insult from which she never recovered. Her arrogance and self-belief turned to bitter resentment against all things English. Since her exile from court she had concentrated all her efforts on promoting her daughter Mary to overthrow the husband who had betrayed her.

Henry now sent the Bishop of Durham, Cuthbert Tunstall, to require her to swear to obey the new Act of Succession, but Catherine lost her temper and assaulted him, raging: 'Hold thy peace, Bishop! These are the wiles of the devil! I am Queen, and Queen I will die! By right, the King can have no other wife.'

When the Bishop recovered, he advised her that to refuse was treason, but Catherine told him she longed to be a martyr. Frustrated, he made her household take the oath, but according to Chapuys Catherine tricked him by having them swear in Spanish, changing the emphasis to make the oath meaningless.

Catherine wrote secretly to her daughter commanding her to follow her example and refuse the oath. This severely compromised Mary, for openly opposing the King would put her in great danger. Up to now she had merely been an irritant, refusing to behave in a civilised manner or to recognise her half-sister Elizabeth. She had thrown teenage tantrums and melodramatically told everyone she would not 'pay court to her unless compelled by sheer force'.[7] But now her mother was telling her to commit treason. This was God's will, Catherine claimed:

Daughter, I heard such tidings today that I do perceive if it be true, the time is come that Almighty God will prove you; and I am very glad of it, for I trust He doth handle you with a good love. I beseech you agree of his pleasure with a merry heart; and be sure that, without fail, He will not suffer you to perish if you beware to offend Him. I pray you, good daughter, to offer yourself to Him. If any pangs come to you, shrive yourself; first make you clean; take heed of His commandments, and keep them as near as He will give you grace to do, for then you are sure armed.

And if this lady [Anne Shelton, Anne's aunt] do come to you as it is spoken, if she do bring you a letter from the King, I am sure in the self same letter you shall be commanded what you shall do. Answer with few words, obeying the King, your father, in everything, save only that you will not offend God and lose your own soul ... one thing I especially desire you, for the love that you do owe unto God and unto me, to keep your heart with a chaste mind, and your body from all ill and wanton company, not thinking or desiring any husband for Christ's passion; neither determine yourself to any manner of living till this troublesome time be past. For I dare make sure that you shall see a very good end, and better than you can desire...

I pray you, recommend me unto my good lady of Salisbury, and pray her to have a good heart, for we never come to the kingdom of Heaven but by troubles. Daughter, whatsoever you come, take no pain to send unto me, for if I may, I will send to you.

Your loving mother, Catherine the Queen.

Little wonder that after receiving this letter Mary suffered an allergic reaction to all the pills she took for stress, headaches and indigestion.

Henry was now being advised by Cromwell, who had been appointed Secretary of State in order to push through the new legislation. Cromwell's aim was to increase and consolidate Henry's power as sovereign. From December plans had been drawn up to transfer much of the Church's wealth to the Exchequer under state control. His *Acta in Consilio Domini Regis* would make Henry the richest prince in Christendom.

Chapuys warned the Emperor in a series of reports: 'What the King intends to do is to usurp part of the Church goods and distribute the remainder to noblemen.' The King 'is very covetous of the goods of the Church, which he already considers his patrimony' and 'intends to take the goods of all the churches'. In the next Parliament Henry 'will distribute among the gentlemen of the kingdom the greater part of the ecclesiastical revenues to gain their goodwill'.[8]

Among these gentlemen were members of the Privy Chamber, including Henry's circle of close companions who enjoyed both access and status and were often in his presence 24 hours a day. Nicholas Carew and Henry Norris had replaced Henry's favourites Compton and Brandon, and there were also Anne's brother George, and Francis Weston, who had taken his place as Henry's favourite page. These men attended Henry day and night, with Norris his most intimate servant as Groom of the Stool, literally in charge of Henry's toilet. Henry had no secrets from this chosen few. They knew all his faults and vices, his health problems, sexual habits and dangerous moods. They lived life on the edge of a volcano; one that would soon erupt and consume them all.

Thomas Cromwell was the odd man out. He had wheedled his way into a position of power by politically radical suggestions which appealed to Henry's autocratic nature. Henry had always believed that the King was God's anointed, but he had grown up as the son of a usurper, whose hold on the crown was constantly under threat. It was through Henry's desire for Anne Boleyn that he was able to grasp the moment and strengthen his own authority by removing the rival power of the Church.

The nobility joined ranks to rid themselves of Wolsey, but now Cromwell showed Henry a way to curb their ambitions.

It has been argued that Cromwell was working to a master plan to centralise power in the hands of the King. More likely, his experience in Italy of Machiavellian *realpolitik* now provided him with solutions that fed Henry's ego in his new role as 'the only Supreme Head on earth of the Church of England'. By centralising political power in the court, the aristocracy would become dependent upon the King's favour and less able to rule their territories as rival private fiefdoms.

It was decided to make an example of William, 4th Lord Dacre, one of Catherine's supporters, who had maintained suspicious links with Scotland and rebels in Ireland. Henry accused him of making 'a wicked and treacherous agreement', dismissed him as Warden of the Western Marches and put him on trial for treason.

But Henry had not calculated that the jury of 24 lords and 12 judges who heard Dacre's seven-hour speech in defence would unanimously acquit him. They saw the attack on him as a presage of a more general assault on their own interests. Over the next few years the new measures would result in uprisings among the old Catholic nobility in northern England and Ireland.[9]

Henry was happy to let Cromwell take the reins of his administration. Reports in the Low Countries record that the King was more in love with Anne than ever and always at her side. By the spring Anne's condition was obvious. Henry had told Chapuys that he was convinced that this time they would have a son and heir. He had ordered a lavish cradle made of silver and jewelled Tudor roses from Cornelius Hayes.[10]

Sir William Kingston noted that 'the Queen hath a goodly belly… Our Lord to send us a prince'.[11] Lady Lisle, wife of the Governor of Calais, sent Anne the gift of a songbird which 'the Queen liked … very well … which doth not cease at no time to give her Grace rejoicing with her pleasant song'. Earlier Lady Lisle had sent a pet dog to Sir Francis Bryan 'which the Queen liked so well that she took it from him before it had been an hour in his hands'.

The little dog became a favourite, like her greyhound, Urian, and was named Purkoy.

Anne refused the gift of a monkey, for she 'loveth no such beasts nor can scant abide the sight of them'.[12]

Anne had dispelled the disappointment of her first pregnancy, becoming absorbed with her daughter Elizabeth and the necessity of ensuring her recognition as Henry's heir. Yet the new pregnancy must have come as a relief, not only proof of Anne's fertility but surely a sign of God's grace.

Anne was with Henry at Hampton Court late in June. He had arranged to go to Calais to meet Francis in August, but early in July Henry sent Anne's brother George to Margaret, Queen of Navarre, to postpone the summit.[13]

Shortly before the time came for her official confinement, it seems that Anne went into labour.

A birth at seven months is always dangerous and this was no exception. The Queen's illness was kept strictly secret and we have no official record of what happened, but Anne must have lost her child.

Perhaps she had exerted herself too much, but, whatever the explanation, this tragedy would have been a devastating blow to both parents.

Henry set out on the summer progress alone, with Anne joining him later.[14]

It was 23 September before the court finally discovered that the Queen was no longer pregnant. If her pregnancy had been known in December then she should have gone into confinement by early August at the latest. Yet it was nearly two months later when Chapuys realised something had gone wrong.[15]

Doubts about Henry's virility were voiced once again. Now people were asking whether Catherine had been to blame after all for the lack of an heir. This doubt is sustained by recalling that during the Blackfriars trial the King had told Parliament that he was not marrying Anne simply out of passion, 'for I am 41 years old, at which age the lust of man is not so quick as in lusty youth'.

Henry had also argued with Chapuys in April 1533 when he had retorted: 'Am I not a man like other men? Am I not? Am I not?'[16]

Of all his wives and acknowledged mistresses only four are known to have conceived: Catherine, Anne, Jane and Bessie Blount. Mary Boleyn had two children, Catherine and Henry, both said to be the King's, but he never officially recognised them. Henry had to consult his doctors after marrying Anne of Cleves because he never 'took any from her by true carnal copulation'. Dr Chamber 'counselled his majesty not to enforce himself, for eschewing such inconveniences as by debility ensuing in that case were to be feared'. He reported that Henry could not 'be provoked or stirred to that act'.[17]

It was alleged that Anne herself had said Henry was impotent: '*Le Roy n'estoit habile en cas de soy copuler avec femme et qu'il n'avoit ne vertu ne puissance.*' It was presumed that it was out of delicacy that she used French to say her husband lacked both skill (*vertu*) and power (*puissance*).[18]

There could have been medical reasons for his problem. We know that in 1528 Henry had recommended to a friend a cure for a tumour of the testicles after suffering bladder trouble himself. Henry had also taken a heavy fall when jousting, which provoked a leg ulcer which failed to heal. This osteomyelitis has led to the conclusion that Henry could have suffered from syphilis.

An epidemic of syphilis had spread across Europe through the armies of Charles V. One theory is that the disease was brought back from the discovery of Africa or the Americas. Migraines, intense fevers and pains in the joints were all symptoms. Mood swings, insanity and sterility were others. Victims were treated with contempt:

> This pestilent infection of filthy lust is a sickness very loathsome, odious, troublesome and dangerous, which spreadeth itself throughout all England and overfloweth as I think the whole world. It is testimony of the just wrath of God against that filthy sin of fornication, the original cause of this infection, that breedeth it, that nurseth it, that disperseth it.

William Clowes called his patients 'lewd wicked beasts' who should be executed as 'a terror to the wicked, the rather to abstain ... from such abominable wickedness'.[19]

Francis I was heavily infected with syphilis, caught from his mistress '*La Belle Ferronnière*'. Henry had shared more than one mistress with him, including Mary Boleyn. When he died his corpse was so putrid that it had to be placed in a lead coffin and no one dared attend the funeral. But Henry's apothecaries' records do not tally with those of a sufferer using the typical mercury cure.[20]

Yet in spite of the rumours about Henry's disabilities, Chapuys was claiming once again that the King was unfaithful to Anne. He asserted that his latest unknown mistress was 'a very beautiful and adroit young lady for whom his love is daily increasing'. He concluded that Henry regretted his marriage to Anne. He also reported that Anne was so jealous that she had asked her sister-in-law, Jane Lady Rochford, to remove her rival from court.[21]

Jane Parker, the daughter of Henry Parker, 8th Lord Morley, had married George Boleyn in 1525. It was not a happy marriage. She was a devoted supporter of Catherine and of Catholic beliefs, quite opposed to her husband and in-laws. Anne had made her one of her ladies, but Jane never shared the friendship of the Queen, as suggested by Chapuys. It is highly doubtful that Anne would ever have confided in her antagonistic and bitter sister-in-law about her husband, his virility or his mistresses.

It was the function of an ambassador to act the role of spy and *agent provocateur*, spreading rumours and supplying false information in the service of his own national interests. An ambassador was required to dissemble, as Sir Henry Wotton said: 'An ambassador is an honest man sent abroad to lie for the good of his country.'

Chapuys was a master in this art. Heavily dependent upon paid informers because he could not speak the language, he conveyed a mangled understanding of events within the King's most intimate circles that can only be regarded with the utmost suspicion.

That autumn the Emperor complained that Catherine was sick and had been ill-treated, which Henry denied furiously. Clearly, Chapuys had been feeding Charles with stories and rumours designed only to enflame his master's outrage with England. Mary also complained how she had been slighted and forced to take second place to her half-sister like a servant. Yet during the summer she had travelled to Richmond in a velvet litter, just like Elizabeth.[22]

That September, when she was ill, she wanted Catherine to visit her. She claimed to be in fear of poisoning and predictably she put the blame on Anne. Mary had taken pills made up for her by an apothecary, 'after which she was very sick and he so much troubled that he said he would never minister anything to her alone'.[23] He was evidently terrified that his patient would accuse him of trying to murder her.

Poison was considered by the English to be a foreign and alien way of acting against your enemies. Herbs such as meconium, henbane, white water hemlock and mandragora could be used to kill or maim. Poison spread on the leaves of a book or the point of a stiletto blade may have been used in the Italian states and France, but they were not the English way to murder. Mary's head had been filled with tales from her mother's Spanish servants and frightening warnings from Chapuys, designed to turn her against her own father. Given Mary's hypochondria, perhaps inherited from Henry, it was easy to create an imagined menace.

On 25 September Pope Clement died, to be replaced by Cardinal Farnese as Paul III. In England the news was received with hope that there might still be some way for reconciliation, with Norfolk approaching the King to make the first move. But one of the first acts of the new pontiff was to finalise Henry's excommunication. Norfolk was soundly rebuked for his suggestion.

In France the religious authorities were now emboldened to take action against reformers. When posters appeared on the streets attacking the Catholic mass, they alleged a Lutheran conspiracy to overthrow Francis I. This 'Night of the Placards' on 24 October convinced Francis to begin a new wave of persecution: 'Let all be seized, and let Lutheranism be totally exterminated!'

A reign of terror began as mobs took to the streets, encouraged by their priests. Their shouts of 'Death, death to the heretics!' reached even the court of the King's evangelical sister, Margaret of Navarre. Her three chaplains, Roussel, Berthaud and Courault, had been seized and now she herself was accused as 'the greatest heretic'. The Constable Montmorency warned the King that: 'He must begin at his own court and especially with his nearest relations if he had a mind to extirpate the heretics out of his kingdom.'[24]

Margaret fled Paris with many of her fellow believers, seeking refuge in her kingdom of Navarre in the Pyrenees. Her daughter Jeanne d'Albret would follow her mother's example in promoting reform and was later murdered for her faith by Catherine de Medici, who sent her a pair of poisoned gloves.

Shortly afterwards the Admiral of France, Chabot de Brion, visited England and was fêted at a state banquet. Anne seems to have taken this opportunity to speak with him, perhaps asking for details of recent events in France. She must have been deeply concerned about the persecution of her fellow believers. Chapuys reports that Chabot treated the Queen coldly.[25]

France was soon to show its true colours. Chabot announced that his King had accepted the new Pope's validation of Catherine's marriage and therefore Anne was not Henry's lawful wife. This could only be seen as betrayal by the French.

Chabot's news put a hold on Henry and Anne's hopes for the betrothal of Elizabeth to one of Francis's sons. From a very early age little Elizabeth became a pawn in her father's strategy. She had been proudly shown off 'quite naked' to a French delegation as the opening move in negotiations for a marriage with the Duke of Angoulême.

In early October, aged 13 months, she was weaned from her wet nurse. This decision was taken at the highest level, put before the King by the Comptroller of the Household, Sir William Paulet.[26]

While Elizabeth remained their only child, Henry and Anne realised it was more important than ever that their marriage be accepted. It was a dynastic necessity.

Parliament now passed a series of acts establishing Henry's control of the Church in England and making it high treason

> to maliciously wish, will or desire by words or writing or by craft imagine, invent, practise or attempt any bodily harm to be done or committed to the King's most Royal person, the Queen's or their Heirs Apparent, or deprive them or any of them of their dignity, title, or name of their royal estates, or slanderously and maliciously publish and pronounce by expressed writing or words, that the King, Our Sovereign Lord, should be heretic, schismatic, tyrant, infidel, etc.[27]

Other acts followed. The Heresy Act, denying the authority of the Pope, and the Act for Submission of Clergy, designed to curb the excesses of the priesthood.

It was now a capital crime to refuse to acknowledge Henry as head of the Church or to contest the line of succession. Cromwell ensured that this would be policed by having 'substantial persons in every good town to discover who speaks or preaches thus'.[28] As a result thousands took the oath, while the few opponents of the new order were arrested. Two friars preaching in support of the Pope were hunted down from Cornwall to Wales. A loose-tongued abbot had rashly said that: 'The King's grace was ruled by one common stewed whore, Anne Bullan.' Another priest, Robert Feron, called her 'the King's wife in fornication; this matron Anne, be more stinking than a sow', while a Suffolk woman, Margaret Chanseler, had called the Queen a 'goggle-eyed whore'.[29]

How popular or unpopular was Anne? In London there were many evangelicals who had lined the streets for her coronation and gave her their wholehearted support in her work for reform and many acts of charity. In other parts of the country she was unknown except for the news reported and stories that filtered through to them. Not everything they heard was accurate, but how much rumour was started by dissidents and Imperial agents? The Catholic lobby was gaining confidence. Anne's failure to produce a male heir meant that her position remained precarious. While Henry lacked a son there could be no uncontested successor for his crown, and Anne's daughter was still threatened by the older, former heir, Mary.

Anne became more protective of Elizabeth, afraid for her safety. She saw that there were forces at work to subvert Henry's reforms and turn back the clock by restoring the old religion and those who had wielded power through its long-established but corrupt traditions. Among these were her very own relatives, her uncle Norfolk and his wife, who still viewed their Boleyn in-laws as upstarts and dangerous 'heretics'.[30]

Anne realised that she was in an increasingly isolated position in the venomous atmosphere of court politics. She was safe only as long as Henry remained in love with her. Therefore it must have been wonderful news when she discovered that once again she was pregnant.

That Christmas the King and Queen kept 'great house', with Henry in 'his most hearty manner'. The celebrations were only spoilt when Purkoy fell out of a window. Anne had 'set much store' on the dog and Henry had to break the news to her. It may be that this was no accident but a warning to the Queen, as shown by Chapuys' sinister description of the King and Queen's shock being 'like dogs falling out of a window'. Such an incident could easily have brought on a miscarriage, which was perhaps the intention.[31]

The French envoy and treasurer of Brittany, Palamedes Gontier, describes meeting Anne briefly on 2 February and reports that she seemed anxious and exhausted. The Queen was 'not at her ease' and he says she told him the delay in negotiations for Elizabeth's marriage had 'caused and engendered in the King her spouse many strange thoughts, of which there was great need that a remedy should be thought of... [or she was] destroyed and lost, for she found herself quite near to that, and more in pain and trouble than she had been since her espousals'.

Anne was alarmed about her safety. She had 'doubts and suspicions' about Henry. Her movements had been restricted and she could not speak freely 'for fear of where she was and of the eyes that were watching her countenance ... she could not write, could not see me, and could no longer talk with me'.[32]

More bad news had come from France the previous month. The persecution of evangelical Christians continued with mass executions on 21 January. Francis himself attended the spectacle, declaring: 'Lutherans still swarming in the realm.' He threatened reformers: 'I warn you that I will have the said errors expelled and driven from my kingdom, and will excuse no one.'[33]

Anne was outraged at the news: 'She has been in a bad humour and said a thousand shameful words of the King of France and the whole nation.'[34]

That spring there were executions in England too. The Prior of the Charterhouse and four Carthusian monks were executed at Tyburn for treason. The hideous spectacle was designed to terrify the watching crowds. The condemned men were dragged through the crowded streets and hanged until they were half-dead. Then they were cut down and while still living suffered castration and the drawing of their entrails. Finally, they were beheaded and their corpses quartered for display around London as a warning to others.

For centuries this had been the accepted punishment for commoners who were traitors. Their rotting heads, set on spikes, were the first thing seen by travellers passing through the city gates. But in this case the fact that it was monks who had suffered this fate became a *cause célèbre*.

But Henry had not turned Protestant. His persecutions were even-handed. After the execution of the monks, it was now the turn of evangelicals to suffer. Twenty-three refugees from the Lowlands, including three women, who had fled to England for safety were arrested and tried as 'heretics' at St Paul's. They were Anabaptists, who believed baptism was not for babies but for adults when they made a commitment of faith. Fourteen were sentenced to burn at the stake, at Smithfield in London and other towns throughout the realm.[35]

On 20 May Pope Paul III created seven new cardinals, including the French envoy, Jean Du Bellay, and Catherine's advocate, Fisher, as Cardinal of St Vitalis. Henry's envoy De Casale told the Pope: 'Your Holiness has never committed a more serious mistake than this.'

It was very clearly a political rebuff to England and provoked immediate retaliation. On 17 June Fisher was taken to Westminster on trial for high treason.

An Act of Attainder took away his office as bishop and he was therefore tried by jury as a commoner and found guilty. Because of Fisher's age – he was 76 – Henry waived the commoner's sentence of hanging, drawing and quartering and on 22 June the bishop was beheaded on Tower Hill. This still sent a shock wave throughout the Catholic courts of Europe. The Vatican now moved against Henry with impunity. At the end of August he was excommunicated from the Roman Church for a second time, so becoming an international pariah.[36]

There was now a massive Catholic conspiracy against England by the European superstate uniting Spain, France and the Papacy. The plan was to depose Henry and replace him with his daughter Mary, who would restore England to the Catholic faith. As an excommunicate, Henry had no right or title to the crown and therefore any rebellion would be sanctioned by the Pope. Mary could be married off to a Catholic prince who would then claim the English crown on his wife's behalf and invade the country in her name. England would become swallowed up as part of the great Holy Roman Empire.

But first Mary must be smuggled out of England and taken abroad. The plans had been in the making for months past. She was at Eltham that spring and it was seen as an excellent opportunity to get her out of the palace by night or while 'going out to sport'. She would then ride to the Thames at Gravesend, taking a boat to board a Spanish warship waiting in the estuary. 'Several Spanish ships' were already on standby.[37]

Chapuys told Granvelle, the Emperor's minister, that the plan

> is very hazardous, but would be a great triumph and very meritorious... she thinks of nothing else than how it may be done, her desire for it increasing every day... If I were to tell you the messages she sent me, you could not refrain from tears, begging me to have pity on her, and advise her as I thought best, and she would obey.[38]

Charles showed less enthusiasm for the plan. On 10 May he warned Chapuys that escape 'is a very difficult and hazardous matter, not to be attempted without good and sure means for its accomplishment; at all events, it would be inadvisable at this time'.[39] He was preoccupied with the Islamic threat on his southern flank, where his troops were preparing for an attack on the Turks in Tunis, their North African stronghold and centre for slavery.

Mary's various illnesses impeded her chances of making the dangerous journey, but she had no qualms about participating in the plan to overthrow the King, her father. She wrote to Chapuys, 'begging him most urgently to think over the matter, otherwise she considered herself lost, knowing that they wanted only to kill her'.[40]

She claimed that after the execution of the Carthusian monks, Lady Shelton was 'continually telling her to take warning by their fate'. Her mother Catherine complained of 'heresies' spreading among the English people. She lamented that she had so few supporters. She wrote in secret to Chapuys:

Mine especial friend,

You have greatly bound me with the pains that you have taken in speaking with the King my lord concerning the coming of my daughter unto me...

As to my seeing of her, you shall certify that, if she were within one mile of me, I would not see her... Howbeit, you shall always say unto his highness that the thing which I desired was to send her where I am... Here have I, among others, heard that he had some suspicion of the surety of her. I cannot believe that a thing so far from reason should pass from the royal heart of his highness; neither can I think that he hath so little confidence in me. If any such matter chance to be communed of, I pray you say unto his highness that I am determined to die in this realm; and that I, from henceforth, offer mine own person for surety, to the intent that, if any such thing should be attempted, that then he do justice of me, as of the most evil woman that ever was born.

The residue I remit to your good wisdom and judgment as unto a trusty friend, to whom I pray God give health.

Catherine the Queen.

Her protests to Henry that she would never countenance a rebellion meant little to the King when he knew for a fact that she was involved in secret negotiations with his enemies.

Catherine and Spain were 'waging war' on Henry and Anne. Lord Bray of Vachery, of the Catholic faction, wanted Chapuys to get hold of the Flanders proclamation that England was on the point of revolution to overthrow Henry. He used code in the secret correspondence, asking for military support from the Emperor, including ships with troops to sail up the Thames to seize London.

In June the King sent a deputation of his Council to Kimbolton to search Catherine's suite for anything incriminating that might be hidden there. Cromwell saw both Mary and her mother as obstacles to acceptance abroad of Henry's marriage to Anne. Without them, relations with the Emperor and the Pope could only improve. On 30 June Cromwell told him that 'if God had taken to Himself the Queen, the whole dispute would have been ended, and no one would have doubted or opposed the King's second marriage or the succession'.

Chapuys reported this as a veiled threat.[41]

Henry feared revolt and a foreign invasion. Imperial ships were at the mouth of the Thames. German mercenaries could land in Scotland or the north. Mary was not only a danger to Elizabeth, but a rival to Henry. Anne believed that while Catherine lived, her own life was in danger. She accused mother and daughter of conspiring her death and of their daughter Elizabeth and the child she now carried.[42]

Yet tragedy must have struck again, for nothing else is known of Anne's third pregnancy. We know that in April the Queen had been obliged to move palaces because one of her ladies had caught measles, but whether this might have triggered a miscarriage is unknown. What we do know is that she was with the court in July and later that month accompanied the King on the summer progress.[43]

On 1 July Thomas More was brought to trial for treason in Westminster Hall. He was charged that he had accepted bribes when Chancellor and admitted receiving a gilt cup from an interested party. When news of this broke, Anne's father was said to have exclaimed of his old enemy: 'Lo! did I not tell you, my Lords, that you would find this matter true?'

But More now found himself in a more dangerous position on the one point of law he had carefully avoided. In treason trials the accused had no right to call witnesses and could only defend himself from the dock. Now More chose to stay silent, afraid that out of his own mouth he would condemn himself.

He never opposed the King's supremacy over the Church, or his marriage to Anne, but refused only to swear an oath imposed by the civil authorities – a lawyer's distinction which failed to convince his judges.[44]

The executioner's axe was turned towards him as the guilty verdict was given.

Even if More was not the close confidant and companion of the King that his son-in-law later claimed him to be, he knew Henry's character well enough to acknowledge that even as he could put an arm around his shoulders he would have his head if it 'could win him a castle in France'. On 6 July, while the King hunted at Reading, More was beheaded on Tower Hill, asserting he died 'the King's good servant, but God's first'.

Anne's later detractors claimed that, like some Salome, she had demanded More's head. But even her worst enemy Chapuys never once said it was Anne's responsibility. For it was plain to everyone at court that Henry was so enraged by the Pope's decision to excommunicate him and to make Fisher a cardinal that he must retaliate by making a supreme example of his opponents. Of More, Henry himself concluded, 'that never was there servant to his sovereign so villainous nor subject to his prince so traitorous as he.'[45]

Days later Chapuys reported that Henry was still celebrating and dancing. He was so supportive of his Queen that when his fool, Will Sommers, made a rash joke, he promptly sent him away in disgrace. Some stories claim that Henry had him killed for calling the Princess Elizabeth a bastard. Either way, the King still clearly loved and protected Anne.[46]

Although it was one of the wettest summers on record, everyone was in good humour as Henry and Anne set out on progress through the countryside. Not only the royal party but a vast convoy of courtiers and hangers-on attended the King and Queen on their tour. A royal progress was a vast operation in logistics, the party arriving at a succession of castles and mansions, often as guests of noblemen and those seeking the King's favour, eating and drinking through a year's provisions and often nearly bankrupting their hosts as a consequence.

The King and Queen would show themselves at a few state functions or relax with hunting and banquets. After five or six days the whole cavalcade moved on, descending on another honoured family.

On 4 September the royal train found its way to Savernake in Wiltshire, to the manor of Wolf Hall, home of the Seymour family.

Sir John Seymour was Sheriff of Wiltshire, Dorset and Somerset and an able local administrator. He had married Margaret, called Margery, the daughter of Sir Henry Wentworth of Nettlestead in Suffolk, around 1500. Before her marriage the poet John Skelton had written a poem, 'To Mistress Margery Wentworth', praising her 'benign, courteous and meek' qualities.

Sir John was incredibly prolific. Of the ten children born of the marriage, four died young, probably of plague. Two of the surviving sons, Edward and Thomas, were political animals, while Henry shunned public life. The daughters included Elizabeth, just widowed, Dorothy and Jane.

The visit of the King and Queen was something of a surprise given the great scandal that attached to the Seymour name. Even the world-weary and promiscuous court of Henry had been shocked when it was revealed that the marriage of the eldest son, Edward, was a sham and masked an incestuous affair between his wife and his own father. The two sons born to Katherine Seymour, John and Edward, were actually not his children at all, but his father Sir John's.

The discovery of this terrible secret came as a devastating blow to Edward Seymour and marked his character for life. All of this was quite recent, the children being born in 1528 and 1529. Edward rejected Katherine and put aside her children, cutting them out of any inheritance. She entered a convent, where she died soon afterwards, leaving him free to marry again. His new bride was the steely and opinionated Anne Stanhope.

All of this was still very much alive in the memories of the court as they came to Wolf Hall. An awkward atmosphere still prevailed between the lecherous Sir John and his wronged eldest son. Edward Seymour was a young protégé of Wolsey, knighted while still a teenager on military campaign in 1522. He became one of Henry's Esquires of the Body in 1530 and was in Calais with the King two years later. Ambitious and shrewd, Edward had been gaining influence in the West Country as well, buying up property and getting into vicious land disputes where, according to Cromwell, he had acted 'very craftily'. He travelled to Wolf Hall from Elvetham, his own home nearby, to meet the King.[47]

Hardly had Henry arrived at Wolf Hall when a messenger arrived from London with serious news from abroad. Emperor Charles had defeated the Islamic forces at Tunis. Although Barbarossa had escaped to Algiers, the Imperial forces had captured thousands of prisoners and much of the fleet. This victory, although very welcome to the leaders of Christendom, was seen as a setback to Henry. It meant that now Charles was no longer preoccupied with battle, he would have more time to pay attention to England and a possible invasion. Now that the Pope had excommunicated Henry there was real danger of Catholic Europe uniting in a 'holy war' against England to put Mary on the throne.[48]

The King was fully aware that Catherine and his daughter were conspiring against him. He had them closely watched and kept them apart so that they could not plot together, but clearly there were others at court capable of stirring up trouble.

Henry sent Bishop Gardiner to France to try to get an alliance against the Emperor. He was even willing to pay for a French army.[49] Henry and Anne masked their frustration at the news of Charles's victory and after just a few days at Wolf Hall the court moved on, arriving in Winchester by 2 October, when Sir Richard Grenville records: 'The King and Queen is merry and hawks daily and likes Winchester and that quarter and praises it much.'

Sir Anthony Windsor confirmed that 'The King and Queen were very merry in Hampshire.' They stayed with Lord Sandes at his house, The Vine, between 15 and 19 October and returned to Windsor by the 26th. Sometime during this happy progress Anne became pregnant for the fourth time.[50]

Meanwhile Catherine harangued the Pope to invade England: indisputably an act of high treason. Embittered and furious, she threw caution to the wind, despising the English as wayward sheep who needed a leader: 'We await a remedy from God and from Your Holiness... It must come speedily or the time will be past!'

Although Mary was sick again she also protested about the delay in plans to get her out of England. She distrusted Chapuys and sent directly to the Emperor, bypassing his ambassador, who, she insisted, was half-hearted in his mission. She warned her cousin that his victory against Islam would be as nothing compared with supporting her bid to take the English throne, which would bring him far more glory. He must 'take brief order and apply a remedy' or their cause would be lost.[51]

That Catherine and Mary were a real threat to England was clear. Chapuys sat at the centre of an espionage ring and in November his agent in the royal household, the Marchioness of Exeter, informed him that the King had spoken in the Privy Council of 'this trouble and fear and suspicion' spread by Imperial agents.

Henry laid the blame squarely at Catherine's door. No longer would he tolerate the danger she posed to the country and to his person, but in the new session of Parliament he would rid himself of both Catherine and Mary. They would become an example of what happened to traitors. It had been said that he had started his reign as gentle as a lamb and would end it more fiercely than a lion.[52]

This appears to have coincided with Anne's discovery that she was again pregnant. This time surely she would bear a son. Their hopes were high, Chapuys reported.[53]

Yet Anne feared an Imperial plot to poison her or her daughter Elizabeth. Chapuys blamed Anne for the King's threat to remove his former wife and daughter: 'the Concubine has for some time conspired for the death of the Queen and her daughter'. He alleges that Anne said of Catherine: 'She is my death, and I am hers… She will be the cause of my death unless I get rid of her first … but I will so manage that if I die before her, she shall not laugh at me.'[54]

But Charles was sceptical of any real intention to harm Catherine and Mary: 'I cannot believe what you tell me. The King cannot be so unnatural as to put to death his own wife and daughter…

'The threats of which you speak can only be designed to frighten them.'

He said they should yield to Henry's will rather than put themselves in danger.

Nevertheless, in December he issued orders to his Captain General in Flanders, the Count de Roeulx, to prepare for Mary's arrival.[55]

Catherine was suffering from chest pains, perhaps cancer, and had taken to her chamber. She believed that God was punishing her for the sins of her father. She was remembering when her father, King Ferdinand, had insisted that before her marriage to Arthur, Henry VII must execute the Yorkist pretenders who threatened his throne, the Earl of Warwick and 'Perkin Warbeck' (possibly Richard, Duke of York, one of the 'Princes in the Tower').[56]

Henry heard regular reports of her illness. Her Spanish doctors, Miguel de la Saa and Balthasar Guersye, claimed that 'if the sickness continueth in force, she cannot remain long'. Accordingly, at New Year Sir Edmund Bedingfield informed Cromwell that the Princess Dowager was 'in great danger of life'.[57]

Chapuys got permission to visit Kimbolton. It was several years since he had last seen Catherine and he was alarmed to find her 'so wasted that she could neither stand nor sit up in her bed'. He spent a few days with her and carried the last letter she ever wrote back to the King. Typically, Catherine had even lectured Henry from her deathbed, urging him to remember

the health and safeguard of your soul…before the care and pampering of your body, for the which you have cast me into many calamities and yourself into many troubles…

I make this vow that mine eyes desire you above all things.

Farewell. Catherine the Queen.

She died on 7 January 1536.

Henry was delighted at the news, 'like one transported with joy'. His first words were of obvious relief: 'God be praised that we are free from all suspicion of war!' He seized little Elizabeth and carried her around for the court to admire. He planned a magnificent banquet on 9 January and a great jousting tournament on St Paul's Eve, 24 January.

For eight years Catherine had been responsible for denying Henry peace and concord in the realm. Her stubborn resistance to his will, refusing to accept the annulment of her marriage – as many others had done – had undermined the Catholic Church, made Henry into a totalitarian tyrant and brought England to the verge of civil war. It was little wonder that he now chose to celebrate. Chapuys reports:

> the King dressed entirely in yellow from head to foot, with the single exception of a white feather in his cap. His bastard daughter Elizabeth was triumphantly taken to church to the sound of trumpets and with great display. Then, after dinner, the King went to the hall where the ladies were dancing, and there made great demonstrations of joy, and at last went to his own apartments, took the little bastard in his arms, and began to show her first to one, then to another, and did the same on the following days.[58]

Elizabeth was two and a half years old, already bright and 'noticing'. Did she perhaps remember this occasion with her father holding her proudly in his arms and Anne watching, perhaps carrying a brother for her?

Anne now took pity on her stepdaughter, writing to Mary about her mother's death, wanting to be a 'second mother' to her, adding she would be welcome at court. Mary rudely refused. But even then Anne did not give up her attempts to win her round. She wrote again to Lady Shelton, hoping she could persuade Mary to change her attitude. Mary did not even reply but smuggled a copy of this letter to Chapuys.[59] On 29 January 'our dearest sister, the Lady Catherine', the Dowager Princess of Wales, was buried in an elaborate ceremony in the abbey at Peterborough.

Five days earlier the King himself had received a greater shock. The great jousting tourney he had planned for St Paul's Eve nearly caused his death when he fell heavily and lay unconscious for two hours.[60]

Henry was nearly 45 and unfit for such strenuous activities. When ordering a new suit of armour the year before, his waist measured 54 inches. But Henry was loath to admit that his youth had vanished. Balding, gross and often in pain from his leg ulcer, he still clung desperately to the fading image of the blond, bluff giant, the people's favourite.

The watching crowd were shocked as he was borne away from the tiltyard. There were immediate rumours that the King was dead.

Norfolk rushed to break the news to Anne. We do not know whether she had been watching or what her uncle may have told her as he hurried with his news. Did he perhaps tell her that Henry was dead? It would have been the kind of crass lack of concern for a pregnant woman that was typical of Thomas Howard. Whatever he said, it was clearly too much of a shock. Anne miscarried.

After some two hours Henry recovered his senses and the official word went out that the King had 'taken no hurt'. Hall records that the King 'fell so heavily that everyone thought it a miracle he was not killed, but he sustained no injury'. But it was too late for his son. Anne miscarried 'a child who had the appearance of a male about three months and a half old, at which miscarriage the King has certainly shown great disappointment and sorrow'.[61]

Chapter Twelve

The Rival

O N THIS OCCASION Anne's miscarriage was not kept secret because the Queen had collapsed in public and became the immediate subject of news. It has since been surrounded in wild speculation and myth, with fantastic stories born out of hindsight.

Chapuys insisted that Anne had never been pregnant at all because he had been reporting for months that Henry no longer had any interest in her.[1] This was nonsense. The King and Queen had been inseparable during the summer progress, with the result that she was three and a half months pregnant by late January 1536.

Later commentators, likewise Anne's enemies, do not deny that she was pregnant but invented intimate conversations between husband and wife as a result of the miscarriage. Nicholas Sander and Jane Dormer, who both detested everything Anne stood for, created dramatic arguments during which the King savagely refused to sleep with her again.

Henry was alleged to have cried: 'I see clearly that God does not wish to give me male children. You will get no more sons from me.' Anne allegedly stood up to him, claiming that he owed her everything. She had been responsible for freeing him from the incestuous marriage to Catherine which had damned him in the eyes of God: 'You should be more bound to me than man can be to woman.'

For commentators writing about these events many years later, it was necessary that the events be made to fit in with the official version of the post-Anne era, when she had become either a non-person or the epitome of evil. By suggesting that Henry had tired of his wife or that she had somehow deceived him, it could be said that Anne 'had miscarried of her saviour'.[2] All the King's actions thus became construed as signs of their estrangement, with his departure for London leaving Anne at Greenwich depicted as a pointer to his disgust with her. The truth is that Henry departed from Greenwich on Shrove Tuesday to open the new session of his Reformation Parliament, and that Anne could not accompany him because for about a month afterwards she was recovering from the miscarriage: she had been 'brought abed before her time with much peril of her life'.[3]

One bearer of tales at the time was Chapuys' spy in the Queen's household, the duplicitous Marchioness of Exeter. She reported a story her husband had heard in the Privy Chamber when Henry allegedly said that God refused to grant him a son and heir. This may very well have been true, but the King is said to have gone on to claim that he had been seduced by Anne – a remarkable suggestion given the seven long years she had resisted his charms: 'I was deceived into this marriage by sorcery... God has shown this to be so because he will not permit me to have sons. I believe I could take another wife.'

On 29 January Chapuys had a secret meeting with Thomas Cromwell, who told him the same story, that Henry had been 'seduced and forced into his second marriage by means of sortileges and charms'. The Imperial ambassador thought this 'incredible', although, since it was from one of the 'principal courtiers', 'authentic'. But he must have been highly suspicious of the reasons why the Secretary of State was breaking such a confidence to an enemy of England. Such suspicion of Cromwell's motives, as we shall see, was fully justified.[4]

Another tale claims that Anne shrugged off the tragedy of her miscarriage, boasting to her ladies that she would soon conceive again: 'It is all for the best. I shall be the sooner with child again, and the son I bear will not be doubtful like this one, which was conceived during the life of the Princess Dowager.'

That Anne would ever cast doubt on the legitimacy of her children is completely unbelievable. This is another fabrication from the

Catholic lobby, which saw Catherine's marriage as valid and Anne's daughter Elizabeth as a bastard.[5]

Anne had no such doubts. The King had overturned a whole system of government in order to bring in a new order confirmed by the Act of Supremacy and Act of Succession, executing dissenters. He had appointed Anne as Regent in the event of his own death, which, on 24 January, had suddenly become a shocking possibility.

Whether Henry was quite so certain is the key question.

Elizabeth's sex had come as a shock, but the tragic loss of a fourth child must have seemed like some portentous omen. Henry could hardly contain the memories of his experiences with Catherine, where pretence and disappointment soon led to bitter frustration. Henry wanted to believe in his divine right as King but had always been insecure about God's support because his father had usurped the crown and murdered every rival, and also because he had been forced to marry his brother's widow, thus bringing a curse on their children.

Henry had been convinced that by putting aside his brother's wife he would gain divine approval for his union with Anne. Had he not restrained himself for seven long years? It was almost biblical. He had waited, just like Jacob, to win the bride to whom he was promised, but now – like Jacob – it seemed the much-desired wife could not live up to her half of the bargain.

Until now it had been impossible for Henry with his vast ego to consider that he might be the cause of these fertility problems, but the cycle of stillbirths and miscarriages seemed to be repeating itself with another wife.

Anne had regularly conceived in the early autumn, when they had returned from their summer progress, where they had been hunting and living in other people's houses.

When she was pregnant all was hopeful, but at other times Henry was moody and spent days 'in the field to divert his ill humour'. Perhaps intermittent sexual problems were one of the causes. Anne and her brother George were said to have discussed Henry's impotency.[6]

Other stories claim that Anne had caught Henry with another woman and her distress provoked the miscarriage: 'Because the love I bear you is much greater and more fervent than Catherine's, my heart broke when I saw that you loved others.'[7]

The question is, why would Henry take other women if he suffered from impotency? Given that he was apparently having difficulties, would he have risked a woman other than his wife discovering his problem and discussing it at court?

The romantic tradition that while on progress the previous September Henry had fallen for plain Jane Seymour does not stand up to close scrutiny. Anne was with him constantly, as recorded, conceiving her fourth child in this period and during the next few months at court they were 'merry' together. Given the crisis in international affairs in the few days that Henry and Anne were staying with the Seymours at Wolf Hall, in September 1535, there was no time at all for a quick wooing.

Henry had no time to even notice Jane Seymour.

Three of the Seymours had returned to court with the King after the progress: Jane and her brothers Edward and Thomas. Henry knew the Seymours very well indeed. Jane was not new to court. She had been there since 1529, when she served Catherine, and was one of Anne's household by the New Year of 1534.[8] Jane Dormer's later account of how Jane first came to court is totally inaccurate. Sir Francis Bryan may have promoted Jane's interests, but he was certainly not her uncle. He had a public quarrel with George Boleyn in what seemed to be a staged demonstration of his break with the Queen's family. His lascivious lifestyle sat ill with Anne's evangelical morals.

Likewise, the story of Jane's broken betrothal appears to be pure fiction. By 1536 she was 28 and still unmarried. Chapuys remarked: 'She is of middle height and nobody thinks she has much beauty. Her complexion is so whitish that she may be called rather pale. She is a little over twenty-five.'[9]

This age is repeated in Nicholas Hilliard's miniature portrait, but this was painted 50 years later, probably based on hearsay. Twenty-nine ladies walked in procession at her death, which also suggests a birth date around 1507.

Holbein's portrait shows a little manikin of a woman lavishly dressed and bejewelled with her distinctive sea-shell headdress. Her face is very plain, with a small, tight-lipped mouth and hard, dark eyes. This formal portrait was based on a preliminary sketch now in the Royal Collection at Windsor.

Chapuys concluded that Jane was not quite as pious or chaste as she liked to appear. He reported scathingly that 'being an Englishwoman and having been so long' at Henry's court, she could not possibly still be a virgin. There were apparently people who could confirm this. He suggested that the King 'may marry her on condition she is a maid, and when he wants a divorce there will be plenty of witnesses ready to testify that she was not'.[10]

It is said that Henry showered Jane with expensive gifts in the hope of getting her into bed. Jane had not scrupled to accept them, while refusing to yield to him.

Henry had given her his portrait set in diamonds, but when he gave a purse of gold, she refused it. She apparently flaunted the locket, constantly looking at the King's picture in front of her mistress the Queen. This kind of behaviour was evidently planned to arouse Anne's jealousy and provoke some kind of hostile reaction. The story from Anne's enemy Sander is that Jane was discovered on Henry's knee and pregnant Anne lost her temper at her bare-faced antics, ripping the locket from about her neck.[11]

When then did these blatant and openly romantic events happen? Did they even happen at all? If it was sometime between October and January, no one seemed to know of it until February. Only in retrospect did commentators claim that their wooing had been blatantly obvious. The French ambassador later claimed that he had seen Henry and Jane together in November and so open was their affair that the court had neglected the Queen in favour of Jane Seymour. Writing in February, Chapuys states the affair began in December, when Anne was pregnant. Then it must have been very short-lived because in January, after Anne miscarried, Henry was away in London while Jane was still at Greenwich with the Queen.

The King had matters other than romance on his mind. He was now desperately in need of funds. Cromwell had pointed out to him that the income of the government was only two-thirds that of the Church, which was England's greatest landowner, with enormous wealth in the form of land, houses and money.[12] Cromwell's report, *Valor Ecclesiasticus*, initiated an inquiry into the abuses of monasteries and convents. Commissioners paid lightning visits around the country, making shocking discoveries.

Their report was presented to Parliament on 4 February. All but the prologue of the Report of the Commission, known as the 'Black Book', was destroyed under the Catholic reign of Mary. Enough survives to give a taste of the alarming revelations that triggered a wave of disgust and outrage against the Church. Far from observing vows of obedience, poverty, and chastity,

> There were found in them not seven, but more than 700,000 deadly sins. Alack! my heart maketh all my members to tremble when I remember the abominations that were there wed out.
>
> O Lord God! ... the iniquities of those religious ... the monstrous lives of monks, friars, and nuns have destroyed their monasteries and churches, and not we.

Moral corruption, venal habits and debauchery were commonplace. Absentee careerists lived off the revenues of sees and parishes they had never even seen.

Monks and nuns confessed to immoral acts, including incest, homosexuality and child abuse. At Langdon Abbey near Dover, Abbot Dyck was discovered *in flagrante delicto*. The monks at Waltham Abbey who visited the convent at Chesham by passing along a narrow path were ambushed by the commissioners. Pregnant nuns were found in various places and at Cartmel one sister had six children. The Abbot of Fountains Abbey kept six women while a prior had seven children.

> Of chastity they monks and nuns make outward shew but very little was fownd amonge them, for it plainlie appered their filthie lusts were not satisfied with maidens wifes and widows but they also practised one with another that detestable sodomitishe and Romishe unnatural Acte whereof St Paul in the first to the Romans [Romans i, 26–7] writeth which was the Cause that horrible vice was made by parliament felonie without helpe or benefit of Clergie.[13]

Pilgrimages were made to shrines such as Canterbury, Walsingham and Compostela to worship saints or to Rome to worship the Pope. Rome was regarded as holy, the 'Eternal City', usurping Jerusalem.

Yet, as Luther found out, the city was more about Mammon than God: 'No one can imagine what sins and infamous actions are committed in Rome; they must be seen and heard to be believed.' The Vatican was at the heart of a bureaucratic business empire controlling millions.

The practice of selling indulgences, whereby sinners could buy redemption if they paid enough money to the Church, was a highly profitable business, bringing in huge revenues. Those who could afford it could also buy a way out of Purgatory, that waiting room of the dead with which priests terrified their congregations. The walls of the cathedrals were painted with graphic images of Purgatory and Hell, with demonic figures torturing those who had not been able to buy their supposed salvation. Tithes were like protection money, taxing the people to buy life after death. Their flocks knew they might sin, receive pardon and then go straight out and sin again. There was no call to reform or to start to live righteously.

The Shrine of Thomas Becket at Canterbury was made of solid gold, rubies, pearls and other jewels, including the diamond known as the Regal of France. The bones of a saint were said to work miracles. People were encouraged in this superstition, grovelling before statues and paying to kiss relics. These included at Marlow the ear of the servant which Peter cut off in Gethsemane (which Jesus had actually restored), some of the Christ child's swaddling clothes and at Peterborough a portion of the five loaves used to feed the 5,000, even a feather from the angel Gabriel's wing. The King himself had given the gift of the 'Crown of Thorns' to Windsor in 1533.

The previous July, when Henry and Anne were in Gloucestershire on progress, the Queen sent her chaplains to nearby Hailes Abbey, famous for its 'holy blood'. They were instructed to 'view, search and examine by all possible means' the authenticity of the relic which was claimed to be the blood of Jesus Christ collected during the crucifixion, which had never congealed since. This was displayed only to those who could pay for a glimpse, making the abbey a fortune from pilgrims. Unfortunately, the Queen's chaplains soon discovered that it was duck's blood, which ran out by a system of hidden levers worked by the monks.

Similarly, Boxley's famous Christ on the crucifix winked at those who paid to see the 'miracle' – thanks to pulleys which made its eyes roll. When he heard all this Henry remarked: 'Upon my word, I do not know whether I ought not to weep rather than laugh, on seeing how the poor people of England have been fooled for so many centuries.'

Such chicanery was proof that the Church ignored biblical warnings against idolatry: 'Do not make graven images' (Exodus 20, 4–5; Psalms 115, 4–8; Isaiah 40, 19–20); 'You were led astray to dumb idols' (1 Corinthians 12, 2); 'idolaters will end in the lake of fire' (Revelation 21, 8).

When Anne told Henry of the trickery at Hailes he ordered that the false relic be removed, but it seems that the monks did this only for a time and it was soon replaced, for they could not afford to lose such a lucrative attraction. Only the dissolution of all monasteries a few years later finally spoilt their business.[14]

The uneducated masses believed what they were told by the priests. They admired the spectacle and colour, the music and rituals. For those who could not read there was no way of testing the validity of teachings by referring to the Bible. Priests were often barely literate, learning their offices by rote, reciting a mantra of prayers in alien Latin. The people had become spectators at the mass, unable to understand the word of God.

Thanks to Anne's influence, Henry was inclining towards greater liberty. In October 1535 Miles Coverdale published a complete Bible in English with a dedication 'Unto the most victorious Prynce and our most gracyous soveraigne Lorde, kynge Henry the eyght ... [and] your dearest iust wyfe and most vertuous Pryncesse, Quene Anne.' Anne's initials were embossed on the cover.

A woodcut attributed to Hans Holbein showed Henry handing the Bible to his lords and bishops from the throne. The name of God is in Hebrew letters at the top of the page, but Henry's name, at the bottom, is even larger.

In early December, when Anne was at Richmond, she visited Syon Abbey. At first the nuns refused to admit her because she was married, but later allowed the Queen to go in, to find the women all prostrate before the altar. Anne asked why they were still using Latin, which they could not understand, when the Scriptures in English were now available. Latimer records that Anne then made 'a brief exhortation' on the stories of immorality which had reached her, bidding them to behave in a more godly manner.

While Anne attacked corrupt Church practices, she also appealed for the preservation of some religious houses: Catesby Priory, which she offered to buy herself, and the convent of Nun Monkton in Yorkshire.[15]

The people had been told that it was through the rituals of the Church that you were saved, but reformers said you simply put out your empty hands to receive this gift from God. They believed that no one needed the intercession of priests, or rituals or ceremonies to get to heaven. The idea that only priests could dispense salvation, that bread could become flesh, the 'Real Presence' in the host at mass, crucifying Christ time and time again, all this was anathema to those who could read the Scriptures for themselves. The doctrine of transubstantiation was, in Luther's words, 'an unspeakable abomination, quite contrary to the principle of justification by faith alone'. The Scripture taught plainly that Christ was sacrificed 'once and for all' and 'one sacrifice for sins forever' (Hebrews 10, 12; 7, 24–27; 9, 27). Ritual had created a mystery religion in which the host in the mass replaced God. The Archbishop of Canterbury, Cranmer, called it a 'confidence trick' and denounced the Pope as the Antichrist. In a sermon in 1535 he announced: 'These many years I had daily prayed unto God that I might see the power of Rome destroyed and … I thanked God that I had now seen it in this realm.'[16]

The entire edifice of the Roman Church was redundant. The theological bankruptcy of late medieval Catholicism and popular anti-clericalism led to rapid expansion of Protestantism and the building of foundations sufficiently strong to resist all subsequent persecution: 'In England as elsewhere, the Protestant Reformation sought first and foremost to establish gospel-Christianity, to maintain the authority of the New Testament over mere church traditions and human inventions.'[17]

The priesthood stood between God and the people, denying access: 'But you have turned from the Way and by your teaching have caused many to stumble' (Malachi 2, 8). Priests were 'the priests of

Jezebel', leading Members of Parliament to cry: 'Let us pull down their houses, and overturn their altars.' These Members fiercely condemned the corrupt priesthood, understanding that only a complete purge of these institutions could cure 'this unthrifty, carnal, abominable living'.

On 11 March 1536 a Bill for the Dissolution of the Monasteries was passed. All religious houses with an income of less than £200 a year must yield their lands to the King for better uses. These numbered fewer than 400, of which only half were immediately shut down. Larger institutions, headed by abbots of the great monasteries, were to be dealt with later.[18]

Catholics argue that the Reformation was rooted only in Henry's will, backed by Cromwell's strong-arm tactics. On the contrary, reform was spreading at grassroots level, particularly in cities and southern England. In Ticehurst in Sussex parishioners openly carried copies of the banned New Testament. There were also many in religious orders who 'sought to put off the habit', including one place, Langley, where 'almost all seek release'. A register at Lambeth records 975 monks who left voluntarily without pensions.[19]

Henry needed the resources of the Church, but Cromwell had major differences with the Queen about where the money should be spent. Anne wanted to influence the policy of the nation in favour of greater education and poor relief. Her charities were already in conflict with clients of Cromwell and he began to resent her growing power.[20]

Chapuys recognised that she was 'the person who manages and orders and governs everything, whom the King does not dare to oppose'. The Bishop of Faenza, papal nuncio in France, was saying the same thing: 'All business passes through the hands of people who depend on the new Queen.'[21]

As Marquess of Pembroke, Anne had already been a power in the land in her own right, a unique situation for any woman. Anne believed she had been placed by God as Queen. Henry had made her more than a consort, crowning her with his crown and by the Act of Succession making her Regent in the event of his death. Anne did not see her role as to be merely a figurehead, but wanted to partner the King to reform and build up the English nation, freeing the people from the shackles of Rome by making great improvements in education and religious instruction.

However much Henry may have shared this progressive vision, his first concern was that Anne should fulfil the traditional role of any wife by providing him with a son and heir, followed by a whole brood of strong, healthy children to make valuable alliances in marriage. He had gambled on a son and heir, but this had now been denied him four times.

Their relationship was changing. Anne had won Henry with her sparkling wit and self-awareness. Her integrity and resolution had been like a breath of fresh air amid the machinations of the court. Her religious scruples and the fortress of her virginity had taunted him until they were so bound together that to retreat would have been the humiliation of King and nation.

He had risked all for her. It was because of Anne that Henry now stood alone against the power of the Holy Roman Empire and the Vatican. It was because of Anne that he was excommunicate, denied the possibility of eternal life, according to Roman tradition. And despite all the changes and reforms, it was still this tradition which superstitiously remained to torment Henry whenever he considered his own mortality.

Anne's independent character, which had been so alluring to him before, now began to irritate. She had proved too clever for Henry. She was more than an equal and too ready to take a lead in political decision-making. Her intellect and involvement in politics and religious reform seemed like presumptuous interference in affairs best left to men. By advancing her appointees, Anne was creating her own power base. This put her into competition not only with Thomas Cromwell but with Henry himself.

Henry said he was 'too old to allow himself to be governed'. Chapuys believed that the King was determined to 'show his absolute power and his independence of anyone'. Henry did 'not choose anyone to have it in his power to command me, nor will I ever suffer it'. D'Aubigny draws the conclusion that:

In the first transports of his affection, Henry had desired to share all the honours of sovereignty with her, and she had taken this high position more seriously than Henry had intended...

This was the beginning of the storm that drove Anne Boleyn from the throne to the scaffold.[22]

Henry's insecurity had always veered towards paranoia. From his youth he had been bred in the dark suspicions of his father's court, where every friend was a potential enemy and even the Queen was suspect. As he grew older he began to demonstrate more traits shared with Henry VII: a miser's attention to money and a usurper's fear of losing his crown. His character had changed, perhaps as a result of the head injuries inflicted by his accidents. He had always been ruthlessly cynical, but from January 1536 his physical and mental health declined. A heightened malice became apparent.

Did he sustain head injuries from the fall at the tournament? He certainly suffered severe headaches and, with the pain from his leg, his temper gave way to terrifying rages against whoever was near. Henry could be malicious, treating those closest to him with open contempt. He called Wriothesley, Cromwell's assistant, 'my pig' and once struck Cromwell about the head and swore at him:

the King beknaveth him twice a week and sometimes knocks him well about the pate; and yet when that he hath been well pummelled about the head and shaken up as it were a dog, he will come out of the Great Chamber shaking off the bush with as merry a countenance as though he might rule all the roost... [he] hath called my lord privy seal villain, knave, bobbed him about the head and thrust him from the Privy Chamber.[23]

It was not only Henry who was traumatised at the thought of his demise. After the King's accident everyone was asking what would have happened if he had died. By law Anne would be Regent for their daughter Elizabeth. For the next decade and more she would rule on Elizabeth's behalf through a council of her own choosing.

Anne's enemies must have trembled at the prospect that the Boleyns, with their evangelical and Protestant beliefs, would take the reins of government. Cromwell increasingly saw the Queen as his rival and a growing danger to his position at the heart of government. Since the previous summer Cromwell had whispered with

Chapuys about his uneasy relations with the Queen. The ambassador reported their strange conversation of June 1535 in which Cromwell claimed that Anne had fallen out with him and bantered that she would have his head. Cromwell had shrugged this off: 'I trust so much on my master that I fancy she cannot do me any harm.' In his report Chapuys showed his disbelief:

> All I can say is that everyone here considers him Anne's right hand... Indeed, I hear from a reliable source that day and night is the Lady working to bring about the Duke of Norfolk's disgrace with the King; whether it be owing to his having spoken too freely about her, or because Cromwell wishes to bring down the aristocracy of this kingdom and is about to begin with him, I cannot say.[24]

Anne was rightly suspicious about Cromwell and his influence on her husband. The idea that Anne and Cromwell were active allies is erroneous. He had been Wolsey's servant after all. It is likely that the Boleyns were always suspicious of Cromwell's evangelical credentials, distrusting his talent for espionage and deceit.

It was not just the channelling of Church funds into the pockets of Henry's cronies but also his alarming interest in opening negotiations with Emperor Charles V that disturbed them.

This would be a complete reversal of foreign policy to date and mean the abandonment of Henry's attempts to join the Protestants of Wittenberg who had established the Schmalkald League. From 1531 Henry had been in communication with them through Robert Barnes, former Cambridge reformer of White Horse Inn fame, who had good relations with the Hanse Steelyard. Calling for a true Church founded on biblical principles, Barnes wrote in his *Supplication to Henry VIII* of 1534: 'they that believe that Christ has washed them from their sins, and stick fast to His merits and to the promise made to them in Him, they are the church'.[25]

Cromwell had used Barnes's contacts abroad to push for a German alliance with Philip Melanchthon, whom his friend Luther once called a 'scrawny shrimp'. It was Melanchthon who had written the Augsburg Confession of 1530, setting out the principles of Lutheran beliefs, a copy of which was sent to Henry by a high-powered delegation from Lübeck and Hamburg which appealed to him to take the vacant throne of Denmark.

Henry wanted the German princes of Hesse, Pomerania, Prussia, Bavaria, Saxony and Poland to know he was 'utterly determined to reduce the Pope's power'. He had boasted to the King of France: 'We shall shortly be able to give unto the Pope such a buffet as he never had before.'

Not everyone was pleased at this prospect. Norfolk had warned the French: 'Things are going at such a rate here that the Pope will soon lose the obedience of England.' English Catholics abhorred the thought of an alliance with the Protestants of northern Europe, but Henry seemed determined to counter the power of the Holy Roman Empire.

Melanchthon wrote to Henry: 'Sire, this is now the golden age for Britain.' He dedicated to the King his 1535 edition of *Common Places*, which became required reading at Cambridge. It was delivered by Alesius, who had been in exile in Saxony. Henry was delighted to welcome Alesius and he became a firm friend of Cranmer, whose secret wife was the daughter of a leading German theologian, and lectured at Cambridge.

Anne and the reform party were active in urging Henry to help the Protestants in Europe, but Melanchthon remained suspicious of Henry's intentions and turned down an invitation to visit England, afraid of a trap. Thomas Boleyn's agent Thomas Tebold relayed information from their exiled friends in Europe on the arrest of reformers, including, in July 1535, William Tyndale himself.

Thomas More had searched for a way to take Tyndale, using friars as spies and mercenaries as reported by Stephen Vaughan. Eventually Henry Phillips betrayed him on the orders of Stephen Gardiner, Bishop of Winchester. Gardiner had been Wolsey's secretary and had hoped to become Archbishop of Canterbury, but was passed over for Cranmer. Gardiner never forgave him for the slight and was determined to use his influence with the King to subvert any Protestant alliance.

Alesius says it was Anne's support for the German Protestants that was the cause of her downfall. As a result of her influence Henry secretly financed Lübeck, a free Imperial state and one of the Hanse towns, in the 'Counts' War', sending money and ships with Bishop Bonner and George Cavendish. English gold paid Frisian *Landsknecht* mercenaries, but the result was defeat when the Duke of Holstein seized the Danish throne first.[26]

Did Cromwell now change his mind about a Protestant alliance? Anne clearly thought so and blamed him for abandoning her fellow reformers. After that betrayal she knew never to trust Cromwell. Also, the King was increasingly unstable in his moods. Anne knew she had enemies, in particular Gardiner, 'Wily Winchester'.

Sir William Paget said Gardiner understood 'his master's nature' but was 'too wise to take upon himself to govern the King'. The Bishop 'with his crafty fetches' had got 'into the King's ear'.[27] When the Germans imposed conditions on any alliance with Henry, it was Gardiner, from France, who warned the King against going too far with these 'heretics'.

The Schmalkald princes wanted some reassurance that Henry and England accepted the Augsburg Confession, where 'the doctrine which is in conformity with Scripture be restored to the whole world'. But Henry was still a Catholic at heart, keeping Catholic rituals and doctrine. He still 'crept to the cross' on Good Friday, went on pilgrimage, revered the mass and believed in the talismanic, magical properties of relics. Ever since the threat of excommunication began to hang over his head he had been superstitiously afraid of the danger to his soul. Perhaps he was still secretly hoping for reconciliation with Rome.

Therefore Henry refused the terms offered, influenced by Gardiner. But the King was cunning, spreading his options. At Christmas 1535 he was still banking on Germany and warned Cromwell that by approaching Chapuys about an Imperial alliance he was exceeding his authority.

Anne's distrust left Cromwell isolated. This base-born figure was the odd man out. Without the Boleyns, he had no natural allies in the Privy Council. He was despised by Norfolk and Gardiner, but he knew what Machiavelli taught:

He who conspires cannot act alone, nor can he take a companion except from those whom he believes to be malcontents, and as soon as you have opened your mind to a malcontent you have given him the material with which to content himself, for by denouncing you he can look for every advantage.[28]

While Catherine was still alive there was an impediment to the restoration of relations with the Emperor, but Chapuys recognised that, 'now that the cause of our enmity no longer exists', there was scope for negotiations.

On the eve of St Matthias, 23 February, Chapuys and Cromwell met in secret at the Church of the Augustine Friars. Cromwell claimed that now he had the full support of the King for such an approach.[29]

How did Chapuys react to Cromwell's news? Could he trust the Secretary of State, the King's right-hand supporter and allegedly a sincere Protestant?

The significance of this meeting was confirmed by Cromwell on that fateful 19 May, when he reminded Chapuys of his prediction that night that Anne would fall.

Alesius later stated unequivocally that it was Anne's support for the Protestants which was the reason why she had to be removed.[30] It was Anne who had persuaded Henry to seek an alliance with the German princes and the English delegation was still at Wittenberg, composed of Henry's experienced ambassador Edward Fox, Bishop of Hereford, and Nicholas Heath, the Cambridge scholar sponsored by Anne's grant, as well as Robert Barnes. On the news of Catherine's death Fox had told the Elector of Saxony:

England is tranquil now. The death of a woman has forever terminated all wrangling. At this moment the creed of Jesus Christ alone is the concern of His Majesty. The King therefore prays you to make an alliance between you and him possible, by modifying a few points of your Confession.

Although Barnes doubted Henry's conversion, Luther was more accommodating to his old enemy: 'It is true that England cannot embrace the whole truth all at once ... but the great doctrines can neither be given up nor modified.'

Negotiations were to continue, with the Protestant faction oblivious to the danger now threatening their patroness, Queen Anne. As the leaders of the Protestant states assembled at Frankfurt, in England a conspiracy was taking shape that would eliminate Cromwell's enemies, exterminating two-thirds of the Privy Council and the Queen herself. The successful draft of the Wittenberg Articles would become the Protestant foundation in England, but prove too late to save its leading proponent, Anne Boleyn.[31]

On 29 February Chapuys had received instructions from the Emperor to pursue an alliance with England. On 3 March Cromwell had begun an assessment of all royal grants of land made to the Boleyns since 1522. This was ominous proof of Cromwell's intention to remove such dangerous rivals.[32]

That Cromwell and the Queen were at loggerheads was confirmed soon afterwards when Chapuys hosted a dinner at his house for his cabal of court spies. These included the Marchioness of Exeter, Thomas Elyot, Lord Montagu and Elizabeth, the Dowager Countess of Kildare, who were all supporters of Imperial intervention to put Mary on the throne and believed 'the whole world of Christendom hangeth yet in balance'.

This group, often characterised as the 'Aragonese faction', was a loose alliance of Catholics who opposed Henry's reforms, for which they blamed Anne and the Boleyns. They included the Chancellor, Thomas, Lord Audley, the King's treasurer, William, Lord Fitzwilliam, and his younger half-brother, Sir Anthony Browne, brought up as Henry's companions and 'minions'. Sent on a diplomatic mission to France in 1519, Browne was ordered home after he lost his temper and struck a colleague. Ironically, it was Thomas Boleyn who saved him by smoothing things over, but Browne's loathing of the French continued unabated. Browne's daughter, Elizabeth, married the Earl of Worcester and acted as a spy in the Queen's household. There was also Sir Edward Neville, Thomas Lord Dacre and the Pole family, the surviving heirs to the House of York.

Chapuys and Montagu reported that the King was looking for a new wife. Since Catherine's death Henry had been a widower in Catholic eyes, free to marry again. As his marriage to Anne was not recognised, Princess Elizabeth was seen as just another royal bastard.

By contrast, they still regarded Mary as his heir, and now that the Pope had excommunicated Henry, she now had a better claim to the English throne than her father. Chapuys claims that Cromwell had told him: 'Although the King has formerly been rather fond of the ladies, I believe he will henceforth live more chastely and not change again.'[33]

Contrary to romantic tradition, it was not an honour for a woman of noble birth to become the King's mistress. This is why Thomas Boleyn had reacted so strongly to the disgrace which Mary had brought on the family. This was why Anne had resisted all but marriage. But now Anne had set the precedent by achieving the impossible: an English noblewoman replacing a foreign princess as Queen.

No one could ever have imagined that a king would put aside a wife of 20 years' standing, and with such high foreign connections, for an unknown Englishwoman. That is why the view of Anne scheming to become Queen is so far-fetched. But once the precedent had been set, it became possible for ambitious families to attempt to promote the daughters of the English nobility to reach for the crown. The Seymours saw this, and later so did the Howards.

Henry needed an heir and the Seymours were notoriously prolific, as their recent scandal had proved. There were those at court who had been waiting for an opportunity to unseat Anne from Henry's affections.

Jane Seymour had lived and served Catherine for many years and the Seymours were still Catholics. Chapuys and the Imperial party now took up Jane's brothers and encouraged their ambitions, convincing them that Anne and her family were dangerous heretics who must be removed.

On 3 March Edward Seymour was appointed to the Privy Chamber, making it simple for him to draw the King's attention to his placid and biddable sister.[34]

Jane was barely literate and uninterested in any of the intellectual pursuits the King had shared with Anne. She was Anne's opposite in her apparent acquiescence and malleable nature, never arguing or daring to contradict the King, but flattering his ego with simpering smiles.

But Jane was as ambitious as her brother. The Seymours and

Chapuys formed an alliance of interests which aimed to use her to bring down the Queen of England and allow the invasion of the country by Imperial forces who wanted to put Mary on the throne. Gardiner, who had stepped into Thomas More's shoes as far as evangelicals were concerned, is cited as one of the ringleaders: 'neither is it unlike, but that Stephen, Bishop of Winchester, being then abroad in an embassy, was not altogether asleep'.[35]

Another party to this conspiracy was Nicholas Carew, brother-in-law of Sir Francis Bryan. They had been the young 'minions' whom Wolsey had exiled briefly in 1518 for overfamiliarity with the King. Carew was one of the King's closest circle, yet working in secret against him, collaborating with Chapuys to give Mary the crown. The ambassador reported in July 1535 that Carew was useful and he would 'keep him in this mood'. When Henry had attacked his fool, Will Sommers, it was Carew who sheltered him in his house. Like the Seymours, Carew was a traditional Catholic who was happy to benefit from the dissolution of Church lands in Surrey and, like them, later proved an opportunist in changing to Protestantism when it served his ambitions.[36]

Jane's meek looks hid a sly and ruthless nature apparently untroubled by qualms of conscience. She was ready to poison Henry's mind against Anne without scruple, regardless of what results might follow. Chapuys could hardly believe his luck. He seemed surprised by her willingness to act as the tool of the Queen's enemies: 'this damsel is quite resolved... I will endeavour by all means to make her continue in this vein.'[37]

It was Carew who coached Jane on how to win the King, yet 'not in any wise to give in to the King's fancy unless he makes her his Queen', for Anne had set the precedent. They assumed that the King was looking for another wife who could give him the son he so wanted, but if Henry was experiencing bouts of impotency, what guarantee did he have that taking a third wife would produce an heir? (In fact it was eight months before Henry managed to get Jane Seymour pregnant.)

By late March Anne recognised that Cromwell had joined her enemies. On 2 April, in a sermon for Passion Sunday, Anne's chaplain, John Skip, preached in the Chapel Royal on the theme 'Which of you convicts me of sin?'. This was Jesus' attack on the liars who spread false tales about him (John 8, 46) and clearly a strong political strike against her own enemies.

Skip preached of good Queen Esther and the deadly plot against her by King Xerxes' councillor, Haman. There could be no doubt in anyone's mind that he was pointing the finger of blame at Cromwell. Haman wanted the destruction of Esther and the Jewish people. Now Skip was warning against a conspiracy aimed at the Protestants around Queen Anne.[38]

Naturally the brave sermon created a sensation. Cromwell must have been appalled that his deception had been revealed. Haman was exposed and paid with his life on the very gallows he had built for Esther's supporters. Cromwell must have been struck with panic that the same fate now awaited him.

If relations between Cromwell and Anne were destroyed, those between Henry and Anne remained strong – at least in public. Cromwell's position was increasingly precarious. When the King returned to Greenwich for Easter, he favoured Edward Seymour by giving him and his wife the suite of rooms connected to his own. The only problem was they were occupied by Thomas Cromwell, who did not take kindly to this very public rebuttal. Coming so soon after Skip's sermon, it made the Secretary of State's future look very black indeed.[39]

On 13 April Cromwell's agent Stephen Vaughan wrote urgently from Antwerp: 'If you will send me a letter for the privy-council, I can still save Tyndale from the stake; only make haste, for if you are slack about it, it will be too late.'

Cromwell did nothing. He did not wish to antagonise the Empire, which controlled the Low Countries, and was cold-bloodedly prepared to sacrifice Tyndale, just as he had with Frith, who had been burned alive.

The next day, Maundy Thursday, Parliament was dissolved for Easter. That Saturday Cromwell told Chapuys that Henry was definitely in favour of an Imperial alliance. The ambassador now asked for an audience with the King to discuss it and Henry granted him a meeting for Tuesday, 18 April.

The events of that day remain a mystery. A series of strange and

unexpected happenings was later said to mark a turning-point and
Anne herself would claim that it was a day of ill omen.

As Chapuys arrived at court, Cromwell delivered a personal message from Henry inviting him to meet the Queen. Chapuys must have
been alarmed, for Cromwell knew very well that he had never met
Anne because the Empire refused to acknowledge her as Henry's wife
and Queen of England. He refused the King's offer, but clearly
Cromwell was under instructions, for he contrived that Chapuys
should come face to face with Anne shortly afterwards. As etiquette
demanded, the Imperial envoy had no choice but to bow to the
Queen before all the court.

The Catholic party were horrified. Chapuys himself was equally
troubled, aware that he had been compromised by the King who had
forced him to acknowledge Anne for the first time as Queen. He must
also have suspected that Cromwell had been deceiving him.

He declined another offer from the King to dine with the royal
couple, but George Boleyn took pity on him, although Chapuys was
aware that guests at the Boleyn table were always subjected to theological discussions.[40] When the time came for his interview with the
King, Chapuys found they were not alone but among a small group of
courtiers which included Edward Seymour, Lord Audley and
Cromwell. Henry took Chapuys to one side and the ambassador
expressed the Emperor's willingness to discuss an alliance with
England. But when he raised the subject of Mary and her status,
Henry burst into a rage, retorting that the Emperor should stay out of
English affairs. He needed no advice from foreigners and would treat
Mary as she deserved, 'for God, of His abundant goodness, had not
only made us a King by inheritance, but also had therewithal given us
wisdom, policy and other graces in a most plentiful sort'.

Chapuys was shocked that Henry's reaction had been the opposite
of what Cromwell had told him it would be. The King now called his
Secretary of State over and had a fierce argument before witnesses,
insisting that he had been presumptuous, exceeding his authority.[41]

What had happened here? Was Henry sincere when he ranted
against Chapuys and Cromwell or was he playing a double game?
While Henry was notorious for his fierce temper, he was also capable
of turning on his emotions, going from fury to tears and tantrums. He

could also conceal his true feelings 'wonderfully well' when it suited him.[42] Was this merely acting, seeking to cover up their secret negotiations?

If Henry's rage was genuine then Anne had won and Cromwell had lost the King's support. The King had demonstrated that he was resolute in promoting Anne as Queen and forcing Chapuys to recognise her at last. If Chapuys and the Seymours had been attempting to divide the royal couple, then they had apparently failed and Anne's position remained strong. As Ives states: 'Where traditional assessment has gone wrong is in failing to recognise the difficulty Cromwell had in finding a way to separate Henry and Anne.'[43]

Since the previous summer Cromwell had been aware of Anne's distrust and dislike. Her growing power was a threat to his influence with the King and now it seemed that unless he could strike first, she would be his ruin.

Like Chapuys, Cromwell reeled from this very public rejection. Although he had always tried to make light of his differences with Henry, it was now plain for everyone to see that the King was seeking someone to blame.

Cromwell knew it must not be him if he was to survive. He was apparently horrified and had to sit down and take a drink. Claiming to be ill, he left court and shut himself away for a week to search for a solution. While Anne was still secure as Queen, Cromwell knew his whole career was at stake. Therefore she had to be removed.

Later Anne remembered these events and insisted that the King 'no longer looked upon her with the same eyes as before'.

Cromwell claims he only moved against the Queen after Henry had rejected the alliance with the Emperor. He later told Chapuys it was only from 18 April that he 'had planned and brought about the whole affair'.

Yet he contradicted this when he reminded Chapuys of their secret meeting on 23 February, and his prediction then of Anne's fall.[44] What is certain is that whatever happened sealed her fate within a mere two weeks.

Had Cromwell been searching all this time for a way to separate Henry from Anne? He hoped that an opportunity would arise to turn the King from the woman for whom he had risked so much. But his attempts had only brought down Henry's anger on his own head. It would need a much greater reason to win the King's support. Now all he had to do was find it, or invent it.

It was either Anne or him. It was not personal, it was business.

Chapter Thirteen

Conspiracy

THE FIRST PUBLIC indication of the gathering storm came on Sunday, 23 April 1536.

The select 'cobrethren and confreres' of the Order of the Garter had gathered for their annual meeting at St George's Chapel in Windsor to elect a new knight to replace the recently deceased Lord Abergavenny. The King, as head of the Order, was expected to nominate the Queen's brother George, Lord Rochford. The Boleyns were in high favour and as recently as 14 April the King had granted Thomas Boleyn rights to the town of King's Lynn and all its lands. Therefore it was astonishing news when it was announced that the new Knight of the Garter was not to be George but Sir Nicholas Carew, 'in regard of the majority of votes, the eminence of his extraction, his own fame, and the many and noble actions he had performed; which ample relation was unanimously applauded by the knights' companions'.[1]

Given that Carew had recently been openly hostile to the Boleyns, this was seen as a sign of the King's changing mood to the Queen and her supporters. Carew and the Catholic party at court were now brazen about their success, boasting that great changes were in the air. Carew had written secretly to Mary encouraging her to be strong because before long the Boleyns would be humbled and forced to 'put water in their wine'.[2]

The political conspiracy was taking shape. Thomas Cromwell had reappeared after his diplomatic illness. He confided to Chapuys that he had been working all the time 'to fabricate and plot' the coup d'état designed to bring down the Queen.[3]

If Cromwell was searching for a conspiracy, he had no shortage of evidence to hand, centred around not Anne and the Boleyns but Chapuys, Carew and the Catholic party. The King himself was fully aware of the ongoing plot being hatched around the unlikely figure of his daughter Mary and her readiness to eject him from his throne. Henry had been irritated beyond measure by her unnatural hatred and had ample cause to eliminate the risk facing the nation from her supporters, who had been loyal to Catherine. There were pockets of discontent, with the new order in rural areas of the north of England and Lincolnshire all too ready to join Mary and the Emperor in rebellion (the uprisings the following year spread to a third of the country); but instead of acting against them, Cromwell had joined with them.

It was a strange alliance: Cromwell, the social climber out for his own advancement, and Chapuys, the spymaster and representative of the great European Empire. The one claimed to be a 'new man', a Protestant and progressive thinker, while the other was a gout-ridden lawyer and Catholic propagandist for a menacing regime which abhorred change and had devised the Inquisition. Between them they hatched an international conspiracy aimed at pulling down the Boleyns, replacing Anne with the pliant Jane Seymour and effectively reversing all the reforms which had overturned the authority of the Pope.

Catholic Europe was willing to collaborate with Cromwell to achieve its aims: the return of England to the Vatican fold. Chapuys was no fool, but he was unscrupulous and clearly recognised in Cromwell a kindred spirit when it came to double-dealing. There was little love lost between Cromwell and his new friends, and but for self-preservation and a shared loathing of the Boleyns, they would still have been natural enemies. Chapuys was a realist, reporting back to his master: 'whoever could help in its execution would do a meritorious work since it would prove … a remedy for the heretical doctrines and practices of the Concubine – the principal cause of the spread of Lutheranism in this country'.[4]

The Boleyns certainly had their share of enemies. Charles Brandon, Duke of Suffolk, remembered the Queen as a young girl disapproving his scandalous affair with Mary Tudor. Norfolk himself, although Anne's uncle, had always viewed his Boleyn relatives as upstarts threatening the status quo with their reformist ideals. He saw Anne's intellect and independence as a woman reaching beyond her natural place in the world.

Rumours were being spread by Anne's enemies that the King was soon to 'dismount' one mare for another. Geoffrey Pole passed the word that the King had asked Bishop Stokesley of London to find some grounds for annulling his marriage. Bishop Gardiner, officially on diplomatic service in France, now returned to England, having been warned that something was afoot. He is alleged to have brought with him the suggestion of adultery as a means to achieve this. Sir Francis Bryan was also away from court, but had been 'sent for in all haste on his allegiance' to meet with Cromwell.[5] These men were traditionalists, standing on the sidelines, quite prepared to watch and wait while the ill-born Cromwell did all the dirty work for them.

That crucial week began on 24 April with the secret device of raising a commission of 'oyer and terminer' ('hear and judge'), composed of 20 peers working to a rota, to investigate the vaguely worded 'misprisions of treason, rebellions, felonies'. This was Cromwell's work, initiated without the King's signature (although not necessarily without his knowledge) as a routine measure when Parliament was not sitting. Thomas Boleyn happened to be one of those peers listed.[6]

Cromwell was still seeking some way to be rid of Anne. He consulted Richard Sampson, the leading expert on canon law. A former ambassador to Charles V, he had acted for the King in his separation from Catherine, and was rewarded in 1533 by being made Dean of Lichfield. For four days these men raked over the old arguments for and against a pre-contract between Anne and Henry Percy a decade before. For his assistance Sampson was later made Bishop of Chichester.

After Percy's wife had sued for divorce on these grounds in 1531, the former Archbishop of Canterbury, Warham, together with the Archbishop of York and the Duke of Norfolk, had examined Henry Percy, now 6th Earl of Northumberland, in 1532. On oath Percy vehemently denied that he had ever promised to marry Anne and the investigation accepted this as the truth.[7] Four years on, Cromwell found this decision inconvenient when he needed to prove the King's marriage to Anne had been illegal. He sent a friend of Percy to show it would be in his interests to admit he had been lying. Whether because of some remaining affection for Anne, or for fear of being caught up in Cromwell's Machiavellian plot, Northumberland refused and stayed loyal to the Queen.[8]

Henry gave every appearance of knowing nothing about this talk of divorce.

On Tuesday, 25 April he instructed Richard Pate, his ambassador in Rome, to oppose Imperial demands because of 'the likelihood and appearance that God will send us heirs male' through 'our most dear and entirely beloved wife, the Queen'.[9]

Yet Thomas Boleyn must have heard rumours at the King's Council and passed on his concerns about her security to Anne. The next day she spoke urgently to her chaplain Matthew Parker. Anne could trust him far more than his relative, her sister-in-law Jane Parker, Lady Rochford. He would remember their meeting on 26 April all his life, confiding to Nicholas Bacon in 1559: 'my heart would right fain serve my sovereign lady the Queen's majesty, in more respects than of mine allegiance, not forgetting what words her grace's mother said to me of her, not six days before her apprehension'.[10]

Deeply troubled about her future, Anne asked Parker to watch over Elizabeth if anything should happen to her. She must have learned that her life was now in great danger. She had previously feared a Spanish plot to poison Elizabeth and herself, but it now seemed clear that her enemy was the King, the man who had pleaded such love for her that he had waited seven years and shaken Europe in order to make her his wife.

Anne obtained Parker's promise that he would care for Elizabeth, a task he honestly fulfilled throughout the dangerous years that followed, until he was appointed her Archbishop of Canterbury. Elizabeth was the legal heir to the throne and Anne believed she had a destiny to rule. Her chief concern was that she should be brought up and educated as befitting a Protestant and future Queen of England.

By Sunday, 30 April Anne had decided to confront Henry face to face. The Council had been in session all week in preparation for the King and Queen's visit to Calais. The arrangements were that the royal party would set out from Greenwich after the May Day tournament the following day. That Sunday evening the Council remained in 'protracted conference' until late at night, finally announcing that the Calais trip was postponed for another week. No reason was given.[11]

Anne went to the King, wanting to know what was so important that he had cancelled their journey at such short notice. She may also have discovered that on 27 April writs had been sent out recalling Parliament. Some crisis must have occurred and, reasonably enough, the Queen wanted to know what was happening.

According to an eyewitness report, Henry turned on her. Alesius was present that day and saw the whole scene, as he later reported to Elizabeth:

Alas, I shall never forget the sorrow I felt when I saw the sainted Queen, your most religious mother, carrying you, still a little baby, in her arms, and entreating the most serene King your father in Greenwich palace, from the open window of which he was looking into the courtyard when she brought you to him. The faces and gestures of the speakers plainly showed the King was angry, although he could conceal his anger wonderfully well. Yet from the protracted conference of the council (for whom the crowd was waiting until it was quite dark, expecting that they would return to London), it was most obvious to everyone that some deep and difficult question was being discussed.[12]

Did Henry accuse Anne of meddling in politics? He would always bluster to cover up his own guilt. The reason why he had cancelled the Calais trip is plain: he knew all along of Cromwell's plot to destroy Anne.

How did Henry's great love turn to ruins? The King in 1536, with his bloated red face, piggy little eyes and ulcerated leg, cut a very different figure from the suitor of ten years before. He was 'of one mind in the morning and quite another after dinner', his violent moods increasingly unpredictable.[13] He had faced humiliation, defying the whole world to make her Queen, but Anne had let him down, betraying her promise to give him a son, a real heir. Yet, after he had risked so much for her, it now required some special reason to put her away without ridicule. That was Cromwell's brief: to create the means to an end, or to suffer the consequences.

That day he had seized his first victim in London for questioning. Mark Smeaton was a groom of the Privy Chamber, a low-born but highly gifted musician, possibly of Flemish origin, but it is an error to suggest that he had anything to do with Anne's book of music with its songs by Josquin Des Prés, whom she had known as a girl at the court of Burgundy. The book is dedicated to 'Mres. [Mistress] A. Bolleyne', showing that she received it long before she was Queen, probably as a gift from her father, whose motto, 'Now thus', is written inside.[14]

It was said that Smeaton had been invited to Cromwell's house for a meal and then set upon and tortured. On the basis of rumours current at the time, the Spanish author claims that a knotted rope wound ever tighter about his head persuaded Smeaton to confess to whatever Cromwell wanted. That torture was used is also reported by George Constantine, one of Sir Henry Norris's servants: 'the saying was that he was first grievously racked, which I never could know of a truth'.[15]

If he was racked, then it must have been in the Tower of London. Alesius stated he heard a cannon fire to announce a prisoner being taken to the Tower late on 30 April, but no one realised Smeaton was missing until later. Thomas Wriothesley, Cromwell's assistant, was noted as an interrogator, perhaps offering pardon in exchange for cooperation. To what did Smeaton confess? Surely even under torture he must have realised the repercussions that would follow. No one received pardon after admitting to 'violating the Queen' three times.

The next day, May Day, the tournament went ahead as planned. It was hot and dry, and the stands were full.[16] George Boleyn and Norris were taking part, but not the King. He watched with Anne from the royal stand set up between the two towers of the tiltyard before the new banqueting hall. Then, halfway through the contest, a message was passed to him and he immediately got up and walked away, calling for Norris and five other attendants to ride with him to London.

He left the tournament to continue without him, saying not a word to Anne.

He would never meet her again.

According to Hall, 'many men mused' at his behaviour.[17] What message had he received? The urgent nature of the news meant that Henry chose to ride rather than take a barge upriver to Westminster. Could Cromwell have warned him that his life was in danger? As the King travelled with just six attendants, it seems unlikely. As two of these were Norris and his servant Constantine, it also shows that the King had no fear that his old friend was involved in any assassination attempt.

As Keeper of the Privy Purse, Chamberlain of North Wales and Groom of the Stool, Sir Henry Norris was Henry's most personal servant, and 'the best beloved of the King'. During the ride the King allegedly turned to him and offered to grant him a full pardon if he would 'utter the trewth' about his relationship with the Queen.

Norris was stunned. Plainly the suggestion that he and Anne were having an affair came as a complete shock to him. He flatly denied the charge and declared he would fight any man who said anything against Anne's honour.

This was pure Camelot, but was the gallant Norris too much a Lancelot to Guinevere? Here was the chivalric knight of old ready to defend his Queen, but times had changed, and this was hardly the answer that Henry was expecting. As they entered London he issued orders that Norris be taken to the Tower at dawn. Norris, accompanied by Constantine, protested to his chaplain that he was innocent. Hearing this, Henry could not control his fury: 'Hang him up then!'[18]

The Queen herself knew nothing of this. On the morning of 2 May she was watching a game of tennis, about to lay a bet on her favoured player when she received news that her uncle Norfolk had arrived, accompanied by Cromwell, Lord Audley, Lord Fitzwilliam and other members of the Privy Council. Confronted with men she knew very well to be her enemies, she must have realised something important had happened.

Even here reports differ, with some accounts claiming this took place in the afternoon, that Anne was immediately told the charges against her, who had been arrested and that they had already confessed to adultery. According to this version, Anne hotly denied everything, saying she was the King's true wife and no other man had touched her.[19]

A different version rings true. Norfolk bluntly informed her that she was under arrest and must come with him to the Tower. He did not tell her why this was happening or anything of future charges that would be brought against her. She was given no time to even change or collect clothes she might need, but taken straight into custody and out to catch the tide. Anne said later that she had been 'cruelly handled' by her unfeeling uncle, and she must have been suffering from shock that the King was doing this 'to prove' her.[20]

There are different opinions on the timing of Anne's journey to London: she could have set out or arrived at any time in the afternoon between two and five o'clock. It was the same route she had taken before her coronation barely three years before. Now she was traumatised and fearful, surrounded only by her enemies, who told her nothing as they travelled up the busy Thames, attracting the attention of passing river traffic.

Later it was said that she entered through the Water Gate, but it was still daylight and she was instead rowed inside by the Court Gate, as befitted her status. As the walls closed around her, she saw waiting for her at the top of the steps the Constable and Lieutenant of the Tower, Sir William Kingston and Sir Edmund Walsingham, her jailers.[21]

Suddenly terrified, Anne fell on her knees and prayed God to help her. As she realised that Cromwell and the others were leaving, she appealed to them to 'beseech the King's Grace to be good unto her'. With great courage she recovered, helped up by Kingston, of whom she asked: 'Will I go into a dungeon?'

He replied: 'No, Madam, you shall go into the lodging you lay in at your coronation.' Kingston was more than 60 and courteous to her, but Anne was under no illusion that she was under close surveillance.

Anne was escorted to the north wing of the Lieutenant's Lodging, called the Queen's House, a new edifice completed just before her coronation. There were five women waiting to attend her, all of whom had served either Catherine or Mary, hand-picked by Cromwell for their hostility to Anne. These included her own aunts by marriage, Anne Lady Shelton and Elizabeth, the wife of her uncle Sir James Boleyn.

The others were Kingston's wife, Mrs Cosyns, wife of Anne's master-of-horse, and Mrs Stoner, wife of the King's sergeant-at-arms. Anne told Kingston she thought it 'a great unkindness in the King to set such about me as I never loved. I would fain have had mine own Privy Chamber, whom I favour most.'

Kingston insisted that 'the King took them to be honest and good women' but they were all under orders to report everything the Queen said in the hope that she would somehow incriminate herself. He duly reported back to Cromwell in a series of six letters.[22]

Anne was to bitterly miss the company of trusted friends to share her ordeal. She then remembered that her father was hunting at Windsor. She must have thought that Lord Fitzwilliam, as keeper of the Great Park, had lured him there to be out of the way while she was seized. She asked about her 'sweet broder' and thought her mother would 'die of sorow' for her.

George had not yet been arrested. He could have been taken any time at Greenwich but it was not until the evening of 2 May that he was brought secretly to the Tower. Their father was left alone, as not even Cromwell could dream up a charge against him, perhaps afraid of the King's long-time trust in him. But Anne was clearly afraid that her entire family would suffer.[23]

The Queen demanded: 'Do you know wherefor I am here?' Kingston then deliberately tried to trap her by saying that Sir Henry Norris, Sir Francis Weston and Mark Smeaton were already in the Tower and had confessed to adultery with her.

Anne's reaction was spontaneous. She laughed at the very idea that anyone could believe such ludicrous charges. Then she went into a panic at the thought that she had been betrayed, crying out: 'Oh, Norris, hast thou accused me?'

According to Kingston's letter to Cromwell, she gained control of herself and vowed: 'My God, bear witness there is no truth in these charges. I am as clear from the company of man as from sin.'[24]

A later footnote to this letter shows that Kingston added a further report from the women spying on Anne: 'The King wist well what he did when he put two such about her as Lady Boleyn and Mistress Cosyns.'[25]

In her state of shock and grief, Anne had been recklessly wondering aloud what grounds they had against her. Sir Francis Weston was a gentleman of the Privy Chamber who had been admitted to the Order of the Bath at Anne's coronation and often played tennis with the King. Convinced that Weston had already been arrested, Anne had recalled an incident the year before when she had told him off for flirting with her ladies. Still in his mid-twenties, Weston had bantered that he was more interested in seeing her, a courtly exchange of pretty gallantry. Yet in Kingston's eyes this innocuous remark could be twisted by innuendo into the most damning evidence.

A conversation Anne had allegedly had with Sir Henry Norris on 30 April was similarly used against her. Norris was ten years older than Anne, a widower whose son Henry was being educated with Anne's ward, Henry Carey, Mary Boleyn's son by the King. For some time he had been betrothed to Madge Shelton, Anne's cousin and lady-in-waiting, who, among others, had caught the King's eye. Anne asked Norris why he did not marry her and put an end to her flirting. He replied that he was content to wait, to which her reply allegedly was: 'You look for dead men's shoes? For if aught but good came to the King, you would look to have me.'

As this conversation was in public it is inconceivable that Anne could be serious. She would hardly have confronted Norris, who had been a good friend for many years, before witnesses to embarrass him. Yet according to the traditional view, they argued and then Anne obliged Norris to swear before her almoner that she was 'a good woman'. This information comes from Sir Edward Baynton, a member of the 'Aragonese faction', who remembered it only after arrests had been made. If their quarrel had been the subject of comment on 30 April, then why did the May Day tournament go ahead as planned, with Norris accompanying the King?[26]

Only in his third letter did Kingston make any mention of Mark Smeaton. Mrs Stoner had told Anne that the musician was being kept in irons in the Tower. Anne allegedly answered that this was because he was not a nobleman. Then she said that he had been in her chamber only a couple of times. Once was at Winchester the year before, when, she said, he had played the virginals for her in a room that was directly below that of the King, as if to point out that her husband would have heard the music stop if anything irregular had been going on. The only other occasion was the previous Saturday, 29 April, when she had seen him looking sad and asked what was troubling him. He seemed surprised that she should even talk to him, to which she is said to have replied: 'You may not look to have me speak to you as I should do to a nobleman' and he responded: 'No, no, Madam. A look sufficed me, and thus fare you well.'[27]

With hindsight it was said that Anne had provided the evidence needed to frame them all.[28] It appears that the whole conspiracy was an invention, with arrests being made long before there were any grounds for official charges. Only when Anne was in custody did Cromwell begin to assemble the evidence against her.

The normal practice of that time was that defendants remained ignorant of charges until their appearance in court. It was necessary to prove innocence, even without any knowledge of the prosecution's case.

No assistance was given to the accused in the way of counsel or documents and no witnesses could be called to support their cause. Anne asked Kingston how she could be expected to defend herself without knowing the charges against her. As another defendant would say later: 'I have had very short warning to provide the answer to so great a matter... I am brought to fight without a weapon.'[29]

But Anne knew from the time of her arrest that there was little hope for her. As he reported to Cromwell, Anne asked the Constable of the Tower, 'Master Kingston, shall I die without justice?' 'The poorest subject of the King hath justice,' he told her. 'And therewith she laughed.'[30]

As word spread of the arrests there was increasing tension among the Queen's supporters. At court the tension was palpable. People feared who might be next on Cromwell's list.

Yet there were other opportunists ready to take advantage of the pickings. On the very day of Anne's arrest, Sir Richard Bulkeley, Norris's deputy in North Wales, was advised by his brother of events and told to come to London immediately. As a lawyer at Gray's Inn, Roland saw it would be open season for the offices and properties of those accused. John Hussey also wrote to Lord Lisle in Calais of the frenzied atmosphere at court: 'Here is nothing but every man for himself.' But Roland warned his brother to hurry, for 'when it is once known that they shall die, all will be too late'.[31]

He certainly saw the arrests for what they were – a coup d'état against the Boleyns by Cromwell and his allies. As Starkey states: 'Their fate was sealed and it remained only to fabricate the detailed charges against them.'[32]

In this Lord Fitzwilliam, the King's treasurer, was a key player. He was so deeply involved that he had neglected writing letters 'since these matters begun'.[33] He had recruited Anne's own Vice-Chamberlain, Sir Edward Baynton, who had his own informers at court. On 3 May he advised Fitzwilliam: 'I have mused much at [the behaviour] of Mistress Margery which hath used her strangely toward me of late, being her friend as I have been. But no doubt it cannot be but that she must be of council therewith; there hath been great friendship between the Queen and her of late.'

'Mistress Margery' was probably Margery Horsman, of the Queen's wardrobe, who would be a useful agent inside the royal household. Baynton was irritated because she had new qualms about betraying her mistress, but he must have found some way to make it worth her while, for Horsman was later rewarded with a place in Jane Seymour's service.[34]

Baynton requested a meeting to speak 'more plainly'. Baynton was worried that Mark Smeaton's confession was the sole piece of evidence they had. He insisted that at least two other men must be made to admit affairs with the Queen:

This shall be to advertyse yow that here is myche communycacion that no man will confesse any thyng agaynst her, but all only Marke of any actuell thynge. Wherefore (in my folishe conceyte) it shulde myche toche the Kings honour if it shulde no farther appeere. And I cannot believe but that the other two bee as ... culpapull as ever was hee.[35]

Fitzwilliam claimed to have obtained some admission from Norris, which the prisoner later denied. Norris's servant Constantine recorded: 'And ... as his chapleyn tolde me he confessed but he sayed at his arrayning, when his owne confession was layed afore hym, that he was deceaved to do the same by the Erle of [South] Hampton that now ys [Lord Fitzwilliam].'

Norris retorted boldly: '[whoever tries to take advantage of] anything of my confession, he is worthy to have (my place here; and if he stand to) it, I defy him'.[36] Another voice was raised in defiance at events. When Anne was arrested her former chaplain and firm supporter Cranmer was at Knole Place. Hearing news of the crisis, the Archbishop hurried back to London hoping to see the King.

This must have proved impossible, for Henry was avoiding all contact with petitioners on his wife's behalf, hiding away and only going out 'in the garden and in his boat at night, at which times it may become no man to prevent him'.[37] So Cranmer sat down on 3 May and wrote perhaps the most difficult and dangerous letter of his life, to plead Anne's cause: 'I am in such a perplexity, that my mind is clearly amazed; for I never had better opinion in woman, than I had in her; which maketh me to think, that she should not be culpable.'

He must have thought that he had gone too far, for now he changed tack, using a more diplomatic tone that would not alienate the King:

And again, I think your Highness would not have gone so far, except she had surely been culpable. Now I think that your Grace best knoweth, that next unto your Grace I was most bound unto her of all creatures living ... and if she be found culpable, considering your Grace's goodness towards her, and what condition your Grace of your mere goodness took her and set the Crown upon her head, I repute him not your Grace's faithful servant and subject, nor true unto the realm, that would not desire the offence without mercy to be punished to the example of all other.

And as I loved her not a little for the love which I judged her to bear toward God and his gospel; so, if she be proved culpable, there is not one that loveth God and his gospel that ever will favour her, but must hate her above all other; and the more they favour the gospel, the more they will hate her...

And though she have offended so, that she hath deserved never to be reconciled unto your Grace's favour, yet Almighty God hath manifoldly declared his goodness towards your Grace and never offended you... Wherefore I trust that your Grace will bear no less entire favour unto the truth of the gospel, than you did before; forsomuch as your Grace's favour to the gospel was not led by affection unto her, but by zeal unto the truth.

Cranmer was in a dilemma. He clearly believed Anne to be innocent because he knew her and her convictions, but he was also a pragmatist and if the King was resolved to be rid of her, then it was his duty as Archbishop of Canterbury to prevent a wider cull that might destroy the Reformation in England. In the postscript he was willing to crawl to the tyrant's will: 'I am exceedingly sorry that such faults can be proved by the Queen, as I heard of their relation. But I am, and ever shall be, your faithful subject.'[38]

More arrests followed. On 4 May another member of the Privy Council was arrested. Sir William Brereton was the seventh son of Sir Randle of Malpas Hall, spending much of his time in Cheshire and Wales. Wyatt described him as 'one that I least knew' but he was closer to Norris and may have been a witness at Anne's wedding. He had given her the greyhound Urian.

The reason for his arrest remains a mystery. His school friend George Constantine 'did ask him and was bold upon him' why he was arrested and he answered 'that there was no way but one with any matter'.

What was layed against hym I know not nor never hearde. But at his deeth these were his wordes: 'I have deserved to dye if it were a thousande deethes, but the cause wherfore I dye judge not: but yf ye judge, judge the best.' This he spake iii or foure tymes. If he were gyltie, I saye therfore that he dyed worst of them all.[39]

Brereton had been Henry's envoy to Rome in 1530 and was deputy to the Duke of Richmond, Henry's illegitimate son. As Chamberlain of Chester, with royal grants valued at over £1,000 per year, he perhaps enjoyed too much influence and independence to suit Cromwell. Married to the Earl of Worcester's sister, Brereton had only one accuser: Worcester's countess, Elizabeth Browne, the daughter of the conspirator Sir Anthony Browne. Given that Anne was betrayed by Lady Worcester, it seems that her opinion of him as a noted seducer was enough to damn him. Even Chapuys says that Brereton was 'condemned on a presumption, not by proof or valid confession, and without any witnesses'.[40]

The next day it was the turn of Sir Francis Weston. He was away from court when the earlier arrests were made and his family were outraged at the false charges. They even offered the King the hand-some sum of 100,000 marks in ransom for his life, but to no avail.[41] Henry was too preoccupied with his plans to marry Jane Seymour the moment he would be free.

Immediately after Anne was taken to the Tower, Henry had arranged for Jane to be taken to the house of Sir Nicholas Carew at Beddington, where Henry could visit her. Chapuys reported to the Emperor on events:

I hear that, even before the arrest of the Concubine, the King, speak-ing with Mistress Jane Seymour of their future marriage, the latter suggested that the princess [Mary] should be replaced in her former position; and the King told her she was a fool, and ought to solicit the advancement of the children they would have between them, and not any others.

Then he exposed the fact that Jane was the instrument of Spain and Mary's rebels:

I will endeavour by all means to make her continue in this vein; I hope also to go and speak with the King within three days, and with members of the council in general. I think the Concubine's little bas-tard Elizabeth will be excluded from the succession, and that the King will get himself requested by parliament to marry. To cover the affec-tion he has for the said Seymour he has lodged her seven miles away in the house of a grand esquire and says publicly that he has no desire in the world to marry again.[42]

In fact the King was openly celebrating, holding lavish banquets and going up and down the river by night in a barge with musicians singing and playing. The people watched these callous antics with growing fury. Public opinion swung in Anne's favour. Jane Seymour was not popular and Henry wrote to assure her he was trying to crush the increasing number of scurrilous ballads against them:

> My dear friend and mistress, the bearer of these few lines from thy entirely devoted servant will deliver into thy fair hands a token of my true affection for thee, hoping you will keep it for ever in your sincere love for me.
>
> There is a ballad made lately of great derision against us; I pray you pay no manner of regard to it. I am not at present informed who is the setter forth of this malignant writing, but if he is found out, he shall be straitly punished for it. Hoping shortly to receive you into these arms, I end for the present.
>
> Your own loving servant and sovereign, H. R.[43]

The purge continued. On 8 May Sir Thomas Wyatt and Sir Richard Page were taken in fetters to the Tower. Like Weston, Page had been away from court and unaware of what was happening. Wyatt, who was more informed, blamed Charles Brandon for his arrest. But 'No one dare say a word for him.'[44]

In the Tower Anne is said to have written to Henry to appeal for mercy for the men condemned with her. Ellis states: 'It is universally known as one of the finest compositions in the English language.' D'Aubigny agrees:

> We see Anne thoroughly in this letter, one of the most touching that was ever written. Injured in her honour, she speaks without fear, as one on the threshold of eternity. If there were no other proofs of her innocence, this document alone would suffice to gain her cause in the eyes of an impartial and intelligent posterity.[45]

The letter, allegedly written on 6 May, was discovered among Cromwell's private papers, which suggests that it may never have reached the King.

> Your grace's displeasure and my imprisonment are things so strange to me, that what to write, or what to excuse, I am altogether ignorant.

Whereas you send to me (willing me to confess a truth and so obtain your favour), by such a one, whom you know to be mine ancient professed enemy, I no sooner received this message by him, than I rightly conceived your meaning; and if, as you say, confessing a truth indeed may procure my safety, I shall with all willingness and duty, perform your duty.

But let not your grace ever imagine that your poor wife will be brought to acknowledge a fault, where not so much as a thought ever proceeded.

And to speak a truth, never a prince had wife more loyal in all duty, and in all true affection, than you have ever found in Anne Bulen – with which name and place I could willingly have contented myself, if God and your grace's pleasure had been so pleased. Neither did I at any time so far forget myself in my exaltation or received queenship, but that I always looked for such alteration as I now find; for the ground of my preferment being on no surer foundation than your grace's fancy, the least alteration was fit and sufficient (I knew) to draw that fancy to some other subject.

You have chosen me from low estate to be your Queen and companion, far beyond my desert or desire; if, then, you found me worthy of such honour, good your grace, let not any light fancy or bad counsel of my enemies withdraw your princely favour from me; neither let that stain – that unworthy stain – of a disloyal heart towards your good grace ever cast so foul a blot on me, and on the infant princess your daughter.

Try me, good king, but let me have a lawful trial, and let not my sworn enemies sit as my accusers and as my judges; yea, let me receive an open trial, for my truth shall fear no open shame.

Then you shall see either my innocency cleared, your suspicions and conscience satisfied, the ignominy and slander of the world stopped, or my guilt openly declared. So that, whatever God and you may determine of, your grace may be freed from an open censure; and my offence being so lawfully proved, your grace may be at liberty, both before God and man, not only to execute worthy punishment on me as an unfaithful wife but to follow your affection already settled on that party for whose sake I am now as I am, whose name I could some while since have pointed unto – your grace being not ignorant of my suspicions therein.

But if you have already determined of me, and that not only my death, but an infamous slander must bring you the joying of your desired happiness, then I desire of God that he will pardon your great sin herein, and likewise my enemies, the instruments thereof; and that he will not call you to a strait account for your unprincely and cruel usage of me at his general judgment-seat, where both you and myself must shortly appear; and in whose just judgment, I doubt not (whatsoever the world may think of me), mine innocency shall be openly known and sufficiently cleared.

My last and only request shall be, that myself only bear the burden of your grace's displeasure, and that it may not touch the innocent souls of those poor gentlemen, whom, as I understand, are likewise in strait imprisonment for my sake. If ever I have found favour in your sight – if ever the name of Anne Bulen have been pleasing in your ears – then let me obtain this request; and so I will leave to trouble your grace any further, with mine earnest prayer to the Trinity to have your grace in his good keeping, and to direct you in all your actions. From my doleful prison in the Tower, the 6th May.[46]

The process continued at a relentless pace. One week after the Queen's arrest a jury decided there was sufficient evidence for the trials to go ahead. This was a foregone conclusion as its members were all hand-picked and the foreman was Sir Thomas More's son-in-law, Giles Heron. The date for the trial of the accused men was set for Friday, 12 May, at Westminster Hall.

Who was it that first hit upon the idea of treason as a solution? Cromwell or Bishop Gardiner? From Gardiner in France came the suggestion of a conspiracy by Anne and her circle of lovers to poison the King so that Anne would become Regent and marry Norris. Chapuys saw Norris as the key figure whom the Queen's enemies needed to remove.[47]

Only the rape of the Queen was an offence under the act of 1352, but adultery was not treason and should have been tried by the Church courts.[48] Treason required a conspiracy to kill the King, Queen or the heir to the throne, plotting with enemies of the nation, or raising an army for war. Henry could have removed Catherine and Mary at any time for the second of these, but where Anne was concerned it required more ingenuity.

Treason had been redefined two years before as the ultimate political crime, where simply to be heard making critical remarks against the King could result in execution. This was one of the charges against Anne, but Henry needed to be sure of a guilty verdict. In 1521 he had successfully removed his Yorkist rival the Duke of Buckingham for 'imagining the King's death', a catch-all charge which could mean as little as a discussion about the King's health and carried overtones of witchcraft and divination.

It was widely recognised that Buckingham had been beheaded for trumped-up charges of paying for prophecies about the King's lifespan. Elizabeth Barton, the 'Nun of Kent', had made far worse predictions when she was being courted by Catherine, Thomas More and the Marchioness of Exeter, yet none of these had been accused of that crime. In 1532, however, Sir William Neville was accused of using divination to discover how long Henry would live. In 1534 it became possible to be charged with treason for simply discussing the possibility of the King's death. By her own admission Anne had talked about this after Henry's fall in January 1536 which provoked her miscarriage later that month. Norfolk had told her the King was unconscious, perhaps even dead. Shock alone had caused her to lose her child, a boy, just three and a half months old. Was it surprising that she had begun to think: what if?

According to the Act of Succession of 1534, Elizabeth was Henry's legal heir and Anne was to be Regent during her minority as Queen. Henry had made Anne more than his consort when his own crown and regalia were used at her coronation. Henry had made certain that if he died without a son to inherit, then Elizabeth, through her mother Anne, would take the throne.

This was the reality in 1536 when Anne had feared that the King had died or might die. She had sought advice about what might happen, but these very natural concerns for her own safety and the rights of her daughter as Queen of England were now viciously turned against her. She was accused of treason under statute 26 Henry VIII c.13, originally designed to protect Anne and Elizabeth against the plots of the Imperial-Vatican alliance, and with slandering the royal issue under 25 Henry VIII c.22, Mar. 1534.

Anne had seemed to build her own power base of evangelical Protestants. In Kingston's second report to Cromwell he says that Anne had expected the bishops she had supported to now support her, but she was to be sorely disappointed.[49] She was the enemy of the Catholic party at court and commented: 'They will not let me live. I am too great an obstacle to their religion.'

In the indictment Anne was accused of 'despising her marriage and entertaining malice against the King, and following daily her frail and carnal lust'. She had seduced these '*adulteros et concubinos*' with 'vile provocations' in order to plot the King's death. Their liaisons were cited by date and location, with the provision of the safety clause 'and on divers other days and places, before and after':

> On 6 October at the palace of Westminster ... and on various other days before and after, by sweet words, kissings, touchings and other illicit means ... she did procure and incite... Henry Norris ... a gentleman of the Privy Chamber of our lord the King, to violate and carnally know her, by reason whereof the same Henry Norris on 12 October ... violated, stained and carnally knew her...

She was accused of adultery with Norris at Greenwich on 12 and 19 November 1533, with Brereton at Greenwich on 16 and 27 November 1533, at Westminster on 3 December and at Hampton Court on 8 December 1533 and 'divers ... at Westminster'. She was charged with adultery with Sir Francis Weston on 8 and 20 May 1534 at Greenwich, and on 6 and 20 June 1534 at Whitehall, and with Smeaton at Greenwich on 13 and 19 May 1534 and at Westminster on 12 and 26 April 1535.

The third count of the indictment accused the Queen of having committed incest with her own brother on 2 November 1535 at Whitehall and on 22 and 29 December at Eltham. She had 'procured her own natural brother to violate her, alluring him with her tongue in his mouth, and his tongue in hers, against the commands of Almighty God and all laws human and divine'.

In this paranoid world, normal events were twisted to appear sinister and suggestive interpretations were put on actions that were quite innocent. Dancing with her brother was now proof of guilt; passing from partner to partner had a sexual connotation. George had once visited Anne alone in her bedroom and they kissed in greeting. But as Erasmus noted:

> Wherever you come you are received with a kiss by all; when you take your leave, you are dismissed with kisses; you return, kisses are repeated. They come to visit you, kisses again; they leave you, you kiss them all round.

John Spelman, one of Anne's judges, was to observe after the trial that 'all the evidence was bawdry and lechery'. It was all sensationalism. Even the fact that Anne had written to her brother with the news that she was pregnant was seen as evidence that he was the father of her child.[50]

Eleven of the 20 offences with which the men were charged are clearly false as the accused were simply not present at the cited location. In the autumn of 1533, when Anne was assumed to be carrying on mad, passionate affairs, she was still recovering from the birth of Elizabeth and waiting to be churched. She was also at Greenwich when the indictment claims she was at Westminster. On 19 May 1534, when she was alleged to have been with Smeaton at Greenwich, she was actually at Richmond.

That these simple facts were not checked shows with what contempt and disdain Cromwell and the King held the nation, assured that a guilty verdict was a foregone conclusion.

Jealousy played a great part in these accusations. Anne was apparently so jealous of her lovers 'that she could scarcely bear any of them to associate with or talk to … any other woman'. The men themselves were full of 'suspicion and jealousy', competing with one another, 'kindled and inflamed with carnal love of the said Queen'. Yet all of them were alleged to have collaborated together in the conspiracy to remove the King on 31 October 1535 and after his fall at the tournament on 8 January 1536. Anne was said to have declared 'she had never wished to choose the King in her heart' and 'had promised to marry one of them when the King died'.

She had always been the only woman in a man's world, sharing their intellectual, political and artistic interests. Was Henry jealous? He saw Anne winning the loyalty of his oldest friends, such as Norris, and he must have wondered, did they discuss him and his inadequacies? The trivia of 'pastime in the Queen's chamber' claims that Henry had been criticised, his clothes mocked, his artistic attempts at poetry turned to scorn. Worst of all, the Queen and her brother had discussed his sexual problems: Henry was impotent, 'having neither vigour nor strength'.[51]

Some suggested that Anne was so desperate to conceive an heir that she took lovers. George was accused of 'having spread reports which called in question whether his sister's daughter was the King's child'. Why he would want to malign his own sister and raise doubts about Elizabeth's paternity was never explained. Chapuys had his own malevolent version: Protestant bishops, he alleged, taught that when a husband proved impotent 'according to their sect, it was allowable for a woman to ask for aid in other quarters, even among her own relatives'. Other Catholics claimed that Smeaton was Elizabeth's father.

The Spanish *Crónica del Rey Enrico* reads like a French farce, in which Smeaton hides in the Queen's closet, while Sander invents the more romantic tale of Henry realising her guilt when she sees her dropping a handkerchief to her lover at the May Day tournament.[52]

The result of all these rumours, according to the indictment, was that the King 'had conceived in his heart such inward displeasure and sadness ... that certain grave injuries and perils ... had befallen his royal body'.

The other charges were all part of the campaign to blacken the reputations of the accused. Norris was the only man not accused of sodomy. Homosexuals were regarded as devil worshippers and a Buggery Statute had been passed in 1534, providing Warnicke with an inventive theory of witchcraft and a deformed foetus which terrified Henry.[53]

The idea that Anne could have been guilty of multiple adultery with a group of secret homosexuals, or committed incest with her own brother is frankly absurd to us today, but this successful ploy was to be used again in 1540, when William Baron Hungerford was executed for buggery, witchcraft and consulting soothsayers about the length of the King's life, and again in 1546, when Henry Neville was also accused of divination.

Weir, never sympathetic to Anne, accepts the official charges without question, that Anne plotted to murder the King so she could rule as Regent and marry her lover Norris. She writes that Anne's own household were so horrified by her acts that they betrayed her. More incredibly, she then asserts that Anne was pregnant when she was executed.

In the normal course of justice, her pregnancy would have saved her from a death sentence, or at least postponed it, but this child could never be allowed to live, because the King would not dare risk a disputed succession.

She claims this is why the trial documents had to be destroyed, in order to conceal Anne's fifth pregnancy before it could be discovered.[54]

Given that the indictment states they were 'performing at night the most services, extraordinary in number', it is strange that no lady of the Queen's bedchamber was accused as accessory.

George's wife has been identified as the source for many of these revelations. Burnet says: 'She carried many stories to the King or some about him', including the news that his deficiencies were being discussed in the Queen's household. Jane Parker, Lady Rochford, had turned against the Queen since she had briefly been sent away from court. She now informed against her own husband and sister-in-law 'more out of envy and jealousy than out of love towards the King'.

Cavendish claims that far from being homosexual, George Boleyn lusted after 'all women'. But even if this was true, and it must remain unlikely given his notable religious convictions, Jane Parker's jealousy seems abnormal in an age when a wife was expected to turn a blind eye to her husband's affairs.

Antony Antony confirms that 'the wife of Lord Rochford was a particular instrument in the death of Queen Anne'. In return for her helpful testimony she would be rewarded with the restoration of her position as lady of the Privy Chamber in the household of Anne's successor. Ironically, her capacity for meddling brought a certain retribution a few years later when she was accused and beheaded for abetting Catherine Howard. The same should have applied to her relationship with Anne, for her collusion in the alleged crimes – notably treason – she ought to have joined her mistress in the Tower, as Wyatt points out.[55]

Before her execution Jane Rochford confessed: 'God has permitted me to suffer this shameful doom as punishment for having contributed to my husband's death. I falsely accused him of loving in an incestuous manner, his sister, Queen Anne Boleyn. For this I deserve to die.'[56]

The charges against Anne overstepped all ordinary bounds of credulity. Henry's hand in the whole sordid business is clearly seen: the real blood-guilt lies with the King. The source of all the horror and brutality was Henry. The whole world revolved around him and his ego. Key players rose and fell at his whim and it was his paranoia which determined everyone's survival. A later ballad by another of his victims, Anne Askew, attacked the tyrant:

> I saw a royal throne where justice should have sit,
> But in her stead was one of moody, cruel wit.
> Absorbed was righteousness as of the raging flood;
> Satan in his excess sucked up the guiltless blood.[57]

Chapter Fourteen

Coup D'état

WITHIN THE BROODING precincts of the Tower of London there are still inscriptions surviving from those May days. In the Martin Tower the word 'boullen' can be seen scratched crudely into the stonework. On the west wall of the first floor of the Beauchamp Tower, in one of the cells where the men were imprisoned, is the tragic symbol of a falcon, Anne's badge, carved by one of those who shared her tragedy to the very end.

The trial of Norris, Brereton, Weston and Smeaton took place on Friday, 12 May 1536. The indictment had made no accusations against the other prisoners, Page and Wyatt, whose families had petitioned Cromwell for their release. On the very day when the indictment was published, 11 May, Sir Thomas Wyatt's father heard that his poet son would not be touched and wrote an immediate and rather pathetic letter to Cromwell in relief. Weston's family was not so fortunate, their offer to buy their son out of trouble ignored. There seemed to be no logic to those who were proscribed, as the Earl of Wiltshire, Sir Thomas Boleyn, and his brother, Sir James Boleyn, were not seized.[1]

The next day the four accused were taken by river to Westminster. Plans to make them walk through the city streets had to be abandoned as Norris in particular was a well-known and popular figure. The people could not understand why the King had turned so dramatically against one of his closest friends and supporters. Even less could they believe that he and the Queen were lovers. Overnight the men closest to the King had become traitors. Fearing a possible rescue attempt, Cromwell made last-minute changes to ensure that the trial brought in a swift verdict. The jury was already primed and knew what the King expected.

Many of those who would judge the case were closely connected to Cromwell or the Catholic faction at court. Edward Willoughby, the foreman, was in debt to Brereton, Thomas Palmer was Lord Fitzwilliam's man, Richard Tempest Cromwell's client, William Askew close to Mary, Sir Giles Alington of Horsheath part of Thomas More's family and Anthony Hungerford related to Jane Seymour.[2]

Barely three years before, Westminster Hall had been the scene of Anne's great coronation banquet. Few of those gathered there that day recognised the ghosts of gaiety behind the proud faces of Norris, Weston and Brereton as they gave their pleas of 'Not Guilty'. Only Smeaton kept apart, head hanging in disgrace as he pleaded guilty in the hope that his life would be saved. Chapuys' account, as usual, assumes Anne's guilt while questioning that of the men accused with her: 'Only the groom confessed that he had been three times with the said whore and concubine. The others were condemned upon presumption and certain indications, without valid proof or confession.'[3]

They were in little doubt of the fate that awaited them. The jury returned its verdict under the watchful eye of the Duke of Norfolk: unanimously guilty. Lord Audley, the Chancellor, gave sentence: as commoners they would face the death reserved for traitors: to be hanged, drawn and quartered and their body parts displayed as a deterrent for others.

This purge exterminated one of the King's oldest friends and split the court apart. But this was just the beginning of a much wider sweep that would bring down a majority of courtiers in the inner circle. As Wyatt, who survived the slaughter, said later: 'These bloody days have broken my heart.'[4]

The guilty verdict against the men accused with Anne meant that her own guilt was now a foregone conclusion. For how could they be adulterers if she was innocent? On hearing the news that they were condemned, she must have given up all hope even if she was unaware that her husband had already sent for an executioner to come from France. The following day, even before she had been tried or found guilty, Fitzwilliam and Paulet dismissed the members of her household.[5]

John Hussey wrote an account of the charges against the Queen to the Lisles in Calais. He was clearly shocked by what he had heard, including a false report that Anne had confessed:

> Madam, I think verily, if all the books and chronicles were totally revolved, and to the uttermost persecuted and tried, which against women hath been penned, contrived, and written since Adam and Eve, those same were I think verily nothing in comparison of that which hath been done and committed by Anne the Queen; which though I presume be not all thing as it is now rumoured, yet that which hath been by her confessed, and others, offenders with her, by her own alluring, procurement and instigation, is so abominable and detestable that I am ashamed that any good woman should give ear thereunto.
>
> I pray God give her grace to repent while she now liveth.
> I think not the contrary but she and all they shall suffer.[6]

Cromwell was also busy writing letters. On 14 May he wrote to Bishop Gardiner in France that evidence against Anne had come from her ladies. When Gardiner later queried what was stated at her trial, the Secretary of State dismissed his concerns by claiming the truth was so vile that most of the proof could not be given.[7]

De Carles states that the 'evidence' was the result of a chance remark by the sister of a member of the King's Council. When criticised for her own behaviour, she allegedly retorted that the Queen was a greater offender. This was then reported to the King, who ordered an investigation.[8] A variation of this story is found in the Lansdowne MSS, in which the brother is named as 'Antoine Brun'. Sir Anthony Browne was, of course, Fitzwilliam's half-brother and another conspirator of the Catholic party. His daughter Elizabeth, Lady Worcester, was named by John Hussey to Lord Lisle as one of the three women who informed against Anne — one unnamed, another Anne Cobham and the third, 'my Lady Worcester beareth the name to be the principal'.⁹ This tight-knit group working in collusion with Cromwell provided what 'evidence' there was to condemn Anne.

Amid a growing tide of public disquiet about the trials, Cromwell judged it too much of a risk for Anne to be tried at Westminster. It was far more secure for the proceedings to go ahead within the fortress of the Tower. There was even concern about a possible rescue bid by Boleyn sympathisers.

Anne and her brother had to wait for their trials. As noble by birth they had to be tried by their peers, unlike the men accused with her. But as the Queen, anointed at her coronation, in reality Anne had no equal other than the King.

In contradiction of the unpopular black legend created by her enemies, Anne had many supporters, particularly in London and southern England, where almost half the population were Protestants. In her brief reign as Queen she had rescued evangelicals and aided the reform in education through her charitable foundations. Her generous alms had helped a great number of people. The £1,500 a year she was said to have distributed to the poor was a fortune by the standards of the day. It was completely inexplicable to those who knew her that Anne could be guilty of any of the crimes attributed to her.

Did Henry himself believe any of the charges? Did he deceive himself that he could kill his wife in good conscience? According to Chapuys' account:

> The very evening the Concubine was brought to the Tower of London, when the Duke of Richmond went to say goodnight to his father, and ask his blessing after the English custom, the King began to weep, saying that he and his sister, meaning the Princess [Mary], were greatly bound to God for having escaped the hands of that accursed whore, who had determined to poison them; from which it is clear that the King knew something about it.

Yet Chapuys had also reported that the King was already planning his wedding to Jane Seymour *before* the trial and that he knew that Anne was not guilty.¹⁰

Did Henry delude himself by imagining what he did was not out of his own desire but for the good of the realm, or did he never even think of it? Did he send Anne away and simply write her out of his life?

Henry refused to see her. He had a coward's fear of death and had always turned his back on the cold-blooded realities of his actions. He had struck out at his rivals without a qualm of conscience. Now he used the same tactics to remove the impediment of an inconvenient wife and her supporters.

He had to be free to get a son elsewhere. But how did he know he would have a son? How could he guarantee that he would still be capable of getting a male heir on any woman? The thought may have been in the back of his mind, but he knew this was his last chance. His mind was made up and he was willing to go along with whatever Cromwell invented to destroy Anne's reputation.

Henry was completely cynical about it. He was so confident of his will being done that he even told Jane Seymour on the morning of the trial, 15 May, that Anne would be condemned and all concluded by three that afternoon.[11]

In the Great Hall of the Tower special stands had been erected for 2,000 spectators. (These were left in place afterwards until the end of the 18th century.)[12] Again the Duke of Norfolk represented the King, assisted by the Chancellor, his justices and a jury of 26 peers. These included the unfortunate Henry Percy of Northumberland, required by the King's malicious cruelty to prove his loyalty by sitting in judgement on the woman he had loved.

Contrary to Sander, Thomas Boleyn was not there and Burnet admits this, having at first followed the false report.[13] Thomas had kept a low profile since the tragedy of his children's sudden arrest. Some have seen his lack of action on their behalf as cowardly or even as betrayal. He had known the King and been his trusted ambassador and companion for many years but, as the treatment of Norris had demonstrated, this was no guarantee of safety. He was a broken man, as Henry must have known he would be, given his closeness and devotion to Anne and George. He was therefore spared the horror of watching their struggle to defend themselves against impossible charges.

Although they were to be tried on the same day, Anne and her brother were not permitted to see each other. George was brought in first, according to an eyewitness, De Carles. He was there as secretary to the French ambassador, reporting back for his master. Chapuys employed a similar agent, although he must surely have wanted to be present to witness in person the downfall of his great enemy.[14]

The prosecution was lead by the Attorney General, Sir Christopher Hales, who had acted as host for Anne and the King on their way to Calais in 1532. He was assisted or supervised by Thomas Cromwell, eager to see the fulfilment of the King's project.

George, Lord Rochford was accused of high treason, having conspired against the life of the King and of incest with the Queen. The evidence was based on information that brother and sister had once spent time alone together. George denied the charges in a scathing attack. The audience was with him as he 'crumbled the royal case to dust'.

Chapuys records: 'To all he replied so well that several of those present wagered ten to one that he would be acquitted, especially as no witnesses were produced against either him or her...' He states that it was George's 'wicked wife' who informed on their 'accursed secret' by letter. According to De Carles, George retorted: 'On the evidence of only one woman you are willing to believe this great evil of me!'[15]

Now Cromwell handed George a document, asking if the Queen had ever discussed such a matter with his wife Jane, Lady Rochford. This was the suggestion that Anne had spoken about Henry's sexual inadequacies. Cromwell clearly meant him only to read the note discreetly to himself, but George had little to lose. He knew very well that his persecutors meant to destroy the Boleyn family and his fate was already determined. Therefore he brazenly read the note out loud before the whole court, exposing the vital question of the King's impotency, as Chapuys says:

I must not omit that among other things charged against him as a crime was, that his sister had told his wife that the King was impotent. This he was not openly charged with, but it was shown him in writing, with a warning not to repeat it. But he immediately declared the matter, in great contempt of Cromwell and some others.[16]

George then refused to answer the question of whether Anne had discussed the matter, refusing to suggest anything against the royal issue according to the 1534 Act of Succession. Cromwell demanded if he had at any time questioned the paternity of the Princess Elizabeth. It was highly improbable that George would have said anything of the kind which might cast aspersions against his own sister, except in the way of a black joke that it was a miracle that Henry, with his problems, had ever produced *any* children. This was in line with the accusation that Anne and George had ridiculed Henry.[17]

As George already knew, whatever the audience might wager, the result of the jury was predetermined. The 26 peers unanimously found him guilty and he faced them with stoical calm. He agreed that all men were sinners and therefore deserved to die, but out of concern for his salvation he read out a list of those to whom he owed money, anxious that the rapacious King he knew so well would confiscate all his wealth without first settling his debts.

He was removed from the court, leaving behind an audience impressed by his courage and humanity. Now the real show could begin.

In the ensuing silence of expectation, Anne was brought in between Lady Kingston and her aunt, Lady Boleyn. She moved with dignity to occupy a chair that had been set for her on the platform. Kingston and Sir Edmund Walsingham were present, but the Queen had no one to assist her or conduct her case. Against her were the benches of the prosecution where Cromwell and Audley had arranged for the best legal team in the kingdom to perform in this kangaroo court.[18]

When the indictment was read out to her, it was the first occasion that Anne had to know the full absurdity of the charges against her. Chapuys described the scene later to the Emperor:

What she was principally charged with was having cohabited with her brother and other accomplices; that there was a promise between her and Norris to marry after the King's death, which it thus appeared they hoped for; and that she had received and given to Norris certain medals, which might be interpreted to mean that she had poisoned the late Queen, and intrigued to do the same to the Princess [Mary].

These things she totally denied and gave to each a plausible answer.[19]

The main accusation was treason, building on the verdict against Norris for 'imagining' the King's death under statute 26 Henry VIII c.13, Dec. 1534. The charge of slandering the royal issue was supplementary to this. Sir John Spelman kept a record of the trial with an emphasis on Anne's allegedly shameful morals which enabled her to carry on adulterous affairs with five men at the same time, including incest with her brother. He wrote that three ladies had testified to the loose behaviour at court, concluding there was 'never such a whore in the realm than the Queen!' Judge Spelman added: 'And note that this matter was disclosed by a woman called Lady Wingfield who was a servant of the said Queen and shared the same tendencies. And suddenly the said Wingfield became ill and a little time before her death she showed the matter to one of those etc.'[20]

Spelman's curt report was based on malicious gossip, hearsay not evidence. Bridget Wingfield had died two years before, probably in childbirth after her third marriage, to Sir Robert Tyrwhit, and there was no written record of any deathbed confession. It seems improbable that a woman whom Anne had regarded as a good friend and supporter could have said anything of a supposed promiscuous past. On the contrary, it was Anne who had written to her after the death of her second husband regarding Bridget's 'indiscreet trouble' which had failed to 'please God'. Once safely married again, Bridget came to court to attend on Anne as Queen, but died shortly afterwards. Of interest is the fact that Bridget's relations by marriage were ominously connected to Anne's enemies, Suffolk and Fitzwilliam. Tyrwhit himself was a leading supporter of Mary's party.[21]

The Queen was of 'excellent quick wit and being a ready speaker, she did so answer all objections'. It was said that she was like an oak withstanding fierce storms. She spoke with such conviction that the whole chamber could not help but be convinced of her innocence. Wriothesley was moved by her astonishing strength: 'She made so wise and discreet answers to all things laid against her, excusing herselfe with her wordes so clearlie, as thoughe she had never bene faultie to the same.'[22]

After she sat down word went out that she would surely be freed, but the jury wasted little time in finding her guilty. De Carles describes how she was then required to surrender her royal honours before Norfolk passed sentence. She was no longer Queen but a condemned traitor. Then her uncle pronounced her punishment, allegedly with 'tears in his eyes':

Because thou hast offended our sovereign the King's grace in committing treason against his person and here attainted of the same, the law of the realm is this, that thou hast deserved death, and thy judgement is this: that thou shalt be burned here within the Tower of London, on the Green, else to have thy head smitten off, as the King's pleasure shall be further known of the same.[23]

Although she had expected the verdict, it was still very hard to bear the indignity of her husband's betrayal. Now Anne gave way to emotion as the full horror of her position created consternation in the hall:

O Father, O Creator! Thou who art the way, the truth, and the life, knowest that I have not deserved this death!

My lords, I do not say that my opinion ought to be preferred to your judgment; but if you have reasons to justify it, they must be other than those which have been produced in court, for I am wholly innocent of all the matters of which I have been accused, so that I cannot call upon God to pardon me.

I have always been faithful to the King my lord; but perhaps I have not always shown to him such a perfect humility and reverence as his graciousness and courtesy deserved, and the honour he hath done me required. I confess that I have often had jealous fancies against him which I had not wisdom or strength enough to repress. But God knows that I have not otherwise trespassed against him. Do not think I say this in the hope of prolonging my life, for He who saveth from death has taught me how to die, and will strengthen my faith.

Think not, however, that I am so bewildered in mind that I do not care to vindicate my innocence. I knew that it would avail me little to defend it at the last moment if I had not maintained it all my life long, as much as ever Queen did. Still the last words of my mouth shall justify my honour. As for my brother and the other gentlemen who are unjustly condemned, I would willingly die to save them; but as that is not the King's pleasure, I shall accompany them in death. And then afterwards I shall live in eternal peace and joy without end, where I will pray to God for the King and for you, my lords.

As De Carles records, Anne's moving and eloquent speech affected even the most hardened of her audience. Chapuys adds the words: 'The judge of all the world, in whom abounds justice and truth knows all, and through His love I beseech that He will have compassion on those who have condemned me to this death.'[24]

A commotion broke out among the jurors as Henry Percy collapsed. He was so overcome by Anne's courage that he had to be carried out. He never did recover from this tragedy. He died the following year, leaving no son to inherit his ancient title, which lapsed until a nephew was old enough to become 7th Earl of Northumberland. The Lord Mayor of London now turned to comment: 'I can only observe one thing in this trial – the fixed resolution to get rid of the Queen at any price.'

Even Chapuys agreed that the Queen had been the victim, not the Messalina whom Cromwell had described, condemned 'without valid proof or confession'. Cromwell himself later praised the spirit of the Boleyns.[25]

There are curious similarities between the figures caught up in these momentous events and some of the characters in Shakespeare's plays. Iago in *Othello* has many elements of Thomas Cromwell, the ambitious servant dropping poison in his master's ear. In *The Winter's Tale* Leontes the King sees his best friend and the Queen together and is suddenly overtaken by jealousy:

Too hot, too hot! To mingle friendship far is mingling bloods.
I have *tremor cordis* on me: my heart dances; but not for joy,
    not joy...
to be paddling palms and pinching fingers, as now they are,
and making practised smiles, as in a looking-glass, and then to
    sigh...
O, that is entertainment my bosom likes not, nor my brows!

Leontes refuses to believe that they are innocent and orders a secret investigation to prove their guilt. Queen Hermione is arrested and accused of adultery, high treason and plotting to murder the King.

Like Anne, Hermione must defend herself against the shameful and absurd charges born out of her husband's paranoia. A masterpiece of internal strength and great dignity, she exemplifies goodness, and is described as a 'most sacred lady'. The parallels with Anne are undeniable, even to the guilty verdict and the figure of her young daughter who will bring new hope for a glorious future, like Elizabeth.

Like Shakespeare, few were fooled by the decision of the Tower court. The public had swung firmly behind Anne, outraged that a Queen of England, whose coronation they had turned out in their thousands to celebrate less than three years before, could so easily be cast out by her husband. It was an act of gratuitous malice. Everyone knew of Henry's affair with the Seymour woman. Such was his open contempt for their opinion that he had flaunted her throughout his wife's imprisonment. They naturally compared the characters of the two women and drew their own conclusions.

Justice had fallen in the gutter. The King was exposed as a tyrant, ready to cold-bloodedly sacrifice the woman he had claimed to love barely days before in a letter to his ambassador in Rome. When he was told of Anne's strength and dignity, he retorted: 'She hath a stout heart, but she shall pay for it!' The transcript of the trials was bagged and removed to conceal the judicial murder.[26]

To celebrate his victory, Henry held a lavish pageant on the river as though to defy Londoners. He went afterwards to a banquet with the Bishop of Carlisle, boasting: 'For a long time back had I predicted what would be the end of this affair, so much so that I have written a tragedy which I have here by me.'

He then pulled out a handwritten book of his poems, perhaps even the same as Anne and George were said to have mocked. As the shocked bishop told Chapuys: 'He believed more than a hundred had to do with her...

'You never saw prince nor man who made greater show of his horns, or bore them more pleasantly.'

Chapuys remarked that Henry's delight was comparable to that 'a man feels in getting rid of a thin old vicious hack in the hope of getting soon a fine horse to ride'. This was sordid and distasteful and the Imperial ambassador recognised that 'already it sounds ill in the ears of the people, that the King … has shown himself more glad than ever since the arrest of the whore…'[27]

George Constantine warned Cromwell that 'there was much muttering of Queen Anne's death'. Even in Europe they knew of Henry's involvement with Jane Seymour. Luther recognised that she was 'an enemy of the Gospel'. Ives states that:

> As Agnes Strickland pointed out even more vigorously, the picture of Jane preparing for marriage to Henry while Anne was under sentence of death in the Tower is repulsive enough, but it becomes tenfold more abhorrent when the woman who caused the whole tragedy is loaded with panegyric.[28]

On the day following Anne's trial, 16 May, Kingston was concerned about the sentence that had been passed upon her. It remained unknown whether the Queen would be beheaded or burned at the stake. He wrote asking Cromwell: 'What is the King's pleasure touching the Queen, as for the preparation of scaffolds and other necessaries?'

Tradition tries to convince us that the King was swayed to mercy, choosing not to burn his wife but sending all the way to Calais for their best executioner to provide her with an easier death.[29] This generosity diminishes when it becomes clear that in order for the headsman to reach London for the date of her execution, Henry must have requested that he set out on his journey long before the jury had even given their verdict on Anne's guilt.

That day the Archbishop of Canterbury came to visit his former patroness. The suggestion that he had come to hear her last confession and grant her absolution is an error made by Catholic writers, for evangelicals and Protestants do not believe in this ritual. As a believer, Anne would have made her own peace with God through the indwelling of the Holy Spirit.

She would have been pleased to see Cranmer, of course. He had been the Boleyn family chaplain and would have offered her comfort in her ordeal, but that was most certainly not the reason that Henry had permitted his visit. The King had denied Anne all contact with her family and insisted that she be kept apart from her brother at their trials. He agreed now to Cranmer's visit simply to suit his own advantage and Anne must have known it.

We come now to the root cause of the whole conspiracy to remove Anne.

It was not enough for the King to cast her down or to blacken her name with scandalous accusations, to defame the woman he had loved so much. After 20 years the insecurity facing the Tudor line remained Henry's motivation.

Anne had failed to produce a son and heir. In this she was, ironically, no better than Catherine had been to him. Henry had no faith in a succession where either one of his daughters would inherit his crown.

The shock of his near-death experience at the tournament in January had been the turning-point. Henry had survived, but he was informed that Anne had been discussing what would happen after his death. This presumption sealed his decision to seek a way to remove her.

Time was running out for him – he was almost 45. It was now, or perhaps not at all, if he was ever to get a legitimate son. If he died without a recognised male heir, civil war would follow. Elizabeth would be the heiress in the eyes of those who supported Henry's divorce from Catherine, while Catherine's supporters would still regard her as illegitimate. Mary's party would never accept Elizabeth as Queen. The Emperor and the Pope would make certain that she was removed, even by foreign invasion. England's independence was under threat. The nation would become a colony of the Holy Roman Empire, with Mary married off to some Catholic prince.

All Henry's new powers and reforms would be erased, the old religion imposed once again. The Inquisition could come to England (and it did).

Henry shared these concerns with Cromwell, threatening his survival if he failed to supply his needs. Cromwell knew his own life was on the line. He had to provide a solution and had few scruples about destroying Anne in order to save himself.

In those April days Cromwell had evolved his plan to kill two birds with one stone: he could appease England's Catholic enemies and still arrange that Henry could name his own successor. If Anne was removed and her marriage proved invalid, then he was free to take a new wife and a new Act of Succession would make Elizabeth as illegitimate as Mary. For suppose a third wife failed to present him with the longed for son. History could repeat itself again, with Jane suddenly in Anne's position and Henry's impotence a confirmed fact. Mary and Elizabeth would be left to battle for the throne unless Henry had named an alternative heir. And if all Henry's children were equally illegitimate then there already existed the perfect candidate and a son of his own blood: Henry Fitzroy, Duke of Richmond.

Richmond was now 17, an assured young man who had been acknowledged as the King's son for years. As a boy he had been given his own household and heaped with honours – Lord High Admiral of England, Knight of the Garter, Duke of Richmond and Somerset, Earl of Nottingham – titles normally reserved for the heir to the throne.

Edward Seymour had served him and Henry Howard, Earl of Surrey, was his closest friend and brother-in-law after his sister Mary married Richmond in 1533.

The King had considered legitimising his son before. In 1527 he had examined the Church's rulings, sending Richmond's tutor, Richard Croke, to Rome. Two years later Henry nominated his son Lieutenant of Ireland, a move which troubled Catherine and Emperor Charles V.[30] When Anne gave birth to Elizabeth, the Act of Succession making Mary illegitimate automatically gave her half-brother Richmond precedence over her.

Richmond had enjoyed an increasingly prominent place at his father's court. He had headed the Garter procession in 1534, attended Parliament regularly and was Henry's choice to lead an army to quell Ireland, gathering his forces at Sheffield, from where he had complained: 'here in this country where I lie I have no park nor game to show sport nor pleasure to my friends when they shall resort unto me'.

The King changed his mind about risking his son in Ireland and sent Surrey in his place while he began planning how he might confirm Richmond as his heir.

Now the opportunity was here, as Cromwell pointed out. The

Secretary of State thought himself so clever that he could contain the Boleyn faction while deceiving the Catholics. He aimed to play one side off against the other, knowing that Henry never intended to make Mary his heir. He would remove Anne and marry the quiescent Jane Seymour and, failing there, he already had sons to succeed him. He had Richmond and he had Henry Carey, his son by Mary Boleyn.

Henry Carey was Henry's reserve. Born in 1526, he was a thriving and bright boy. As Anne's ward since 1528, he was tutored by the great French poet Nicholas Bourbon, along with Henry Norris's son. The King had never recognised his bastard by his wife's sister. In 1528 this had been an impediment to their marriage, but now the marriage was an impediment to his acknowledgement of the child.

Cromwell had been searching for grounds to prove that Henry's marriage to Anne was as illegal as his marriage to Catherine. He did not want to claim that the 1533 annulment was false because that would have restored Mary's legitimacy and made her heir to the crown. A way had to be found to erase both marriages, both wives and daughters, leaving Henry free to marry again and choose his own successor.

For days he had been closeted with Sampson, the expert on canon law, as they went over the alleged pre-contract between Henry Percy and Anne. Even though the verdict of the 1532 inquiry had confirmed Percy's story that there was no betrothal between them, Cromwell had tried to make him renege on his vow. But Percy stood strong, writing back on 13 May, when he knew that he would be a juror at Anne's trial, to refuse to cooperate in Cromwell's scheme. He had told him boldly that he would keep his vow 'to his damnation'.[31]

Cromwell had no option but to set Cranmer to convince Anne to admit that her marriage was false. For this, it was necessary to wait until the trial was over and she was at her most vulnerable, awaiting death. Cromwell was certain that Anne would trust the Archbishop, who had been her chaplain and friend, and agree once she heard the offer he brought from the King.

Cranmer himself was willing to go through with this once he realised the Queen was doomed. Cromwell was offering her the one way out of her terrible predicament if she would only take it. Surely he thought that if she consented to a divorce her life would be spared? Even more, once he had her signature on the papers, the King would permit her to go into exile abroad with her daughter. Elizabeth would become illegitimate and of no importance, therefore they could be freed.

Cranmer had even found a way. Although the 1534 Act of Supremacy had made all papal dispensations null and void in England, the 1528 papal bull had granted a dispensation against consanguinity which applied to Henry's liaison with Anne's sister Mary. If this was overturned, then Henry's marriage to Anne was not legal under statute 25 Henry VIII c.21. This convenient get-out clause now provided Cranmer with a last chance to save Anne's life.

Did she believe him? He was an honest friend but she must have realised that he was being used as the instrument of her husband's gross desire to be free of her. So death was not enough for Henry. He needed more: he needed to clear the succession by disinheriting Elizabeth, as he had done with Mary. If Anne agreed to sign away her daughter's birthright, then they would be sent away – as Catherine was banished – leaving Henry free to take another wife.

If she signed then the verdict of the trial would be meaningless, for if she and Henry were never married, then how could she be guilty of adultery? Henry no longer had any reason to kill her, for she was not a threat.

She signed. Cranmer gave thanks to God for her cooperation and took away the papers annulling her marriage, certain that soon she would be released in secret and allowed to go abroad. Perhaps they even discussed where she might go. He had many contacts in the Protestant German states, where she would receive a warm welcome.

The chance of a future for Elizabeth and herself now gave Anne hope. She was heard to say, 'I will go to Antwerp',[32] but in this she was deluding herself, and perhaps she knew it, for Henry was not only a coward but a murderer. She knew his character well enough to doubt his good intentions, but she had risked all on Cranmer's word and the possibility of freedom.

As for Henry, he had no intention of saving Anne. To relent now, after the whole sordid business of her very public trial, would make him look a fool. Anne remained too dangerous an opponent to be permitted to live. Removing his problem meant removing it permanently.

Chapter Fifteen

Bloody Days

THE FIRST EXECUTIONS took place on Wednesday, 17 May. Some accounts claim that they occurred on Tower Green and that Anne was forced to watch her brother and accused lovers suffer. Chapuys says the sight cruelly 'aggravated her grief'. This is surely incredible, as the *Lisle Letters* state they were executed on Tower Hill, a traditional site located outside the Tower's walls. For Anne to view this sorry spectacle she would have had to be moved to a better vantage point, presumably the Bell Tower, from where Thomas Wyatt witnessed events. That Wyatt was a witness was confirmed only in 1959 by the discovery of one of his lost manuscripts at Trinity College, Dublin.[1]

Again there is controversy about the way they died. The King had agreed to commute the sentence of hanging, drawing and quartering even for Smeaton, although some writers say he was hanged. In fact they were all beheaded that May morning, having made their final speeches to a watching crowd.

Before being marched out of the Tower, George Boleyn had asked to take communion one last time and on the scaffold he took the chance to defend his religious beliefs.[2] In the tradition of the time, he did not speak of injustice or his innocence, aware that the King confiscated all property from those condemned and could refuse to aid their families or honour their debts. This was very much George's concern, not wishing that anyone should suffer by his death, and even Kingston interceded with Cromwell, pleading: 'You must help my lord of Rochford's conscience.' George's last words were widely reported in England and abroad and three conflicting versions exist: 'Masters all, I am come hither not to preach a sermon but to die, as the law hath found me, and to the law I submit me. I was born under the law, I am judged under the law and I must die under the law, for the law has condemned me.'

As any sinner, he said, he deserved death but his fate was a warning to all not to trust in fortune:

Trust in God, and not in the vanities of the world, for if I had so done, I think I had been alive as ye be now.

Men do common and say that I have been a setter-forth of the word of God and one that hath favoured the Gospel of Christ; and because I would not that God's word should be slandered by me, I say unto you all that if I had followed God's word in deed as I did read it and set it forth to my power, I had not come to this.

Truly and diligently did I read the gospel of Christ Jesus, but I turned not to profit that which I did read; the which, had I done, of a surety I had not fallen into so great errors.

Wherefore I do beseech you all, for the love of our Lord God, that you do at all seasons hold by the truth, and speak it, and embrace it.

He asked forgiveness from anyone he had offended, but did not mention the King.[3]

Sir Francis Weston followed George's Christian speech, admitting to having led a sinful life, although this in no way suggested he was guilty as charged. With disturbing honesty he told the crowd: 'I had thought to have lived in abomination yet this twenty or thirty years and then to have made amends. I thought little it would have come to this.'

He warned his listeners to learn by 'example at hym'. In his farewell letter to his family he had echoed his conscience, confessing to be 'a great offender to God'.

By contrast, Norris 'sayed all most nothinge at all'. He had denied his guilt many times, but now it was too late. Brereton alone spoke out against the judgement: 'I have deserved to die if it were a thousand deaths. But the cause whereof I die, judge not. But if ye judge, judge the best.'

He had sent his wife a last token before his death, a golden bracelet. He was executed 'shamefully, only of old rancour', claimed Cavendish, and John Hussey agreed: 'By my troth, if any of them were innocent it was he. For either he was innocent or else he died worst of all.'[4]

Smeaton alone could say in truth: 'Masters, I pray you all pray for me for I have deserved the death.' He had not retracted his confession, even on the scaffold.

Each man had taken his turn to kneel on the scaffold, placing his neck in the semicircle of the block. They faced death 'charitably', following one another as the axeman did his work, showing each head to the crowd in turn as the trunk was quickly removed. The bodies were taken by a wagon back into the confines of the Tower and hastily buried, George in the Chapel of St Peter ad Vincula and the others in the churchyard.[5]

The attitude of the crowd watching the executions on Tower Hill had been remarkable. There was no crying out or jeering, but a respectful silence, even awe.

Cromwell was sufficiently troubled by the thought of popular protest that he revised the plans for Anne's execution.

Anne waited to hear about events from Kingston. Following her encounter with Cranmer, she had been in growing desperation for news from Cromwell or the King that she would be released. But Kingston came only to confirm what she had dreaded.

She was to die the next day, Thursday, 18 May.

The King had decided that she was not to be burned alive at the stake, nor would she suffer the crude blows of the axe; for the expert swordsman he had sent for from Calais would take off her head swiftly. Kingston reassured her that her execution would not prove painful, for his touch was 'so subtle'.

She bore the news well, coming to terms with the truth that she had been betrayed. Cranmer's offer of a reprieve was all deceit: he had been used by the unscrupulous King and Cromwell. The confirmation was proved by Henry's summons for the swordsman. She knew now that he must have been sent for many days before her trial by a husband who cared nothing for her innocence.

Her dignity impressed her jailer. She asked for details of her brother's death. Kingston gravely informed her of the morning's brutal executions and she suffered greatly to hear of George's bravery. She would have been comforted to know that already his last speech was being written down and copied in London.

Kingston told her that all men except Smeaton had insisted on their innocence on the scaffold. Anne had hoped that the musician who had betrayed her under torture would have had the courage to retract his false confession. She thought he had put his immortal soul in danger by his lies, but she still had compassion on him for his weakness. According to a later account, she said: 'Alas! Has he not then cleared me of the public shame he has brought me to? Alas, I fear his soul suffers for his false accusations!

'But for my brother and those others, I doubt not but they are now in the presence of that Great King before whom I am to be tomorrow.'[6]

With all hope gone, she openly laid the blame on Chapuys. When he heard reports of this later, the ambassador admitted: 'I was flattered by the compliment, for she would have cast me to the dogs!'[7] Anne recognised that her constant enemy, the representative of the Holy Roman Emperor, had been part of the plot to destroy her and that Cromwell, an alleged fellow believer, had betrayed her to save himself.

She had come to the throne through her sense of mission and destiny, Queen Esther interceding for the advance of reform in the kingdom, and now she was paying the price of leading the great revolution against Catholic Europe. Many were to see her as a martyr, sacrificed by men of no principle, the first casualty of the coming wars of religion that would dominate the next century and more.

Anne is said to have written two poems during her time in captivity. Although their authenticity is in question, they do convey the bitter betrayal of these days:

> Defiled is my name full sore
> Through cruel spite and false report,
> That I may say for evermore,
> Farewell, my joy! adieu comfort!

> For wrongfully ye judge of me
> Unto my fame a mortal wound,
> Say what ye list, it will not be,
> Ye seek for that can not be found.

The other poem was later set to music written by Robert Jordan, one of her chaplains, and remains highly popular for its great poignancy:

> O Death, O Death, rock me asleepe,
> bring me to quiet rest;
> Let pass my weary guiltless ghost
> out of my careful breast.
> Toll on, thou passing bell;
>
> Ring out my doleful knell;
> Thy sound my death abroad will tell,
> For I must die,
> There is no remedy.
>
> My pains, my pains, who can express?
> Alas, they are so strong!
> My dolours will not suffer strength
> My life for to prolong.
> Toll on, thou passing bell;
> Ring out my doleful knell;
> Thy sound my death abroad will tell,
> For I must die,
> There is no remedy.
>
> Alone, alone in prison strong
> I wail my destiny:
> Woe worth this cruel hap that I
> Must taste this misery!
> Toll on, thou passing bell;
> Ring out my doleful knell;
> Thy sound my death abroad will tell,
> For I must die,
> There is no remedy.

Farewell, farewell, my pleasures past!
Welcome, my present pain!
I feel my torment so increase
That life cannot remain.
Cease now, thou passing bell,
Ring out my doleful knoll,
For thou my death dost tell:
Lord, pity thou my soul!
Death doth draw nigh,
Sound dolefully:
For now I die,
I die, I die.[8]

Anne's strength and great resilience helped her through this time of endurance. She prayed with her almoner late into the night. Outside on the green they were building her scaffold and the tapping of their hammers marked out her last hours.

Before dawn she invited Kingston to take communion. She had composed herself to face death and swore twice on the sacrament that she was innocent of all charges the King had brought against her. She wanted Kingston to make that public and he reported the occasion to Cromwell by letter: 'This morning she sent for me, that I might be with her at such time as she received the good Lord, to the intent I should hear her speak as touching her innocency alway to be clear.'[9]

After he left, she waited for nine o'clock, the hour appointed for her death. She must have dressed and prepared herself, but when Kingston returned it was not to conduct her on her last walk. He brought news that the executioner was delayed on his way there and her death must be postponed until noon.

Anne was certain that this was one last act of cruelty on Henry's part. Recovering herself, she announced bitterly: 'Master Kingston, I hear say I shall not die afore noon, and I am very sorry there for, for I thought to be dead by this time and past my pain. I have heard say the executioner was very good, and I have a little neck.' And she began 'laughing heartily'.[10]

She spent the morning in an agony of waiting, but when midday came, allegedly the executioner had still not arrived. Kingston came to say that the time was now set for nine the next morning, 19 May.

Reporting back to Cromwell, Kingston was worried about the growing unrest in the city, fearing that Anne's supporters would overwhelm the Tower's security. He recommended that the time of the execution should remain a secret so that few people would hear her speech from the scaffold. He was afraid that 'she will declare herself to be a good woman for all men but the King at the hour of her death... I have seen men and also women executed and they have been in great sorrow; but to my knowledge this lady has much joy and pleasure in death.'

As a result of Kingston's warning, Cromwell decided to ban all foreigners from the Tower.[11]

Was it mere cruelty that lay behind Henry's decision to postpone Anne's death? There was a more practical reason for the delay which had nothing to do with the Calais swordsman. Henry was giving time for his tame Archbishop Cranmer to finalise the annulment of his marriage to Anne. As she had suspected, her death was not enough for Henry: he needed to erase the memory of their relationship by illegitimating their daughter Elizabeth.

On 18 May Cranmer convened an ecclesiastical court at Lambeth to confirm the annulment of Anne's marriage. It was over quickly, with no grounds being cited and all the relevant papers were then destroyed. An official announcement merely stated that the marriage was null and void, thereby making Princess Elizabeth as illegitimate as her half-sister Mary. Now all of Henry's children were bastards.[12]

Further business on their agenda was a dispensation permitting Henry to marry Jane Seymour. Ironically, this was necessary because Henry's great grandmother, Cecily, Duchess of York, and Jane's grandmother, Elizabeth Neville, were cousins.

As they prepared for their wedding, the Tower was being made ready for the first public execution of a Queen of England.

Anne is said to have been able to send a final message to Henry via a member of the Privy Chamber:

Commend me to his Majesty, and tell him that he has ever been constant in his career of advancing me. From a private gentlewoman he made me a marchioness, from a marchioness a Queen; and now that he has no higher degree of honour left, he gives my innocence the crown of martyrdom as a saint in heaven.[13]

Her own ladies, including Wyatt's sister Margaret, Lady Lee, had finally been allowed to attend her and prepare her for this last ordeal. Her mood was resolute, calm, even cheerful as she tried to console her friends. She had no qualms as she faced her own mortality, assured by her faith of her future salvation.

Dressed in black damask, Anne, with her women, was escorted by Kingston out into the May sunshine. Before them, just a few yards away, stood the rough-hewn scaffold, draped in black cloth and laid with straw.

There was an audience waiting. Her enemy Cromwell was there with his son Gregory, who was shortly to be married to Jane Seymour's widowed sister Elizabeth. Other eager conspirators were there as well: Lord Audley, the Chancellor, and Charles Brandon, Duke of Suffolk, who had hated her from her youth; but her uncle Norfolk had not the stomach to witness the sad spectacle of his niece's death. Also standing in the shadows of the scaffold was Henry's son and intended heir, young Henry Fitzroy, Duke of Richmond, and behind him a crowd of hundreds of onlookers to witness this historic moment.

A great hush fell over them all as Anne appeared. She was 'never so beautiful', her serenity noted by everyone as she came to the steps of the scaffold 'with an untroubled countenance'.[14]

There was no sound as Anne began to speak from the raised platform. Her voice was surprisingly strong, echoing the last words of her brother George:

Good Christian people, I have not come here to preach a sermon; I have come here to die, for according to the law and by the law I am judged to die, and therefore I will speak nothing against it. I am come hither to accuse no man, nor to speak of that whereof I am accused and condemned to die, but I pray God save the King and send him long to reign over you, for a gentler nor a more merciful prince was there never, and to me he was ever a good, a gentle, and sovereign lord.

And if any person will meddle of my cause, I require them to judge the best. And thus I take my leave of the world and of you all, and I heartily desire you all to pray for me.[15]

This was no time to protest her innocence, she knew it was far too late for recriminations which could only endanger her daughter Elizabeth. In her last moments Anne's sole concern was to depart this life with grace and forgiveness for those who had wronged her, many of whom now stood waiting to witness her death.

She turned to her ladies, removing her headdress, divesting herself of her necklaces and handing her Bible to Margaret Wyatt. This was said to be the illustrated Book of Hours now found at Hever, in which Anne had written: 'Remember me when you do pray, that hope doth lead from day to day.' Another volume believed by some to be the one she handed to Margaret Wyatt is a book of psalms by Sir John Croke MP, formerly in the possession of the Wyatt family and now in the British Library.[16]

Then Anne forgave her executioner and paid him to do his work well. By contrast with the English headsman's traditional method, where the prisoner almost had to lie prostrate at the low block, the swordsman from Calais performed his task without a block, his victim kneeling upright. Anne now sank down on her knees, praying: 'O Lord have mercy on me, to God I commend my soul. To Jesus Christ I commend my soul; Lord Jesu receive my soul'; 'which words she spake with a smiling countenance', according to John Stow, who adds: 'and with that word suddenly the hangman of Calais smote off her head at one stroke with a sword'.

Every source confirms the blow was swift and sure: 'before you could say a paternoster'.[17] Her spirit had fled the body as the cannons fired, announcing to the city that it was finished.

Anne's long-time friend and fellow prisoner Thomas Wyatt was a witness from the Bell Tower. He later wrote these verses in an attempt to exorcise the memories of these terrible days:

'V. Innocentia Veritas Viat Fides Circumdederunt me inimici mei':

> Who list his wealth and ease retain,
> Himself let him unknown contain.
> Press not too fast in at that gate
> Where the return stands by disdain,
> For sure, *circa Regna tonat.*

> The high mountains are blasted oft
> When the low valley is mild and soft.
> Fortune with Health stands at debate.
> The fall is grievous from aloft.
> And sure, *circa Regna tonat.*

> These bloody days have broken my heart.
> My lust, my youth did them depart,
> And blind desire of estate.
> Who hastes to climb seeks to revert.
> Of truth, *circa Regna tonat.*

> The Bell Tower showed me such sight
> That in my head sticks day and night.
> There did I learn out of a grate,
> For all favour, glory, or might,
> That yet *circa Regna tonat.*

> By proof, I say, there did I learn:
> Wit helpeth not defence too yerne,
> Of innocency to plead or prate.
> Bear low, therefore, give God the stern,
> For sure, *circa Regna tonat.*

As the spectators moved away, Anne's ladies wrapped her body in a sheet and removed it to the Church of St Peter ad Vincula, where her brother already lay interred.

Kingston, writing later to Cromwell, could not conceal the respect he had for his former prisoner: 'The Queen died boldly. God take her to His mercy.'[18]

Across the river the Scots reformer Alesius accompanied Thomas

Cranmer as he walked in the gardens of Lambeth Palace. They may have heard the cannon fire from the Tower, signalling the end, for the Archbishop looked up and proclaimed: 'She who has been the Queen of England on earth will today become a Queen in Heaven.'

Then he sat down on a bench and wept, as Alesius later reported to Elizabeth.[19]

Chapter Sixteen

The Legacy

ACCOUNTS DIFFER AS to Henry's whereabouts as the cannon fired from the Tower of London announcing he was free. One source states that he was at Richmond, ready to set off for Wiltshire, where his future bride waited. Others say he was at White-hall, where he dressed himself all in white before taking his barge to Sir Nicholas Carew's house, as had been his practice every night. Other sources claim that Jane heard the news herself from Sir Francis Bryan in the palace in the Strand, where she was trying on her wedding dress.[1]

The very next day Henry and Jane moved together to Hampton Court and were betrothed before witnesses. According to canon law, this had the same validity as marriage. Henry had no time to lose, desperate for a son. He now issued orders that his daughter Elizabeth be removed from his sight to live at Hatfield. He clearly wanted no reminders of her mother to raise inconvenient ghosts.

The wedding ceremony took place just 11 days after Anne's execution, on 30 May, performed by Bishop Gardiner.[2] The speed with which this was conducted left the English people in little doubt that Henry's lust for Jane was the root cause. Suspicions about the trials were widespread with increasing hostility across the country as the King was mocked and openly despised for his callous butchery. He was called 'a tyrant more cruel than Nero' and 'it were better he had broken his neck'. People took great risks in decrying the King but so strong was the tide of popular disgust that they saw him as 'a beast and worse than a beast'. Within days there were new ballads in circulation denouncing Henry and defending Anne. It was believed that if he knew the extent of the nation's loathing 'it would make his heart quake'.[3]

Thomas Wyatt was released from the Tower after his narrow escape. Ignoring the dangers of committing his thoughts to paper, he recalled the deaths of innocent men:

> In mourning wise since daily I increase,
> Thus should I cloak the cause of all my grief;
> So pensive mind with tongue to hold his peace
> My reason sayeth there can be no relief:
> Wherefore give ear, I humbly you require,
> The affect to know that thus doth make me moan.
> The cause is great of all my doleful cheer
> For those that were, and now be dead and gone.
>
> What though to death desert be now their call,
> As by their faults it doth appear right plain?
> Of force I must lament that such a fall
> Should light on those so wealthily did reign.
> Though some perchance will say, of cruel heart,
> A traitor's death why should we thus bemoan?
> But I alas, set this offence apart,
> Must needs bewail the death of some be gone.
>
> As for them all I do not thus lament,
> But as of right my reason doth me bind;
> But as the most doth all their deaths repent,
> Even so do I by force of mourning mind.
>
> Some say, 'Rochford, haddest thou been not so proud,
> For thy great wit each man would thee bemoan,
> Since as it is so, many cry aloud
> It is great loss that thou art dead and gone.'

Ah! Norris, Norris, my tears begin to run
To think what hap did thee so lead or guide
Whereby thou hast both thee and thine undone
That is bewailed in court of every side;
In place also where thou hast never been
Both man and child doth piteously thee moan.
They say, 'Alas, thou art far overseen
By thine offences to be thus dead and gone.'

Ah! Weston, Weston, that pleasant was and young,
In active things who might with thee compare?
All words accept that thou diddest speak with tongue,
So well esteemed with each where thou diddest fare.
And we that now in court doth lead our life
Most part in mind doth thee lament and moan;
But that thy faults we daily hear so rife,
All we should weep that thou art dead and gone.

Brereton farewell, as one that least I knew.
Great was thy love with divers as I hear,
But common voice doth not so sore thee rue
As other twain that doth before appear;
But yet no doubt but thy friends thee lament
And other hear their piteous cry and moan.
So doth each heart for thee likewise relent
That thou givest cause thus to be dead and gone.

Ah! Mark, what moan should I for thee make more,
Since that thy death thou hast deserved best,
Save only that mine eye is forced sore
With piteous plaint to moan thee with the rest?
A time thou haddest above thy poor degree,
The fall whereof thy friends may well bemoan:
A rotten twig upon so high a tree
Hath slipped thy hold, and thou art dead and gone.

And thus farewell each one in hearty wise!
The axe is home, your heads be in the street;
The trickling tears doth fall so from my eyes

I scarce may write, my paper is so wet.

But what can hope when death hath played his part,

Though nature's course will thus lament and moan?

Leave sobs therefore, and every Christian heart

Pray for the souls of those be dead and gone.[4]

Anne herself proved too dangerous a subject to discuss. Among her enemies there was rejoicing. The English envoy reported from Rome that at news of Anne's fall the Pope had exclaimed: 'I have never ceased praying to heaven for this favour.' Other rulers were cynical, the Emperor's sister Mary of Hungary, now Regent of the Netherlands, commenting on Henry's new wife: 'When he is tired of this one he will find some occasion of getting rid of her.'[5]

Nicholas Bourbon and other evangelicals left England with news of the travesty of the trials. Etienne Dolet declared that Anne had been condemned 'on a false charge of adultery'. German Protestants believed that the attack on Anne was the price for Henry's reconciliation with Rome. Melanchthon saw great dangers ahead: 'The Queen, accused rather than convicted of adultery, has suffered the penalty of death and that catastrophe has wrought great changes in our plans.' And he knew who to blame: 'that blow came from Rome. In Rome all these tricks and plots are contrived.'[6]

The Catholic party in England were certain they now had Henry in their pocket.

Mary had always been taught by her mother that the entire blame for their troubles was due to the 'heretic' Anne and her influence. Now that Anne had been removed, Mary was certain that she would soon be restored as princess and heir to the throne. She called Cromwell 'one of her chief friends' and conspirators such as Carew, Audley and Fitzwilliam, who had used Jane Seymour as a lure, were now expecting great advances from Henry's third wife and her relatives.

They were to be sorely disappointed. Although Jane had been proclaimed Queen of England on 4 June and her brother Edward was created Earl of Hertford, there was no coronation. Even if she could give him a son, Henry had no intention of raising another woman to the same power he had given to Anne. When Jane tried to give her opinion on the dissolution of the monasteries, Henry quickly reminded her of the fate of her predecessor and delivered an ominous warning not to interfere in politics.[7] As the Earl of Sussex told the King, now that all his children were of equal status, all illegitimate, 'it was advisable to prefer the male to the female for the succession to the crown'. Henry was ready to name Henry Fitzroy, Duke of Richmond, as his heir. The King's son walked with him in the procession at the formal opening of Parliament in June and attended proceedings every day.[8]

By contrast with the way he treated his son, Henry did not reply to the stream of frantic letters from Mary. Although the Catholic party pressed for her restitution, as far as the King was concerned nothing had changed in their strained relationship. Until Mary agreed to submit to the Act of Supremacy and recognise her illegitimacy, she was still a rebel to the crown.[9] In a panic, Chapuys advised Mary to save herself and take the oath of supremacy. He told her she could always get a dispensation from Rome when she broke it. Chapuys was certain that Henry's daughter would prove to be an able liar.[10]

But Cromwell made her grovel 'most humbly prostrate before the feet of Your Most Excellent Majesty', for she had 'so extremely offended Your Most Gracious Highness, that my heavy and fearful heart dare not presume to call you father'. She signed, acknowledging Henry as supreme head of the Church in England, refusing 'the Bishop of Rome's pretended authority, power and jurisdiction within this realm, heretofore usurped' and admitting that 'the marriage heretofore had between His Majesty and my mother the late Princess Dowager was by God's law, and man's law, incestuous and unlawful'.[11]

Henry graciously responded, referring to the 'imbecility of her sex', which limited her intelligence and made her subject to manipulation by the enemies of England. Mary was rewarded with her own household at the end of June and her father actually visited her soon afterwards, although she was not restored as she had expected on Anne's death.[12] Henry had insisted on reforms to the Act of Succession in order to nominate his son as heir to the throne, but while the bill was still in Parliament Richmond died suddenly at St James's Palace on 22 July.

Tradition says he died of tuberculosis, but for three weeks he had attended Parliament every day without comment on any signs of illness. His death was immediately covered up. Henry sent Norfolk, Richmond's father-in-law, to remove the body in secret without the accustomed autopsy or any of the ceremonial due to someone of his high rank and position.

The body was duly encased in lead and smuggled out of the palace under a cartload of straw. Norfolk took it to Thetford, where the burial took place. When his daughter, Richmond's widow Mary Howard, wrote to the King about a pension, Henry refused to grant her anything. In a further demonstration of his increasingly violent moods, Henry now attacked Norfolk and threatened him with jail for not giving his son the full honours due to him.[13]

Chapuys was soon reporting that 'the party of the Princess Mary is naturally jubilant at his death'. But Cromwell now turned against his former allies. Exeter and Fitzwilliam were dismissed from court and the Marchioness of Exeter was imprisoned in the Tower.

Sir Francis Bryan and Sir Anthony Browne were questioned about their loyalty to Mary, the Pope and the Emperor.[14]

In July Cromwell had succeeded Thomas Boleyn as Lord Privy Seal and became ennobled as Baron of Oakham. Thomas had retired to Hever, broken by the tragedy that had destroyed his family. Henry left him alone; whether out of regard for his qualities or the friendship they had shared for many years is impossible to judge. He died in 1538 and was buried in the local church.

George's betrayer, his widow Jane, Lady Rochford, begged Cromwell 'as a power desolat wydow' and was allowed to retain part of her husband's property. She was reinstated as a lady of the Privy Chamber and served Henry's subsequent wives, but was executed in 1542 with Catherine Howard, ironically for similar indiscretions in the royal household.[15]

The other conspirators fared no better. The Marchioness of Exeter was in the Tower for more than a year, her son for nearly 15 years and her husband was beheaded in December 1538. Richard Tempest, a member of the jury, died in the Fleet prison in August 1537, while the jury foreman, Giles Heron, was hanged, drawn and quartered in August 1540. Sir Nicholas Carew, who had coached Jane Seymour, also fell foul of his erstwhile ally Cromwell and was executed on Tower Hill in March 1539. Ironically, according to Hall, he gave thanks for his imprisonment, during which he had undergone a religious conversion by reading a copy of the Bible in English. In his last words 'he exhorted all to study the evangelical books, as he had fallen by hatred of the Gospel'.

'Seventy-two thousand persons are said to have perished by the hand of the executioner in the reign of King Henry.'[16] 'As he lay dying, Henry confessed the many injustices of his reign and allegedly was truly repentant, and among other things, on account of the injury and crime committed against the said Queen [Anne Boleyn].'[17]

Matthew Parker had no doubt that Queen Anne was in 'blessed felicity with God' but for years it was as if she had never even existed. Her falcon badges had been torn down in the royal palaces, her interlocking initials roughly painted over in the haste to erase her memory. Portraits and documents were destroyed as the truth about Anne was airbrushed from history.[18]

Cardinal Pole called Anne 'a Jezebel and a sorceress' and the 'author of all the mischief that was befalling the realm'. The Treshams of Rushton blamed Anne for all the sufferings of Catholics under her daughter Elizabeth, claiming that she 'did beget a settled hatred of them against her and hers ... Anne Boleyn – the bane of that virtuous and religious Queen Catherine, the ruin of man ... the first giver of entrance to the Protestant religion'. In Catholic eyes

Anne had committed an unpardonable crime: she had separated England from the papacy and accordingly their savage hatred has known no bounds and they have never ceased to blacken her memory with their vile calumnies... Anne Boleyn has had her full share of slander in this huge conspiracy of falsehood.[19]

Her daughter Elizabeth was now officially a bastard, with her mother's enemies insinuating that she was not the child of the King but of Norris. Her half-sister Mary often declared there was a likeness to Smeaton. Cardinal William Allan declared that Elizabeth was 'an incestuous bastard, begotten and born in sin of a famous courtesan'.[20]

After Anne's death her child was neglected if not forgotten. Lady

Bryan wrote to Cromwell complaining that her charge had long out-grown her clothes and needed attention: 'Elizabeth is put from that degree she was afore and what degree she is at now, I know not... For she is as toward a child, and as gentle of condition as ever I knew in my life. Jesu preserve her Grace.'[21]

By Christmas 1536 Elizabeth was received at court, but here she became aware of a mother whom no one ever mentioned. Jane Seymour's brother greeted a remark about the town of Boulogne with the retort: 'No words of Boleyn!'

Yet Elizabeth was educated as her mother had insisted, by Protestant scholars like Sir John Cheke and Roger Ascham. She soon proved herself to be something of a child prodigy, speaking several languages and translating *The Mirror of the Sinful Soul* by Anne's friend Margaret of Navarre from the French as a present for her stepmother, Katherine Parr. As Elizabeth later said herself: 'It is said that I am no divine. Indeed, I studied nothing but divinity till I came to the throne.'

Elizabeth was born to rule and prepared for this destiny. She had no doubts at all of her mother's innocence, for as Foxe says: 'whatso-ever can be conceived of man against that virtuous Queen, I object and oppose again the evident demonstration of God's favour, in main-taining, preserving and advancing the offspring of her body, the lady Elizabeth, now Queen'.[22]

Elizabeth was preserved through many dangers to finally ride in tri-umph through the streets of London, where her mother was hon-oured in the pageantry. She adopted as her own her mother's badge and motto, '*Semper eadem*' (Always the same). She summoned Matthew Parker to be her Archbishop of Canterbury, to which he replied: 'If I had not been so much bound to the mother, I would not so soon have granted to serve the daughter in this place.'[23]

She asked Parker to trace the papal dispensation for her parents' marriage (which he did, in 1572). In Parliament she restored Anne's legal title as Queen and her own as heir. Her purpose was to vindicate her mother, boasting that she was 'the most English woman of the kingdom'. She even had a ring made which opened to reveal secret portraits of herself and Anne in enamel.[24]

Elizabeth chose to make a family for herself from those who knew her mother. She appointed George, Anne's brother's son, Dean of Lichfield. She considered Mary Boleyn's children as her half-brother and half-sister. She made Henry Carey Baron Hunsdon, Knight of the Garter and a member of her Privy Council. He became her the captain of her personal bodyguard and in November 1569 during the Revolt of the Northern Earls, was lieutenant-general of the royal army. He was also Lord Chamberlain when a company of actors, the Lord Chamberlain's Men, performed Shakespeare's plays. He died in July 1596.

His sister Catherine was treated as Elizabeth's half-sister and closest friend. She married Sir Francis Knollys, Privy Councillor and Vice-Chamberlain of the royal household, and their daughter Lettice became Countess of Essex and of Leicester.

Elizabeth also recognised that Sir Henry Norris had 'died in a noble cause and in justification of her mother's innocence', she created his son Lord Rycote.

With Protestant rule re-established, the memory of Anne was at last resurrected. Those who had known her personally were finally able to speak openly. Anne's chaplain, William Latimer, and Alesius wrote accounts for Elizabeth in which they blamed her mother's death on her Catholic and Imperial enemies. Anne's role in bringing the Reformation to England was illustrated by the scholar John Aylmer: 'Was not Queen Anne, the mother of the blessed woman, the chief, first and only cause of banishing the beast of Rome with all his beggarly baggage?'

As the chronicler Holinshed recorded:

> Because I might rather say much than sufficiently enough in praise of this noble Queen as well for her singular wit and other excellent qualities of mind as also for her favouring of learned men, zeal of religion and liberality in distributing alms in relief of the poor, will refer the reader unto that which Mr Foxe says…

George Wyatt, grandson of Sir Thomas Wyatt and Anne's first biographer, compiled his collection of reminiscences from members of his family and those who had personally known her, such as her former maid of honour, Anne Gainsford. He concluded that 'this princely lady was elect of God'.[25]

Elizabeth was her mother's daughter in many ways. The restoration of Protestantism as the faith of England, advances in education, sponsorship for poor scholars and new ideas in literature and music were all first started by Anne Boleyn.

The rise of an English national spirit and sense of independence from the rest of Europe were the result of Anne's intervention on the political scene. Her capacity to move and participate in areas which had been exclusively the preserve of men was also due to her mother's radical breakthrough, leading directly to her death.

In other ways, too, Elizabeth inherited qualities from her mother: her looks, her skill at languages and music, also perhaps her opinions on love and marriage: 'Affection? Affection is false!' she once declared. It was noted that 'for her part she hated the idea of marriage every day more, for reasons which she would not divulge to a twin soul'.[26]

Did the young child remember more about her mother and her execution than anyone had assumed? In the following years her own bitter experiences would only reinforce these early fears as others close to her followed Anne to the scaffold.

Elizabeth had learned a hard lesson well.

Notes

Abbreviations used in notes

BIHR *Bulletin of the Institute of Historical Research*

BL British Library

BM British Museum

EHR *English Historical Review*

SP Span *Calendar of Letters, Despatches, and State Papers, relating to the Negotiations between England and Spain, preserved in the Archives at Vienna, Simancas, Besançon and Brussels*, ed. Pascual de Gayangos, G.A. Bergenroth, M.A.S. Hume, Royall Tyler and Garrett Mattingly, 13 vols., HMSO, London, 1862–1954

SP Ven *Calendar of State Papers and Manuscripts Relating to English Affairs, Existing in the Archives and Collections of Venice and in Other Libraries of Northern Italy*, ed. R. Brown, G. Cavendish-Bentinck, H.F. Brown and A.B. Hinds, 38 vols., London, 1864–1947

GEC G.E. Cokayne, *Complete Peerage of England, Scotland, Ireland, etc.*, 13 vols., reproduced edn. 1982

Lisle Letters *The Lisle Letters*, ed. M. St Clare Byrne, 6 vols., Chicago, 1981

LP *Letters and Papers, Foreign and Domestic of the Reign of Henry VIII*, ed. J.S. Brewer, J. Gairdner and R.H. Brodie, 21 vols., London, 1862–1932

PRO Public Record Office

SP *State Papers of King Henry VIII*, 11 vols., London, 1830–52

Documents are referred to by number except in a few instances where a page reference is more helpful.

CHAPTER 1 Into the Vortex

1. Paget, pp. 162–70; LP. x.450.
2. LP. iii.1994.
3. LP. i.438; LP. viii.71.
4. Cavendish, *The Life and Death of Cardinal Wolsey*, p. 29; De Carles, lines 53–4.
5. D'Aubigny, vol.1. pp. 111–12.
6. LP. iii.1559; SP Span. suppl. 42, pp. 69–73; Hall, p. 631.
7. More, *Epigrammata*, published 1520.
8. SP Ven. ii.1287.
9. Giustinian, i.85–90f.; LP. ii.395.
10. Giustinian, ibid.
11. Mancini, pp. 67, 69.
12. Byrne, p. 63; House of Commons, i.456; GEC.x.137–40.
13. Hall, p. 518; LP. ii.1500–2,1490.
14. SP Ven.
15. Loades, *The Tudor Court*.
16. SP Ven; Chapuys: SP Span.
17. Sir Robert Naunton, *Fragmenta Regalia*, 1653.
18. BL.Sloane MSS.
19. SP Span., suppl. to vols. I and II, p. 39.
20. Cited in Loades, *The Tudor Court*.
21. Hall, pp. 597–8; LP. iii, 246–50; SP Ven.ii, 1220, 1230; Giustinian, ii.270–1.
22. SP Ven. Li.1220; BL.Cotton MS. Cal. D vii, fo. 118; LP. iii.246.
23. Rebholz, *Wyatt*, Poem CLI.68.
24. Sir Anthony Denny to Roger Ascham: Ellis, p. 14.
25. Zagorin, pp. 113–14; Starkey, 'The Court: Castiglione's Ideal and Tudor Reality', pp. 232–9.
26. Erasmus Collected Works, *De Conscribendis epistolis*.
27. Sander, p. 21; William Camden, *Annales*, 1612, p. 2; Clifford, p. 80.
28. Friedmann, vol. 2, p. 315; J. Gairdner, 'Mary and Anne Boleyn' and 'The Age of Anne Boleyn', *EHR*, 8, 1893, pp. 53–60; Round, pp. 12–23; Brewer, ii.170.
29. Sander, p. 25.
30. De Carles, lines 55–8.
31. George Wyatt, p. 18.
32. De Carles, line 61; Simon Grynee, *Original Letters*, ii.553.
33. Grynee, ii.553.
34. Historical Manuscripts Commission, *Manuscripts of the Marquess of Ormonde*, new series, 1902–20, vii.507; Ives, *Anne Boleyn*, pp. 52–6; E.W. Ives, 'The Queen and the painters: Anne Boleyn, Holbein and Tudor Royal Portraits', *Apollo*, July 1994, pp. 36–45; Roland Hui, 'A Reassessment of Queen Anne

Boleyn's Portraiture', from a lecture at the Concordia University Art History Forum, Montreal, Quebec, Canada, 18 January 2000.

35. *Garland of Lavrell*, lines 864–77.

36. P. Somerset Fry, *Chequers, the Country Home of Britain's Prime Ministers*, 1977, p. 52; *Catalogue of the Principal Works of Art at Chequers*, HMSO, 1923, no. 507.

37. SP Ven. iv.824.

38. De Carles, lines 62–8.

39. Wyatt, *Papers*, v. p. 141; Sander, p. 25.

40. *Privy Purse Expenses of King Henry VIII*, ed. N.H. Nicolas, London, 1827, pp. 222–3.

41. HM the Queen, Windsor; Parker, *Drawings*, no. 63; BM, Department of Prints and Drawings: 'Portrait of a Lady', 1975-6-21-22.

42. J. Rowlands and D.R. Starkey, 'An old tradition reasserted: Holbein's portrait of Queen Anne Boleyn', *Burlington Magazine*, 125, 1983, pp. 88–92.

43. Foxe, v.60–1.

44. LP. vi.613.

45. Friedmann, vol. 2, p. 315; Parker, *Drawings*, pp. 7–20, 53, 63; J. Rowlands, 'A portrait drawing by Hans Holbein the Younger', in *British Museum Yearbook*, 2, 1977, pp. 231–7; Rowlands and Starkey, pp. 88–92.

46. Roy Strong, *The English Renaissance Miniature*, London, 1983, pp. 36–7, 189; Roy Strong, *Artists of the Tudor Court: The Portrait Miniature Rediscovered 1520–1620*, London, 1983, pp. 18, 39–40.

47. BM, Department of Coins and Medals: G. Hill, *Medals of the Renaissance*.

Chapter 2 The Marriage Market

1. Bryce, James, *The Holy Roman Empire*, 1978; Heer, Friedrich, *The Holy Roman Empire*, trans. Janet Sondheimer, 1968.

2. GEC, x.137.

3. Riley, *Croyland Chronicle*.

4. LP. i.1338; *Chronicle of Calais*, pp. 71–6.

5. Machiavelli, *The Prince*, ch. 23.

6. LP. viii.1448.

7. De Boom, *Marguerite d'Autriche*, p. 118.

8. Baldwin de Bolon came from Boulogne, which in the *Chronicles of Calais* is spelt 'Boleyn', so the spelling 'Boleyn' for the family name is more correct than 'Bullen'.

9. Cal. Close Rolls, Henry VII, i.143; Cal.Inquisitions Post Mortem, Henry VII, i.322; *Vergil*, vol. 74, pp. 52, 94.

10. LP. xi.17; Cal.Close Rolls, Henry VII, ii.179.

11. LP. xi.13; GEC, x.139.

12. See the brasses at Hever and Penshurst: M. Stephenson, *List of Monumental Brasses*, 1926, vol. 2, pp. 236, 251.

13. Parker, *Correspondence*, p. 400.
14. LP. ii.1501; LP. iv.5462; LP. iv.1939; SP. vii.219; Du Bellay, i.105.
15. Friedmann, pp. 319–20; Gairdner, 'Mary and Anne Boleyn', viii, pp. 58–9; Ives, *Anne*, p. 21.
16. Warnicke, *Anne*, p. 16.
17. De Carles, lines 43–8.
18. Paget, p. 163 n.9.
19. S110, Royal Genealogies, 42; S443, royalfam.ged.
20. Paget, pp. 163–6; LP. i.2655.
21. Ives, p. 31.
22. Hall, p. 569.
23. Cited in Richardson, *Mary Tudor*, 1970.
24. Erasmus Correspondence, vol. 2, p. 278.
25. SP Ven. ii.482.
26. De Carles, lines 37–42.
27. Ives, p. 33 n.25; LP. ii.3348; BL. MS Cotton Vitellius cxi, fo. 155v refers to 'Madamoyselle Boleyne'.
28. LP. ii.15.
29. LP. ii.68; Pollard, *Henry VIII*, p. 51; Knecht, *Francis I*, p. 38.
30. LP. ii.i.223; BL. MS Cotton Cal DVI, ff. 163–265; LP. ii.106, 133–5.
31. LP. ii.222.
32. LP. ii.113, 203.
33. LP. ii.225.
34. LP. ii.227.
35. Brantôme.
36. LP., ii.80.
37. SP Ven.
38. LP. ii.224.
39. Richardson, *Mary Tudor*, p. 140.
40. LP. ii.399.
41. LP. x.18, 450.
42. Brewer, ii.168, i.168 n.2; Friedmann, vol. 1, pp. 55.
43. Watson (ed.), *Vives and the Renascence Education of Women*, p. 96.
44. Herbert, *Henry VIII*, p. 30; Sander, p. 56; George Wyatt, *Papers*, p. 143; LP. iii.1994.
45. Knecht, pp. 88, 103.
46. BL. Sloane MSS.
47. SP Span. 422.
48. Russell, *Cloth of Gold*, pp. 124–5, 159–61, 195, 202, quoting Oxford, Bodleian MS Ashmole 1116; SP. vi.56.
49. Friedmann, app. B.
50. LP. ii.1230, 1269; LP. ii.1277; iii.1646, 1628, 1583, 1830.

51. Fox, *Politics and Literature*, pp. 56–72; LP. ii.124, 125; Ives, *Anne*, p. 15.
52. Giustinian, i.320, 326.
53. LP. ii.3446, 3455; SP Ven. 918–920.
54. Gwyn, *The King's Cardinal*.
55. LP. iii.1762.
56. Ives, *Anne*, p. 45; LP. iii.1628; iv.1279, 2433.

CHAPTER 3 The King's Desire

1. Cavendish, *Wolsey*, pp. 29, 34, 58–64.
2. LP. vii.171.
3. Cavendish, *Wolsey*, pp. 31–7.
4. LP. ii.1893, 1935, 1969–70, 3819, 3820.
5. Cavendish, *Wolsey*, pp. 29–34, 58–64.
6. Burnet, *History of the Reformation in England*, 1865.
7. Fraser, *The Wives of Henry VIII*, pp. 124–7.
8. House of Commons, iii.419; LP. iii.3358.
9. GEC, x.140–2.
10. LP. iv.i.639.
11. Starkey, 'The Court: Castiglione's Ideal and Tudor Reality', pp. 232–9.
12. LP. ii.395.
13. Roper, pp. 20ff.
14. Reese, *Music in the Renaissance*, 1954, pp. 769ff, 842, 850; BL. Sloane MSS.
15. LP. ii.410, 4024.
16. Castiglione, *The Book of the Courtier*, p. 74.
17. SP Ven. ii.780; Reese, pp. 769ff, 842, 850; Lisa Urkevich, *Anne Boleyn, a Music Book, and the Northern Renaissance Courts*, PhD diss., University of Maryland, 1997, pp. 100–1.
18. John Stevens (ed.), *Musica Britannica*, vol. 18, 'Music at the Court of Henry VIII', London, 1973, p. 18.
19. BL. Add. MS 31922, ff. 71v–73 attributed to Henry VIII; John Stevens, *Music and Poetry in the Early Tudor Court*, London, 1961, pp. 411–12.
20. Pace to Wolsey: LP. iii.447, 1188.
21. Motto, Christmas 1530.
22. Hebel, J. William and Hoyt H. Hudson, *Poetry of the English Renaissance*, New York, 1941, pp. 8–9.
23. George Wyatt, *Papers*, p. 10; *Wolsey*, ed. Singer, pp. 426–7.
24. Rebholz, CLI.68; Thomson, pp. 194, 196–200; K. Muir and P. Thomson (eds.), *Collected Poems of Sir Thomas Wyatt*, Liverpool, 1969, p. 5; Zagorin, 'Sir Thomas Wyatt and the Court of Henry VIII', pp. 113–41.
25. Ives, *Anne*, pp. 92–3.
26. *Norton Anthology of English Literature*, 6th edn. vol. 1, New York, 1993, p. 447.

27. Mattingly, *Catherine of Aragon*, p. 182; Ives, *Anne*, p. 108.

28. Byrne, *Letters*, p.15.

29. Savage (ed.), *The Love Letters of Henry VIII*, pp. 40–1; Fraser, pp. 128–9.

30. Ridley, *Letters*, pp. 13–18, notes that Hever passed to the Catholic Edward Waldegrave, who could have forwarded the letters.

31. LP. iv.3219; Ridley, *The Love Letters of Henry VIII*, p. 49; Savage, p. 39 n.1.

32. Byrne, p. 368

33. George Wyatt, in *Wolsey*, ed. Singer, p. 426: BL. Sloane MS 2495, fo. 3.

34. LP. iv.3219.

35. Bernard, *Rise of Sir William Compton.*

36. Savage, pp. 32–4; LP, iv.3218.

37. Hall, *The triumphant reigne of King Henry the VIII*, p. 707.

38. Ives, pp. 92–3; Knecht, *Francis I*, p. 192.

39. Savage, pp. 29–30; LP. iv.332, 635; Ridley, *Love Letters*, pp. 37, 53.

CHAPTER 4 The Curse

1. *Correspondencia de Gutierre Gomez de Fuensalida*, ed. Duque de Berwick y de Alba, Madrid, 1907, p. 449.

2. Commynes, *Mémoires*, i.455; ii.64–5.

3. York Civic Records, i.122.

4. LP. vi.618; vii.1368.

5. *Croyland Chronicle.*

6. SP Span. i.164, 178.

7. Buck, George, *History of Richard III*, 1646, in Kennett, *History of England*, vol. 1, p. 568; Gairdner, James, *Letters and Papers of Henry VII*, pp. 203–4.

8. Francis Bacon, *History of Reign of Henry VII*, Folio Society, London, 1971.

9. Denys Hay (ed.), *Polydore Vergil.*

10. *Vergil*, pp. 127–9, 146–7.

11. SP. Milanese, i.299.

12. SP Span. I.

13. D'Aubigny, vol. 1, pp. 111–12.

14. Hume, *Wives*, p. 151 n.1.

15. LP. iv.5774, 5778.

16. LP. 5681; Hall, 494.

17. SP Span. i.265.

18. Burnet, i.35.

19. Hall.

20. Scarisbrick, pp. 13, 42; LP. iv.5774.

21. Scarisbrick, p. 13 n.2; Fraser, p. 38 n.24.

22. Scarisbrick, pp. 186–94; Mattingly, pp. 48–52.

23. Burnet, iv.17f.

24. Vatican Archives, Arm.34, 23, 689.

25. SP Span. ii. suppl. 19.
26. Mattingly, p. 90.
27. Burnet, i.36.
28. SP Span. ii.38.
29. LP. iv.1638.
30. SP Ven. ii.479.
31. Brewer, ii.162; Scarisbrick, p. 152.
32. Erickson, *Bloody Mary*, pp. 56–9; Strickland, vol. 3, p. 514n.
33. Brewer, ii.102–3; LP. iv.1431, 1500, 1510.
34. BL. Harleian MS 6807, fo. 3; Scarisbrick, p. 154; Beverley Murphy, *Bastard Prince: Henry VIII's Lost Son*, Sutton Publishing, 2001.
35. SP Ven. iii.455, 1037, 1053.
36. LP. v.136; Virginia Murphy, 'Debate over Henry VIII's First Divorce,' PhD in 'Literature and Propaganda of Henry's Divorce', cited in MacCulloch, *Henry VIII*, ch.6.
37. LP. iii.1193.
38. BM. Add. MSS 4729.
39. SP Ven. iii.195, 210.
40. LP. ii.4257; iii.1233, 1297.
41. Just as John F. Kennedy's Pulitzer prize-winning *Profiles in Courage* is said to have been ghosted by his speechwriter, Ted Sorensen.
42. Cranmer, Letter to Wolfgang Capito.
43. SP Span. v.i.9.
44. Roper, p. 67f; LP. iii.1233, 1450, 1574, 1772.
45. LP. iii.1450, 1510; Leo X Bull, 11 October 1521; Ellis, 1, vol. 1. p.292.

Chapter 5 The Turning-Point

1. Cited in Williams, Neville, *Henry VIII and His Court*, p. 171.
2. Foxe, v.52–3, 60.
3. Wood, M.A.E., *Letters of Royal and Illustrious Ladies*, 1846, ii.15–16; Savage, pp. 27–48; LP. iv.3218–21, 3990, 4383, 4403, 4410, 4477, 4537, 4539, 4597, 4648, 4742, 4894.
4. LP. iii.1284–8, 1290–3; SP Ven. iii.213, 219; SP Span. ii.336; Hall, 622–4; LP. iii.18–137.
5. E.W. Ives, 'Henry VIII: The Political Perspective', in MacCulloch, *Henry VIII*, p. 31.
6. Walter Raleigh, *History of the World*, ed. C.A. Patrides, 1971, p. 56.
7. Pollard, *Henry VIII*, 429, 434, 439–40; William Thomas, *The Pilgrim*, pp. 9, 54–5.
8. Ridley, *Love Letters of Henry VIII*, no. 10.
9. George Wyatt, *Papers*; This in the indictment at her trial: Wriothesley, 222; LP, x.876.

10. Wyatt, *Poems*, vii. 'sithens' = seeing that; George Wyatt says Anne's motto was: 'I am Caesar's all, let none else touch me', George Wyatt, *Papers*, p. 181.

11. Warnicke, 'Eternal Triangle', pp. 565–79.

12. Dowling, 'Anne Boleyn and Reform', pp. 30–46; Foxe, iv.656–8, v.53, 58, 135, 137; Ives, pp. 161–3.

13. Anderson, *Annals of the English Bible*, vol. 1, p. 584, 42f.

14. George Wyatt, *Anne Boleigne*, p. 14.

15. Harpsfield, *Pretended Divorce*, p. 213.

16. *Crónica del Rey Enrico*, 89–91; Muir, *Life and Letters of Wyatt*, pp. 22–3.

17. Friedmann, vol. 1, p.190, n.i; George Wyatt, *Papers*, p. 27.

18. Wyatt, *Poems*, v.

19. Muir, *Life and Letters*, pp. 37, 85.

20. Wyatt, *Poems*, xcvii.

21. Muir, *Life and Letters of Wyatt*.

22. LP. iv.3326–35; Ridley, *Letters*, pp. 34–7, 53; LP. iv.3325: last line = 'looks for no other'.

23. LP. iv.3221, 4537.

24. cited in Paul, p. 78.

25. Scarisbrick, pp. 243–4; Ives, p. 293; Warnicke, pp. 27, 109.

26. BL. Add. MSS 43, 827, fo. 2.

27. P.E. Hughes, *Lefèvre*, vol. 13, pp. 35–40; Ives, p. 293.

28. SP Span. iv.ii.i.972; v.i.179.

29. LP. iii.3386.

30. LP. iv.5416. For Morley: BL. Harleian MS 6561.

31. Foxe, iv.183–155.

32. Ridley, *Statesman*, pp. 31–2, 124, 126–8, 135–6, 253–8; Wood, *Broken Estate*, pp. 3–15.

33. *Reply to Luther: More's Works*, v.41, 57, 79, 181, 223, 225, 227, 311, 341, 355, 403, 429, 437, 439, 611, 677, 683.

34. Stapleton, T., *The Life and Illustrious Martyrdom of Sir Thomas More*, 1928, p. 34.

35. *More's Works*, v.61, 685, 689, 691.

36. Ridley, *Statesman*, pp. 133–5.

37. *More's Works*, v.823–5.

38. *More's Life*, 134.

39. MS de Brienne, quoted in J. Lingard, *History of England*, Dublin, 1878, iv.237 n3.; LP. iv.1413–14; Hall, 722.

40. Cavendish, *Wolsey*, p. 230.

41. Ibid.

42. Kaulek, p. 131.

43. Greenblatt, p. 137.

44. Scarisbrick, pp. 152–4.

45. Plowden, *Tudor Women*, p. 54.
46. Stemmler, *Letters*, 13; Ridley, *Love Letters*, 15.
47. Harpsfield quoted by Warnicke, p. 84.
48. *Lisle Letters*, v.276–7, 280.
49. LP. iv.3913, 4251.
50. Cavendish, *Wolsey*, pp. 31–7.

CHAPTER 6 A Renaissance Family

1. SP Span. iii.ii.432–3.
2. LP. iv.3625, 3664, 3761, 4141, 4173, 4296, 4310, 4414.
3. SP Span. v.i.122, 170; LP. viii.909.
4. SP Span. iii.ii.550; iv.ii.993; SP Ven. iv.761; Gunn, *Brandon*, p. 228.
5. Cavendish, *Wolsey*, pp. 35–6.
6. LP. iv.3757, 3783.
7. LP. iv.4251; Pocock vol. 1, pp.141.
8. LP. iv.4251, 4289, 4355, 4358, 4359, 4361, 4390.
9. LP. iv.4649, p. 2021; D'Aubigny vol. 1, p. 331.
10. D'Aubigny vol. 1, pp. 321–2.
11. LP. iv.4649; SP i.289, LP. iv.4335.
12. Du Bellay, iii.129, 143; LP. iv.1924, 1925, 1941.
13. Carlson, James R., Hammond, Peter W. 'The English Sweating Sickness, 1485–1551', *Journal of the History of Medicine*, 54, 1999, pp. 23–54.
14. Christopher Hibbert, *The English*, p. 201.
15. LP. IV.ii.1924.
16. LP. ii.1547; iii.198.
17. Du Bellay, iii.137.
18. LP. iv.4391.
19. LP. iv.4403.
20. Foxe, v.689.
21. LP. i.2610, 2634.
22. Dr A.S.Currie, 'Notes on the Obstetric Histories of Catherine of Aragon and Anne Boleyn', *Edinburgh Medical Journal*, vol.1, 1888, pp. 1–34.
23. A.S. MacNalty, *Henry VIII: a Difficult Patient*, London, 1952, pp. 180, 199; Ove Brinch, 'The Medical Problems of Henry VIII', *Centaurus V*, 3, 1958, p. 367.
24. *Inventories*, p. 57.
25. SP. i.296ff.
26. LP. iv.4408, 4409; SP i.312–16; Brewer, ii.274.
27. D'Aubigny, vol. 1, pp. 343–6.
28. Savage, p. 44.
29. LP. iv.1932.
30. LP. iv.4391, 4398, 4408, 4440.

31. LP. iv.4383, 4408–9, 4277; SP. i.296–301.

32. LP. iv.4358, 4359, 4361, 4390; Scarisbrick, pp. 210–11.

33. LP. iv.4360.

34. SP. i.305, 312; LP. iv.4486, 4507.

35. LP. iv.4410.

36. LP. v.11, 306; LP, iv.4410.

37. LP. iv.4197, 4477, 4488, 4507; Knowles, D., 'The Matter of Wilton', *BIHR*, 31, 1958, pp. 92–6.

38. LP. iv.4538, 4649.

39. LP. iv.4539, 4649.

40. SP Span. iii. 432, 790; Cavendish, p. 36.

41. LP. iv.4537, 4647.

42. Fraser says Honey Lane was in Oxford: p. 145; Dowling, 'Anne Boleyn and Reform', pp. 30–46; LP, iv.6401, 4004, 4017, 4030, 4073, 4175; Foxe, v. 802–9, 829–33; see also S. Brigden, *London and the Reformation*, Oxford, 1989.

43. Foxe, v.428.

44. LP. x. 891; Foxe, v.421–8.

45. J. Venn, *Biographical History of Gonville and Caius College*, Cambridge 1897, i.17; J. A. Giles (ed.), *Whole Works of Roger Ascham*, London 1865, i. ep. 60 to Thomas Wendy.

46. Latimer, *Chronicle,* fo. 28.

47. BL. Sloane MS 1207; Foxe, v.35; LP. iv.5925; v.982; vi.299; Foxe, Strype and George Wyatt; R. Triphook, ed., *Extracts from the Life of the Virtuous, Christian and Renowned Queen Anne Boleigne*, London, 1817; SP Span. iv.ii.i.972.

48. Hughes, *Lefèvre*, pp.35–40; Ives, p. 293; E.F. Rogers (ed.), *Letters of Sir John Hacket*, Morgantown, 1971, pp. 155–251.

49. BL. Harleian MS 6561; LP. iv.126–7.

50. Latimer, *Chronicle*, fo. 28.

51. LP. iv.2652, 2677, 2697; Foxe, iv.670–1; Hall, pp. 762–3; More, *The Confutation of Tyndale*, 1532.

52. Foxe, v.117.

53. Strype, vol. 3, pp.171–3 quotes a written memorandum by John Louthe found among the Foxe papers, iv. 657–8; v. 53, 58, 135, 137; George Wyatt, *Life of Anne Boleigne*, pp. 16–17 record the memories of Anne's maid, Anne Gainsford later Zouche; Dowling, *Anne and Reform*, p. 36.

54. *Tyndale's Works*, edited by Russell, vol. 1, p. 212.

55. Simon Fish, *A Supplication for Beggars*; Dickens, *English Reformation*.

56. Foxe, v.53; iv.657–8; LP. iv.2607; LP. iv.4779; Louth's account is printed in J.G. Nichols, *Narratives of the Days of the Reformation*, Camden Society, 1859, pp. 52–7; George Wyatt, pp. 422, 429, 438–40.

57. SP Span. iv.i.539.

58. SP Span. iii–ii.541, 550.
59. Ridley, *Love Letters*, p. 65.
60. SP Span. iii.ii.789.
61. Latimer, fo. 22; SP Ven. iv.873, 923.
62. Zahl, p. 5.
63. D'Aubigny, vol. 1. p.338.

CHAPTER 7 The King's Great Matter

1. Hall, 144; SP Ven. iv.177–8.
2. Burnet, vol. 1, pp. 54, 55, 58; Strype, vol.1, p.171.
3. LP. iv.3802.
4. LP. iv.4246, 4257.
5. Brewer, vol. 2, pp. 303–4.
6. LP. iv. 2108, 4875.
7. SP Span. iii.ii.38, Suppl. 34.
8. Hall, 754f.; LP. iv.2145; Du Bellay, iii.217–8; Harpsfield, p. 177; LP. iv.5702.
9. SP Ven. iv.184; Du Bellay, iii.231; LP. iv.2177; Hall, 149; Harpsfield, p. 83.
10. Campeggio to Salviati, February 18, 1529, Brewer, vol. 2, p. 486.
11. LP. iv.5368–73, 5314, 5325, 5375, 5571, 5599; SP Span. iii.ii.652, 676–7.
12. LP. iv.2096; SP Span. iii.ii.861.
13. Burnet, vol. 5, p. 444.
14. LP. iv.5518, 5519.
15. LP. iv.5481.
16. SP Span. iii.ii.789.
17. Cavendish, pp. 113–16; Hall, pp. 756–7; BL. MS Cotton Vitellius BXII, 2–164.
18. Cavendish, p. 118.
19. Cavendish, pp. 121, 225–6; D'Aubigny, vol. 1, pp. 409–10.
20. LP. v.360; vi.775; Burnet, vol. 4, p. 15f.; Scarisbrick, pp. 186–94.
21. LP. iv. 4251, 5791.
22. *Daily Telegraph*, 14 May 2002.
23. LP. iv.iii.5679.
24. Hall, p. 758; LP. iv.5791.
25. LP. iv.5749–50; Skelton, *Poetical Works*.
26. Loades, *George Wyatt*, p. 29.
27. SP Span. v.ii.54, 120; G. Mattingly, 'A Humanist Ambassador,' *Journal of Modern History*, 4, 1932, pp. 175–85.
28. LP. iv.5859; Scarisbrick, p. 246.
29. LP. iv.113.
30. Du Bellay, iii.342.
31. Cavendish, pp. 113, 129–131, 176.
32. D'Aubigny, vol. 1, p. 433.

33. LP. iv.6035.
34. Cavendish, pp. 136, 188.
35. LP. iv.6738.
36. LP. iv.6019.
37. LP. iv.6026.
38. LP. iv.6075.
39. Strype, vol. 1, p. 204; Act 25 Henry VIII, 19.
40. Herbert, p. 321.
41. LP. iv.5996; Ives, p. 152.
42. LP. iv.6459.
43. SP Span. iv.i.351–2.
44. SP Span. iv.196.
45. LP. iv.5276.
46. Cavendish, p. 120f.

CHAPTER 8 The Grand Enemy

1. LP. iv.6030.
2. LP. v.110.
3. LP. iv.6114; Cavendish, p. 121.
4. LP. iv.2715; D'Aubigny, vol. 1, p. 469; SP Span. iv. i.450.
5. SP Span. iv.i.368.
6. LP. iv.6094, 6181–2, 6411, 6436, 6447.
7. SP Span. iv.i.366, 368.
8. SP Span. iv.i.647, 804–5.
9. Du Bellay, iii.408–9, 454; LP. iv.6256.
10. D'Aubigny, vol. 2, p.24.
11. Al-Masudi, 10th century; Said ibn Ahmad, Qadi of Toledo, 1068; Bat Yeor, *Islam and Dhimmitude: Where Civilizations Collide*, Associated University Press, 2001.
12. D'Aubigny, vol. 2, pp. 24–6.
13. Sanders, p. 63; SP. vii.194; Herbert, *Life of Henry VIII*, p. 287.
14. SP Span. iv.ii.28; LP. v.45.
15. LP. iv.3802; SP Span. iv.i.634.
16. SP Span. iv.i.692.
17. Hall, p. 771.
18. Latimer's *Remains*, pp. 297, 305.
19. *A Copy of the Letters*, London, n.d., sig.A8.
20. *More's Works*, viii.18–20; ix.117–19, 247; Roper, p. 35.
21. SP Span. iv.i.598, 599, 616.
22. SP Span. iv.i.354; LP. iv.6688.
23. SP Span. iv.iii.6738; LP. iv.iii.6738.
24. Cavendish, pp. 37-8.

25. Kamen, *Inquisition*, pp.62,311,328 n.100; Netanyahu, *Origins of the Inquisition*, p.1085; Roth, Cecil, *A History of the Marranos*, New York, p.20.

26. Roth, *Spanish Inquisition*, p.27.

27. Bataillon, Marcel, *Erasmo y España*, Mexico, 1966, p. 490.

28. Cited in Kamen, p. 256.

29. Foxe, v.

30. SP Span. iv.i.449, 708–9; LP. v.216.

31. SP Span. iv.i.535.

32. SP Span. iv.i. 422.

33. SP Ven. 637; LP. iv.6579, 6688.

34. Cavendish, p. 132.

35. SP. vii.212; LP. iv.6763; SP Span, iv.i.819.

36. LP. iv.3035, 6720, 6733; SP Span. iv.ii.71, 445, 819; LP. v.50; Ives, p. 158.

37. Hall.

38. Cavendish, i. 313, 314, 319–20.

39. D'Aubigny, vol. 1, p. 425.

40. Machiavelli, *The Prince*, ch.18; Starkey, 'Castiglione's ideal', pp. 232–9.

41. Machiavelli, *The Prince*, ch. 22.

42. Ibid., ch.18.

43. Sir Anthony Denny to Roger Ascham in Ellis, *Original Letters*, p. 14.

44. Machiavelli, *The Prince*, ch. 23.

45. Roper, pp. 56–7.

46. Machiavelli, *The Prince*, ch. 21.

47. Ibid., ch. 17.

48. Ibid., p. 59.

49. LP. v.216, 238.

50. SP Span. iv.i, 814, 818–19; LP. v.238, 1164; vi.474–5.

51. SP Span. iv.ii.3.

52. LP. v.492, 1114; SP Span. iv.i.386; iv.ii.8.

53. LP. v.65.

54. Foxe, v.99.

55. Wood, pp. 3–15.

56. Foxe, iv.689, 698, 705; Guy, 'More and the Heretics', pp. 14–15.

57. Strype, vol. 1, p. 211.

58. D'Aubigny vol. 1, p. 17; SP Span. 63, 71, 75; LP.v.105, 112.

59. LP. v.105; SP Span. iv.ii.71.

60. G.W. Bernard, 'Henry VIII and the search for the middle way', *Historical Journal*, 41, 1998, pp. 321–49.

61. George Ashdown in Michael de Semlyen, *All Roads Lead to Rome?*, 1993, p. 33.

62. Jeremiah, 7, 18; 44, 17–25; Ezekiel, 8, 14.

63. Hall.

64. LP. v.171.
65. SP Span. iv.ii.212, 228, 239; LP. v.16.

CHAPTER 9 **England's Queen**

1. SP Span. iv.i.351; LP. v.239.
2. LP. v.340, 361, 696.
3. LP. v.696, 762; SP Span. iv.880, 897.
4. D'Aubigny, vol. 2, p. 79.
5. SP Span. iv.i.445.
6. SP Span. iv.ii.699; Warnicke, pp. 146–7.
7. SP Span. iv.ii.487; LP. v.1202.
8. Du Bellay, iii.553–7.
9. Starkey, p. 92.
10. LP. v.1377.
11. LP. x.864.
12. MacCulloch, *Cranmer*, p. 54.
13. MacCulloch, ibid., pp. 613–14.
14. LP. v.1274, 1370.
15. SP Span. iv.ii.528.
16. SP. vii.565; LP. vi.692; LP. ix, 378; SP. vii.566; LP. viii.378.
17. Mattingly, *Catherine*, p. 253.
18. LP. v.529.
19. LP. iv.6511; v.12, 686, 1711.
20. LP. vi.32; vii.1672.
21. LP. v.662.
22. Hall, ii.215, 220, 793; LP. v.625, 1109, 1541, 1546.
23. Ives, pp. 200–1.
24. SP Ven. iv.365–8, 823.
25. Hall, p. 794.
26. LP. vi.438.
27. Friedmann, vol. 1, p. 183.
28. MacCulloch, *Cranmer*, pp. 637–8, app.2.
29. SP Span. iv.ii.i.1003; LP. v.1579.
30. Ellis, vol. 3, pp. 34–9.
31. SP. vii.410.
32. SP Ven. 846; Ridley, *Cranmer*, pp. 52–3; Kelly, *Matrimonial Trials*, p. 40n.
33. LP. v.327; Hall, ii.p. 222.
34. Lehmberg, *Reformation Parliament*, pp. 161, 168.
35. LP. iv.5679, v.594; SP Span. iv.ii.i.872; iv.ii.ii.1077; SP Ven. iv.768; Friedmann, vol. 1, p. 190.
36. SP Span. iv.ii.i.1047, 1048, 1055.
37. SP Span, iv.592–8, 1025; LP. v.1532, 1536, 1567; vi.142.

38. SP Span. iv.i.623; LP. vi.235.

39. SP Span. iv.ii.i.1056, 1061; SP Ven. iv, 867, 893; SP. vii.427; LP. vi.230.

40. SP Span. iv.ii.628; LP. v.150.

41. SP. i.392–3.

42. SP. i.ii.415–17.

43. LP. vi.324, 351; SP Span. iv.1058, 1061.

44. LP. v.723, 1142, 1299, 1525; vi.115, 116, 168, 334, 512, 1264.

45. LP. vi.180, 296.

46. LP. vi.1453.

47. LP. vi.1164, 1249.

48. LP. vi.1528.

49. LP. vi.391.

50. LP. vi.465, 918, 1125.

51. LP. vi.661; Ellis, vol. 3, pp. 34–39.

52. SP Span. iv.ii.ii.1061, 1062, 1077; SP Ven. iv.870, 873; LP. vi.528, 737.

53. LP. vi.661; Ellis, vol. 3, pp. 34–9.

54. LP. vi.264.

55. SP Span. iv.ii.693; LP. vi.240, 241.

56. Cranmer.

57. Hall, ii.231–2; LP. vi.250, 276; SP Ven. iv.912.

58. LP. vi.661; Ellis, vol. 3, pp. 34–9.

59. Hall, ii.232.

60. LP. vi.265, 277; Hall, ii.232–6.

61. Hall, ii.234; SP Span.iv.ii.740; LP. vi.356.

62. Furnivall, *Ballads*, i.374–6.

63. Hall, ii.232–3.

64. SP Span. iv.ii.646, 1077.

65. Cranmer in LP. vi.661; Ellis, vol. 3, pp. 34–9; Hall, ii.236–7.

66. SP Ven. iv.426, 873

67. LP. vi.661; Ellis, vol. 3, pp. 34–9.

68. Hall, pp. 798–805.

69. LP. vi.266–78; Hall, ii.237–41.

70. LP. x.450.

CHAPTER 10 Child of Promise

1. LP. vi.1427.

2. LP. vi.1572.

3. LP. vi.453.

4. LP. vi.890, vii.923.

5. SP Span. iv.ii.756; vi.397, 918.

6. LP. vi.890–1948, 1004; SP Ven. iv.971; SP Span. iv.ii.ii.1124.

7. SP Span. iv.ii.788; LP. vi.453.

8. BM. Julius B XII, fo. 56.

9. LP. vi.282; SP Span. iv. i.224, 249; ii, 788, 1123, 1186.

10. SP. i.ii.407 n.2; LP. vi.1089.

11. SP Span. iv.ii.789; LP. vi.1112.

12. De Carles; *Crónica del Rey Enrico.*

13. Ackroyd, *More*, ch.1.

14. Hall, ii.242–4; SP Span. iv.ii.ii.1107, 1123; LP. vi.1111.

15. Hall, ii. 244.

16. LP. vi.1125, 1112, 470; SP Span. iv.ii.795.

17. Smith, *Henry VIII*, p. 231; A.S. MacNalty, *Henry VIII: a Difficult Patient*, pp. 180, 199; Brinch, 'The Medical Problems of Henry VIII', p. 367.

18. SP Span. iv.ii.842; LP. vi.557.

19. LP. viii.174; Warnicke, p. 168.

20. SP Span. iv.ii.1058.

21. LP. vi. 472, 584–7.

22. Cranmer, *Letters and Remains*, p. 273.

23. D'Aubigny, vol. 2, pp. 172, 174.

24. Ibid.

25. LP. vi.399–400.

26. LP. vi.399–400, 733; viii.736; SP Span..iv.i.373; v.i.60; Foxe, v.136.

27. SP Span. iv.1153; LP. vi.418, 624, 584–9.

28. Rebholz, *Wyatt Complete Poems*, p. 72.

29. LP. iv.7; SP Span.v.i.90, 97, 118, 155; LP. vii.1172.

30. LP. vii.9, 21, 24, 126, 1062.

31. LP. v.1553; vi.6, 1364, 1382, 1591; vii.137, 1475; viii.209, 937; ix.850, 892; Ives, *Anne*, p. 287.

32. LP. vi.222, 225–6, 456, 670, v.1453, vii.112, 964, viii.1031, 1057; ix.450.

33. LP. vii.922; vii.632; Wyatt, *Anne Boleigne*, p. 18; Latimer: Bodleian MS C. Don. 42, ff. 20–33: *A Brief Treatise or Chronicle of … Anne Bulleyne, late Queen of England.*

34. Foxe, v.60–1; Zahl, p. 5.

35. Latimer, fo. 31v.

36. Foxe, v.605.

37. LP. vii.122, 923; v.363; ix.85.

38. LP. iv., app. 99, 2599, 4476, 4488, 1939, 3448, 4520, 6748; v.755, ix.729, v.747, 753, 757–8; xi.164.

39. Wyatt, *Anne Boleigne*, 18.

40. *Correspondence of Matthew Parker*, Parker Society, 1853.

41. SP. i.ii.1303, 532.

42. J.E. Cox (ed.), *Miscellaneous Writings and Letters of Thomas Cranmer*, 1846, ii. 308–9; Latimer, 'Treatyse', Oxford, Bodl. MS Don. C. 42 fo. 30; LP, v.1366; vi.1460; viii.412; ix.1091; Foxe, v.60.

43. Dowling, 'Anne Boleyn and Reform', pp. 30–46; LP. viii.722, 834, 1056.

44. LP. iv.2699; vii.171.

45. Foxe, v.175; Thomas S. Freeman, 'Research Rumour and Propaganda: Anne Boleyn in Foxe's Book of Martyrs', *Historical Journal*, 38, 1995, 797–819.

46. BL.Add. MSS 43, 827. fo. 2.

47. LP. vi.559, 917, 934; x.827.

48. Latimer, fo. 31.

49. D'Aubigny vol. 2, p. 192; LP.vii.664; ix.746.

50. *Nugarum*, vii.90, 402.

51. Ibid. iv.81, 251.

52. Latimer, fo. 28; Ives, *The Common Lawyers*, pp. 319–21; Ives, 'A Frenchman at the Court of Anne Boleyn', *History Today*, August 1998.

53. *Parker Correspondence*, ep. iii; Foxe, v.60; LP. xi. 63, 337, 344; vii.964; *Lisle Letters*, iii.112–13.

54. *Nugarum*, vii.15, 378.

55. Foxe, v.60; Latimer, ff. 23–7b; LP. ix.186.

56. Wyatt, *Anne Boleigne*, p. 19; Burnet, vol. 1, p. 314.

57. LP. vi.1543, 1558, 1571; SP Span. iv.1164–5.

58. LP. vii.8; SP Span. iv.ii.839.

59. SP Span. v.i.ii.

60. LP. vii.69, 323, 871.

61. LP. vii.296.

62. LP. vii.1013.

63. LP. vii.127, 634.

64. LP. v.101; viii.167.

65. LP. vii. 14–16, 214, 254.

CHAPTER 11 Tragedy

1. Hall, ii.242; LP.vi.1111; viiii.509; Foxe, v.62.

2. LP. vi.1249; SP Span. iv.1133.

3. Roper, p. 70.

4. Rogers, E.F., *The Correspondence of Sir Thomas More*, Princeton, 1947, p. 466.

5. *More's Works*, viii.17–21; ix.45, 60.

6. LP. vii.289 .

7. SP Span. iv.ii.894; v.95.

8. LP. vi.1486, 1487; vii.45, 70, 324, 449, 1355.

9. SP Span. v.i.225; LP. vii.389.

10. LP. vi.1065; vii.94, 1668.

11. LP. viii.919.

12. *Lisle Letters*, i,447–8; ii.299; LP.vii.92; ix.991.

13. LP. vii.556, 682, 784–5, 888.

14. LP. vii.958; viii.1013.

15. LP. vii.1193.
16. LP. vi.351.
17. Strype, vol. 1, pp. 460–1.
18. SP Span. v.ii.126–8; LP. x.378, 908; Friedmann, vol. 2, pp. 280; Smith, *Henry VIII*, pp. 64–6; Ives, pp. 238–9.
19. William Clowes, 1579.
20. Knecht, pp. 418–19; Dr A.S. Currie, 'Notes on the Obstetric Histories of Catherine of Aragon and Anne Boleyn', *Edinburgh Medical Journal*, I, 1888, pp. 1–34; Sir John Dewhurst, 'The Alleged Miscarriages of Catherine of Aragon and Anne Boleyn', *Medical History*, 28, 1984, pp. 49–56; Hall, ii.209; Scarisbrick, pp. 211, 485.
21. LP. vi.1054.
22. LP. vii.497.
23. LP. vii.445.
24. LP. vii.378.
25. SP Span. v.i.331, 376; LP. vii.551; viii.15.
26. SP. i.ii.426.
27. Act 26 Henry VIII, 1; Act 37 Henry VIII, 17.
28. LP. viii.974; Harpsfield, pp. 183–97, 258–64; Roper, pp. 86–97.
29. LP. v.907; viii.196.
30. SP Span. v.i.355; LP. viii.1.
31. LP. x.357.
32. LP. VIII, 355; Friedmann, vol. 2, pp. 50–1.
33. *Bulletin de la Société de la Histoire du Protestantisme*: *François I*, Paris, p. 828.
34. SP Span. v.i.476; LP. viii.312.
35. LP. viii.771, 826, 846; SP Span. v.i.170.
36. LP. ix.207; x.82.
37. SP Span. v.i.410; LP. viii.103.
38. LP. viii.194, 253.
39. LP. viii.200, 501–2, 697.
40. LP. viii.210.
41. LP. viii.165, 370.
42. SP Span. v.i.454; LP. viii.251.
43. Sir John Dewhurst, 'The Alleged Miscarriages of Catherine of Aragon and Anne Boleyn', *Medical History*, 28, 1984, pp. 49–56; LP. vii.463; viii.516.
44. Roper, pp. 225–6; *More's Works*, viii.128.
45. Roper, pp. 21, 74; Elton, *Reform*, pp. 180–5, 193; LP. v.472; vii.498–500; SP Span. iv.ii.i,646, 805; v.i.174, 208.
46. SP Span. v.i.156, 170, 174; LP. viii.1056–7.
47. LP. ix.620, 639.
48. LP. ix.326, 356–7.
49. LP. ix.443.

50. LP, ix.525, 571, 639.
51. SP Span, v.i.68, 134, 142, 211; 559–60; LP. vii.871; viii.189, 200, 429.
52. LP. ix.288, 290; 862; SP Span. v.1.570.
53. SP Span. v.ii.40; LP. x.117.
54. SP Span. v.i.573; LP. ix.8731.
55. LP. ix.262, 288, 290.
56. SP Ven. v.257–8.
57. SP. i.ii.451.
58. LP. xi.51; SP Span. v. ii.19; Hall ii.266.
59. Hall ii.266; LP. x.48, 65, 69, 117–18, 141, 307; SP Span. v.ii.3, 4, 9, 12, 27, 44.
60. Giustinian, ii.101; LP. x.71, 172, 200, 294, 838; SP Span. v.ii.35, 58, 67; Wriothesley, i.33.
61. LP. x.282; Hall ii.266.

CHAPTER 12 The Rival

1. LP. x.282–3, 351, 450.
2. SP Span. v. i.454; LP. v.202, viii.251, xi.29, x.1134, xiii.981; Sander, p. 132; Clifford, p. 79.
3. LP. x.134.
4. LP. x.103, 199, 282; SP Span. v.ii.13, 39; Friedmann, vol. 2, p. 203.
5. LP. x.352.
6. LP. x.908.
7. Friedmann, vol. 2, p. 199; LP. x.134.
8. LP. vii.9.
9. LP. x.374.
10. SP Span. v.ii.158; LP, x.450.
11. SP Span.Cal.v.ii.39, 40; LP, x.103, 245; Sander, p. 132.
12. Savine, A., *English Monasteries on the Eve of the Dissolution*, Oxford, 1919.
13. Fuller, *Church History*, 1655, p. 317; Loades, *George Wyatt*, p. 156.
14. LP. viii.989; ix.747, 1118; x.192.
15. Latimer, fo. 31; LP. ix.639, 850, 897; G.W.O. Woodward, 'The exemption from suppression of certain Yorkshire priories', in *EHR*, 76, 1961, pp. 385–401; LP. xii.786; x.383, 858.
16. BL.Cotton MS Cleopatra EVI ff. 234–5.
17. Dickens, p. 13.
18. Act 27 Henry VIII, 28; LP.x.406; D'Aubigny vol. 2, p. 243.
19. LP. x.137–44; xiii.i.1199; xvi.101; Duffy, pp. 422, 479–80.
20. Ives, *Anne*, pp. 399–400.
21. LP. viii.909.
22. Giustinian i.237; D'Aubigny, vol. 2, p. 191.
23. Foxe, v. 564.

24. LP. viii.317, 355; SP Span. v.i.484.

25. Tjernagel, *Barnes*.

26. Scarisbrick, pp. 401–2.

27. LP. xvii.22–3; Foxe, v.261.

28. Machiavelli, *The Prince*, ch. 19.

29. LP. x.243–4, 308, 351, 410, 699; SP Span. v.ii.29, 55.

30. Foxe, v.137; Ales, 'Letter', pp. 525–7.

31. The Act of 39 Articles of Elizabeth I closely resembled the Wittenberg agreement.

32. SP Span. v.ii,55, 123; Ives, 355, 358; LP. x.409.

33. LP.vii.1040; viii.263, 1074, 1084; x.601; SP Span. v.i.70, v.ii,43; Warnicke p. 207; Friedmann, vol. 2, p. 227.

34. LP. x.495, 601, 752.

35. Foxe, v.136–7.

36. LP. x.315.

37. SP Span. v.ii.84–5, 106; LP. x.245, 315.

38. LP. x.615.

39. Ives, pp. 395–9, 398–9; G. Bernard, 'Anne Boleyn's Religion', *Historical Journal*, 36, 1993, pp. 12–18.

40. LP. x.699, 720; Ives, pp. 351–2.

41. LP. x.291, 292, 699–700.

42. Ales, 'Letter' in Calendar of Foreign Papers, Elizabeth I, 1303, p. 528.

43. Ives, *Anne*, pp. 352, 360; Weir, *King and Court*, pp. 376–9.

44. SP Span. v.ii.61, 137; LP. x.441, 782, 1069.

CHAPTER 13 Conspiracy

1. Anstis, *Order of the Garter*, i.249, ii.398.

2. LP. x.315.

3. SP Span. v.ii.61.

4. SP Span. v.ii.85.

5. SP Span. v.ii.47; LP. x.635, 669, 715, 748, 752, 864, 926, 1000.

6. Ives, *Anne*, p. 361.

7. LP. x.753, 864.

8. LP. x.864; SP Span.v.ii.107, 108.

9. LP. x.726.

10. Parker, *Correspondence*, pp. 59, 400.

11. LP. x.789, 793, 797; Foxe, v. 553–8.

12. LP. x.789, 793, 797; Foxe, v. 527, 553–8; PRO, SP 70/7, ff. 5–6.

13. Foxe, v.

14. Cavendish, *Metrical Visions*, pp. 36–7; Lowinsky, in *Florilegium historiale*, pp. 192–200.

15. *Crónica del Rey Enrico*, pp. 80–1; Constantine, *Archaeologia*, 64.

16. LP. x.338.

17. Hall.ii.268.

18. LP. x.782, 799; SP Span.v.ii.107.

19. LP. x.793, 797; Cavendish, *Wolsey*, 451, 452, 456.

20. Hall.ii.268; LP. x.797.

21. LP. x.782; *Lisle Letters*, 694.

22. Cavendish, *Wolsey*, pp. 451–60.

23. LP. x.793, 797; *Wolsey*, ed. Singer, p. 461.

24. LP. x.793.

25. Cavendish, *Wolsey*, 452, 455, 454.

26. LP. x.675, 738, 748, 779, 902; *Lisle Letters*, iii.677, 684, 687, 689; Ives, pp. 364–7.

27. LP. x.798, 808.

28. LP. x.793, 799, 876.

29. The Duke of Norfolk, 1572.

30. Ellis, i.ii.56.

31. LP. x.785, 820, 870; *Lisle Letters*, iv.420.

32. Starkey, *Henry VIII: Personalities and Politics*, p. 113.

33. *Wolsey*, ed. Singer, p. 456; *Lisle Letters*, iii.695; LP, x.865.

34. LP. iv.5243; LP. x.499, 793, 797, 799, 953; LP. xi.117, 1165; *Lisle Letters*, iv.863.

35. BL. Cotton MS Otho CX, fo. 209.

36. Constantine, in *Archaeologia*, p.64; *Wolsey*, ed. Singer, p. 455.

37. *Lisle Letters*, iii.698; LP. x.919.

38. Cranmer, *Works*, ii.323–4; BL. Cotton MS Otho CX, fo. 230; LP. x. 792.

39. Wyatt, *Poems*, CXLIX; Constantine, in *Archaeologia*, p.65.

40. LP. x,908–9.

41. LP. x.865, 908.

42. LP. x.908–9.

43. LP. x.909.

44. Ives, *Anne*, p. 368n., 370n., 373n., 374n.

45. D'Aubigny, vol. 2, pp. 279–97.

46. LP. x.808; Burnet, 4, pp. 291–2.

47. LP. x.785, 908; Wriothesley, pp. 189–226.

48. 28 Henry VIII, 7; 33 Henry VIII, 21.

49. LP. x.797–8.

50. LP. x.1107.

51. LP. x.377–8.

52. *Crónica del Rey Enrico*, pp. 68–76; Sander, p. 133.

53. G. Bernard, 'The Fall of Anne Boleyn', *EHR*, 1991; Warnicke, pp. 191–233; A. Bray, *Homosexuality in Renaissance England*, London, 1982, pp. 14–31; H.A. Kelly, 'English Kings and the Fear of Sorcery', *Medieval Studies*, 39, p. 235.

54. Weir, *King and Court*, pp. 376–8.
55. SP Span. v.ii.126; LP. x. 378, 908; Burnet, vol.1, p. 316; Cavendish, *Metrical Visions*, pp. 301–7.
56. Ellis, i.ii.128.
57. Elton, *Henry VIII*, p. 13; cited in Wilson, 423.

Chapter 14 Coup D'état

1. Hammond, Peter, *Royal Fortress*, HMSO; *Treasures of the Tower, Inscriptions*, HMSO; LP. x.1131; xi.17.
2. House of Commons, i.307–8, 342–3; ii.52–3, 60–1, 409–10, 646–8; iii.54–6, 430–1, 597–9.
3. LP. x.908–9.
4. Rebholz, p. 155; Starkey, *Personalities and Politics*, p. 119.
5. LP. x.902; Hall, 819.
6. LP. x.866.
7. LP. x.873.
8. De Carles, lines 339–458.
9. *Lisle Letters*, iii.703; iv.847; LP. x.953, 964.
10. LP. x.908–9.
11. LP. x.908.
12. SP Span. v.ii.125; LP. x.377, 908.
13. Burnet, addenda to Book Three.
14. De Carles, *Histoire de Anne Boleyn Jadis Royne d'Angleterre*, BL. Addit. MS 40662: Brussels, Bibliothèque Royale Albert 1er, MS 19378 ff. 1–19; Wriothesley, p. 39; SP Span. v.ii.126; LP. x.378.
15. LP. x.908; De Carles, lines 861–4; Ives, p. 388.
16. LP. x.908–9; SP Span. v.ii.54–5.
17. LP. x.908; Friedmann, vol. 2, p. 280.
18. Wriothesley, pp. 37–9.
19. LP. x.908–9.
20. Spelman, *Reports*, i.71.
21. LP. xi.533–4, 539.
22. Crespin, *Anne Boleyn*, pp. 200–1; Wriothesley, i.37–8; SP Span.v.ii.126–7; LP. x.378.
23. Wriothesley, i.38; LP. x.908; xii.i.361.
24. Hall, p. 819; Wriothesley, i.41–42; Friedmann, vol. 2, p. 295 n. 2; De Carles, 1002–12, 1235–9.
25. LP. x.908–9, 1069; SP Span. v.ii.125.
26. Wriothesley, i.189–226; Ives, 'Faction' pp. 169–88.
27. SP Span. v.ii.121; LP. x.380.
28. SP Span. v.ii.121, 127–8; LP. x.378, 380, 908–9; xi.188; Ives, *Anne*, p. 338; Strickland, vol. 2, p. 273.

29. LP. x.902, 965; xi.381.
30. SP Span. iii.ii.37, 39.
31. *Wolsey*, ed. Singer, pp. 464–5; Wriothesley, pp. 1–41.
32. LP. x, 890; Cavendish, *Wolsey*, p. 459.

CHAPTER 15 **Bloody Days**

1. SP Span. v.ii.128; LP. x.379, 908; *Crónica del Rey Enrico*, p. 68; Wyatt, *Poems*, CXLIII.
2. *Wolsey*, ed. Singer p. 460.
3. *Chronicle of Calais*, 27.
4. Constantine, in *Archaeologia*, 23.65; *Lisle Letters*, iii.698; LP. x.738, 793, 869, 919.
5. *Lisle Letters*, iii.698; LP. x.919.
6. *Epistre*, p. 207.
7. SP Span. v.ii.120, 121; LP. x.380.
8. Anne Boleyn, 'O Deathe, rock me asleepe', *Historical Anthology of Music by Women*, Indiana University Press, 1991, 'O Death Rock Me Asleep', on *Henry VIII and his Six Wives*, The Early Music Consort of London; Anne Boleyn, 'Defiled Is My Name', Robert Johnson, *Full Well She Sang: Women's Music from the Middle Ages and Renaissance*, Toronto Consort, 1993.
9. LP. x.908; *Wolsey*, ed. Singer, p. 461.
10. LP. x.380, 910; SP Span. v.ii.131;*Wolsey*, ed. Singer, pp. 460–1.
11. LP. x.453, 910.
12. LP. x.896; Kelly, *Matrimonial Trials*, pp. 250–9.
13. Strype, 437.
14. *Wolsey*, ed. Singer, pp. 4–61; LP. x.908, 918; *Lisle Letters*, iii.697; Antony Antony in Herbert, *Henry VIII*, p. 385.
15. Hall, ii.268; LP. x.908, 920, 1107; George Wyatt, *Papers*, p. 189; *Lisle Letters*, iii.698.
16. BL. Stowe MS 956.
17. Hamy, *Entrevue*.
18. LP. xi.381.
19. Calendar of Foreign Papers, Elizabeth I, 1303, pp. 528, 530–1.

CHAPTER 16 **The Legacy**

1. LP. x.908, 926.
2. LP. x.926, 1205; xii.i.1212, ii.908; xiii.ii.307, 986; xiv.i.1239.
3. Constantine; in Archaelogia, 23.64; LP, x.926, 1205, xii.i.1212, ii.908, xiii.ii.307, 986, xiv.i.1239; Ales, 'Letter', pp. 530–1.
4. Wyatt, *Poems*, cxlix; LP. x.1131; xi.17; Rebholz, p. 155.
5. D'Aubigny, vol. 2, p. 295; LP. x.401, 965.

6. Ives, 'A Frenchman at the Court of Anne Boleyn', *History Today*, August 1998; D'Aubigny, vol. 2, p. 302.

7. Du Bellay, ii.453; LP. xi.860, 1250.

8. SP Span. v.ii.139; Wriothesley, i.45.

9. LP. x.908, 1134, 1150, 1187; xi.7, 9–10, 230.

10. SP Span. v.ii.183; LP. xi.40, 101, 219.

11. SP. i.457–9.

12. LP. x.422–4, 1187.

13. LP. xi.221, 233.

14. LP. xi.250.

15. LP. x.502, 566, 1010–1, 1257; xi.17.

16. House of Commons, ii.35O; iii–430–1.

17. D'Aubigny, vol. 2, p. 491;

18. Parker, *Correspondence*, p. 70.

19. LP. x.888, 956, 1043; xi.41; Prescott, p. 254; SP Ven. vi.iii.1274; D'Aubigny, vol. 2, p. 267.

20. William Allen, 'An Admonition to the Nobility and People of England and Ireland concerning the Present Wars', Antwerp, 1588.

21. LP. x.920, 1165; xi.29, 203.

22. Foxe, v.136–7.

23. *Correspondence of Matthew Parker*, p. 391.

24. Statutes of the Realm: Mary, 2, iv.i.200–1; 1 Eliz.3, 23, iv.i.358–9, 39.

25. Oxford, Bodl. MS. C. Don. 42. ff. 20–33.7; Holinshed, *Chronicles*, 1565–8.

26. SP Span. iii.252.

Bibliography

Primary Sources

Bacon, Francis, *The History of the Reign of Henry VII*, Folio Society, London, 1971

Bergenroth, G.A. (ed.), *Supplement to Vols. I and II of the Calendar of State Papers, Spanish*, London, 1868

Bourbon, Nicolas, *Nugarum libri octo*, Lyons, 1538

Brantome, Pierre de Bourdeille, Seigneur de, *Lives of Fair and Gallant Ladies*, trans. R.A. Allinson, Liveright, New York, 1933

Brewer, J.S. and R.H. Brodie (eds.), *Letters and Papers, Foreign and Domestic, of the Reign of Henry VIII*, 21 vols., HMSO, London, 1862–1920

Castiglione, Baldesar, *The Book of the Courtier*, trans. C.S. Singleton, New York, 1959

Cavendish, George, *The Life and Death of Cardinal Wolsey*, ed. Richard S. Sylvester and Davis P. Harding, Yale University Press, New Haven and London, 1962

Cavendish, George, *Metrical Visions*, ed. A.S.G. Edwards, Columbia, South Carolina, 1980

Chronicle of Calais in the Reigns of Henry VII and Henry VIII, ed. Nichols, J., Camden Society, 1846

Clifford, Henry, *The Life of Jane Dormer, Duchess of Feria*, transcribed by Canon E.E. Estcourt and ed. Rev. Joseph Stevenson, Burns and Gates, London, 1887

Coates, Tim (ed.), *The Letters of Henry VIII, 1526–1529*, HMSO, London, 2001

Commynes, Philippe de, *Mémoires*, Paris, 1901

Constantine, George, Memorial to Thomas Lord Cromwell, ed., Amyot, Thomas, in *Archaeologia*, xxiii, 1831, pp. 56–78

Cranmer, Thomas, *Works*, ed. J. and E. Cox, 2 vols., Parker Society, Cambridge, 1844–6

Crónica del Rey Enrico, ed. Marquis de Molins, Madrid, 1874, trans. M.A.S. Hume, London, 1889

De Carles, Lancelot, *La Grande Bretagne devant L'Opinion Française*, ed. G. Ascoli, Paris, 1927

Du Bellay, Joachim Le Grand, *Preuves de L'Histoire du Divorce de Henri VIII*, 3 vols. Paris, 1688

Ellis, Henry, *Original Letters*, London, 3 series, 10 vols., 1825–46

'Epistre contenant le Procès Criminal faict à l'encontre de la Royne Anne Boullan d'Angleterre', 1545, in G.A. Crapelet, ed., *Lettres de Henri VIII*, Paris, 1826

Erasmus, Correspondence, ed. Corrigan, B., University of Toronto Press, 1992

Fish, Simon, *A Supplication for Beggars*, 1528, ed. E. Arber, London, 1880

Foxe, John, *The Acts and Monuments of John Foxe*, ed. G. Townsend and S.R. Cattley, 8 vols., 1838, reprinted New York, 1975

Giustinian, Sebastian, *Four Years at the Court of Henry VIII*, London, 1854

Hall, Edward, *The triumphant reigne of King Henry the VIII*, ed. Whibley, London, 1904

Harpsfield, N., *A Treatise on the Pretended Divorce Between Henry VIII and Catherine of Aragon*, ed. N. Pococke, Camden Society, new series, xxi, London 1878, reprinted New York 1965

Harpsfield, Nicholas, *The Life and Death of Sir Thomas More*, London, 1932

Hay, D. (ed.), *The Anglica Historia of Polydore Vergil*, Camden Society, 3rd series, lxxiv, London, 1950

Kaulek, Jean, *Correspondance politique de Castillon et de Marillac*, Paris, 1885

Latimer, William, 'A brief treatise or cronikelle of the most vertuous

Ladye Anne Bulleyne, late Queen of England, Bodleian MS C. Don. 42

Machiavelli, Niccolò, *The Prince*, trans. W.K. Marriott, Knopf, New York, 1992

Mancini, Dominic, *The Usurpation of Richard III*, trans. C.A.J. Armstrong, Sutton Publishing, 1969

Merriman, R.B., *The Life and Letters of Thomas Cromwell*, 2 vols., Oxford, 1902

More, Thomas, *Works*, ed. W.E. Campbell et al., 1963–79

Muir, Kenneth, *Life and Letters of Sir Thomas Wyatt*, Liverpool University Press, 1963

Parker Correspondence 1535–75, ed. Bruce, J. & Perowne, TT., Parker Society, 1853

Rebholz, *Wyatt: Complete Poems*, Yale University Press, 1981

Riley, H.T., *Croyland Chronicle*, London, 1854

Roper, William, *The Life of Sir Thomas More*, London, 1935

Sander, Nicolas, *The Rise and Growth of the Anglican Schism*, ed. D. Lewis, 1877

Savage, Henry (ed.), *The Love Letters of Henry VIII*, University of Colorado Press, 1949

Skelton, John, *Poetical Works*, ed. Alexander Dyce, Boston, 1885

St Clare Byrne, Muriel, *The Lisle Letters*, University of Chicago Press, 1980

Strype, John, *Ecclesiastical Memorials*, London, 1820–40

Tyndale, William, *The Obedience of a Christian Man*, 1528

Vergil, P., *Anglica Historia*, ed. Hay, D., Camden Society, lxxiv, 1950.

Vives, Juan Luis, *De Instructione Feminae Christianae*, 1523, trans. 1529

Wriothesley, Charles, *A Chronicle of England during the Reigns of the Tudors from A.D. 1485 to 1559*, Camden Society, xi., London, 1875–7

Wyatt, George, *Papers*, ed. D.M. Loades, Camden Society, iv. 5, London, 1968

Wyatt, George, 'The Life of Queen Anne Boleigne', in S.W. Singer (ed.), *The Life of Cardinal Wolsey by George Cavendish*, London, 1827

Wyatt, Thomas, *Collected Poems*, ed. Kenneth Muir, Routledge and Kegan Paul, 1949

Secondary Sources

Ackroyd, Peter, *The Life of Thomas More*, Random House, 1998

Archer, John, *Sovereignty and Intelligence: Spying and Court Culture in the English Renaissance*, Stanford University Press, 1993

Beckingsale, B.W., *Thomas Cromwell: Tudor Minister*, Macmillan, London, 1978

Bellamy, John G., *The Tudor Law of Treason: An Introduction*, London, 1979

Bernard, G.W., 'Anne Boleyn's Religion', *Historical Journal*, xxxvi, pp. 1–20

Bernard, G.W., *War, Taxation and Rebellion in Early Tudor England: Henry VIII, Wolsey and the Amicable Grant of 1525*, Brighton, 1986

Bernard, G.W., 'The Fall of Anne Boleyn', *English Historical Review*, 106, pp. 584–610

Bernard, G.W., 'The Fall of Wolsey Reconsidered', *Journal of British Studies*, xxxv, pp. 277–310

Bernard, G.W., 'The Rise of Sir William Compton', *English Historical Review*, 96, 1981

Block, J.S., *Factional Politics and the English Reformation 1520–1540*, Royal Historical Society 1993

Brewer, J.S., *The Reign of Henry VIII from his Accession to the Death of Wolsey*, ed. James Gairdner, 2 vols., John Murray, London, 1884

Brigden, S., *London and the Reformation*, Oxford, 1989

Brigden, S., *New Worlds, Lost Worlds: The Rule of the Tudors*, Penguin, 2000

Bruce, Marie Louise, *Anne Boleyn*, London, 1972

Buck, George, *The History of the Life and Reign of Richard III*, 1973

Burnet, *History of the Reformation in England*, 1681, ed. Pocock, N., 7 vols., London, 1865.

Carlson, James R. and Peter W. Hammond, 'The English Sweating Sickness, 1485–1551', *Journal of the History of Medicine*, 54, 1999, pp. 23–54

Chapman, Hester W., *Anne Boleyn*, London, 1974

Cunnington, C.W.P., *Handbook of English Costume in the Sixteenth Century*, Boston, 1970

D'Aubigny, J.H. Merle, *The Reformation in England*, 2 vols., London, 1962–3

Daniell, D., *William Tyndale: A Biography*, London, 1994

Davis, J.F., *Heresy and Reformation in the South-East of England 1520–1559*, London, 1983

Dickens, A.G., *The English Reformation*, London, 1991

Dickens, A.G., 'The Early Expansion of Protestantism', in Margo Todd (ed.), *Reformation to Revolution: Politics and Religion in Early Modern England*, Routledge, London, 1995

Donaldson, Peter, 'Bishop Gardiner, Machiavellian', *Historical Journal*, xxiii.i., pp. 1–16

Dowling, M., 'Anne Boleyn and Reform', *Journal of Ecclesiastical History*, xxxv, 1984, pp. 30–46

Dowling, M., 'The Gospel and the Court', in P. Lake and M. Dowling (eds.), *Protestantism and the National Church in Sixteenth Century England*, London, 1987, pp. 36–77

Dowling, Maria, 'Debate: The Fall of Anne Boleyn Revisited', *English Historical Review*, July 1993, pp. 450–1

Dowling, M., 'New Perspectives on the English Reformation', *Journal of British Studies*, xxx, 1991, pp. 99–105

Drummond, Jack C. and Anne Wilbraham, *The Englishman's Food: A History of Five Centuries of English Diet*, London, J. Cape, 1939

Duffy, E., *The Stripping of the Altars*, Yale University Press, New Haven, 1992

Eisenstein, E., *The Printing Press as an Agent of Change*, Cambridge, 1979

Ellis, S.G., *Tudor Frontiers and Noble Power: the Making of the British State*, Oxford, 1995

Elton, G.R., *The Tudor Revolution in Government: Administrative Changes in the Reign of Henry VIII*, Cambridge, 1953

Elton, G.R., *Reform and Reformation: England, 1509–1558*, Cambridge, Mass., 1977

Elton, G.R., *Policy and Police*, Cambridge, 1972

Elton, G.R., 'The Political Creed of Thomas Cromwell', *Transactions of the Royal Historical Society*, v.vi., 1956, pp. 69–92

Elton, G.R., 'Sir Thomas More and the Opposition to Henry VIII', *Bulletin of the Institute of Historical Research*, xli, 103, May 1968, pp. 19–34

Elton, G.R., *Reform and Renewal: Thomas Cromwell and the Common Weal*, Cambridge, 1973

Emmisson, Frederick George, *Tudor Food and Pastimes*, London, 1965

Erickson, Carolly, *Bloody Mary*, London, 1978

Erickson, Carolly, *Mistress Anne*, New York, 1984

Fox, Alaistair, *Politics and Literature in the Reigns of Henry VII and Henry VIII*, Oxford, 1989

Fraser, Antonia, *The Wives of Henry VIII*, New York, 1993

Friedmann, Paul, *Anne Boleyn*, London, 1884

Gairdner, James, 'The Draft Dispensation', *English Historical Review*, v, pp. 544–50

Gairdner, James, 'Mary and Anne Boleyn', *English Historical Review*, viii, pp. 53–60

Greenblatt, Stephen, *Renaissance Self-Fashioning*, University of Chicago Press, 1980

Gunn, S.J., *Charles Brandon, Duke of Suffolk, c. 1484–1545*, Oxford, 1988

Gunn, S.J., *Early Tudor Government, 1485–1558*, London, 1995

Guy, J.A., 'Wolsey, the Council and the Council Courts', *English Historical Review*, xci, pp. 481–505

Guy, J.A., *The Public Career of Sir Thomas More*, Yale University Press, New Haven, 1980

Guy, J.A., 'Sir Thomas More and the Heretics.' *History Today*, 30, pp. 11–15

Guy, J.A., 'The King's Council and Political Participation', in A. Fox and J.A. Guy (eds.), *Reassessing the Henrician Age*, Oxford, 1986, pp. 121–47

Guy, J.A., 'The Privy Council: Revolution or Evolution?', in C. Coleman and D. Starkey (eds.), *Revolution Reassessed*, Oxford, 1986, pp. 59–85

Guy, J.A., *Thomas More*, London, 2000

Gwyn, P., *The King's Cardinal: The Rise and Fall of Thomas Wolsey*, London, 1990

Haigh, Christopher, *English Reformations*, Clarendon Press, 1993

Harris, Barbara, 'Women and Politics in Early Tudor England', *Historical Journal*, xxxiii, pp. 259–81

Herbert, Lord Edward of Cherbury, *The Life and Reign of Henry VIII*, 1649, repr.1870.

Hughes, P.E., Lefevre, William Eerdmans, 1984

Hume, Martin, *The Wives of Henry VIII*, Bretano, New York, 1905.

Ives, E.W., *Faction in Tudor England*, Historical Association, London, 1979

Ives, E.W., *Anne Boleyn*, Oxford, 1986

Ives, E.W., 'The Fall of Wolsey', in S.J. Gunn and P.G. Lindley (eds.), *Cardinal Wolsey: Church, State and Art*, Cambridge, 1991, pp. 286–315

Ives, E.W., 'Anne Boleyn and the Early Reformation in England', *Historical Journal*, xxxvii, 1994, pp. 389–400

Ives, E.W., 'Debate: The Fall of Anne Boleyn Reconsidered', *English Historical Review*, 107, pp. 651–64

Kamen, Henry, *Inquisition and Society in the 16th and 17th Centuries*, Bloomington, 1985

Kelly, Henry Ansgar, *The Matrimonial Trials of Henry VIII*, Stanford University Press, 1975

Knecht, R.J., *Francis I*, Cambridge, 1982

Knowles, D., 'The Matter of Wilton', *Bulletin of the Institute of Historical Research*, 31, 1958, pp. 92–6

Lehmberg, Stanford E., *The Reformation Parliament 1529–1536*, Cambridge, 1970

Lerer, Seth, *Courtly Letters in the Age of Henry VIII*, Cambridge, 1997

Loach, J., *Parliament under the Tudors*, Oxford, 1991

Loades, David, *The Tudor Court*, Historical Association, London, 1989

Loades, D., *Revolution in Religion: The English Reformation 1530–1570*, Cardiff University Press, 1992

Lowinsky, Edward, 'A Music Book for Anne Boleyn', in J.G. Rowe and W.H. Stockdale (eds.), *Florilegium historiale: Essays Presented to Wallace K. Ferguson*, University of Toronto Press, 1971

MacCulloch, D. (ed.), *The Reign of Henry VIII: Politics, Policy and Piety*, London, 1995

MacCulloch, Diarmaid, *Cranmer*, Yale University Press, 1996

MacCulloch, D., 'The Myth of the English Reformation', *Journal of British Studies*, xxx, pp. 1–19

Marius, R., *Thomas More: A Biography*, London, 1986

Mattingly, Garrett, *Catherine of Aragon*, Boston, 1941

Murphy, V., 'The Literature and Propaganda of Henry VIII's First Divorce', in D. MacCulloch (ed.), *The Reign of Henry VIII: Politics, Policy and Piety*, London, 1995, pp. 135–58

Netanyahu, Benzion, *Origins of the Inquisition*, New York, 1995

Paget, Hugh, 'The Youth of AB', *Bulletin of the Institute of Historical Research*, 55, 1981, pp. 162–70

Parmiter, Geoffrey de C., *The King's Great Matter: A Study of Anglo-Papal Relations 1527–1534*, London, 1967

Paul, John E., *Catherine of Aragon and Her Friends*, London, 1966

Pollard, Albert F., *Henry VIII*, London, 1905, 1951

Pollard, Albert F., *Wolsey: Church and State in Sixteenth-Century England*, London, 1929

Prescott, H.F.M., *Spanish Tudor: The Life of Bloody Mary*, London, 1940

Rex, Richard, *Henry VIII and the English Reformation*, New York, 1993

Richardson, W.C., *Mary Tudor: The White Queen*, London, 1970

Ridley, Jasper, *The Statesman and the Fanatic*, London, 1982

Ridley, Jasper, *Statesman and Saint: Cardinal Wolsey, Sir Thomas More*, London, 1982

Ridley, Jasper, *The Love Letters of Henry VIII*, Weidenfeld & Nicolson, 1988

Roth, Cecil, *The Spanish Inquisition*, New York, 1960

Round, John Horace, *The Early Life of Anne Boleyn: A Critical Essay*, London, 1886

Russell, J.G., *The Field of the Cloth of Gold*, London, 1969

Scarisbrick, J.J., *Henry VIII*, London, 1968

Smith, Lacey Baldwin, 'English Treason Trials and Confessions in the Sixteenth Century', *Journal of the History of Ideas*, xv.iv., pp. 471–98

Smith, Lacey Baldwin, *Henry VIII: The Mask of Royalty*, Boston, 1971

Starkey, David, *The Reign of Henry VIII: Personalities and Politics*, London, 1985

Starkey, David, 'Court, Council and Nobility in Tudor England', in Ronald G. Asch and Adolf M. Birke (eds.), *Princes, Patronage and the Nobility*, Oxford, 1991

Starkey, David, 'The Court: Castiglione's Ideal and Tudor Reality', *Journal of the Warburg and Courtauld Institutes*, 45, 1982

Stevens, John, *Music and Poetry in the Early Tudor Court*, University of Nebraska Press, 1961

Strickland, Agnes, *Lives of the Queens of England*, 8 vols. repr. edn. 1972

Strong, Roy, *Holbein and Henry VIII*, Routledge and Kegan Paul, London, 1967

Strype, John, *Ecclesiastical Memorials*, London, 1820–40

Sylvester, R. (ed.), *George Cavendish: The Life and Death of Cardinal Wolsey*, Early English Text Society, ccxliii

Tjernagel, N.S., *Henry VIII and the Lutherans*, Concordia, St Louis, 1965

Tjernagel, N.S. (ed.), *The Reformation Essays of Dr Robert Barnes*, London, 1963

Urkevich, Lisa, *Anne Boleyn, a Music Book, and the Northern Renaissance Courts*, PhD diss., University of Maryland, 1997

Warnicke, Retha M., *The Rise and Fall of Anne Boleyn*, Cambridge University Press, Cambridge and New York, 1989

Warnicke, Retha M., 'The Rise and Fall of Anne Boleyn: Family Politics at the Court of Henry VIII', *Historical Journal*, xxx, 1987

Warnicke. Retha M., 'The Eternal Triangle and Court Politics', *Albion*, 18.iv, 1986, pp. 565–79

Watson, Foster (ed.), *Vives and the Renascence Education of Women*, London, 1912

Weir, Alison, *The Six Wives of Henry VIII*, New York, 1993

Weir, Alison, *Henry VIII: King and Court*, London, 2001

Williams, Neville, *Henry VIII and His Court*, London, 1971

Williams, Neville, *The Cardinal and the Secretary: Thomas Wolsey and Thomas Cromwell*, London, 1975

Wilson, Derek, *In the Lion's Court*, London, 2001

Wood, James, *The Broken Estate: Essays on Literature and Belief*, New York, 1999

Zagorin, Perez, 'Sir Thomas Wyatt and the Court of Henry VIII', *Journal of Medieval and Renaissance Studies*, Winter 1993, pp. 113–41

Zahl, P.F.M., *Five Women of the English Reformation*, William Eerdmans, Cambridge, 2001

Zimmerman, T.C. Price, 'A note on Clement VII and the divorce of Henry VIII', *English Historical Review*, lxxxii, 324, pp. 548–52

Picture credits

Index